# Strategic Survey 2019
# **The Annual Assessment of Geopolitics**

*published by*

 Routledge
Taylor & Francis Group

*for*

The International Institute for Strategic Studies

# The International Institute for Strategic Studies

Arundel House | 6 Temple Place | London | WC2R 2PG | UK

# Strategic Survey 2019
# The Annual Assessment of Geopolitics

First published October 2019 by **Routledge**
4 Park Square, Milton Park, Abingdon, Oxon, OX14 4RN

for **The International Institute for Strategic Studies**
Arundel House, 6 Temple Place, London, WC2R 2PG, UK

Simultaneously published in the USA and Canada by **Routledge**
52 Vanderbilt Avenue, New York, NY 10017

*Routledge is an imprint of Taylor & Francis, an Informa business*

© 2019 The International Institute for Strategic Studies

DIRECTOR-GENERAL AND CHIEF EXECUTIVE Dr John Chipman

EDITOR Dr Nicholas Redman

ASSOCIATE EDITORS Alice Aveson, Alex Goodwin
EDITORIAL Sara Hussain, Jill Lally, Michael Marsden, Jack May, Jeff Mazo, Bao-Chau Pham,
Sam Stocker, Jessica Watson, Carolyn West
GRAPHICS RESEARCH: Frederik Florenz
COVER/PRODUCTION/CARTOGRAPHY John Buck, Carolina Vargas, Kelly Verity
COVER IMAGES BJ Warnick/Kyodo via Newscom/Alamy

British Library Cataloguing in Publication Data
A catalogue record for this book is available from the British Library

Library of Congress Cataloguing in Publication Data

ISBN 978-0-367-27357-6
ISSN 0459-7230

# Contents

# Chapter 1

# Key Events

July 2018–June 2019

## July

**1** **Yemen:** The United Arab Emirates announces a pause in its military campaign in the Yemeni port city of Hudaydah to allow for the unconditional withdrawal of Houthi fighters following UN-brokered talks.

**1** **Mexico:** Andrés Manuel López Obrador is elected as the new president of Mexico.

**6** **China–US:** The US imposes new tariffs on US$34 billion-worth of goods coming from China, which retaliates with equivalent tariffs on US exports.

**8** **Iran:** Iran surpasses the limit of uranium enrichment imposed by the 2015 nuclear deal, marking its first violation of the terms.

**9** **Eritrea–Ethiopia:** Eritrea and Ethiopia sign a declaration to end their lengthy cold war, agreeing to reopen embassies, ports and phone lines between the two countries.

**9** **South Sudan:** Rebels supporting opposition leader Riek Machar reject a power-sharing proposal between Machar and President Salva Kiir, setting back prospects for peace.

**12** **Syria:** Russia initiates an offensive in coordination with the Syrian army, reconquering the city of Daraa and sparking a new wave of refugees to flee towards Jordan and Israel.

**12** **South Sudan:** The South Sudanese parliament extends President Salva Kiir's term to 2021.

**12** **Sudan:** President Omar al-Bashir extends the unilateral ceasefire with rebels in the country until the end of the year.

**14** **Israel–Palestine:** Fighting between Israeli forces and Palestinian forces increases significantly, culminating in the largest bombardment of Gaza since the start of the war in 2014.

**18** **Syria:** The Syrian government and rebel groups reach a deal that allows for the evacuation of two towns in northern Idlib province.

**19** **Israel:** The Israeli parliament passes a new law declaring the country a Jewish 'nation-state', which grants only Jews the right of self-determination in Israel, and revokes Arabic as an official language.

**24** **Israel–Syria:** The Israel Defense Forces (IDF) shoot down a Syrian plane, saying that it crossed into the airspace of the Israeli-occupied Golan Heights.

31 **Iran:** Protests against falling living standards and rising prices break out in Iran and spread across multiple cities.

## August

7 **Ethiopia:** The Ethiopian government signs a peace deal with the Oromo Liberation Front (OLF) to end the conflict between Ethiopia and the rebel group, which was established in the 1970s.

8 **South Sudan:** President Salva Kiir grants amnesty to rebels involved in the country's civil war, including his former deputy Riek Machar, three days after both parties signed a ceasefire and power-sharing deal along with other group leaders.

12 **Caspian Sea:** Russia, Iran, Azerbaijan, Kazakhstan and Turkmenistan sign a convention defining a special legal status for the Caspian Sea after more than 20 years of talks.

26 **Zimbabwe:** President-elect Emmerson Mnangagwa of the African National Union–Patriotic Front (ZANU–PF) is sworn in as president, amid a controversial election marked by several protests, following the ousting of Robert Mugabe.

31 **Palestine–US:** A week after cutting more than US$200 million in aid to the Palestinian territories, the US Department of State announces an end to funding for the United Nations Relief and Works Agency (UNRWA) for Palestinian refugees.

## September

6 **Djibouti–Eritrea:** The two countries sign a peace agreement to end the border conflict, symbolising a further move towards peace in the Greater Horn of Africa region.

10 **US:** The US threatens to impose sanctions on the International Criminal Court (ICC) if it decides to prosecute US soldiers over alleged abuses committed in Afghanistan.

12 **European Union–Hungary:** The European Parliament votes to take disciplinary action against Hungary, following accusations of a breach of the EU's founding principles by Prime Minister Victor Orban's government. This marks the first time the European Parliament has voted to initiate such proceedings against a member state.

17 **Russia–Syria–Turkey:** Russia and Turkey agree to establish a demilitarised zone in Syria's Idlib province to enable the withdrawal of rebels from the region.

17 **US:** US Secretary of State Mike Pompeo announces plans to cap the admission of refugees into the US at 30,000 for the 2019 fiscal year.

17 **US:** The US announces trade tariffs on US$200bn-worth of Chinese goods, at an initial rate of 10%, marking the third and highest set of tariffs imposed so far in the US–China trade war. China retaliates the following day by announcing new tariffs on US$60bn-worth of US goods, amounting to approximately half of all US exports to China.

28 **Syria:** Russia delivers an advanced S-300 missile-defence system to Syria, a move that is met with criticism and concern by a range of international actors.

## October

2 **Saudi Arabia–Turkey:** Saudi journalist and regime critic Jamal Khashoggi is murdered in the Saudi consulate in Istanbul.

6 **US:** Following weeks of hearings related to sexual-assault allegations, the US Senate votes in favour of Brett Kavanaugh as Supreme Court judge. The lifelong appointment shifts the highest legislature of the US decisively to the right.

7 **China:** Interpol chief Meng Hongwei, who has been reported missing for two weeks, resigns as Chinese law enforcement confirms that it is holding him for investigation relating to alleged corruption charges.

8 **IPCC:** The Intergovernmental Panel on Climate Change (IPCC) releases a report calling on states to limit temperature increase to a maximum of 1.5°C to avoid potentially far-reaching and irreversible consequences of global warming.

10 **US–Syria:** US Secretary of State Mike Pompeo announces the United States' refusal to provide additional reconstruction assistance to Syria if Iranian-backed forces remain within the country.

13 **Afghanistan:** The US and the Taliban initiate talks, without representation from the Afghan government, to discuss the prospects for peace in Afghanistan.

25 **Ethiopia:** Parliament appoints Sahle-Work Zewde as the new president of Ethiopia, the country's first female president.

28 **Brazil:** Far-right candidate Jair Bolsonaro wins the Brazilian presidential election.

29 **US–China:** The US blocks Chinese state-owned company Fujian Jinhua Integrated Circuit from buying American components over concerns that the company poses a national-security threat to the US, in a series of escalating tensions between the two countries.

## November

4 **UAE:** The UAE sentences a Shia cleric to life imprisonment over charges of spying for Qatar.

5 **US:** The US reimposes sanctions on Iran, previously removed in 2015, to curb its oil revenue and coerce it into halting its nuclear fuel-enrichment programme.

6 **US:** The Democratic Party gains control of the House of Representatives, while the Republican Party maintains control over the Senate in the midterm elections.

14 **UK–European Union:** The UK and the EU agree a draft withdrawal agreement for the UK's separation from the EU. However, members of Parliament reject all amendments to the proposed Brexit plan. The UK is due to leave the EU on 31 October 2019.

25 **Sea of Azov:** The Russian coastguard fires at and eventually captures three Ukrainian vessels crossing the Kerch Strait to enter the Sea of Azov. This marks the first time that Russian forces openly engage Ukrainian forces since the annexation of Crimea in 2014.

30 **US–Mexico–Canada:** The US, Mexico and Canada sign the United States–Mexico–Canada Agreement (USMCA) to replace the North American Free Trade Agreement (NAFTA).

## December

1 **Canada:** Canadian authorities arrest Meng Wanzhou, Huawei's chief financial officer and daughter of Huawei founder Ren Zhengfei, at the request of US authorities who accuse her of circumventing sanctions on Iran.

3 **Qatar:** Qatar announces its decision to leave the Organization of the Petroleum Exporting Countries (OPEC) and to focus on exporting liquefied natural gas instead.

4 **France:** The French government suspends its planned fuel-tax increase in response to the violent protests in Paris by the so-called 'yellow vests' movement.

7 **Germany:** Annegret Kramp-Karrenbauer is elected to succeed Angela Merkel as leader of the Christian Democratic Union (CDU). Merkel remains in office as chancellor.

12 **Philippines:** The Philippine Congress approves President Rodrigo Duterte's request to extend martial law in Mindanao for another year.

12 **US–Saudi Arabia:** The US Senate votes to end US military support for the Saudi-led coalition in Yemen in view of the severity of the conflict as well as the killing of Jamal Khashoggi. However, the bill does not pass in the House of Representatives.

13 **European Union:** The European Central Bank ends its €2.6 trillion (US$2.95trn) quantitative-easing policy, established to save the eurozone following the 2009 financial crisis.

14 **Kosovo:** Parliament votes to establish a Kosovan army, drawing criticism from Serbia and NATO.

18 **Yemen:** A UN-brokered ceasefire agreement between the conflict parties in Yemen comes into effect, although fighting continues.

19 **US–Syria:** US President Donald Trump announces plans to withdraw all remaining US forces from Syria, claiming that the Islamic State, also known as ISIS or ISIL, has been defeated. This contradicts the assessments of other states in the US-led coalition against ISIS in Syria. The decision is later partially revoked, with a smaller US contingent remaining in Syria.

21 **US:** President Donald Trump signs a law that punishes Chinese officials who have barred American citizens from going freely into Tibetan areas.

## January

**5** **Russia–Ukraine:** The Ukrainian Orthodox Church splits from the Russian Orthodox Church, formally gaining its independence.

**20** **Democratic Republic of the Congo (DRC):** The Constitutional Court confirms Félix Tshisekedi as winner of the presidential election. The main opposition claims that outgoing president Joseph Kabila changed the vote tallies to deny it victory, having done deals with Tshisekedi.

**29** **Iran–Syria:** Syria and Iran agree on future trade deals, including plans for Iran to build a power plant in Syria and to support post-war reconstruction.

## February

**1** **European Union–Japan:** The Economic Partnership Agreement (EPA) between the EU and Japan enters into force, substantially lowering trade barriers.

**2** **US–Russia:** US President Donald Trump announces that the US will suspend its compliance with the Intermediate-Range Nuclear Forces (INF) Treaty and will formally withdraw within six months, unless Russia destroys new missiles that violate the treaty.

**5** **Afghanistan:** Representatives of the Afghan Taliban meet Afghan politicians in Moscow to hold peace talks, in one of the first intra-Afghan negotiations. Another meeting is scheduled in Doha, Qatar.

**12** **Republic of North Macedonia:** The Republic of Macedonia formally changes its name to the Republic of North Macedonia, days after signing a NATO accession agreement.

**14** **India:** A Jaysh-e-Mohammad (JeM) suicide attack kills 40 Indian Central Reserve Police Force (CRPF) personnel. In response, Indian and Pakistani air-force jets conduct airstrikes, resulting in the capture of an Indian pilot who is later released.

**28** **Israel:** The attorney general announces his intention to indict Prime Minister Benjamin Netanyahu on charges of bribery, fraud and breach of trust. The indictment is subject to a hearing that is postponed until October 2019.

## April

**11** **Sudan:** President Omar al-Bashir is removed from power by a military coup following months of civilian protests. A Transitional Military Council is established to act as an interim government.

**18** **US:** Special Counsel Robert Mueller publishes the final report of his investigation into allegations that Donald Trump conspired with Russia to manipulate the result of the 2016 presidential election. The report concludes that there is not enough evidence for conspiracy, yet it does not explicitly exonerate Trump from collusion or obstruction of justice.

**21 Ukraine:** Volodymyr Zelensky wins the presidential election against incumbent Petro Poroshenko with more than 73% of the vote.

## May

**7 US–China:** The US imposes new tariff rates of 25% on US$200bn-worth of Chinese goods, the highest tariffs imposed in the trade war between China and the US.

**14 Syria:** Syrian and Russian forces intensify their offensive in Syria's Idlib province, due to the continuous presence of Hayat Tahrir al-Sham (HTS) forces, which were supposed to have left the region under a previously agreed deal between Russia and Turkey.

**16 US:** Citing national-security concerns, the US adds Chinese company Huawei to the Entity List, making the firm subject to specific licensing agreements for trade with the US.

**23 India:** Prime Minister Narendra Modi secures another term in office as his Bharatiya Janata Party (BJP) wins 303 out of 543 seats in the Lok Sabha (the lower house of parliament).

**26 European Union:** After three days of voting, the European People's Party group wins the largest share of seats in the European Parliament elections.

## June

**3 Sudan:** After the ousting of Omar al-Bashir, the Sudanese armed forces forcefully break up a pro-democracy protest in Khartoum, killing more than 100 people.

**5 Thailand:** Parliament elects former military general Prayuth Chan-ocha as prime minister in the country's first elections since the 2014 military coup.

**9 Mali:** An attack on a Dogon village in Mali leaves 35 dead and 60 missing. It underscores the increasing violence between the Dogon and Fulani since the start of the Islamist uprising in 2012.

**13 Gulf of Oman:** Unidentified assailants attack two oil tankers in the Gulf of Oman. The US blames Iran, which denies responsibility for the attack. This is the second such incident in the Gulf of Oman in two months.

**14 Sudan:** The Sudanese Armed Forces admit to having carried out a disproportionally violent crackdown against civilians protesting at the establishment of the military interim government.

**15 Hong Kong:** Chief Executive Carrie Lam indefinitely suspends a proposed extradition bill in response to weeks of protests. The new law would have enabled extraditions from Hong Kong to mainland China.

**26 Myanmar:** Prosecutor Fatou Bensouda of the International Criminal Court (ICC) announces that she will request permission for judges to open an investigation into 'two waves of violence' committed in Myanmar's Rakhine State. This follows the report of a UN fact-finding mission in August 2018 that described how Myanmar's security forces had committed the 'gravest crimes under international law' and demanded action.

# Chapter 2

# **Prospectives**

The trends of 2018–19 have all confirmed the atomisation of international society. Neither 'balance of power' nor 'international rules-based governance' serve as ordering principles. International institutions have been marginalised. The diplomatic routine of meetings continues, yet the competing exertions of national efforts, too rarely coordinated with others, matter more – and most often they are erratic in both execution and consequence. Almost all international strategic issues of importance (whether the Middle East peace process, the conflict in Ukraine or the tensions on the Korean Peninsula) are either in a constant state of feckless negotiation, or artificially and dangerously frozen. Outcomes are fleeting, partial and then subject to review. There is no predictable rhythm to international affairs – the disruptors carry most of the advantage; those clinging to the status quo are losing their grip. The effort to master advanced technologies, data and information has added a new field of competition, with control of 5G mobile-network technology and the future of the internet as key battlegrounds. The US is pricing itself out of alliance politics – complaining that its European allies contribute too little and seeking to charge allies in Asia multiples of what they now pay for American bases. China is advancing a model of development through its Belt and Road Initiative (BRI) that is intended to ensure more states stand with it or are usefully neutral. Some small powers feel horribly squeezed by these pressures and the loss of certainty; others have gained disproportionate bargaining power in the new diplomatic bidding wars; still others are able to carry out ruthless domestic policies, in the sure knowledge that there is no effective 'international community' willing, or able, to check their excesses.

In time, some new order will emerge from this, but the indications are that politically, and possibly technologically, the world will simply divide into separate ecosystems with their own rules and customs. Perhaps power will accrue to those who can navigate best between them, lead effective networks in the absence of institutions and build coalitions when alliances have withered. The evolving world order is not likely to mimic past power shifts. If the Pax Americana is ending, that does not mean a Pax Sinica is beginning. China is rising with its own characteristics and sense of purpose, and into an environment where power is subtly diffused. It will perhaps hold sway over more countries and have a wider array of political relationships, but it is neither in its diplomatic style, nor in its power, to have the sort of cooperative alliance relationships that the US developed in the past. For its part, the US is not likely voluntarily, reluctantly or after some sort of battle, to pass any strategic baton to China. The shifts will be more tectonic than sudden. As this happens, other countries will assert their national interests with greater force, sensing, rightly, that there is less resistance to their unilateral impulses. The US and China, and to a degree the EU, Iran and Russia, will aim to retain power in their neighbourhoods. Yet the operation of 'sphere-of-influence politics' will be difficult for modern-day geopoliticians. Nationalist impulses create antibodies to foreign clout. An atomised world order is resistant to tutelage from afar. This is true no matter how compelling the ideology and model of governance promoted by ambitious states.

As China has risen strategically, it has developed its own theory of 'exceptionalism' to define its external engagement. Its 'community of human destiny' is rhetorically designed to support China's image as a benevolent power whose foreign-policy ambitions are to support international development and prosperity. This may not succeed in winning friends and influencing neighbours. The survivability of this doctrine is heavily predicated on the success and perception of the BRI. Scepticism towards it has risen in parts of Africa and Asia, including even in close partner Pakistan. China has renegotiated some contracts and, in its own interests, also decided to judge more carefully the ability of countries to sustain the debt burdens that BRI arrangements create. There are indications, too, that it intends to concentrate more efforts in Southeast Asia where, reputationally, the success of the BRI is more strategically vital. While much attention has focused on the large traditional infrastructure projects of ports, railways and roads, it is the ambitions of the so-called Digital Silk Road (DSR) that may permit China to exert more influence over time, with less risk of ostentatious resistance, and then to collect the data that can help its accession to data-superpower status.

The appreciation that China is firmly focused on advancing technologically at speed, in the 5G domain in particular, has animated much of the present US–China geopolitical competition. The commanding lead that the US and its Western allies had in the technology realm is slipping. The national resources that China is devoting to this area are massive. America's concern over China's intellectual-property theft was an important element spurring the so-called 'trade war'. The fear that China would gain a further march on the US through its internet development and 5G expansion has mixed toxically with that initial charge. The risk of data theft by China when joined to the artificial-intelligence (AI) capacities it is generating for itself could create a stunning array of assets for China. This would pose a new kind of threat to international stability and order if the power that these developments provided to Beijing were not checked. The US strategic complaint is that once the DSR is consummated, China will own the data and potentially sensitive information of dozens of countries and use this as a lever to manage its diplomatic relations. In general, the idea that the US might trail China technologically has added a new dimension to the rivalry and a fresh theatre of competition. No one can credibly assess what the true dangers are in this realm, but the presumption that the ICT domain can be used at least as often for malign activities as for wholesome community-building is sufficiently settled for the US to begin erring on the side of extreme caution and for cyber 'space' to be confirmed as a core arena of contest. There is now a geopolitical operating premise that the ills of the internet are potentially more consequential than its benefits. Where physical control of territory was once the principal indicator of external power successfully wielded, supremacy in the cyber, AI and data domains – especially when combined – is a new key indicator.

This is even more powerfully the case given the rise of 'influence operations' as a central instrument of statecraft. A good deal of influence operations take place through conventional means – the funding of friendly political actors abroad or the insertion of one's citizens into prestigious foreign universities – but more now take place through social media and the invidious use of the internet. Russia has sought to use the instruments of state television to sow international propaganda but has also been propitious in the use of Twitter and internet bots to amplify the voices of disruptive forces in other, especially Western societies. Terrorist organisations have become first-class communications specialists, adopting personalities on the web and creating instruction manuals to animate and guide their adherents. More conventionally, Iran has developed a sophisticated network of influence in the Middle East that enables it to shape outcomes through local proxies, friends, allies and partners. Iran's 'persistent engagement' in these neighbouring jurisdictions is hard for others in the region or outside to match because it has honed a specialist strategy for building its own support system within fragile states. Its opponents struggle to fight Iran's embedded capacities. Within Asia, more countries are alert to the way in which China, in its efforts to be an uncontested regional power, is using its diasporas to spread the message of Greater China. Sometimes the means used to promote the Chinese point of view have been clumsy, inspiring some countries, such as Australia, to pass legislation that while generically crafted, is evidently aimed at constraining the way in which China can influence overseas electoral politics.

It is striking in these circumstances, where 'grey-zone warfare' has become so prominent, how much the soft power of the US and Europe has shrunk. Their ability to project power and inspire positive change has dramatically receded. This is partly a collateral effect of 'strategic self-determination' (especially in the Middle East), where an emerging political class is less inclined to accept Western guidance; partly a result of a loss of strategic self-confidence in the West and the failure of past efforts to export its own political model; and partly a consequence of domestic politics demanding the near-exclusive attention of Western political leaders.

At the height of US post-war power, in the late 1990s and early 2000s, the US and some of its allies made an effort not just to support democracy where it existed, but to promote it where it was absent. This was done on the strategic judgement that more democracies in the world would increase compliance with the rules-based order as a natural consequence, not requiring external enforcement. However, it later proved that democracies were difficult to install; elections in countries with limited prior experience of democratic values often invested illiberal leaders with power; and authoritarian regimes came to see real or imagined support by the West for 'colour revolutions' as an assault on their rules and governance models that required a vigorous response. Democracy promotion was perceived as a new imperial project, and in some societies, genuine democratic impulses were snuffed out before they had a chance to flourish naturally. Western powers began to moderate their international goals in proportion to their ability to implement them. The irony is that the democracy movements that pop up in different corners of the world today are more likely to have grown organically and domestically, rather than to have been fertilised from abroad.

As nationalism and populist policies have taken hold in several key Western states, the appetite for extrovert foreign policies has receded and so has the will to defend the rule of law, or to rally organised opposition to its more dangerous ruptures. While in the aggregate Western military power remains impressive, it is not harnessed cooperatively, as shown by the difficulty in late summer 2019 in mounting a maritime coalition to defend commercial shipping in the Strait of Hormuz. More importantly, the political authority that was once assumed as a matter of right by Western states, and was so often conferred on them by those who lived under different systems, has been greatly depleted. Military strength and technical prowess divorced from political reputation and moral authority are commensurately weaker and less effective. The rise of populist politics in the US and in a number of EU countries has consumed political attentions. It has rendered introvert and self-obsessed states that were previously open in outlook and guided by a notion of enlightened self-interest. These states are less interested today in promoting new rules or norms of behaviour; rather, they are focused on maintaining their own national and regional orders relatively intact. The main adherents to a 'rules-based order' are in countries more used to following than leading.

In a world that is fragmenting, powers such as Russia, Iran and China will strive to rewrite the rules in their own regions. Smaller powers will tend to heed some of the preferences of the would-be regional hegemon, while still aiming to import external support to watch over and perhaps constrain more extreme ambitions. Pretenders to regional leadership will not find the going all smooth: Russia will not always have its way in Eurasia; Iran will not control the Persian Gulf uncontested; China will discover that others in Asia will not pay it automatic tribute; both South Africa and Nigeria accept Africa's reluctance to acknowledge a continental overseer; and the US is struggling to uphold its Monroe Doctrine in Venezuela. For its part, Europe is simply finding its 'near abroad' coming uncomfortably close to its own borders, as people and instability migrate north from Africa and the Levant.

Maintaining defensive regional positions will coexist with the efforts in the digital domain to create specific internet ecosystems. The physical and virtual will potentially conflate and then divide into separate universes. While most would prefer to see a global internet sustained by trust as the main connective tissue, the trends are moving in the other direction: Europe legislating its own digital space; China perfecting its own great firewall; Russia contemplating a large intranet of its own; and the US, and its leading ICT industry, potentially finding the global internet contracting. This is not inevitable, but given how political power and cyber/AI dominance have been fused, the competition in cyber and over internet futures raises the prospect of the internet fracturing into different formations.

The same is true of legal regimes. A global rules-based order, to the degree it was ever established, is now clearly deposited in the banks of Western strategic nostalgia. Much the same can be said of international law, now so honoured in the breach rather than in the observance that it cannot make a credible claim to global force. Law is made and sustained by politics. When law cannot settle disputes, they are shunted back to the political realm for resolution. If this is true of municipal law, it is all the more so for international law. As compliance with international law shrinks, the rules will be made by those who command the most political power. Quite possibly, international law will cease to have true international pretensions. Universality then cedes to regionalism. The separate regional political orders and internet ecosystems might then be replicated in separate international legal arrangements. A global rules-based order may in time be re-established. That will only happen with the determined application of statecraft, rather than by the earnest convening of international summits. The process will be competitive. It will be upsetting. It will be draining and dynamic. The questions are: whose rules will they be, and how many different orders might they govern? This is the international strategic competition, foretold in the events of 2018–19, that will play out in the coming years, and which we anticipate in the analysis that follows in these pages.

# Chapter 3

# Strategic Policy Issues

## The Advent of 5G Technology

The world is on the cusp of rolling out fifth-generation (5G) mobile-network technology. Compared with 4G technology, 5G will allow for a vastly increased number of devices to be connected to mobile networks and, through increased capacity and speed, will enable new uses including ultra-high-definition video and virtual reality. In time, it will enable remote surgery and driverless cars on a large scale, and later smart cities in which traffic, utilities and public services are managed through the use of huge volumes of real-time data. 5G has become an area of contention between China and the United States. There are grounds for concern about the potential for espionage and sabotage, in the latter case because the 'Internet of Things' (IoT) will increase the attack surface of Western societies. However, America's principal preoccupation is that China will win the race to roll out and set standards for 5G, giving it a platform to become a technology leader in related fields.

The evolution of wireless telephony is classified into roughly decade-long generations. The first generation was rolled out in the 1980s and provided for voice calls. In the early 1990s, 2G provided the first digitally encrypted telecommunications, also enabling text messaging.

Later iterations of 2G, using General Packet Radio Services (GPRS) and Enhanced Data Rates for GSM Evolution (EDGE) standards, introduced data transmission via packet switching – a process by which messages or data are digitised and divided into packets for faster, efficient routing around a network. The improved data rates of 2G enabled basic web browsing and emails. The introduction of 3G, from the late 1990s, led to the full transition to data packet switching, increasing speed and enabling video calls, faster communication and mobile television. The roll-out of 4G from 2008 and the Long Term Evolution (LTE) standard a few years later provided for vastly faster data transmission by leveraging all-IP networks and relying entirely on packet switching. This fuelled the growth of video services such as YouTube.

The precise features and capabilities of 5G are still to be determined. It is expected not only to bring faster data speeds, allowing for a high-definition film to be downloaded in seconds rather than ten minutes via a 4G network, but also to handle massive numbers of devices and to support applications that require reliable communications with minimal lag. 5G has three primary network layers to deliver on these features. Firstly, enhanced mobile broadband (eMBB) enables data-driven usage that depends on fast data rates across a large coverage area such as high-quality video calls and streaming of high-definition films. Initially using existing 4G infrastructure, eMBB will be among the first 5G services commercially available, as early as 2019. Secondly, ultra-reliable low-latency communications (uRLLC) will enable usages that depend on little or no time gap in data transfer and very high levels of reliability, such as driverless vehicles or remote surgery.

The final layer is massive machine-type communications (mMTC), also known as the IoT, which is designed to provide wireless connectivity to billions of sensors and other edge devices. That in turn will enable fully smart homes, and by extension smart neighbourhoods and smart cities, in which it will be possible to capture huge efficiencies in the production and distribution of energy and civic services. Industry and agriculture are also expected to become 'smarter' thanks to the IoT. An early example is the networking of weather stations with soil moisture and salinity sensors, and watering systems, to provide real-time action-able intelligence that will boost agricultural yields.

The roll-out of 5G will be an evolutionary process. The first stage will be non-stand-alone 5G in which existing 4G LTE services are leveraged to gradually implement 5G, and later stages will move to stand-alone 5G technology. While the deployment cost of low- to mid-band 5G networks will be similar to current 4G/LTE networks, high-band 5G will require different architecture with much denser networks. Whereas LTE requires two to five sites per square kilometre in urban areas, high-band 5G will need 15–20 sites to deliver the promised performance improvements. High-band 5G is therefore likely to be selectively deployed initially.

The potential economic benefits of 5G are considerable, yet some of the world's richest economies now face a difficult choice between capturing those benefits at an early stage through reliance on foreign-owned technology or delaying the process to allow national companies or those from allied states to achieve the technological sophistication necessary to roll out 5G. The US government was a leader in communications technology for much of the second half of the twentieth century, but in the 1990s it handed primary responsibility to the private sector. The transfer has generated enormous wealth through the establishment of technology giants such as Amazon, Apple, Facebook and Google. However, this wealth has not been funnelled back into fundamental research in a way that has positioned the US to lead the global roll-out of 5G and the development of related technologies such as quantum computing and artificial intelligence (AI).

## The 5G patent race

The standards for 5G are overseen by an industry consortium known as the 3rd Generation Partnership Project (3GPP) and the International Telecommunication Union (ITU). As part of the standards-development process, companies disclose patents to the European Telecommunications Standards Institute (ETSI) as Standard Essential Patents (SEPs), which are those patents required to implement a technology within the wireless standard. Companies began increasing their filings of 5G-related patents around 2016. Owning patents serves both as a source of protection from lawsuits and a way to profit from licensing. In other words, it drives both how 5G networks are built and who profits from them.

Different datasets are available on SEPs related to 5G. According to one study (by Morten Springborg of C Worldwide Asset Management) drawing on ETSI data, of the 8,707 patents registered as of February 2019, Huawei owned 3,036 and ZTE 1,473, giving them a 52% share of the total. A different dataset by IPlytics, which runs to March 2019 but covers proposed as well as approved patents, gives the Chinese companies just over 34% of the SEPs for 5G. It is worthwhile putting these estimates into context. SEPs for 2G were almost completely dominated by Western companies such as Ericsson, Nokia, Nortel and Qualcomm. For 3G, roughly 10% of the SEPs were owned by Datang, Huawei and ZTE. Their share of 4G SEPs doubled to more than 20%.

Chinese firms' leading share of 5G patents underscores Western concerns about Beijing's 'Made in China 2025' plan to be a world leader in next-generation technologies such as 5G, AI, quantum computing and microchips (although, realistically, this will be limited to some aspects of 5G, AI and quantum communications). To an extent, winning the 5G race will give China an advantage in some of those related technologies. China's technology strategy is increasingly about shaping the global information and communications technology (ICT) environment to suit its interests, making use of its status as a global manufacturing hub for ICT products and its growing economic and political reach. Huawei and ZTE play a central role. They have achieved extensive penetration overseas in 4G, particularly in the developing world, where they have built and operated core networks, and in Europe and South Korea. Huawei is reportedly spending US$10 billion a year on research and development related to 5G base stations – significantly more than its main rivals. Paul Triolo of the Eurasia Group consultancy says it is the only telecommunications company in the world that can produce and deploy all the elements of a 5G network at cost and scale; other experts are sceptical.

## Geopolitical and security implications

Since 2018, several governments have expressed strong concerns over Chinese telecommunications equipment, although there is no consensus over the scale of the problems or the correct policy response. Perceptions of vulnerability as well as the realities could have knock-on effects for Western states and particularly for the Five Eyes alliance with regard to intelligence-sharing. US Deputy Assistant Secretary of State for Cyber and International Communications Policy Rob Strayer indicated in April 2019 that the US would not share information with allies over networks it considered insecure.

In 2018 Australia ran ahead of its fellow Five Eyes states by issuing guidance to dissuade telecoms companies from using Chinese 5G equipment; the US followed suit. Canada, New Zealand and the UK, however, have indicated a willingness to permit Chinese telecommunications companies' involvement in non-essential parts of their 5G infrastructure. The division reflects existing dependencies on Chinese telecoms, and specifically Huawei technology, as well as concerns on the part of the UK and Canada that it is desirable to have a global set of standards for 5G security that cannot be achieved if one major country or company is completely excluded.

Some politicians worry that Chinese domination of 5G technology would enable Beijing to conduct espionage more effectively. The US government started to publicly acknowledge systematic Chinese data exfiltration in August 2006, after Chinese actors had successfully intruded into the US Department of Defense's network for exchanging sensitive but unclassified information and downloaded up to 20 terabytes of data. Private threat-intelligence companies have a longer history of reporting on Chinese cyber-enabled espionage. Some argue that with more devices connected under 5G networks, the potential for data theft will increase. In reality, the effective use of encryption and other cyber-security measures would probably mean the risk of espionage under 5G is much the same as under 4G. In addition, ubiquitously used commercial applications now encrypt by default much of the data travelling across global networks. The giant US technology companies that mainly provide those applications have the best potential access to the underlying data and, if US legal thresholds are met, the US government via those companies. This dwarfs anything that China would be able to do by merely providing the hardware for parts of a mobile network in a Western country. Similarly, it is worth noting that Five Eyes' secret intelligence is especially strongly encrypted and is anyway not allowed to be transmitted over public networks, mobile or otherwise.

Likewise, carrying out cyber disruption (sabotaging a network, for example) in a 5G environment is not straightforward. Mobile networks in most advanced countries are part of a much larger and highly complex telecommunications infrastructure, with inbuilt redundancy and resilience. The UK, for example, has so many connections to the internet that only the failure of multiple nodes would noticeably impact the functioning of the system. The UK plans to roll out 5G within this ecosystem and to have built-in redundancy.

This is not to say that 5G does not introduce new risks for states, however. As the technology reaches maturity, more and more services and activities will depend on internet connections and the provision of real-time data. These would potentially be subject to sabotage in times of war or acute strategic crisis. Furthermore, a vast range of vital services could be taken down by interrupting the power supply on which all internet-enabled services would depend.

While the prospect of 5G roll-out has some potentially negative implications for the vulnerability of states to espionage and sabotage, the principal risks relate to economic advantage and the shape of the future technological landscape. 5G will have cascading effects on robotics, AI and machine learning, for instance, across the economy (there will also be military applications). The US finds itself in the odd position, having been the world's leading technology power for decades, of lagging behind China in this crucial area. It instinctively rejects the notion of relying on Chinese technology to capture the full benefits of smart neighbourhoods, cities, agriculture and manufacturing. China, for its part, wishes to break its dependence on the US for hardware (including microchips) and software (including mobile-phone applications).

The controversy surrounding 5G is part of a broader contest between the US – which until very recently took its supremacy for granted – and China over which of them will dominate the internet-related technologies of the future. With China currently better placed to roll out 5G, it is little wonder the US is seeking to delay its rival and so buy the time needed to catch up. US concerns over the security implications of China providing 5G to its allies and other states are but one symptom of American disquiet over China's technological challenge.

# China's Concept of World Order: Theory and Practice

The trade war between the United States and China that began in June 2018 with the decision by US President Donald Trump to impose tariffs on a range of Chinese imports has brought into stark relief the degree to which China is now seen as challenging the US-led international order. From the outset, it was clear that the friction between the world's two largest economies was about far more than just trade. At issue were long-simmering differences of ideology and values and a contest for global geostrategic influence that was increasingly being played out in the economic and technological spheres.

For some time, both states have been setting out their respective visions of how the world should be run. In its December 2017 National Security Strategy report, the US government characterised China as a disruptive revisionist power. In October 2018, US Vice President Mike Pence delivered a speech at the Hudson Institute that was unremittingly critical of China's behaviour. In April 2019, Kiron Skinner, the Director of Policy Planning at the State Department, said that the US was in a 'fight with a really different civilization' and that it was the first time that the US 'will have a great power competitor that is not Caucasian'. China, on the other hand, has been increasingly vocal in questioning the fitness for purpose of the global governance order established by the US and its allies after the Second World War. As an alternative, China has offered Chinese wisdom, the Chinese development model and the idea of a world built around a 'community of common destiny for mankind' – *renlei mingyun gongtongti* – now more commonly (though less accurately) translated as 'a community of common future'.

The significance of the term 'community of common destiny' has largely escaped the notice of Western policy makers. First used by President Xi Jinping in 2013 in a speech at the Boao Forum, it has since become clear that this concept enjoys the status of an official policy formulation – *tifa* – and as such needs to be taken seriously as a statement of Chinese government intent. Chinese strategy often emerges in this manner, starting with a broad general formulation that sets the direction of travel and serves as a starting point for a more detailed elaboration. The significance of this particular formulation can be inferred from the fact that the Belt and Road Initiative (BRI), seen by Beijing as the primary vehicle for implementing the community of common destiny strategy, has been incorporated into the Chinese constitution. Western incomprehension is unsurprising given China's failure to date to offer a detailed account of what the concept entails. There is, however, a body of Chinese-language writing that does provide greater specificity. Some valuable work by Western scholars has also illuminated the intellectual context within which the concept has arisen. More pertinently, it is also possible to track actions by the Chinese state that have sought to promote and normalise this concept within the international discourse on global governance.

## Reinvigorated ideology

During the 1990s, a vibrant debate began to take place among China's intellectual elite about the direction the country should take at a time of rapid economic growth and rapidly growing economic inequality. Various strands of leftism and authoritarianism contended with liberalism and social democracy, but of particular salience were the views of a group of new leftist intellectuals, as distinct from old leftist intellectuals motivated by a nostalgia for the Maoist era. The new left, comprising thinkers such as Hu Angang, Wang Shaogang and Jiang Shigong who were mostly Western-trained, rejected the idea that there could be only one (Western) path to development. They saw a strong centralised state as the only way to mitigate inequalities and rejected Western notions of electoral democracy, civil society and the neutrality of law as at odds with achieving that outcome. They were influenced by the ideas of the Weimar intellectual and Nazi collaborator Carl Schmitt on issues of state sovereignty and the law and the impossibility of achieving a modus vivendi with political opponents. The key elements of their thinking reinforced the superiority of political sovereignty over the rule of law:

they argued for a repoliticisation of the state, rejected universalism and asserted Chinese exceptionalism.

Such ideas were hardly novel in the context of a Marxist–Leninist culture. Nonetheless, they provided important validation for established ideology at a time when the Chinese Communist Party (CCP) was navigating the uncertainties and social dislocation generated by rapid economic development, and was facing a period of international isolation following the violent suppression of the 1989 student protests. They also served as a basis for what was to become a more unapologetic articulation of distinctive Chinese values under Xi Jinping. In China, it is always hard to determine whether intellectuals influence policy or whether their output is merely designed to add credibility to predetermined party policy goals – though it is generally more the latter than the former. However, there can be no doubt that the intellectuals of the new left moved closer to the locus of power under Hu Jintao.

Another important intellectual influence during that period was Wang Huning, a Shanghai-based academic who was the architect of the contributions to the Marxist–Leninist theory of Jiang Zemin, Hu Jintao and Xi Jinping. Wang, who in an unprecedented move for an academic was appointed to the Politburo Standing Committee in 2016, had been very critical of what he saw as the unbridled individualism of US society, as depicted in his 1991 book *America Against Itself* (*Meiguo Fandui Meiguo*), and was a consistent advocate of a statist model.

During the 1990s and early 2000s, China was able to cultivate a largely benign international image as a status quo power. As China became more globally prominent, it sought pre-emptively to allay concerns that its emergence as a major power would be globally disruptive or even lead to war with established powers (i.e., the US). In the late 1990s, China promoted a new security concept that held that Cold War concepts of competing and antagonistic blocs were outdated and that the way for states to enhance their security was through diplomatic and economic engagement. Implicit, though not yet explicit, in this concept was China's concern about a continuing network of US alliance relations, with states around China's periphery seen as part of a containment strategy. This security concept evolved into the concept of China's peaceful rise, subsequently renamed China's peaceful development. This concept, first enunciated by former Central Party School vice-president Zeng Bijian in a speech at the 2003 Boao Forum, sought to persuade the world that China would be sufficiently self-aware to avoid what Graham Allison was later to refer to as 'the Thucydides Trap', where anxiety about a rising power drives the hegemonic state to wage war. China went to some lengths to promote good-neighbourly relations with the Association of Southeast Asian Nations (ASEAN) and many of its outstanding border disputes with neighbouring states were resolved.

The period between 2007 and 2012 – the latter part of Hu Jintao's tenure as secretary-general – came to be widely perceived within China as a time of drift, characterised by the entrenchment of vested interests that inhibited further economic reform and by levels of corruption that increasingly challenged the CCP's credibility. This period also witnessed a gradual move away from relative liberalism towards a somewhat more authoritarian approach at home, as well as the emergence of a more assertive approach internationally. This was fuelled by a number of key developments: international protests about Tibet in the run-up to the 2008 Beijing Olympics (which China's leadership saw as the country's coming-out party and which the West seemed determined to spoil); the 2008 global financial crisis (which hit China's economy particularly hard and called into question the fitness for purpose of the Washington Consensus); the Obama administration's pivot to Asia (which reinforced existing perceptions that the US was seeking to contain China); and a succession of 'colour revolutions' that Beijing perceived as being instigated by the US and which gave rise to concern that China might be next on the hit list – a concern further exacerbated by evidence of continued Western attachment to 'neo-interventions' in Libya and Syria. In addition, while China's leaders saw the adoption of modern information and communications technology (ICT) as essential for the country's economic development, they had from the outset been concerned about the potential of a US-dominated internet to serve as a vector for the transmission of subversive ideas, a concern that was only enhanced by the

2012 Snowden revelations. Meanwhile, China's efforts to establish a different modus vivendi with the US based on a 'new kind of great power relations', interpreted by some analysts as amounting to a G2 world, were met with studied indifference.

The appointment of Xi Jinping as the CCP secretary-general in 2012 came at a point when China's domestic politics had become more than usually convoluted and contested. Former leaders, in particular Jiang Zemin, were manoeuvring to ensure that their and their families' interests would be protected by whoever replaced Hu Jintao. In the western megalopolis of Chongqing, Bo Xilai, who had made a name for himself by promoting a kind of neo-Maoist governance based on mass mobilisation – the shorthand term for which was 'singing red songs'– was engaged in a very un-Chinese campaign of self-promotion for the top job. Vested interests in the security and military communities had become independent fiefdoms which were increasingly unresponsive to central party control. Xi, who up to that point had maintained a low profile and hence was something of an unknown quantity, moved quickly to mark out his territory once appointed. In 2013, Central Party Document Number Nine was circulated. This document listed seven taboo topics: Western constitutional democracy (including the separation of powers, a multiparty system, general elections, an independent judiciary and a 'nationalised' army); universal values; civil society; promoting economic neo-liberalism; advocating a free press; promoting historical nihilism (i.e., focusing on the party's mistakes and failures); and questioning the 'reform and opening-up' policies initiated by Deng Xiaoping and 'socialism with Chinese characteristics'. This set the tone for a relentless crackdown on civil-society activism and the expression of heterodox views that, together with a wide-ranging and sustained anti-corruption campaign, have had a chilling effect on public discourse and behaviour.

Internationally, China's leadership was motivated by perceptions of both opportunity and threat. The sense of strategic opportunity, which had become a trope in Party documents since the mid-1990s, was driven by China's seemingly unstoppable economic and technological advance but also by a perception that the US and the West more generally was in a state of irrevocable decline and that China's moment had come. The US had demonstrated its inability to exercise effective stewardship over the global financial system; was bogged down in the Middle East and Afghanistan; and had, contrary to Chinese expectations, failed to take meaningful action to curtail China's programme of building military facilities on disputed islands and reefs in the South China Sea. Meanwhile, Europe was mired in the eurozone crisis and falling victim to a divisive and debilitating populism. Western liberal democracy no longer seemed to have the answers and a Chinese model of authoritarian state capitalism enjoyed increasing allure in the developing world. Still, China's approach to global governance was first and foremost defensive in nature, driven by the need to maintain the CCP's power by seeking explicit international legitimation of China's Marxist–Leninist system and preserving and promoting an international trading system that was essential to China's continued economic prosperity. Concern that the US under Donald Trump appeared to be resiling from the international trading system led to the unlikely spectacle of Xi at the 2018 session of the World Economic Forum presenting China as the leading advocate of globalisation and world trade.

In promoting its vision of global governance, China emphasised a commonality of interests with the developing world. At the second of two Politburo study sessions on global governance held in 2015 and 2016, Xi observed that 'China must make the international order more reasonable and just to protect the common interests of China and other developing countries'. In an op-ed in the *People's Daily* in December 2017, Foreign Minister Wang Yi argued for the centrality of the United Nations' role in upholding the interests and values of China and other developing countries. China also sought to highlight the shortcomings of the status quo. In 2017, then-state counsellor Yang Jiechi observed that it had become 'increasingly difficult for Western governance concepts, systems and models to keep pace with the new international situation'. Issues discussed at the June 2018 Central Foreign Affairs Work Conference included a decline in the quality of global governance; persistent slow global economic growth; climate change; violations of international norms; and the pervasive nature of transnational terrorism: all issues of real concern to China and which the US-led status quo increasingly struggled to address. China may have experienced a sense of schadenfreude in the face of a perceived US decline, but it was aware of the risks that might arise in the event of a wholesale US withdrawal from an international policing role that China was both unwilling and unable to fill.

## Global governance with Chinese characteristics for the new era

Academic writings on the community of common destiny concept began as soon as Xi's appointment was announced and quickly gathered momentum following the inauguration in 2013 of One Belt One Road (subsequently renamed the BRI). The community of common destiny concept still lacks formal definition and is subject to continuing debate within China's policy and intellectual elite, with numerous study centres being set up to research the concept. However, there is broad convergence around the centrality of economic development and the need for the concept to exercise the broadest possible international appeal. An article by Professor Zhang Yaojun in the journal of the Beijing International Studies University's Belt and Road Research Institute in 2017 gives a good overview of the key elements on which there is consensus.

Zhang sees the BRI as the principal means of implementing the theoretical concept of the community of common destiny. This concept offers a new framework of international relations that he regards as being forward-looking, comprehensive and offering leadership, and is linked to China's success in economic development and poverty reduction, industrialisation and infrastructure development. Zhang argues that existing global governance arrangements are not in line with new global economic realities. The Chinese model is designed to move beyond political and military alliances, ideologically based foreign-development assistance and cartels and small groups. It abjures hegemonism and colonialism, interference in the internal affairs of other states, the imposition on others of specific political and ideological systems and the establishment of spheres of influence. It rejects Western international-relations theories based on great-power contestation and alliance relations, and the proposition that globalisation and modernisation must equate with Westernisation. Zhang emphasises that the community of common destiny is a work in progress and will take time to realise. It faces numerous challenges from historical inertia and old thinking; US hegemony (which seeks to use 'smart power' – *qiao shili* – to contain and suppress rising powers); and regional instability, fuelled in the case of the Asia-Pacific region by the existence of US alliance structures.

A key element of the community of common destiny concept is the self-image of China as a morally superior power concerned about the well-being of all humankind, in contrast to the US, which is depicted as being motivated by narrow and selfish concerns and whose politics are dominated by special-interest groups. This approach draws on traditional Chinese concepts of governance that date back to the pre-Christian era, in particular the concept of *tian xia* ('all under heaven'). This concept, which first appears in the *Shang Shu*, an ancient compilation of the sayings of the mythical emperors Yao and Shun and the rulers of the Shang and Zhou dynasties, was developed by Confucius and later Confucian philosophers such as Mencius (Mengzi) into the political ideal of a state in which peoples coexist harmoniously under an enlightened ruler upon whom has been conferred the Mandate of Heaven (*tian ming*) – as supposedly happened during the Western Zhou dynasty (1046–771 BCE). It is also bound up with a self-image of China as a peaceful non-expansionist power, a characterisation that is at odds with much of China's recorded history. Although China decries the Western alliance system, the community of common destiny has been described by Yang as a 'non-aligned alliance' in which participating states are expected to 'stand on the side of China, or at least, be neutral'.

## Implementation

The consensus assumption is that binding states to China's vision must begin with the development of economic links, with the primary focus on the BRI. The expectation is that as economic links grow closer, states will appreciate the benefits of also developing close political and security links with China, and with closer engagement will come a greater identity of interests and values. Beyond the development of physical infrastructure (in the form of ports and rail links), the digital component of the BRI will enable China to develop a wide range of communications infrastructure, including under-sea fibre-optic cables and core backbone ICT networks, together with the capacities for surveillance and social control that these networks can enable. The same is likely in due course to be true of concepts such as smart cities, which in China constitute an interface in which technologies deployed to minimise the frictions and maximise the efficiencies of urban life also facilitate the state's ability to monitor and control populations. Like the community of common destiny, the BRI is seen as a work in progress and has been subject to revisions in the face of international criticism of issues such as debt entrapment and corruption.

In working to create a receptive environment for its concepts of global governance, China is, in the words of a 2019 report by the Center for a New American Security, 'increasingly using its economic, political and institutional power to change the global governance system from within. The CCP ... has become more proactive in injecting its ideological concepts into international statements of consensus and harnessing the programmatic dimensions of global governance to advance its own foreign policy strategies.'

To achieve these aims, China is:

- promoting a particularist view of human rights, enabling governments to cite unique circumstances to justify disregarding individual or minority rights;
- redefining democracy in terms of economic and social rights;
- emphasising the inviolability of state sovereignty;
- infusing consensus global goods with Chinese ideological terms; and
- resolving political disputes with other states through bilateral negotiations rather than resorting to a rules-based approach.

Such techniques are part of a wider effort to develop China's discourse power – *huayuquan* – and normalise the narrative of the Chinese party-state at a global level. The overt dimensions of this campaign include the promotion of Confucius institutes, significant expenditure on new international media outlets such as China Global Television Network (CGTN) and investment in Hollywood with a view to the production of more China-friendly films. It also includes exercises such as the Conference of Dialogue on Asian Civilizations that took place in Beijing in May 2019 with the theme of 'exchange and mutual learning among Asian civilisations and a community with a shared future'.

## An uneasy peace?

Notwithstanding the vagueness of the formulation thus far, it is possible to discern the broad outlines of a concept that looks very much like a form of Chinese hegemony that may have global aspirations but which more realistically conceives of the world in concentric circles, with a primary focus on the Asia-Pacific region. States seen as falling within the scope of the community of common destiny would accept the legitimacy of China's political system; internalise China's core interests and not act against them on pain of sanction; acknowledge that the interests of great powers (i.e., China) take precedence over customary international law; and accept that disputes should be resolved bilaterally rather than through a rules-based order, thereby conferring a permanent advantage on China. In return, states would be largely left to their own devices in terms of ideology and political organisation. Comparisons have been offered with the tributary state model of foreign relations, although the concept is perhaps better understood as a political framework for ensuring regional stability, and hence China's national security, rather than the active exercise of political dominance.

The community of common destiny concept, though needing to be taken seriously as an indication of how China views the world and aspires to reshape it, is better viewed as an aspiration rather than a blueprint for global domination. China's leaders have looked at the British and US models of global hegemony and appear to have concluded that the costs of either model outweigh any potential benefit. There is a risk that current US alarm about China's potential emergence as a peer competitor and the impasse over trade and technology could translate into an escalatory dynamic that China is probably loath to embark on. It remains to be seen whether the Sino-US relationship will turn into a fully fledged confrontation or whether the situation will be as described by Chinese scholar Yan Xuetong in his 2019 essay 'The Age of Uneasy Peace', with the two countries opposed in strategic interests but evenly matched in terms of power. Such a situation suggests a world defined more by realpolitik than rules and a more fluid system of international alliances that are issue-specific. In such a world, tensions will continue to simmer and to play out through economic and technology competition and, possibly, proxy conflicts. However, rather as in the Cold War, broad military parity (which China aims to achieve by the middle of the century) between the two major powers will limit the risk of all-out conflict.

# Prospects for New START

On 28 June 2019, US President Donald Trump and Russian President Vladimir Putin began their bilateral meeting in Osaka by affirming their 'very good' relationship and suggesting that it could lead to progress on a number of fronts, including arms control. However, there have been no major accomplishments that either can point to as a product of their personal chemistry, let alone an improvement in bilateral relations. In the field of arms control, there is a looming test case: the future of the New Strategic Arms Reduction Treaty (New START). Extending New START is an action that could be done in a day with a decision by Trump and Putin to move forward – a unique circumstance in today's world of US–Russia relations, where domestic and international complexities and constraints abound. For this reason, many observers have assumed that, at some point, it will simply get done, but prospects for New START's survival are in fact dim – perhaps far dimmer than is commonly understood. Whether the June 2019 Trump–Putin bilateral meeting fundamentally alters what has so far proven to be an unpredictable and uncertain pattern for the United States' Russia policy and provides an incentive for extending New START is one of the key variables in plotting the treaty's fate.

## The erosion of arms control

New START entered into force on 5 February 2011 and will expire on 5 February 2021, unless Washington and Moscow agree to extend it. New START limits the number of deployed nuclear warheads of the US and Russia to 1,550 each, and limits the number of long-range intercontinental and submarine-launched ballistic missiles and heavy bombers. These legally binding constraints also include provisions for data exchanges, notifications and on-site inspections, providing a significant degree of transparency and predictability.

Today, New START stands as one of the last remaining pillars of an arms-control regime that for decades has regulated both nuclear and conventional forces. The unravelling of the arms-control fabric began in 2001 with the decision by the administration of George W. Bush to withdraw from the 1972 Anti-Ballistic Missile (ABM) Treaty in 2002. The quick demise of ABM was followed by the slow disintegration of the 1990 Conventional Armed Forces in Europe (CFE) Treaty, with first Russia and then the US and NATO suspending their obligations in 2007 and 2011, respectively.

More recently, under Trump, the 1987 Intermediate-Range Nuclear Forces (INF) Treaty – which banned ground-launched nuclear-capable ballistic and cruise missiles with ranges of 500–5,500 kilometres – was set to expire in early August 2019, after the US and Russia decided to withdraw from the treaty following the deployment of prohibited missiles by Russia and Russian allegations of US violations. The future of the Comprehensive Nuclear-Test-Ban Treaty (CTBT) appears in doubt, as the Trump administration is now alleging that Russia is failing to comply with the treaty's ban on nuclear-explosive testing, coinciding with a letter by four Republican senators asking if the president would consider 'unsigning' the CTBT. How relevant this crumbling edifice is to the survival of New START is an open question; however, it is fair to say that the extension of New START in this environment would cut against the trendline.

## A bad deal?

Scepticism by Trump regarding agreements negotiated by presidents other than himself – and former president Barack Obama in particular – appears to be a significant factor in the Trump administration's decision-making regarding the fate of a range of security and trade agreements. While Trump has been known to change course on an issue, he has consistently and continuously repudiated agreements of his predecessors, including the Trans-Pacific Partnership, the North American Free Trade Agreement, the Paris Agreement on climate change and the Joint Comprehensive Plan of Action (JCPOA), also known as the Iran nuclear deal. In his first phone call with Putin on 28 January 2017 – only days after Trump's inauguration as president – Trump reportedly referred to New START as a bad deal for the US in response to Putin inquiring over the possibility of extending the treaty. There has been no evidence of the president having a change of heart.

Within the Trump administration, opposition to an extension has also hardened. Over the past two years, senior Trump administration officials who appeared at times sympathetic to New START – including secretary of state Rex Tillerson, secretary of defense James Mattis and national security advisor Lt-Gen. H.R. McMaster – have departed. In at least two cases, their replacements – Mike Pompeo at the State Department and John Bolton at the White House – appear more sceptical with respect to Russia policy writ large, and arms control more specifically. National Security Advisor Bolton has been a long-standing and vocal critic of arms control in general and New START in particular, writing in a 2010 November *New York Times* op-ed that the treaty's faults were 'legion' and thus it should be rejected or amended so that it didn't 'weaken our national defense' by constraining strategic launchers that could be used for conventional capabilities. He also cited inadequate verification, ignoring Russian tactical-nuclear-weapons capabilities, and hindering American missile-defence programmes. On 18 June 2019, Bolton spoke of a New START extension, saying 'there's no decision, but I think it's unlikely'.

There is also a lack of support from Republicans in general for an extension. While leading Democrats in the House and Senate strongly support New START extension, at present there is no discernable pushback from elected Republicans against the president's stated scepticism towards New START, in particular in the US Senate. On the contrary, there is criticism, including from former Republican presidential nominee now US Senator from Utah Mitt Romney – often thought to be a sensible moderate in today's Republican Party – who wrote in a 2010 July *Washington Post* op-ed that

> By all indications, the Obama administration has been badly out-negotiated. Perhaps the president's eagerness for global disarmament led his team to accede to Russia's demands, or perhaps it led to a document that was less than carefully drafted. Whatever the reason for the treaty's failings, it must not be ratified: The security of the United States is at stake.

Nine years later, Romney has not forgotten his original critique. In a 2019 May Senate Foreign Relations Committee hearing, Romney noted his earlier opposition to New START and reiterated that the treaty did not address non-strategic nuclear weapons and had other 'loopholes' that Russia was taking advantage of. At the same hearing, the Foreign Relations Committee Chairman, Republican Senator Jim Risch from Idaho, repeatedly emphasised his opposition to a 'gratuitous' five-year extension.

## Time running out

As the Obama administration took office in 2009 and considered its options for nuclear arms control, the existing agreement regulating strategic nuclear arms – the 2002 Strategic Offensive Reductions Treaty (which relied on the 1991 Strategic Arms Reduction Treaty for verifying implementation) – was due to expire on 31 December 2012. Consistent with the policies of presidents dating back to John F. Kennedy, the Obama administration placed a high priority on ensuring that the world's deadliest weapons would not go unregulated, and moved quickly to begin new talks with Russia that resulted in a new treaty, albeit with modest reductions, in two years.

In many respects, the Trump administration entered office in 2017 facing the same dilemma as that of the Obama administration: whether and if so how to continue regulating US and Russian strategic nuclear forces, looking ahead to when the existing treaty was due to expire. Rather than move quickly, however, for two years there was no clear direction from the White House and no talks with Russia on the future of New START and strategic arms control.

Finally, at the June 2019 G20 meeting in Osaka, Japan, Trump and Putin reportedly agreed to instruct their foreign ministers to begin consultations on nuclear arms control. However, despite the image of partnership projected by Trump and Putin at the summit, the underlying reality of US–Russia relations is more complex, with the direction of US policy towards Russia at the heart of uncertainty over New START. On the one hand, Trump's professed willingness to improve US–Russia relations is one of the few constants that ran through his campaign, transition and the first two and a half years of his presidency. Yet whatever plans Trump might have had for moving quickly and substantively to pursue better relations with Moscow have consistently been shelved and replaced by a more aggressive Russia policy, including additional US sanctions and other actions – including withdrawal from INF.

The year leading up to the November 2020 US elections also will be crucial to whether Trump has any political space to pursue better relations with Moscow. One can be certain that Democrats and Republicans will campaign hard this election cycle against Russian interference in US domestic politics – and implicitly if not explicitly against the prospects of closer ties between Trump and Putin's Russia. As a result, under any circumstances, there will be a steep political hill to climb for Trump and his administration to improve ties with Moscow.

On the Russian side, Moscow's position on extending New START may appear favourable at the moment – Putin has recently reiterated that Russia has said 'a hundred times that we are ready for talks [on New START]' – but it is unclear that Russia would agree to simply extend the treaty for five years, if that were to become Washington's position late in the day. At that moment, Moscow might seek revisions to the agreement (relating to procedures for converting launchers from nuclear to conventional roles) or concessions in other areas unrelated to New START (constraints on missile defence, long-range conventional 'prompt-strike' systems, or space-based weapons), either one of which could frustrate New START's extension. Russian Ambassador to the US Anatoly Antonov, who served as the chief Russian negotiator for New START, has underscored this point: 'The extension of the New START is not a simple technicality that could be resolved in a couple of weeks … Serious issues must be settled.' Despite progress in discussing arms control at Osaka, Putin said that 'we cannot yet say whether this will lead to an extension of New START treaty'.

Trump's volte-face at Osaka not only put the extension of New START belatedly back on the agenda, but even opened the possibility of expanding the arms-control framework, despite the limited time. After the Trump–Putin Osaka meeting, a White House statement reported that 'The Presidents agreed the two countries will continue discussion on a twenty-first-century model of arms control, which President Trump stated as needing to include China'. However, a new model of arms control that includes China would be an ambitious undertaking that most experts believe would be a multi-year project – and many believe is a framework constructed by Bolton to sabotage a simple extension of New START. That said, on 6 May 2019, Secretary of State Mike Pompeo appeared to take a more measured stance, acknowledging that a trilateral deal involving China might be 'too ambitious', noting that there are 'just a couple years left before New START expires' and that it may be necessary to address the expiration of the treaty 'on a bilateral basis'.

Of course, it is possible that Trump will lose his bid for re-election when the votes are counted in November 2020. This would open the door to his successor moving quickly during the first two weeks of the new president's term – before New START expires on 5 February 2021 – to seek a clean five-year extension, but this would require both alacrity in Washington and complete cooperation from Moscow, neither of which is guaranteed. Moreover, the prospects of losing in November 2020 could prompt Trump to act more aggressively to ensure New START's demise by simply informing Moscow that the US intends to withdraw from the treaty in three months' time, as allowed under the treaty, arranging the calendar so that the treaty would terminate before Trump leaves the White House.

### In the absence of New START

The unwillingness or inability of Washington and Moscow to extend New START prior to its expiration in 2021 February would be another blow against any restoration of more positive relations between Washington and Moscow, which could impact bilateral issues such as Crimea and Ukraine, election interference and US sanctions, which are arguably more significant at present.

That said, one should not underestimate the longer-term significance for bilateral relations between Washington and Moscow of eliminating the most important of the few remaining constraints on US and Russian nuclear forces, as well as US recognition of Russia as a peer – its sole peer indeed – in the field of nuclear arms. The expiration of New START would be rightly perceived as yet another breakdown in relations between the two countries, and another failure of the nation's two leaders to agree on a path forward on a crucial security issue. Over time, the deregulation of strategic nuclear arms – including the removal of limitations and means for verification – will inevitably increase suspicions over what each side is doing now, or planning to do in the future. This will lead to a further erosion of trust and feed arguments in both capitals for accelerating nuclear-weapons development and deployment. It could well signal the beginning of a new and more dangerous arms race.

Failing to extend New START would also undermine the 1970 Treaty on the Non-Proliferation of Nuclear Weapons (NPT), which remains central to limiting the spread of nuclear weapons. Any action that calls into question the commitment of the NPT nuclear-weapons states, in particular the US and Russia, to pursue their NPT-related disarmament obligations weakens the non-proliferation–disarmament framework that is at the core of the NPT 'bargain' between non-nuclear and nuclear-weapons states.

New START was rightly perceived to be a concrete demonstration by the two states who together control 90% of global nuclear inventories that they remained committed to limiting and reducing their nuclear stockpiles. In the absence of New START – and with no new agreement on the horizon, the collapse of INF and new questions over CTBT – the perception will be that disarmament has stalled or even been abandoned on the eve of the NPT's 50th anniversary in 2020.

### Reason to hope?

Optimism regarding the future of New START rests in two quarters. Firstly, both the US military and intelligence community place great value on the treaty's monitoring regime, which provides transparency and visibility into Russian nuclear forces beyond what can be obtained solely through national technical means of verification. Moreover, the treaty limits the size and structure of America's most potent potential nuclear adversary. One would expect these arguments to be made to Trump – and for the same reasons, to Putin by the Russian military and intelligence services. Together, this could help tilt the balance in favour of a simple five-year extension of New START – in particular if reinforced by close US allies, such as France, Germany and the United Kingdom. That logic, however, may not carry the day – particularly if filtered through White House hawks and the president's hostility to 'anything Obama'. Indeed it was the US defence and intelligence communities which, joined by European allies, reportedly argued in favour of Washington's continued adherence to the JCPOA – and that agreement fell when confronted by Bolton and Trump.

The second – and perhaps most compelling – force that might lead to an extension of New START is political. Both Trump and Putin could benefit from what would be a relatively easy win, especially as extending New START could be done with a stroke of a pen, not subject to any legislative review or approval process in either country. It would be perceived positively internationally and in both countries, and lay a foundation for a more robust bilateral relationship that could benefit both leaders, and both nations.

While this political dynamic on its own may be enough to save New START, the forces against the treaty appear now to be more salient and potentially ruinous. Time will soon be of the essence in extending New START, but so far the Trump administration has taken time off – and now appears committed to a new course that would require more time than is available.

# The Climatic Consequences of a Limited Nuclear War

At the height of the Cold War, the prospect of a devastating nuclear exchange was in the consciousness of publics in North America, Europe and the Soviet Union. In 1979, the US Office of Technology Assessment (OTA) published a report stating that a major nuclear war between the United States and the Soviet Union might kill more than 200 million people – approximately 5% of the world's population at the time – within the first 30 days, with millions more dying from starvation, exposure, radiation effects and inadequate medical care in the aftermath.

The end of the Cold War and reductions in the number of nuclear arms substantially downgraded those risks throughout the 1990s. The number of nuclear weapons currently deployed by the US and Russia is only about 5% of what they collectively held in the mid-1980s, while the arsenals of the other seven nuclear-weapons states amount to several hundred weapons each at most. India, Pakistan and North Korea have

Figure 1: **Nuclear warheads, 1945–2017**

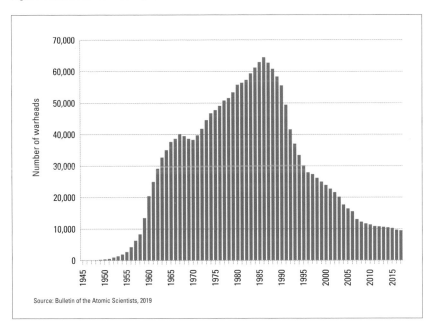

Source: Bulletin of the Atomic Scientists, 2019

arsenals of relatively low-yield (10–40 kilotonne–kt) fission weapons. An exchange between nuclear powers with arsenals of this sort would cause immense human suffering and economic damage, but on a scale comparable to what most combatant nations experienced in the major wars of the twentieth century.

Yet the global framework of arms-control treaties is coming under increasing strain. Important treaties such as the 1972 Anti-Ballistic Missile (ABM) Treaty have been revoked, while both the United States and Russia have announced that they are suspending their obligations to the 1987 Intermediate-Range Nuclear Forces (INF) Treaty, with the US intending to withdraw in late 2019. The 2010 New Strategic Arms Reduction Treaty (New START) may follow suit: as of June 2019, negotiations to extend the treaty, which expires in February 2021, had yet to be scheduled.

Meanwhile, the US and Russia are modernising their arsenals and changing their doctrines in ways that facilitate nuclear use, while the dispute between India and Pakistan over Kashmir remains a potential flashpoint for the use of nuclear weapons. The possibility of proliferation cascades – and consequent risk that nuclear weapons might be used through accident, misjudgement or deliberate aggression – is real, especially in the Middle East and South Asia, while the trend of increasing geopolitical competition and systemic insecurity is likely to continue.

## Nuclear Winter

For more than three decades after Hiroshima, concerns about nuclear war focused on the immediate effects of blast, heat and radiation from nuclear explosions. In the early 1980s, however, the possibility that a nuclear exchange could affect the world's climate entered, and even at times dominated, the discussion.

In 1983, a team of five scientists calculated that the smoke and dust generated by an all-out nuclear war with then-current arsenals, or even the detonation of ten 100-kt weapons over each of 100 major cities, could block enough sunlight to lower summer-time continental temperatures in the Northern Hemisphere to below freezing and to inhibit or halt plant growth for several months. Some of the authors speculated in public that such a 'Nuclear Winter' might even be severe enough to destroy civilisation, or even lead to the extinction of humanity.

The theory behind Nuclear Winter is that detonations in urban areas will ignite thousands of small fires directly through the initial flash and indirectly through blast effects on gas and electricity mains, stored chemicals and fuel, and so on. These widespread fires then combine into mass fires that in turn generate firestorms, where an updraft creates strong winds blowing inwards from all directions, consuming all combustible material and lofting the smoke high into the lower atmosphere (troposphere) through convection, and then up into the stratosphere through the solar heating of soot particles. (The effect is not unique to nuclear weapons: major firestorms occurred after the conventional firebombing of Hamburg, Dresden and Tokyo in the Second World War.) Smoke in the troposphere would cause short-term cooling and reduced sunlight locally or regionally, while smoke in the stratosphere would spread throughout the hemisphere or even globally, and persist for months or even years. The soot would also absorb solar radiation, heating up the stratosphere and causing ozone depletion through several different chemical processes.

After a decade of further research and vigorous debate in the scientific and public arenas, a consensus emerged that the Nuclear Winter effect, though real, was only about half as severe as originally suggested (more of a 'Nuclear Autumn') and had few or only minor implications for deterrence, war fighting or arms control. It was evident, too, that Nuclear Winter was not an inevitable consequence of a nuclear war; its likelihood was strongly dependent on the time of year of an attack, targets, number and size of weapons, civil-defence measures, the local weather conditions at the time of an attack, whether ground- or air-bursts were used, and other factors.

Beginning in 2007, however, a team from Rutgers University and the University of Colorado, including three authors of the original Nuclear Winter study, published a series of studies based on a nuclear-exchange scenario involving 100 low-yield (15kt) detonations in city centres (the

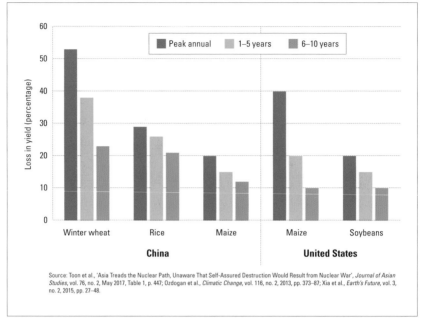

Figure 2: **Maximum and average annual loss in yield following 100 low-yield (15kt) detonations in urban centres in South Asia in spring: selected crops and locations**

same size of bomb used on Hiroshima in the Second World War, which resulted in a firestorm). They concluded that smoke from the resulting urban firestorms would rise into the stratosphere, where it could significantly affect the global climate, especially if the exchange took place in the sub-tropics. The amount of soot varied from around 2.8 teragrams (Tg; one teragram is equivalent to one megaton) to around 8.9Tg depending on the countries assumed to be involved, compared to the 150–225Tg assumed in various studies in the 1980s. An India–Pakistan exchange would produce around 6.6Tg, and subsequent work on climate effects and agricultural impacts used 5Tg injected into the atmosphere in mid-May over South Asia as a starting point. Using a modern, global climate model, the Rutgers–Colorado group calculated that the scenario would result in unprecedented global ozone losses of 20–50% over populated areas, the coldest average global temperatures for a thousand years, a shortening of mid-latitude growing seasons by 10–40 days over the first five years, and reduced temperatures for more than 25 years, rather than the months that less sophisticated models had indicated two decades earlier. Based on detailed climate and crop modelling for China (wheat, rice and maize) and the American Midwest (maize and soybeans), extrapolated to other regions and crops, the group estimated that global grain production could fall to 80% of normal levels for the first five years after a regional nuclear war, and remain at 85–90% for another five years. These figures mask a great deal of variability; China's May/June winter-wheat harvest one year after the nuclear exchange could be more than cut in half (see Figure 2).

## Food insecurity

To put these reductions in context, severe weather in Russia, Ukraine, Canada and Australia in 2010 reduced global wheat crops by 5%, with Russia's harvest falling by one-third. At the same time China, facing a drought, began to import wheat. Global wheat prices more than doubled between July 2010 and January 2011, and the world dipped into its stock as consumption exceeded production. Russia imposed a ban on the export of wheat, barley, rye and maize. The UN Food and Agriculture Organisation's Food Price Index increased by 43% between 2009 and 2011, to what is still its record peak. Acute global food inflation was a significant aggravating factor in the wave of protests, uprisings and civil war that swept the Middle East and North Africa in the Arab Spring. A similar price spike in 2008 saw food-export restrictions imposed by more than 30 governments, panic-buying by importing governments and more than 60 countries experiencing some form of civil unrest, which turned violent in one-third of the affected countries.

The projected food-price spike in the year following a regional nuclear war would likely be on the same order as those in 2008 and 2010, or slightly higher. However, those were short-term events, with overall food prices recovering within one year in the case of 2008 and four years in the case of 2010. A decade-long depression in agricultural output, coupled with the direct physical effects of the war, would have complex effects on markets and supply chains. The advocacy group International Physicians for the Prevention of Nuclear War suggests that two billion people globally – over a quarter of the world's population – would be at risk of starvation, malnourishment or heightened food insecurity in the aftermath of a regional nuclear war.

This is not the same, however, as saying that as many as 2bn people could be affected. It is rather a reflection of great uncertainty over whom among these 2bn would be affected. The number includes, for example, the entire population of China, since the country would no longer be a net food exporter and would either have to import in a world of scarcity, or go without. The average caloric intake of Chinese citizens would only decline by about 10% in the latter case, although since the reduction would not be uniform across the population, there would be immense human suffering and social disruption, but it would not mean national extinction.

Nevertheless, it is clear that the effect of smoke from burning cities in a regional nuclear war could dramatically cool the planet, and that this would have serious consequences for human security and geopolitics. A major criticism, in fact, of the idea that unprecedented global warming poses a threat to the stability or cohesion of modern societies and states is the overwhelming evidence that, in the past, it has been cooling rather than warming that has led to famine, instability and violence. (Paradoxically, a Nuclear Autumn might make long-term global warming even worse, if temporary cooling and lowered emissions in a post-war global depression, coupled with the distraction of dealing with the literal and figurative fallout from a nuclear exchange, created a lack of urgency among policymakers and negatively affected efforts to slow or reduce greenhouse-gas emissions.)

The historical example that best illustrates the impact of short-term but substantial cooling is probably 1816, known as the 'year without a summer' or, to contemporaries, 'eighteen hundred and froze to death'. In April 1815, the largest volcanic eruption in recorded history, that of Mount Tambora in the Indonesian archipelago, injected enough sulphur dioxide into the stratosphere to reduce the average global temperature by 0.7°C, about half what might result from a regional nuclear war. In Western and Central Europe, temperatures were 1–2°C colder in summer 1816 than the average for the decade and 3°C colder than the mid-twentieth-century average. Repeated frosts from June to August along the eastern seaboard of North America (as far south as North Carolina) cut the growing season in half and resulted in almost total crop failure. Crops were affected in China and India from both cooling and disruption to the monsoon. Crop failures in Northern Europe approached 75%, Canada banned grain exports and global grain prices doubled. Famine and food scarcities prompted a financial panic and depression; riots, looting and arson; and a sharp political shift to the right across Europe. Historian John D. Post called the period 1816–19 'the last great subsistence crisis in the Western world'.

## A plausible scenario?
Nearly all the recent work on the climatic effects of nuclear war has come from the same group of around a dozen scientists, including several of the authors of the original Nuclear Winter study in the 1980s. Most researchers with the relevant expertise have different priorities, as do funding bodies; since the early 1990s, the focus in climatology has been on global warming. In fact, it has been the improvement (stimulated by concern about global warming) in climate models that allowed the Nuclear Winter calculations to be updated and refined. This has involved a variety of climate and crop models, all producing similar results, but these all rely on the assumption that 5Tg of soot would be injected into the upper troposphere from a limited nuclear exchange. One of the few studies not conducted by this small group, published in 2018 by a team from the US National Nuclear Security Administration based at Los Alamos National Laboratory, used different models and concluded that the 100-weapon scenario would produce less soot (3.69Tg), a much smaller proportion would reach the upper troposphere for lofting into the stratosphere, and thus the climate effects would be only about one-fifth as severe, and much shorter-lived.

Overall, there are still too many uncertainties or assumptions about the amount and type of combustible material in particular potential targets, how much soot is produced from burning different materials, the optical effects of soot from different sources, how soot particles evolve in the atmosphere over time, how quickly soot is removed, how the soot circulates in the atmosphere and so on. The history of Nuclear Winter theory in the 1980s, and of global-warming research over the last 25 years, does suggest that as better knowledge becomes available, such uncertainties do tend to cancel each other out. The only real-world case that might confirm and help quantify the Nuclear Winter effect – the strategic bombing campaign against Japanese cities in 1945 – shows a small global cooling trend that is consistent with the models, but tanta-lisingly just below the level of statistical significance. A broader question, however, is the plausibility of the scenario. The 5Tg scenario assumes an attack in late spring, with clear, dry weather and wind conditions within a narrow range. Changing any of these conditions could substan-tially reduce the size of the fires (or even the chances that a firestorm is ignited at all), the amount of smoke produced, or the amount of soot that makes it into the stratosphere, and hence reduce the long-term climatic effect. It also assumes that both sides will deliberately target the other's population centres rather than military or industrial targets. With high-yield weapons, targeting such sites near but not within dense population centres could still ignite urban firestorms, but this is less probable with the lower-yield weapons likely to be used in a regional exchange.

It is unlikely that these idealised conditions, and hence the worst-case cooling scenarios, would all occur simultaneously in a real attack. Setting aside the possibility that planners might deliberately avoid launching an attack when conditions favoured a Nuclear Winter, the experience of strategic bombing in the Second World War suggests that it is not so easy to ignite firestorms, even deliberately. Moreover, given the minimum-deterrent postures of nuclear-weapons states other than the US and Russia, it is unlikely that a nuclear war between regional adversaries would start with an exchange of attacks against enemy cities. Nor would such an exchange necessarily be targeted so as to maximise fatalities (population density is closely correlated with available fuel for urban firestorms, and in fact is used as a proxy for it in these studies). Retaliatory strikes might just as likely be planned to maximise economic damage – transport hubs, industrial facilities and so on.

## Policy implications

Some of the scientists working on limited-nuclear-war scenarios, as well as other analysts, have argued that their results imply that the existence of even small nuclear arsenals is an existential threat. Others have argued that the results argue for 'winter-proofing' national deterrents by reducing numbers to levels below which they would individually or collectively risk a global environmental catastrophe.

It is by no means clear, however, that even the worst-case scenarios materially change the calculus behind nuclear-arms control, reduction and non-proliferation, or on civil defence, war fighting and deterrence theory. Even as the scientific merits of Nuclear Winter theory were debated during the 1980s, there was a parallel debate among strategic analysts over the implications if it were validated. When the dust settled, there had been little or no impact on policy. There is, for example, no evidence – other than a coincidence in timing – that the threat of Nuclear Winter was a significant factor in concluding the 1987 INF Treaty or the 1991 START I and its 2010 successor New START, which sets the maximum levels for current US and Russian arsenals. Nor did the new research into limited nuclear war and Nuclear Autumn appear to influence the famous 2007 *Wall Street Journal* op-ed 'A World Free of Nuclear Weapons' by George Shultz, William Perry, Henry Kissinger and Sam Nunn, and the subsequent launch of the 'Global Zero' campaign. The direct consequences of a potential nuclear attack, rather than the climatic effects of nuclear-weapons use, have proven more than enough to motivate such policies.

The key issues for current and potential nuclear-weapons states are whether a potential Nuclear Autumn is likely enough or would be severe enough to make using their deterrent suicidal, effectively converting an unacceptable damage doctrine into one of mutual assured destruction, and whether it might raise or lower the size of their calculated minimum deterrent. Neither is close to being quantifiable with current knowledge. All that can be said with reasonable certainty is that a limited, regional nuclear exchange could, under some circumstances, have severe global environmental effects. But under other circumstances, the effects could be minimal. The best guess – and it is still only a guess – is that the indirect consequences of a regional or limited nuclear war – social, economic and environmental – would be at least as severe as the direct consequences, and on a level comparable to the major wars of the twentieth century. Climatic disruption is an important part of these indirect consequences, but whether it is the most important has yet to be determined.

# The UN's Travails in the Middle East: Syria, Yemen and Libya

Besides sub-Saharan Africa, the Middle East is where the United Nations has seen its values, ambitions and performance most challenged. Since 1948 the UN has had little success in the Middle Eastern conflicts it has been tasked with resolving. Instead it has tended to become the alleviator of their humanitarian consequences and political repercussions, freezing conflicts in the hope that great-power engagement with the warring parties would lead to progress or de-escalation. Indeed, whether during the Arab–Israeli and Gulf wars, the Yemeni and Lebanese civil wars, or when the US injected new momentum into Arab–Israeli talks after the Cold War, the UN played an essentially subordinate and *post facto* validating role, rather than that of a proactive peacemaker.

The UN's travails in the Middle East have become even more pronounced with the three major wars resulting from the 2011 Arab uprisings: Syria, Yemen and Libya. The great powers have outsourced to the UN the difficult work of stabilising those three countries by building inclusive political frameworks, while pursuing in parallel their own military and counter-terrorism campaigns against extremist and rebel groups such as the Islamic State (also known as ISIS or ISIL), al-Qaeda and others. This prioritisation of security operations over political processes has undercut the UN's ability to broker solutions. With weak mandates and limited tools, vulnerable to local warlords and regional whims, and hostage to geopolitical competition, the UN's peace missions have unsurprisingly delivered meagre results.

At the core of the UN's troubled record in the Middle East today are deep divisions within the Security Council. Permanent Western members have expected that the UN would facilitate political transition in strife-torn countries while endorsing Western policies, including armed interventions. In contrast, Russia and China have since 2011 seen the Security Council as an arena in which to counter Western hegemony, frustrate regime change in states not beholden to the West and shape a new balance of power.

Whether paralysed by struggles within the Security Council or by the unchecked assertiveness of global or regional powers, the UN has in effect lost the initiative in advancing conflict resolution in the Middle East region. It has become the marginalised overseer of protracted conflicts, generating expectations it cannot meet and crystallising frustrations it cannot address. Bereft of great-power leverage, its envoys have often been compelled to bend to local and regional powers to maintain relevance and access, to cajole international powers for support and to find the lowest common denominator for joint diplomatic action.

## UN missions in Syria, Yemen and Libya

The wars in Syria, Yemen and Libya have tested the UN's ability to broker ceasefires, design and implement peace processes, deliver humanitarian assistance, obtain genuine regional cooperation and rally international powers. These wars have exposed the limitations, dilemmas and weaknesses of the UN, and its increasing vulnerability to global, regional and local indifference, competition or pushback. Its alarm over humanitarian catastrophes and the growing disregard for international humanitarian law reveals the concern about receding norms of war and new challenges to the rules that have governed conflict.

UN peacemaking strategies have differed considerably, alternating between or combining bottom-up and international approaches, prioritising political dialogue or humanitarian tracks, alternatively counting on international attention for high-profile negotiation rounds or eschewing it in favour of more discreet dialogue, as well as direct or proximity talks. In each case, progress has been at best halting and reversible; perversely, failed diplomacy has often incentivised escalation.

The difficulty of managing each of these three high-profile missions is best illustrated by the high turnover among the envoys: since 2011 the UN has appointed five envoys for Libya, four for Syria and three for Yemen, due to a mix of complex local situations, diplomatic stalemate and personal frustrations. The mandates of those envoys also differ considerably. The envoy in Yemen has been constrained by UN Resolution 2216, adopted at the onset of the conflict. In contrast, his counterpart in Libya has great latitude to design a political process. The envoy in Syria has had to switch between markedly different formulas for peace, as battlefield and international circumstances have changed. In each case, however, battlefield dynamics and external support for the various factions have been more influential than mandates in determining the envoy's margin for manoeuvre.

The nature of each conflict has also set boundaries for each envoy. In Syria, the president is firmly in control of his capital and heads a unified military command structure. In Yemen, the president has fled the country, living in exile in Saudi Arabia, and is only nominally in control of an array of pro-government militias. In Libya, authority is contested between a UN-backed transitional government in Tripoli, which has little control over security forces, and the government in Tobruk, which claims parliamentary legitimacy and can rely on a more coherent military organisation.

The three missions also differ with regard to another key issue: whether or not there is a UN-mandated arms embargo and sanctions regime. Libya has been under an arms embargo and sanctions regime since 2011, although the UN panel of experts has identified continuous and significant breaches by all sides. In Yemen, only the Houthis and their allies are under an arms embargo and sanctions regime, while the UN resolution endorses the Saudi-imposed blockade to interdict their resupply. Syria is under no UN embargo or sanctions: government forces have been generously supplied with weapons by Russia and Iran, while rebel forces were armed by Western and Arab states until 2017, since when Turkey has continued to arm militias in the north of the country.

The UN's humanitarian missions have faced significant difficulties and dilemmas. In each conflict the UN has struggled to balance aid neutrality and humanitarian access. In Syria, the government, Iran and Russia have obstructed aid deliveries to besieged areas across the country. Over time, UN agencies in Damascus have become ensnared with regime actors in delivering aid, thereby jeopardising their impartiality. In Yemen, two of the main funders of the humanitarian response are Saudi Arabia and the United Arab Emirates (UAE) – who are also the combatants responsible for most of the infrastructural destruction and civilian casualties, as well as the actors who have imposed a blockade over Houthi-held regions. Yet without their cooperation, the UN would be unable to restore humanitarian access, and Gulf funding for reconstruction and stabilisation is essential for Yemen's future. The Houthis, for their part, in control of most of the population, have amplified the humanitarian crisis by diverting or impeding aid on a large scale as part of their strategy of controlling local communities and also in order to increase their revenues through the illegal taxation or sale of humanitarian donations. In Libya, UN agencies oversee centres for migrants seeking refuge in Europe but are at the mercy of local militias involved in trafficking or providing security. Such entanglements have damaged the credibility of the agencies and reduced their ability to deliver aid.

## Syria

In Syria, the UN has often been marginalised and left dependent on major powers. Early on, the US and Russia had hoped to reach a deal through UN-facilitated talks. The result was the Geneva communiqué of 2012 that foresaw a 'transitional government body with full executive powers … on the basis of mutual consent'. However, the US and Russia differed on the fate of President Bashar al-Assad: the American interpretation of the agreement was that Assad's future would remain an open question, while Russia insisted otherwise. The UN envoy at the time, Kofi Annan, failed to bridge this gap. This disagreement, and the increasingly bitter US–Russian relationship, limited the prospects of UN mediation. Indeed, several iterations of a political dialogue from 2014 under UN auspices in Geneva by the second UN envoy, Lakhdar Brahimi, failed. Seeking to build on the 2013 US–Russian deal on Syria's chemical weapons, UN envoys hoped that a US–Russian rapprochement would restrain their respective regional allies and in turn create an opening for UN diplomacy and local truces. This top-down approach failed utterly: not only were the positions of the US and Russia irreconcilable, but Iran, Saudi Arabia, Qatar and Turkey opposed de-escalation. Taking stock of this failure, the third envoy, Staffan de Mistura, started his mission with a bottom-up plan aimed at halting the fighting in Aleppo: the hastily arranged initiative quickly fizzled out as there was no trust or enforcement mechanism for such a ceasefire to hold. Other attempts at local ceasefires with UN facilitation were merely surrenders without political compromises, such as the one in Homs in 2014, which further tarnished the UN's reputation because its humanitarian terms were not implemented.

In 2016, after Russia intervened to support Assad and the US prioritised the fight against ISIS in Syria, the two countries designed a de-escalation process that the UN was asked to help sustain. However, there was once again no monitoring or enforcement mechanism, allowing local actors to act as spoilers. The process predictably failed, leading to a massive escalation and major rebel defeats. Soon after, Russia initiated a parallel track at talks in Astana that only included Turkey and Iran, the main patrons of Syrian militias, with the aim of advancing their various political and territorial interests. The UN's fear that Astana would marginalise its own efforts led to a debate over whether to embrace the Russian track, in the hope of later being able to shape it, or to ignore it in the expectation that it would fail. By 2019 it was unclear whether the UN could succeed. The most recent envoys, de Mistura and his successor Geir Pedersen, have prioritised constitutional reform, an aspect of the political transition mandated by Resolution 2254, but they both struggled to get any traction with the Syrian government or to explain why and how a regime accused of committing large-scale atrocities and flouting international humanitarian law would be constrained by constitutional revisions. Indeed, a victorious Damascus saw no need for meaningful engagement with the UN envoys, rebuffing them on questions of constitutional reform, prisoners, refugees and aid.

The UN experience in Syria points to a hard truth: despite repeated claims by UN envoys and Western officials that there was no military solution to the conflict, battlefield dynamics rather than negotiations have been decisive in ushering the conflict towards a conclusion. This was mainly because of the lack of enforcement mechanisms and the success of the Russian–Iranian intervention in restoring Assad's fortunes.

In the process, the UN lost standing and was accused of compromising its values in a futile effort to remain relevant.

## Yemen

The UN mission in Yemen has also been politically fraught. The civil war that started in 2014 was multi-sided and the 2015 Saudi intervention began with considerable international support, before the humanitarian toll and military stalemate caused the international community to call for a halt.

The UN envoy is constrained by Resolution 2216, adopted in April 2015, which demands unconditional Houthi concessions, supports President Abd Rabbo Mansour Hadi's government-in-exile and endorses the Saudi-led intervention. However, the resolution failed to reflect important realities: that the Houthis had effectively captured the state and large parts of the country; that Hadi had minimal local support and influence; and that the unconditional UN endorsement of the Saudi intervention would make diplomacy more difficult.

By 2017, Yemen had replaced Syria as the worst crisis in the Middle East. A famine there was due more to the collapse of the economy and the destruction of livelihoods than to a lack of food. The paramount importance of not aggravating the humanitarian crisis guided the actions of the dogged UN diplomat Martin Griffiths. This meant prioritising a ceasefire, a mutual withdrawal and an agreement regarding the management of transport routes from the port city of Hudaydah, the key to providing Yemen with food supplies. (This also meant temporarily ignoring other flashpoints around the country. Indeed, the UN focus on Hudaydah diverted attention from Ta'izz and other places, where fighting increased.) In December 2018, Griffiths sought to leverage mounting international outrage over the extent of the human suffering and widening criticism of Saudi Arabia to force a breakthrough during a round of negotiations in Stockholm. He succeeded in passing the Stockholm agreement regarding Hudaydah, but its language was vague and allowed the Houthis to postpone their agreed withdrawal from the port. They finally withdrew in May 2019 but left in charge a force that contained Houthi fighters disguised in different uniforms. The Saudi-led coalition has also faced accusations that it was slow to abide by its commitments in Hudaydah, and that it has done so only partially. This showed how difficult it is for the UN to implement such agreements. A small monitoring mission has been deployed but its efficacy remains questionable.

Fundamentally, the UN envoys to Yemen have struggled to build leverage with the main parties to the conflict. As a hardened, low-maintenance and reclusive insurgency, the Houthi movement does not seek international acceptance and has shown little concern for the humanitarian consequences of the war. The political and financial power of Saudi Arabia and the UAE led key members of the Security Council either to support their military actions or remain silent. Ultimately, it was the increasing international criticism of Saudi Arabia over Yemen but also non-Yemen matters such as the assassination of journalist Jamal Khashoggi that provided the leverage needed.

## Libya

The conflict in Libya further exposed the UN's limitations and vulnerabilities. After the 2011 uprising, at the request of the Libyan transitional authorities the UN adopted a support and advisory role, notably helping to organise elections. The descent into civil war in 2014 forced a change in the UN role. In 2015, then backed by key powers, the UN facilitated the Libyan Political Agreement (LPA), which created a presidential council and the Government of National Accord (GNA). However, multiple factions soon denounced the LPA, meaning that the GNA's credibility and power derived almost entirely from the UN. The consensus among permanent members of the Security Council also frayed quickly, as France, quickly followed by Russia, began supporting Khalifa Haftar, the commander of the self-styled Libyan National Army (LNA), the most powerful militia in eastern Libya, against Islamist and jihadi militias.

From 2017 the current envoy, Ghassan Salamé, patiently put together a complex process that was intended to culminate in spring 2019 with a national conference. However, in April 2019 Haftar launched a campaign to conquer Tripoli and expel the UN-backed government, thereby delivering a serious and potentially mortal blow to the UN dialogue process.

Salamé's progress was further undermined by two rivalries. The first was between France, a Security Council member that prioritised counter-terrorism missions in Libya and in the Sahel region and sponsored Haftar, and Italy, which prioritised migration control and worked through the GNA. The second rivalry pitched the UAE, Egypt and Saudi Arabia, intent on helping the like-minded Haftar to win decisively, against Turkey and Qatar, which sponsored Islamist militias and supported the GNA. Haftar chose to ignore the UN process because of the strength of his alliances and the political cover and military support they generated. In turn, Salamé's efforts were derided by Haftar's enemies, which they saw as too accommodating towards him. Shortly afterwards Salamé delivered a scathing condemnation of the various Libyan and external players, predicting a protracted civil war. Even this warning was not enough to deter the US from blocking a Security Council statement introduced by the United Kingdom in favour of an immediate ceasefire, with some in Washington betting on a quick Haftar victory.

## Regional competition

The UN missions in Syria, Yemen and Libya have faced complex regional dynamics that have often undermined diplomacy and local peacebuilding efforts. Regional powers have often fuelled the fighting through weapons deliveries, support for local partners and the articulation of maximalist objectives.

Indeed, conflicts in the Middle East since 2003, and more so since the Arab uprisings of 2011, have attracted and been sustained by considerable regional initiative. Saudi Arabia, the UAE, Qatar, Turkey, Egypt and Iran have competed for influence across battlefields, nurturing and arming local partners and proxies and intervening directly in support of their allies.

Regional rivalries have greatly complicated the work of UN envoys. Aggressive behaviour has been fuelled by limited Western attention to enforcement of norms and by Russian tolerance for the use of violence. Regional states have often dismissed or circumvented UN rules. In Libya, the UAE, allied with Saudi Arabia and Egypt, conducted airstrikes in May and July 2019 in support of its partner, Khalifa Haftar's LNA, despite a UN embargo. Soon after, Turkey, allied with Qatar against the UAE, provided weaponry to Haftar's enemies. In Syria, Iran has deployed large numbers of militiamen and weaponry in support of the Assad government despite UN, US and EU sanctions on Iran's arms exports.

Regional powers have often shunned UN criticism and recommendations. Iran has rejected UN appeals to suspend fighting and sieges in Syria, often denying its combat role there or justifying its actions as necessary to combat terrorism. In 2018, in Yemen, the UAE and Saudi Arabia proceeded with a campaign to seize the port city of Hudaydah despite stern warnings by Griffiths, the UN envoy, that the battle would precipitate a major humanitarian crisis. International condemnation of Saudi Arabia following the murder of Khashoggi and intense pressure by the US ultimately forced the two countries to halt their operation.

Regional powers have also relied on their allies among the permanent members of the Security Council to block or tone down language that was critical of their actions and those of their local partners, and notably to deflect accusations of war crimes. Despite brutal tactics Turkey has avoided criticism of its military intervention and occupation of Afrin in northwest Syria, in large part because the US and Russia feel compelled to placate an important partner. In 2017 and 2018, UN reports on Yemen did not list the Saudi-led coalition among the perpetrators of violations against children during wartime, even though the coalition's airstrikes have been identified as a main cause of civilian casualties including children.

To circumvent opposition from permanent members of the Security Council or powerful regional players, countries have appealed to the General Assembly or other UN bodies. In 2011 the UN Human Rights Council set up the Independent International Commission of Inquiry on the Syrian Arab Republic, and in 2018 the Group of Eminent International and Regional Experts on Yemen. These two bodies conduct investigations and collect information but have no prosecutorial powers or authority to sanction individuals. Such mechanisms have so far failed either to precipitate action by the Security Council or to restrain the warring parties.

## Great-power divisions

The backdrop for the UN's woes in the Middle East has been the competition and resulting paralysis in the Security Council in recent years. Russia's reassertion of power since 2012, when Vladimir Putin returned as president, has significantly complicated UN action as advocated by Western powers since the 1990s. In 2011 Russia chose not to veto but instead abstained over UN Security Council Resolution 1973, which sought an immediate ceasefire during the Libyan civil war but also authorised 'all necessary measures' to protect civilians in Libya, including the establishment of a no-fly zone. The NATO intervention that followed, and that contributed to the fall of the Gadhafi regime, was interpreted by Moscow as a deliberate manipulation of the mandate by Western powers to pursue regime change, which Russia has resisted in favour of upholding the principle of non-interference in the internal affairs of sovereign states. Since then, Russia, already incensed by the Western interventions in Kosovo and Iraq, has sought to use the Security Council to frustrate Western policy in the Middle East and deny Security Council legitimacy to coercive Western policies.

The conflict in Syria has been the central issue in this regard. Between 2011 and 2018, Russia (often joined by China) vetoed 12 UN resolutions on Syria, blocking condemnation of government repression and demands for immediate ceasefires as well as proposals to investigate the use of chemical weapons. Russia has steadfastly shielded Assad and his officials against international criticism and referral to the International Criminal Court. Russia's defence of Syria in the Security Council stiffened after 2015, when it committed forces to the fight, and made it pivotal to Syria's future. Russia's own military has been blamed for attacks on civilian and health infrastructure and on humanitarian convoys, and the presence on the ground of Russian troops when chemical weapons were used suggests either deliberate ignorance or complicity.

Only after Russia succeeded in changing the battlefield in Syria and solidifying Assad's control did it agree to Resolution 2254, whose diluted terms included an ill-defined political settlement. Russia further undercut the UN by creating parallel tracks: the Astana process starting in

2017 was designed to bring together Russia, Turkey and Iran to manage the battlefield without UN supervision, while the Sochi conference in 2018 was aimed at setting political parameters for the settlement of the conflict on terms favourable to Russia and Assad. This challenge posed a significant dilemma for the UN: refuse to engage with the political manoeuvring of a permanent Security Council member and the military victor in Syria, and therefore face irrelevance; or lower its objectives and engage with Russia at the risk of being trapped and manipulated.

Yet Syria also illustrates the enduring relevance of the UN. Russia's parallel tracks have not delivered the expected results. Instead it has been compelled to work to obtain the imprimatur of the Security Council in order to translate its military gains into political currency: the rehabilitation of the Assad regime, the lifting of Western sanctions and the delivery of international funding for reconstruction. This effort has so far met with opposition from Western and Arab powers, which still seek a political agreement.

Faced with Russian obstructionism in the Security Council, the US has also bypassed the UN on questions of war. In April 2017 and again in April 2018, the US conducted strikes against Syrian military targets after the use of chemical weapons by the Assad regime. France participated in both strikes, and the UK in the later one. In neither case did these powers seek UN approval for their military operations; they relied on their own intelligence findings to determine that proscribed chemical attacks had been conducted, rather than wait for those of the special investigation mission of the Organisation for the Prohibition of Chemical Weapons (OPCW).

Security Council divisions alone do not explain the UN's shortcomings. In Yemen and Libya the rise of regional actors, compounded by great-power confusion and equivocation, was a significant hurdle to UN action. In Yemen, Saudi Arabia, thanks to its partnership with the US and other powers, secured a favourable resolution (2216) that demanded the restoration of the Saudi-allied government and the rollback of the Houthi expansion, and imposed an arms embargo; Russia abstained. Later, Moscow initiated a rapprochement with Saudi Arabia that shielded

Riyadh from overt Security Council condemnation. However, this did not translate into better UN performance. Libya is another case of the UN mediation efforts being undercut by great powers. While nominally supportive of the UN process, at least two permanent members of the Council, France and Russia, have often worked at cross purposes with the UN peace mission, assisting regional powers keen on landing military victories.

In conclusion, the UN's struggles in the Middle East are more a function of the divisions between regional and great powers than a reflection of the organisation's weaknesses. The more intractable the conflict, the greater the reliance on the UN. The advent of strategic self-determination in the Middle East, exemplified by Saudi Arabia and the UAE but by no means limited to them, has rendered peacemaking an ever-more challenging endeavour, compounded by an increasingly rivalrous relationship between the Western and Eastern permanent members of the Security Council. In these circumstances the UN has become an instrument to manage or freeze conflicts, at the cost of its credibility with local actors and populations.

Table 1: **Great-power and regional intervention in key Middle Eastern conflicts**

| 2011–18 | Syria | Libya | Yemen |
|---|---|---|---|
| Regional proxy support | Iran, Qatar, Saudi Arabia, Turkey, UAE | Egypt, Qatar, Saudi Arabia, Turkey, UAE | Iran, Qatar, Saudi Arabia, UAE |
| Direct regional intervention | Iran, Turkey | Egypt, UAE | Iran, Saudi Arabia, UAE |
| UNSC permanent members most involved | Russia, US | France, Russia, US | Russia, UK, US |
| Direct intervention by UNSC permanent members | Russia, US | France, Russia, US | US |

**Map 1: Main UN political and peacekeeping missions in the Middle East, and specialised UN agencies**

©IISS

The UN has an extensive political, humanitarian and military presence across the Middle East. Its oldest monitoring mission there is the United Nations Truce Supervision Organisation (UNTSO), founded in 1948, and its oldest agency is the United Nations Relief and Works Agency for Palestine Refugees in the Near East (UNRWA), founded in 1949. Since then it has had political, humanitarian and/or peacekeeping missions in Libya, Yemen, Syria, Israel–Palestine, Iraq, Lebanon, Western Sahara and Somalia – all of which are ongoing.

**Israel–Palestine**

United Nations Special Coordinator for the Middle East Peace Process (UNSCO) (since 1993)

United Nations Relief and Works Agency for Palestine Refugees in the Near East (UNRWA) (since 1949)

**Lebanon**

United Nations Special Coordinator for Lebanon (UNSCOL) (since 2007)

United Nations Interim Force in Lebanon (UNIFIL) (since 1978)

Special Envoy of the Secretary-General for the Implementation of Security Council Resolution 1559 (since 2004)

**Syria**

Special Envoy of the Secretary-General for Syria (since 2012)

United Nations Disengagement Observer Force (UNDOF) (since 1974)

**Yemen**

Special Envoy of the Secretary-General for Yemen (since 2012)

United Nations Mission to Support the Hudaydah Agreement (UNMHA) (since 2018)

**Iraq**

Special Representative of the Secretary-General in Iraq (since 2003)

United Nations Assistance Mission for Iraq (UNAMI) (since 2003)

**Somalia**

Special Representative of the Secretary-General for Somalia (since 2013)

United Nations Assistance Mission in Somalia (UNSOM) (since 2013)

**Libya**

Special Representative of the Secretary-General in Libya (since 2011)

United Nations Support Mission in Libya (UNSMIL) (since 2011)

**Western Sahara**

Personal Envoy of the Secretary-General (since 1997)

United Nations Mission for the Referendum in Western Sahara (MINURSO) (since 1991)

WESTERN SAHARA

L I B Y A

I R A Q

SYRIA

LEBANON

ISRAEL
GAZA

Y E M E N

S O M A L I A

# Asia: Drivers of Strategic Change

- China has developed a pattern of coercive behaviour towards Southeast Asian states with competing claims in the South China Sea. Beijing has continued to militarise atolls and islands in support of its territorial claims and for strategic reasons; it has also tested weapons and undertaken military exercises in the area.

- China has also sought to discourage Western navies from conducting freedom-of-navigation operations in Asian waters, while its navy has sought to normalise its presence around Japan's Senkaku islands, which Beijing claims.

- Chinese President Xi Jinping set a deadline of 2049, the 100th anniversary of the foundation of the People's Republic of China, for reunification with Taiwan. Internationally, Beijing is working steadily to reduce the number of states that recognise Taipei. However, domestic developments in Taiwan are not currently conducive to reunification and the credibility of Beijing's 'one country, two systems' model has been damaged by the curtailment of freedoms in Hong Kong and a popular backlash there.

- The US has made no appreciable progress in its efforts to persuade North Korea to curtail and eventually close its nuclear programme. The Trump administration has not fulfilled the fears of some Americans and Asians who suspect it seeks a deal at any price, but its interest in achieving an agreement appears undimmed.

- Across Asia, US allies are seeking partial accommodation with China as a hedge against the possibility of US abandonment, which seems more real since the Trump administration adopted a more transactional approach to its alliance relationships.

- India's prime minister, Narendra Modi, won an absolute majority in the May 2019 parliamentary election, which was held against the background of the most serious military exchanges with Pakistan in 20 years. Many expectations for the second term centre on economic reform, but the scope for Modi to give greater expression to Hindu nationalism in the domestic politics of the multiconfessional country might be as important.

## DEMOGRAPHY

POPULATION AND MEDIAN AGE
(IMF, April 2019; UN Department of Economic and Social Affairs, Population Division, 2019)

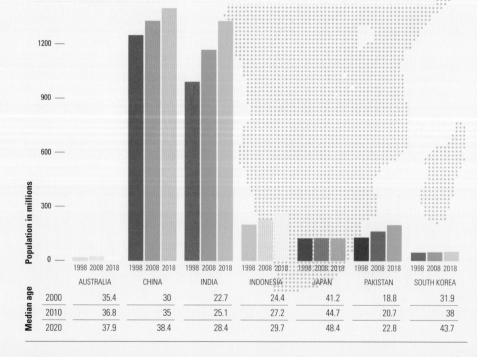

| Median age | AUSTRALIA | CHINA | INDIA | INDONESIA | JAPAN | PAKISTAN | SOUTH KOREA |
|---|---|---|---|---|---|---|---|
| 2000 | 35.4 | 30 | 22.7 | 24.4 | 41.2 | 18.8 | 31.9 |
| 2010 | 36.8 | 35 | 25.1 | 27.2 | 44.7 | 20.7 | 38 |
| 2020 | 37.9 | 38.4 | 28.4 | 29.7 | 48.4 | 22.8 | 43.7 |

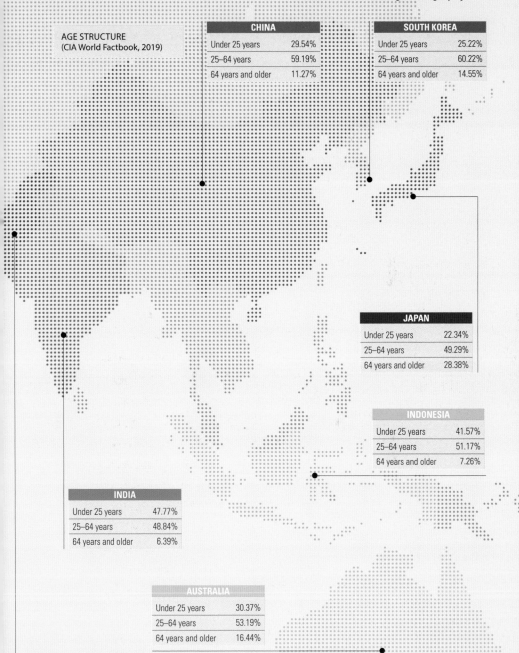

**AGE STRUCTURE**
(CIA World Factbook, 2019)

| CHINA | |
|---|---|
| Under 25 years | 29.54% |
| 25–64 years | 59.19% |
| 64 years and older | 11.27% |

| SOUTH KOREA | |
|---|---|
| Under 25 years | 25.22% |
| 25–64 years | 60.22% |
| 64 years and older | 14.55% |

| JAPAN | |
|---|---|
| Under 25 years | 22.34% |
| 25–64 years | 49.29% |
| 64 years and older | 28.38% |

| INDONESIA | |
|---|---|
| Under 25 years | 41.57% |
| 25–64 years | 51.17% |
| 64 years and older | 7.26% |

| INDIA | |
|---|---|
| Under 25 years | 47.77% |
| 25–64 years | 48.84% |
| 64 years and older | 6.39% |

| AUSTRALIA | |
|---|---|
| Under 25 years | 30.37% |
| 25–64 years | 53.19% |
| 64 years and older | 16.44% |

| PAKISTAN | |
|---|---|
| Under 25 years | 51.70% |
| 25–64 years | 43.74% |
| 64 years and older | 4.56% |

# ECONOMICS AND DEVELOPMENT

## GDP AT PPP
Constant 2011 international dollars (IMF, April 2019)

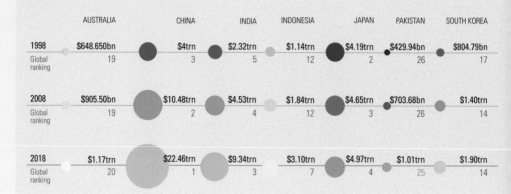

| | AUSTRALIA | CHINA | INDIA | INDONESIA | JAPAN | PAKISTAN | SOUTH KOREA |
|---|---|---|---|---|---|---|---|
| **1998** | $648.650bn | $4trn | $2.32trn | $1.14trn | $4.19trn | $429.94bn | $804.79bn |
| Global ranking | 19 | 3 | 5 | 12 | 2 | 26 | 17 |
| **2008** | $905.50bn | $10.48trn | $4.53trn | $1.84trn | $4.65trn | $703.68bn | $1.40trn |
| Global ranking | 19 | 2 | 4 | 12 | 3 | 26 | 14 |
| **2018** | $1.17trn | $22.46trn | $9.34trn | $3.10trn | $4.97trn | $1.01trn | $1.90trn |
| Global ranking | 20 | 1 | 3 | 7 | 4 | 25 | 14 |

## GDP PER CAPITA AT PPP
Constant 2011 international dollars (IMF, April 2019)

| | AUSTRALIA | CHINA | INDIA | INDONESIA | JAPAN | PAKISTAN | SOUTH KOREA |
|---|---|---|---|---|---|---|---|
| **1998** | $34,675.89 | $3,206.64 | $2,343.35 | $5,669.45 | $33,168.32 | $3,293.04 | $17,386.99 |
| Global ranking | 18 | 125 | 146 | 102 | 26 | 122 | 47 |
| **2008** | $42,163.40 | $7,893.96 | $3,883.75 | $7,949.43 | $36,383.68 | $4,273.53 | $28,588.37 |
| Global ranking | 24 | 110 | 142 | 109 | 33 | 136 | 46 |
| **2018** | $46,554.63 | $16,097.76 | $6,998.93 | $11,759.71 | $39,313.41 | $5,048.72 | $36,756.43 |
| Global ranking | 20 | 78 | 126 | 101 | 31 | 140 | 32 |

## HUMAN DEVELOPMENT INDEX (HDI)
(UN Development Programme, 2019)

AUSTRALIA — 2 2
CHINA — 99 102 86
INDIA — 112 135 130
INDONESIA — 95 114 116
JAPAN — 14 21 19
PAKISTAN — 119 146 150
SOUTH KOREA — 29 25 22

0.0    0.2    0.4    0.6    0.8    1.0

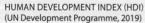

● Global ranking 1998   ● Global ranking 2008   ● Global ranking 2018

Score between 0 and 1, where 0 denotes a low level of development and 1 a high level of development.

## INTERNATIONAL INTEGRATION

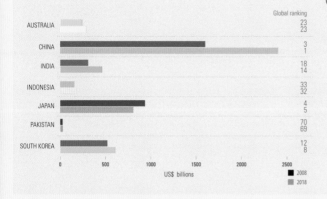

**TRADE**
Exports of goods and commercial services, constant 2010 US dollars
(World Trade Organization, 2019)

Global ranking

| | | |
|---|---|---|
| AUSTRALIA | | 23 / 23 |
| CHINA | | 3 / 1 |
| INDIA | | 18 / 14 |
| INDONESIA | | 33 / 32 |
| JAPAN | | 4 / 5 |
| PAKISTAN | | 70 / 69 |
| SOUTH KOREA | | 12 / 8 |

0    500    1000    1500    2000    2500
US$ billions
■ 2008   ■ 2018

**INTERNATIONAL NETWORK**
Total number of diplomatic missions, 2017
Lowy Institute Global Diplomacy Index
(2017)

| | Missions abroad | | Global ranking |
|---|---|---|---|
| AUSTRALIA | 116 | | 28 |
| CHINA | 268 | | 2 |
| INDIA | 181 | | 12 |
| INDONESIA | 133 | | 19 |
| JAPAN | 229 | | 5 |
| PAKISTAN | 116 | | 27 |
| SOUTH KOREA | 172 | | 13 |

## DIPLOMACY AND DEFENCE

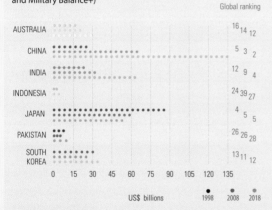

**DEFENCE BUDGET**
Constant 2010 US dollars (Military Balance 1998,
and Military Balance+)

Global ranking

| | |
|---|---|
| AUSTRALIA | 16 14 12 |
| CHINA | 5 3 2 |
| INDIA | 12 9 4 |
| INDONESIA | 24 39 27 |
| JAPAN | 4 5 5 |
| PAKISTAN | 26 26 28 |
| SOUTH KOREA | 13 11 12 |

0   15   30   45   60   75   90   105   120   135
US$ billions
● 1998   ● 2008   ● 2018

**OFFICIAL DEVELOPMENT AID**
Constant 2015 US dollars (OECD, 2019)

| | 1998 | | 2008 | | 2018 | |
|---|---|---|---|---|---|---|
| AUSTRALIA | $2bn | 13 | $3.19bn | 12 | $3.15bn | 24 |
| CHINA | n/a | | n/a | | n/a | |
| INDIA | n/a | | n/a | | n/a | |
| INDONESIA | n/a | | n/a | | n/a | |
| JAPAN | $10.89bn | 2 | $8.73bn | 5 | $9.92bn | 5 |
| PAKISTAN | n/a | | n/a | | n/a | |
| SOUTH KOREA | $324.9m | 21 | $935.8m | 21 | $2.34bn | 17 |

* Global ranking

**POLITICAL SYSTEM**
(Economist Intelligence Unit, 2008, 2018)

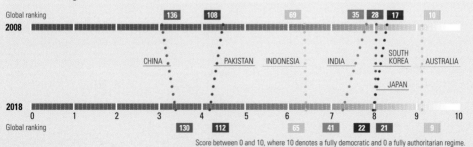

Global ranking
2008    136   108   69   35 28 17   10

CHINA   PAKISTAN   INDONESIA   INDIA   SOUTH KOREA   AUSTRALIA

JAPAN

2018
0    1    2    3    4    5    6    7    8    9    10
Global ranking
130   112   65   41   22 21   9

Score between 0 and 10, where 10 denotes a fully democratic and 0 a fully authoritarian regime.

Ulan Bator ■

**MONGOLIA**

Beijing ■     **NORTH KOREA**
                Pyongyang ■
              ■ Seoul
Kabul ■        **SOUTH**
              **KOREA**
**AFGHANISTAN**        Tokyo ■
  Islamabad ■

**PAKISTAN**  ■ **NEPAL**
              Thimpu ■
  New Delhi ■ Kathmandu ■ **BHUTAN**
              **BANGLADESH**        ■ Taipei
**I N D I A**    ■ Dhaka              **TAIWAN**
          **MYANMAR**  ■ Hanoi
          Naypyidaw ■  **VIETNAM**
              Vientiane ■
              **THAILAND**
          Bangkok ■  ■ **CAMBODIA**
                Phnom
                Penh      Manila ■  **PHILIPPINES**
Colombo ■
**SRI LANKA**              **BRUNEI**
          Kuala Lumpur ■ **MALAYSIA**
              **SINGAPORE** ■
                            **PAPUA**
              **I N D O N E S I A**  **NEW**
          Jakarta ■              **GUINEA**
                    Dili ■  Port
                  **TIMOR-LESTE**  Moresby ■  **SOLOMON**
                                            **ISLANDS**

**JAPAN**

*Pacific Ocean*

*Indian Ocean*

**VANUATU**            **FIJI**

                    **NEW**
                  **CALEDONIA**

**A U S T R A L I A**

                Canberra ■

                              **NEW**
                            **ZEALAND**
                              ■ Wellington

©IISS

Chapter 4

# Asia

## 2018–19 Review

Beijing's relentless advance as the central player in Asia's geopolitics continued to preoccupy foreign-policy actors in much of the region, and to challenge the Trump administration in the United States, in the year to mid-2019. Even with its economic vulnerabilities highlighted by the major bilateral trade dispute that Washington opened in June 2018, China was more than ever a powerful economic magnet for other Asia-Pacific states, including India and Japan. Despite concerns about issues involving national security, these states all had little choice but to accept that China was, as a trading partner, of long-term importance for their own economic well-being. Security concerns focused particularly on Beijing's growing assertiveness in its littoral (notably in the South China Sea but also in relation to the East China Sea and Taiwan), its increasing presence and activities in the Indian Ocean and South Pacific, and its efforts to use economic power and other instruments to influence the domestic politics and foreign policies of smaller regional states.

Contrary to repeated assertions by Beijing that the situation in the South China Sea had become calm – or 'generally stable and positive', as Chinese Minister of National Defence General Wei Fenghe said in his plenary address at the IISS Shangri-La Dialogue in Singapore in June

2019 – the reality was different. China continued to militarise features that it occupied there, including the seven islands in the Spratlys group that it had enlarged since 2013. In early 2018 it placed anti-ship and anti-aircraft missiles on three of them; deployed combat aircraft to Woody Island in the Paracels group over the following year; built a platform – probably for radar or signals-intelligence purposes – on Bombay Reef, also in the Paracels, in November 2018; test-launched anti-ship ballistic missiles close to the Spratlys in June 2019; and held a major military exercise between the Paracels and Spratlys in July 2019.

Beijing undoubtedly had long-term strategic rationales for militarising the South China Sea, most importantly a desire to complicate or prevent US military intervention in China's littoral; to protect China's maritime trade (and particularly its seaborne energy supplies); and to protect its nascent submarine-based nuclear deterrent. But a pattern of coercive behaviour in relation to Southeast Asian countries' claims and resource exploitation in the South China Sea has become increasingly evident. In January 2019 and again over the following months, 275 or more fishing vessels operating under the control of China's maritime militia blocked access to fishing grounds around Thitu Island, the largest outpost occupied by the Philippines in the Spratlys. In late May 2019, a Chinese coastguard vessel patrolling near the Luconia Shoals, off the coast of the Malaysian state of Sarawak, harassed supply vessels in an effort to stop authorised operations by a gas-drilling rig within Malaysia's exclusive economic zone (EEZ).

From mid-June, the same Chinese vessel conducted similar operations off the coast of southern Vietnam in waters that it claimed were 'under Chinese jurisdiction', with the intention – as in earlier incidents in 2017 and 2018 – of forcing Vietnam to stop drilling work, this time by Russia's Rosneft. Moreover, while attempting to impede resource exploitation by Southeast Asian states, China has stepped up its own exploration for resources in the South China Sea: a Chinese government survey ship escorted by Chinese coastguard vessels started to survey a large area within Vietnam's EEZ in early July 2019. Vietnam sent its own coastguard vessels to the area and, later in the month, Hanoi announced that it had 'staunchly demanded China to stop all unlawful activities and withdraw its ships from Vietnamese waters'.

Economic considerations significantly complicated Southeast Asian responses to Chinese pressure, in some cases apparently constraining regional states from defending their interests. This has most obviously been the case with the Philippines where, since 2016, President Rodrigo Duterte's government has signed a series of agreements with China on infrastructural development. At the same time, it put aside the ruling by the international Permanent Court of Arbitration in a case brought by a previous administration that China's claims in the South China Sea were incompatible with the United Nations Convention on the Law of the Sea, and has agreed to discuss the conflicting claims bilaterally with Beijing. In March 2019, Philippine Secretary of Foreign Affairs Teodoro Locsin visited Beijing and said that his country had 'nothing to fear' from China's rise. Meanwhile, Vietnam's continuing efforts to strengthen its navy and air force, to deter the use of force by Beijing, showed that Hanoi had no illusions about the dangers China poses to its maritime interests. The Vietnamese Communist Party, however, simultaneously recognised the reality of China's economic power and its increasing importance to Vietnam, particularly after the incoming Trump administration abandoned the Trans-Pacific Partnership, a prospective multilateral regional trading arrangement to which Hanoi had made a major commitment. The potential economic consequences of escalation encouraged Vietnam to respond in a measured way to China's maritime assertiveness.

While pressing its own interests to the detriment of those of Southeast Asian countries, China continued to protest freedom-of-navigation operations in the South China Sea by US naval vessels and aircraft. In September 2018, a Chinese warship engaged in what the US Navy called 'unsafe and unprofessional' behaviour during an encounter with the American destroyer USS *Decatur*, which was conducting such an operation – the first such incident since the US and Chinese defence establishments agreed in 2014 on rules of behaviour for air and sea encounters. China also attempted to dissuade US allies from patrolling in the South

China Sea. In early September 2018, for example, a Chinese navy frigate and two helicopters challenged the British amphibious-warfare ship HMS *Albion*, which was, according to the Royal Navy, 'exercising her rights for freedom of navigation' close to the Paracel Islands. China also stepped up its activities in the East China Sea around the Japanese-held Senkaku/Diaoyu islands, which Beijing claims as its own. By early June 2019, Chinese coastguard ships had patrolled close to the Senkakus continuously for two months, sometimes entering Japanese territorial waters, with the apparent aim of normalising China's presence in the disputed area. Probing flights also increased, with the Japan Air Self-Defense Force scrambling 638 times during 2018 to intercept Chinese military aircraft, mainly close to Okinawa and the East China Sea.

In a major speech in January 2019, Chinese President Xi Jinping set a deadline of 2049 for the reunification of the mainland with Taiwan, which Beijing sees as a renegade province. He also made it clear that Beijing did not rule out the use of force to achieve this. China's growing military capabilities have certainly shifted the balance across the Taiwan Strait in Beijing's favour. Using force would, on balance, be a highly risky option as long as US military intervention in support of Taiwan remains possible, so China has taken a multidimensional approach to coerce the island into political submission. This has included efforts to isolate Taiwan diplomatically; in August 2018, for example, El Salvador succumbed to Chinese pressure, becoming the latest country to abandon diplomatic relations with Taipei in favour of formal links with Beijing. Beijing has also tried to influence Taiwan's domestic politics through economic incentives in advance of the island's January 2020 presidential election. The opposition Kuomintang party is more positively disposed towards China than the Democratic Progressive Party of President Tsai Ing-wen, whose efforts to enhance Taiwan's identity, agency and economic independence have angered Beijing. China's aspirations to reunify with Taiwan on the basis of the 'one country, two systems' model offered to Hong Kong were harmed in the first half of 2019 by escalating protests in Hong Kong. They started after the territory's government put forward legislation in February to establish an extradition regime between Hong Kong and the People's Republic. By June, an estimated 2m of Hong Kong's 7m people marched peacefully to vent their frustration over living conditions, the assault on Hong Kong's autonomy in previous years and the Hong Kong authorities' lack of accountability. A smaller, youthful subsection engaged in more direct and occasionally violent activities.

China's growing geopolitical assertiveness was not restricted to its littoral. As Beijing's closely interrelated economic and security interests in the wider Asia-Pacific grew, so did its efforts to influence states in and around the Indian Ocean and in the South Pacific. The use of economic levers (particularly loans to support infrastructure construction) to gain geopolitical advantage in Sri Lanka and in the Maldives, Mauritius and Seychelles, which had raised concerns in India and the West in 2017–18, was followed in 2018–19 by similar efforts in Fiji, Papua New Guinea, Samoa, Vanuatu and other Pacific states. Responses from traditional South Pacific powers such as Australia, France, New Zealand, the United Kingdom and the US included an enhanced political and economic role for Australia in the region, which Minister for Foreign Affairs and Trade Marise Payne described in September 2018 as 'an imperative' for her country.

Despite encountering challenges, China's approach to the Asia-Pacific was characterised by an impressive drive and unity of purpose. Meanwhile, the United States' approach changed with the new Trump administration. Speaking at the 2019 Shangri-La Dialogue, Singapore Minister for Defence Ng Eng Hen described this as 'a shift to a more transactional foreign and security policy', asking rhetorically how this might affect the outlook of 'other nation-states, friends and even allies' towards the US. A particular focus for Washington continued to be the potential of North Korea's nuclear-weapons and long-range-missile programmes to threaten the US homeland. Although the June 2018 Singapore summit between US President Donald Trump and North Korean leader Kim Jong-un, alongside Kim's simultaneous dialogues with China and South Korea, had removed the immediate prospect of war, and Pyongyang had desisted from further nuclear-weapons and long-range-missile tests, US intelligence estimates indicated that in the absence of a verifiable process of denuclearisation North Korea continued to present a serious threat to the US and its allies.

A second summit between Trump and Kim, in Hanoi in February 2019, ended with the US president departing unexpectedly early after claiming that North Korea wanted an end to the economic sanctions that had been imposed on it in return for dismantling its main nuclear complex at Yongbyon, rather than the complete denuclearisation demanded by Washington. At the end of June, however, the two leaders unexpectedly met again, this time in the Korean Demilitarized Zone (DMZ), with Trump becoming the first incumbent US president to set foot inside North Korea. Trump and Kim also joined South Korean President Moon Jae-in in the DMZ for a brief but unprecedented trilateral meeting. Importantly, Trump and Kim agreed to restart bilateral negotiations on North Korean denuclearisation. Pyongyang's release in late July 2019, however, of photographs showing Kim inspecting a large submarine potentially capable of carrying intercontinental-range nuclear missiles seemed to provide new evidence that the North Korean regime was continuing the nuclear and missile programmes that potentially threatened the US.

In the face of serious challenges from China and North Korea, and also tangible unease (deriving in large measure from Trump's unpredictability) in regional capitals over the future of America's regional security role, the US administration encapsulated its regional strategy in a 'Free and Open Indo-Pacific' (FOIP) vision, unveiled in late 2017. Important elements included an emphasis on the importance of international rules and norms, and particularly freedom of navigation and overflight, in the region, as well as the strengthening of US alliances and security partnerships including defence relations with Taiwan. In his plenary address at the 2019 Shangri-La Dialogue, which coincided with the launch of the US Department of Defense's first Indo-Pacific Strategy Report, the acting US secretary of defense, Patrick Shanahan, elaborated on the implications of FOIP for US allies and security partners in the region. Both the report and Shanahan's speech stressed the importance of allies and partners investing 'sufficiently' in their own defence – a long-running theme of Trump's expressed views on relations with Japan, South Korea and other friendly regional countries, second in importance only to his arguments for the correction of imbalances in bilateral trade relations.

Japan, America's largest and most important ally in the region, was a particular target; Trump criticised Tokyo not only for supposedly low defence spending but also for the alleged unfairness of the bilateral Mutual Security Treaty. One response by some regional allies and partners to such criticism was to commit themselves to high-profile defence-equipment deals with the US. When Trump visited Japan in late May 2019, for example, Tokyo confirmed that it would purchase an additional 105 F-35 Joint Strike Fighter combat aircraft.

Many states in the region thus found themselves in the uncomfortable position of facing an increasingly assertive China while simultaneously having good reason to question the reliability of the US as an ally, security partner or (in the case of countries without formal security relations with the Washington) a 'regional balancer'. While most did what they could to maintain their relations with the US, even countries that the US was engaging in its FOIP strategy simultaneously sought closer ties with China, which sought to compensate for the impact of its trade dispute with the US. Japanese Prime Minister Shinzo Abe visited Beijing in October 2018 and signed 52 memoranda of cooperation.

Southeast Asian governments felt particularly exposed to the tension in US–China relations and sought to avoid taking sides. Despite this sense of vulnerability, however, little progress was made towards turning their regional group, the Association of Southeast Asian Nations (ASEAN), into a stronger institution with a more developed politico-security dimension that might provide its members with greater agency in their relations with larger powers. The ASEAN Summit Meeting in Bangkok in June 2019 adopted the 'ASEAN Outlook on the Indo-Pacific', which originated with Indonesia, to 'help guide ASEAN's engagement and cooperation in the wider Indo-Pacific region'. The leaders of ASEAN member states, however, continued (at least at the declaratory level) to place their hopes with regard to the most important regional geopolitical issue on the progress of negotiations with Beijing for 'an effective and substantive Code of Conduct in the South China Sea'. This process had been under way since 2002 and was hardly an effective response to China's persistent pursuit of strategic advantage in Southeast Asian waters.

India, by contrast, improved ties with China after the nadir of 2017, when their armed forces faced off on Bhutan's Doklam plateau. At a summit in Wuhan in April 2018, Xi Jinping and Indian Prime Minister Narendra Modi established a pragmatic working relationship. In May 2019, China lifted its long-standing veto on the addition of the Pakistan-based group Jaysh-e-Mohammad (JeM) and its leader Masood Azhar to a UN blacklist of terrorist groups. Sanctions included a travel ban, asset freeze and embargo on arms supplies. In June, moreover, China joined 54 other states in the UN's Asia-Pacific Group to endorse India's bid for a non-permanent seat on the UN Security Council in 2021–22.

India balanced improving relations with China with deepened cooperation with the US. In September 2018, the two powers inaugurated a long-awaited '2+2' dialogue between their defence and foreign ministers. This yielded an agreement that will facilitate Indian access to advanced US defence systems and enable India more fully to use its US-made military equipment. Washington and New Delhi also agreed to establish new bilateral tri-service exercises, the first of which was set to be held by the end of 2019.

The US and India also found common cause in the Maldives. In the September 2018 presidential election, Ibrahim Solih led a four-party coalition to victory over the government of President Abdulla Yameen. The latter's policies, including his embrace of China, were highly controversial and the new government struggled to ascertain its level of indebtedness to China. Estimates were in the range of US$1.5 billion–3.2bn, potentially as much as 80% of its total foreign debt. As of mid-2019, the new administration was also auditing various Chinese projects in the Maldives with the support of Western governments. Modi also offered his support to Solih, and attended the new president's inauguration in November 2018.

A spike in India–Pakistan tensions in the months before the May 2019 Indian general election, to the highest level in two decades, made security a central theme. In February, an Indian Kashmiri carried out a suicide-bomb attack in Pulwama in the state of Jammu and Kashmir, killing 40 Indian paramilitary personnel. JeM claimed responsibility, while the Pakistani government denied it was either responsible or complicit. In response to the bombing, 12 Indian Air Force *Mirage*-2000 aircraft crossed the Line of Control (LoC), the de facto border between Indian- and Pakistani-controlled parts of Kashmir, to bomb an alleged JeM training camp in Balakot, a town in Pakistan's Khyber Pakhtunkhwa province. Pakistan responded with airstrikes against unspecified targets on the Indian side of the LoC, shooting down an Indian MiG-21 sent to repel the incursion in the process.

Both strikes were unprecedented. It was the first time India had attacked Pakistan proper since 1998, after Islamabad conducted a series of nuclear tests, and the first time the Indian Air Force had mounted an offensive operation against Pakistan since the two countries' last full-blown war in 1971. Pakistan's response was the first time that its aircraft had mounted operations across the LoC. Tensions subsided after 1 March, when Pakistan returned the downed Indian pilot, but de-escalation would have been much harder if there had been casualties – civilian or military – on either side; in the event, the only fatalities after the original terrorist attack were suffered by JeM.

In May 2019, Modi's Bharatiya Janata Party (BJP) won a landslide victory in the general election, marking the first time in nearly 50 years that an incumbent government had won an absolute majority and an increased mandate. The BJP's electoral sweep expanded from the north and west to the east and northeast of the country, winning seats in 22 of the country's 29 states. By contrast, the principal opposition party, the Indian National Congress (INC), won seats in only 16 states, with one seat each in Uttar Pradesh, the largest state, and Madhya Pradesh. The INC won no seats in Rajasthan, where it had triumphed in the 2018 State Assembly elections. The BJP's campaign gave greater expression to Hindu nationalism than in previous elections and, after the crisis of the preceding months, it pushed national-security concerns to the fore. This raised the possibility that Modi, in his second term, might revisit sensitive questions over the status of the state of Jammu and Kashmir within India.

The Kashmir episode was the first major test for Pakistani Prime Minister Imran Khan, who had come to power following elections in July 2018. This was the second time (after 2008) that a civilian government in Pakistan completed a five-year term and then transferred power to another elected administration. This norm appeared to be gaining traction, but the military remained a powerful political actor.

Khan took office in the face of a building economic and fiscal crisis. For years, Pakistan had run a large trade and current-account deficit, and external debt more than doubled to over US$90bn in the previous decade. Debt-servicing obligations were proving onerous and foreign reserves had fallen to dangerously low levels. Initially Khan looked to China and Gulf states, rather than the IMF, for assistance. In March 2019, Pakistan received US$2.1bn from China in commercial loans and safe deposits. Saudi Arabia agreed to loan Pakistan US$3bn for one year as balance-of-payments support, as well up to US$3bn for a one-year deferred payment facility for the import of oil. The United Arab Emirates also provided US$2bn in cash deposits, while in June 2019, Qatar announced US$3bn in foreign-currency deposits and direct investments for Pakistan. In mid-2019 the government concluded a three-year US$6bn package with the IMF, which the latter said would allow Pakistan to access US$38bn over three years from other international partners, including the Asian Development Bank and the World Bank.

In June 2019, Khan established a new decision-making body, the National Development Council, to boost economic growth. Its membership included the army's chief of staff, General Qamar Bajwa, who had previously blamed Pakistan's macroeconomic troubles on fiscal mismanagement. In an early sign that the army was prepared to contribute to greater fiscal discipline, it was announced that the defence budget would remain flat in nominal terms in the fiscal year 2019/20. Islamabad's economic challenges were compounded by a June 2018 decision of the intergovernmental Financial Action Task Force (FATF) to 'greylist' Pakistan for failures to combat terrorist financing. This is the final step before a state is blacklisted and subject to swingeing penalties; it carries no mandatory sanctions, although greylisting can impair a state's financial operations with third parties. The task force gave Pakistan until October 2019 to undertake 27 action points to avoid being blacklisted. As of June 2019, Pakistan had failed to complete 25 of them, although thereafter it sought to clamp down on Lashkar-e-Taiba and its fundraising group Jamaat-ud-Dawa, as well as JeM. Despite patchy progress, Pakistan hoped that China, which assumed the FATF presidency in July 2019, would spare it from the blacklist.

In April 2019, Sri Lanka suffered its worst-ever terrorist attack, with eight suicide bombers carrying out coordinated attacks across the capital Colombo and on the western and eastern coasts that killed over 250 people. The government blamed two local Islamist groups, National Thowheed Jamaath (led by Zahran Hashim) and Jamathei Millathu Ibrahim, although the Islamic State, also known as ISIS or ISIL, later claimed responsibility. Intelligence warnings by the US and India about a terrorist attack were not properly shared across the state's institutions; a stand-off between the president and prime minister, which began in late 2018 (involving a bid by the president to dissolve parliament which was overturned by the Supreme Court), had created political dysfunction, which was expected to continue until presidential elections scheduled for December 2019.

# US–China Trade Dispute

The US–China trade dispute that began in June 2018 with US President Donald Trump's decision to impose tariffs on imports from China appeared to take China's leadership by surprise, but the warning signs had been evident for some time. During the preceding decade, US officials had been warning their Chinese counterparts that failure to address a growing range of US concerns about China's anti-competitive policies and behaviours would, if left unaddressed, have repercussions. Trump had made no secret during his campaign for the US presidency of his belief that China was to blame for much of the national malaise caused by de-industrialisation as US manufacturing was relocated to China, and addressing the US trade deficit with China was a key component of his offer to the US electorate.

Since the latter part of the Obama administration, the Office of the US Trade Representative (USTR) had been seeking to build a coalition of like-minded states to take collective action against China within the World Trade Organization (WTO) grievance mechanism. Issues of concern included pervasive intellectual-property (IP) theft; the forced transfer of technology as a condition for US and other foreign firms to operate within China; a failure to live up to promises to open China's markets in areas such as financial services and insurance; and large-scale state subsidies to Chinese industries. In the view of USTR, a command economy the size of China's was something for which the WTO had not been configured and was bending the entire structure out of shape. In 2017, US Trade Representative Robert Lighthizer opened a formal investigation into China's unfair trading practices. Meanwhile the Trump administration's first National Security Strategy report (published in December 2017) reclassified China as a disruptive power that was using predatory economic and growing military power to intimidate its neighbours.

China either missed or failed to take adequate account of the warning signs for a variety of reasons. This was not entirely China's fault. Few within the US policy community believed that Trump would make good on all his campaign promises, with many supporters arguing that he should be taken seriously but not literally. The early Trump White House came across as chaotic and unstable, with a high turnover of staff and little in the way of clearly enunciated policy. China's traditional interlocutors within the US policy community had few contacts with the new administration and hence few insights to offer. The US business community, significant parts of which had long been among the most consistent advocates of close engagement with China, had also become disenchanted with China's restrictive practices and unrealised promises.

The situation was compounded by the fact that under Chinese President Xi Jinping, restrictions on the ability of Chinese scholars to travel overseas meant that most of China's experts on the US had little opportunity to conduct in-depth field research – and even less incentive to report findings they knew would not be well received. China's intelligence services were of little help, preoccupied as they were with the tasks of collection against traditional national-security targets including the pursuit of ideological opponents and pervasive industrial cyber espionage. In any case, a strategic problem of this nature, which is as much about judgement as hard fact, is not something that intelligence services are well configured to address. Moreover, it appears that China's leadership were guilty of the failings that can easily affect any administration, namely mirror-imaging. To China's leaders, steeped in rationality, Trump's action in disrupting a relationship that appeared mutually beneficial made little sense and was simply not something they would have contemplated.

China's leadership could not, however, ignore the evidence that the Trump administration had a very different view of globalisation and international trade from that of previous post-Second World War US administrations. Though China had been advocating for changes to global governance structures since Xi came to office in 2013, the prospect of a global power vacuum brought about by an abdication of US leadership without an effective replacement was not something they relished. China's economy was far too globally entangled and export-dependent for China's leadership to contemplate a breakdown of the global trading system.

## Negotiations begin

China's initial response to the imposition of 25% tariffs on US$50 billion of Chinese imports was cautious and measured. Countervailing tariffs were imposed on a variety of US goods with a particular focus on agricultural produce, apparently in the belief that the US farming lobby would pressure the US government to rethink its position. Commentary in China's state-controlled media was relatively restrained, focusing on the benefits of a global trading system and arguing that historical experience showed trade wars never produced winners. The Chinese Ministry of Commerce produced a report illustrating US gains from Sino-US economic and trade cooperation, citing a report by the Carnegie Endowment for International Peace that if the US reduced current export restrictions to China to the level applied to France, its trade deficit with China would be reduced by up to one-third. Formal talks began in December 2018, headed on the Chinese side by Vice Premier Liu He, a respected economist.

China's approach to the talks was dictated by the fact that its delegation comprised financial experts and administrators with collectively little experience of international trade talks, in contrast to a US delegation made up primarily of international trade lawyers. The latter's efforts to negotiate an agreement based on detailed and legally binding commitments was fundamentally at odds with a Chinese mindset that sees laws as indicative rather than prescriptive and prefers to effect change through the more flexible option of administrative measures. China's initial approach was to offer concessions (including the purchase of more US goods) to reduce the trade deficit and the reiteration of earlier promises to open Chinese markets to foreign companies. They were encouraged by evidence of differences in approach on the part of US principals, with US Treasury Secretary Steven Mnuchin apparently keen to reach a quick settlement, in contrast to Lighthizer, who was seeking to drive a much harder bargain.

In February 2019, the Chinese negotiators proposed the signing of a Memorandum of Understanding (MOU), a familiar Chinese device that amounts to little more than a broad statement of intent. Under the direction of Lighthizer, the US side responded with a demand for concrete commitments from China to amend laws on IP protection (in effect demanding that China admit to a long and detailed list of IP infringements and make specific and verifiable undertakings to desist – according to Professor Shi Yinhong of Renmin University, the US was 'demanding enormous, even hundreds of changes to Chinese laws to protect intellectual property'); to commit to bringing state subsidies into line with WTO provisions (having originally demanded an end to all such subsidies); to address the issue of forced technology transfers (which China for the first time acknowledged as a legitimate US concern); and to agree to the establishment of a committee to review progress in achieving agreed objectives, on pain of tariffs being re-applied in the event of non-compliance.

In May 2019, a draft agreement was returned to the US with roughly a third of the text, containing much of the above detail, struck out. In response, the Trump administration raised tariffs on US$200bn of Chinse imports from 10% to 25% just as Liu He was about to arrive in Washington for another round of talks which had originally been expected to set the seal on an agreement. Predictably, the talks made no progress. Although the Chinese government denied having backtracked on issues thought to have been agreed, there can be no doubt that this is what had happened. To make matters worse, the Trump administration added China's information and communications technology (ICT) national champion Huawei to its Entity List, effectively banning US corporations from doing business with it and in the process dealing a potentially massive blow to China's ambitions to become a major global technology power.

Huawei had already become a serious irritant in Sino-US relations as a company perceived to have benefited from the theft of US IP, enabling it to develop products that undercut US suppliers. Added to this was concern about Huawei's role in breaching US sanctions against Iran and North Korea, the investigation of which had led in December 2018 to the arrest in Canada of Meng Wanzhou, Huawei's Chief Financial Officer and daughter of Huawei founder Ren Pengfei. The US government had for some time expressed reservations about the security risks inherent in using Huawei technology in US phone networks, but the realisation that Huawei might be the vector that would enable China to steal a march on the US in relation to 5G – an important enabling technology providing the levels of hyper-connectivity essential for artificial intelligence (AI), the Internet of Things, robotics and autonomous systems – appears to have come as a wake-up call equivalent in impact to the 1957 Sputnik moment. The result has been what China sees as a strategy aimed at containing China and preventing it from achieving its technology ambitions.

For China, the US approach to the negotiations had unwelcome resonances of Japan's experience with the 1985 Plaza Accord – it was not seen as coincidental that Lighthizer had been involved in those talks, the outcome of which had been a revaluation of the US dollar relative to the yen to make US exports more competitive. The Plaza Accord led to a speculative bubble in Japan which, when it burst, resulted in over a decade of economic stagnation, the effects of which are arguably still apparent.

## China's response and options

Speculation in the Western media that China's efforts to amend the joint text were a response to objections raised by hawkish members of the Politburo are almost certainly wide of the mark. It is far more likely that Xi himself authorised the changes precisely in order to outflank some of his more hawkish colleagues and hence retain the initiative. More problematic for Xi was the argument advanced by many of China's intelligentsia that the US–China trade conflict was a self-inflicted injury brought about by China's excessively assertive approach and espousal of 'techno-exuberance' at a time when it was still not in a position to challenge the US and still heavily dependent on some key US technologies. Critics of Xi's approach, some of whom went public in an appropriately cautious way, argued that the best way to deal with the current dispute was a return to Deng Xiaoping's strategy of 'hide and bide', seek a solution to the dispute by taking account of justified US concerns and focus on the next phase of economic reform and the opening up of the Chinese economy.

The degree to which this line of thinking was problematic for Xi can be determined by the number of articles and op-eds in the state media that forcefully rebutted such thinking. Examples included a *People's Daily* op-ed entitled 'Did this misfortune really come about because China overplayed its hand [*gaodiao*]?' and another in the People's Daily Online entitled 'Can China get what it wants by eating humble pie [*weiqu*]?'. An article in the intellectuals' newspaper *Guangming Daily* excoriated people it described as 'worshipping the USA, fawning on the USA or living in terror of the USA'. At the same time as pushing back on the naysayers, China quietly ceased referring publicly to its 'Made in China 2025' strategy, which aimed at increasing the indigenously manufactured components in strategic technologies to 70% and which has been the focus of US animus – though the actual strategy remains alive and well.

It was clear that the China's leadership was discountenanced by the US decision to publicise the substance of the talks, something they had hoped to avoid. Faced with this fact, China produced a White Paper setting out its version of events. The key points were that frictions in any bilateral relationship were inevitable but should be dealt with by negotiation, not coercion; that China's technological evolution was the product of its people's hard work and allegations that it had been achieved by theft and uncompetitive practices were unfounded; that it was incorrect to say that China had reneged on commitments, modifications to texts under negotiation being standard practice; and that responsibility for the breakdown of the talks rested entirely with the US side. China was prepared to continue negotiating but could not compromise on its core interests. At the same time, China demonstrated its well-established propensity for more intimidating behaviour by summoning the representatives of US and other Western technology companies and threatening them with serious repercussions if they enforced the ban on sales of US high-tech inputs: in effect, demanding that they violate the laws of the countries in which they were incorporated.

The most authoritative open-source analysis of how China viewed the trade dispute was set out in a 14 June 2019 article in the Chinese Communist Party (CCP)'s theoretical journal *Qiushi* entitled 'Clearly understand the essence, clearly address the main issue, struggle to the end: aspects of the US-China trade friction [*moca*] that need to be clarified'. The article makes the following points: the dispute is the product of a US zero-sum mentality which makes it unable to accept gains made by other states; the US approach to free trade is akin to the German economist Friedrich List's 'kick away the ladder' analogy (where a dominant trade nation protects its position by denying others the 'ladders to her greatness'); technical hegemonism cannot succeed – China's technical achievements are the product of a sustained and bitter struggle by millions of Chinese workers; US efforts to pressure China show that the US, while appearing brave, is actually fearful [*seli neiren*]; there is no evidence that the current trade conflict will result in the re-industrialisation of the US and though in the short term the US economy might not suffer too badly, in the longer term markets will start to have doubts about US solvency; and the Chinese economy will survive the dispute as its earlier high dependence on exports has been reduced. The article ends with the words 'China doesn't want a fight but isn't afraid of a fight and if needs must will certainly fight [*zhongguo buyuan da, bupa da, biyaoshi budebu da*]'.

China, which had initially imposed tariffs of between 5% and 10% on US$110bn of US goods between July and September 2018, applied tariffs of up to 25% on a further US$60bn of goods in June 2019 and also opened its own equivalent of the US Entity List, but for all the brave talk, China's options for retaliation are limited by the fact that US exports to China are much lower than vice versa. The United States' most valuable exports, namely advanced technology inputs such as semiconductors, are precisely the items that China cannot afford to forgo. Although it is true that reliance on exports has been substantially reduced – from 35% of GDP in 2007 to 18% in 2018, according to the World Bank – as China rebalances its economy through the promotion of domestic consumption, China's private-sector companies – which now account for most of China's economic growth and almost all new employment – are reliant on export-generated finance to fund domestic expansion. Meanwhile, there are still many towns and cities in China whose economies depend on medium-sized state-owned enterprises (SOEs), the collapse of which could feed into widespread social discontent in a country whose social-security systems are still weak to non-existent.

China did hold out the threat of denying the US access to rare earths, substances that constitute critical inputs for a range of civilian and military technology products, including smartphones, satellites, lasers, jet engines and missiles. China, which is estimated to hold some 37% of the world's rare-earth reserves, had previously applied a similar ban to Japan in 2010 in response to Japan's detention of a Chinese fisherman in a disputed area. However, rare earths are, despite their name, relatively abundant – though costly and environmentally damaging to process. China's effort to deny Japan access to rare earths elicited much international criticism and was judged by the WTO to be a violation of global trade rules. Japan quickly established an alternative supply chain that caused China's share of global rare-earth production to decline from 95% in 2010 to 70% in 2018. The US has ample supplies of rare earths, as do a number of other friendly countries including Australia, Canada, South Africa, Brazil and India. The most China could hope to achieve would be a temporary disruption of some manufacturing activity while the US developed alternative supply chains – which would have the effect of further reducing China's global market share.

If the US were to sustain its ban on US companies conducting business with Huawei and other Chinese national champions, the implications for China's wider high-tech ambitions could be serious. Although Huawei has moved far from its origins of imitating and undercutting US telecommunications equipment to become a genuine innovator (it spends a tenth of its revenue on research and development), it remains critically dependent on US technology inputs, notably semiconductors and software. Although Huawei is redoubling its efforts to make good these deficits, it is debatable whether it will be able to do so quickly enough to achieve its aim of becoming a first mover and global standard setter for 5G technologies. The knock-on effect on other strategic technologies – such as AI, robotics and autonomous systems – could adversely affect China's declared ambition to become a world leader in these areas by 2035. Following the meeting between Xi and Trump at the G20 Osaka summit in June 2019, the Huawei ban appears to have been rescinded, predicated on the condition that any dealings with Huawei would not impact national-security issues. That decision may owe more to the financial losses being sustained by US companies, a significant portion of whose revenues derive from sales to China, than any desire to let Huawei off the hook. In any case, it is unlikely to affect the determination of the Chinese government to move away from dependence on US technical inputs as early as possible.

It remains to be seen whether and how the currently stalled talks can make progress. Xi retains considerable flexibility, though the longer the propaganda war persists, the less leeway he may have. It is, however, unlikely that he will be able to sanction a resumption of talks while China's exports remain subjected to high tariffs, with the threat of yet more to come. For China, the trade dispute has also been a wake-up call, reinforcing a determination to cut itself free of dependence on US technology by redoubling efforts at indigenous innovation. At present, most successful Chinese technology entrepreneurs have focused on developing lucrative consumer-facing services designed to reduce or eliminate the frictions of life in China's crowded urban environment. There has been much less focus on genuine scientific and technical innovation, where returns on investment are less certain. However, the Chinese state has deep pockets and is capable of constructing a system of incentives that would encourage greater focus in this area. At the same time, China is acutely aware of its vulnerabilities and is signalling that it does not wish to move in the direction of the global technology decoupling that it perceives current US strategy is driving it towards – and which it correctly assesses would have adverse implications for US technology companies for whom the China market has, by virtue of its size and sophistication, served as an important catalyst for US technical innovation.

Xi has to walk a fine line, balancing strong feelings of nationalism (which China's state media have to some degree been fuelling) with the practicalities of an economy that is dependent on access to global markets and to US technology inputs. He has some cards up his sleeve, most notably the fact that genuine efforts are now in hand to open up China's financial sector to foreign participation in 2020 and that rules limiting foreign ownership have now been somewhat relaxed. If China does make concessions to US demands, it can plausibly claim that these represent action China was always intending to take – and which might genuinely enhance China's economic performance. Xi can rely on his propaganda apparatus to present the outcome in a positive light, and any such concessions will appease those of his critics who object to the current confrontational posture with the US. When the talks broke down, Xi immediately invoked the spirit of the Long March in 1934–35, an important part of the CCP's foundation myth. This was interpreted as preparing the Chinese people for a long and arduous struggle. It might equally be seen as preparing them for a tactical climbdown in the interest of achieving longer-term strategic objectives that are unlikely to change whatever the outcome of the negotiations with the US.

## US–China Trade Conflict

In June 2018, the US and China embarked on a trade war that has raised concerns not only for businesses within the two countries, but all around the world. The significant US trade deficit with China gives Washington a strategic advantage because it allows the US escalation dominance within a tariff fight. Although the trade war has featured hostile rhetoric from both sides, the largest tariffs have not yet affected the most important trade sectors. China has not put tariffs on much-needed imports of US technology, while the US has sought to spare its consumers by eschewing hefty tariffs on products such as toys and clothing.

### TIMELINE

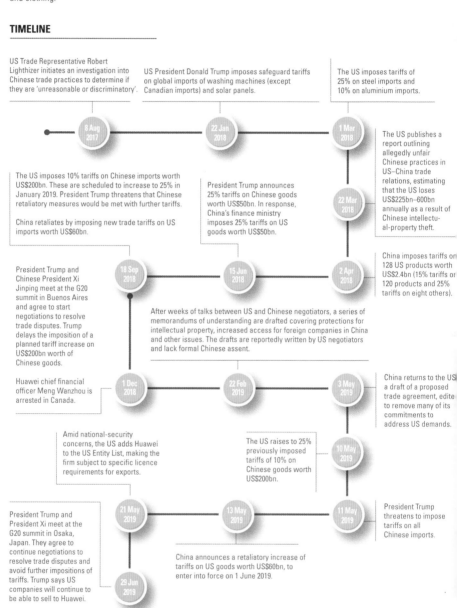

US Trade Representative Robert Lighthizer initiates an investigation into Chinese trade practices to determine if they are 'unreasonable or discriminatory'. **8 Aug 2017**

US President Donald Trump imposes safeguard tariffs on global imports of washing machines (except Canadian imports) and solar panels. **22 Jan 2018**

The US imposes tariffs of 25% on steel imports and 10% on aluminium imports. **1 Mar 2018**

The US publishes a report outlining allegedly unfair Chinese practices in US–China trade relations, estimating that the US loses US$225bn–600bn annually as a result of Chinese intellectual-property theft. **22 Mar 2018**

The US imposes 10% tariffs on Chinese imports worth US$200bn. These are scheduled to increase to 25% in January 2019. President Trump threatens that Chinese retaliatory measures would be met with further tariffs.

China retaliates by imposing new trade tariffs on US imports worth US$60bn.

President Trump announces 25% tariffs on Chinese goods worth US$50bn. In response, China's finance ministry imposes 25% tariffs on US goods worth US$50bn.

China imposes tariffs on 128 US products worth US$2.4bn (15% tariffs on 120 products and 25% tariffs on eight others). **2 Apr 2018**

President Trump and Chinese President Xi Jinping meet at the G20 summit in Buenos Aires and agree to start negotiations to resolve trade disputes. Trump delays the imposition of a planned tariff increase on US$200bn worth of Chinese goods. **18 Sep 2018**

**15 Jun 2018**

After weeks of talks between US and Chinese negotiators, a series of memorandums of understanding are drafted covering protections for intellectual property, increased access for foreign companies in China and other issues. The drafts are reportedly written by US negotiators and lack formal Chinese assent.

Huawei chief financial officer Meng Wanzhou is arrested in Canada. **1 Dec 2018**

**22 Feb 2019**

China returns to the US a draft of a proposed trade agreement, edited to remove many of its commitments to address US demands. **3 May 2019**

Amid national-security concerns, the US adds Huawei to the US Entity List, making the firm subject to specific licence requirements for exports.

The US raises to 25% previously imposed tariffs of 10% on Chinese goods worth US$200bn. **10 May 2019**

President Trump and President Xi meet at the G20 summit in Osaka, Japan. They agree to continue negotiations to resolve trade disputes and avoid further impositions of tariffs. Trump says US companies will continue to be able to sell to Huawei. **21 May 2019**

**29 Jun 2019**

China announces a retaliatory increase of tariffs on US goods worth US$60bn, to enter into force on 1 June 2019. **13 May 2019**

President Trump threatens to impose tariffs on all Chinese imports. **11 May 2019**

Sources: Office of the United States Trade Representative, 2019; International Trade Administration, US Department of Commerce, 2019; Bown, Chad P., Zhang, Eva (Yiwen), 'Will US–China Trade Deal Remove or Just Restructure the Massive 2018 Tariffs?', Peterson Institute for International Economics (PIIE), April 2019

## S–CHINA MARKET-SIZE COMPARISON, 2018

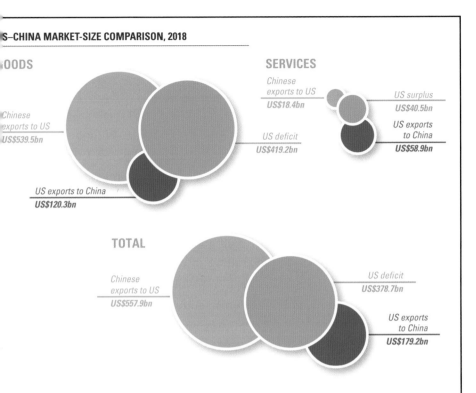

**OODS**

Chinese
exports to US
US$539.5bn

US exports to China
US$120.3bn

**SERVICES**

Chinese
exports to US
US$18.4bn

US surplus
US$40.5bn

US exports
to China
US$58.9bn

US deficit
US$419.2bn

**TOTAL**

Chinese
exports to US
US$557.9bn

US deficit
US$378.7bn

US exports
to China
US$179.2bn

## XPORTS AND TARIFFS BY SECTOR, 2018

### US EXPORTS TO CHINA

| Sector | Amount (US$bn) | Percentage hit by Chinese tariffs | Value of tariffs (US$bn) |
|---|---|---|---|
| Transportation equipment | 27.66 | 52% | 14.38 |
| Machinery | 14.20 | 59% | 8.38 |
| Electronics and electrical machinery | 12.88 | 41% | 5.28 |
| Chemicals | 12.27 | 69% | 8.47 |
| Miscellaneous | 10.31 | 85% | 8.76 |
| Fuels | 8.45 | 56% | 4.73 |
| Wood products | 6.82 | 100% | 6.82 |
| Plastics and rubber | 6.40 | 84% | 5.38 |
| Vegetable products | 4.99 | 99% | 4.94 |
| Metals | 4.82 | 100% | 4.82 |

### CHINESE EXPORTS TO US

| Sector | Amount (US$bn) | Percentage hit by US tariffs | Value of tariffs (US$bn) |
|---|---|---|---|
| Electronics and electrical machinery | 155.95 | 45% | 70.18 |
| Machinery | 119.57 | 51% | 60.98 |
| Miscellaneous | 56.43 | 66% | 37.24 |
| Textiles and clothing | 42.40 | 13% | 5.51 |
| Metals | 29.90 | 86% | 25.71 |
| Toys and sports equipment | 27.93 | 7% | 1.95 |
| Plastics and rubber | 24.98 | 70% | 17.49 |
| Transportation equipment | 20.27 | 92% | 18.65 |
| Chemicals | 19.06 | 56% | 10.67 |
| Footwear | 18.90 | 7% | 1.32 |

# Moon Jae-in's Quest for Peace on the Korean Peninsula

South Korean President Moon Jae-in, elected in 2017, has staked his presidency on achieving a major breakthrough in South–North relations and institutionalising a peace regime on the Korean Peninsula. Without his intervention, United States President Donald Trump and North Korean leader Kim Jong-un would probably not have met for the first summit in June 2018, although Trump was instrumental in forging ahead with his two additional meetings with Kim in the last year. Like previous progressive presidents such as Kim Dae-jung (1998–2003) and Roh Moo-hyun (2003–08), Moon regards the crafting of a peace regime for the Koreas as the ultimate accomplishment. Yet while those predecessors conducted the first and second inter-Korean summits, in 2000 and 2007 respectively, Moon has gone further in pursuing inter-Korean detente. He is determined to put into place a set of irreversible agreements including the signing of a permanent peace treaty, major arms reductions and confidence-building measures (CBMs) with North Korea, and to modernise the Republic of Korea (ROK)–US alliance by securing wartime operational control (OPCON) as soon as permissible. In these endeavours he may be assisted by Trump, who like Moon is eager to create a legacy. Yet for South Korea this is a risky manoeuvre, in which the weakening of its key alliances is a near-certain cost, while the benefits may not endure or amount to much.

When Moon Jae-in was inaugurated on 10 May 2017 following the impeachment of former president Park Geun-hye, he was little known outside South Korea. He had lost to Park in the presidential election in December 2012 but thereafter was able to exploit Park's increasingly obstinate and alienating leadership style, while making a quiet but driven effort to become the polished face of the South Korean left. The 'Candlelight Revolution' that began in late 2016, in which cascading crises crippled the Park government and led to her impeachment in March 2017, opened Moon's path to power. He entered the Blue House on the back of nationwide, peaceful protests.

## Remaking Korea

For Moon, the Candlelight Revolution was a mandate to forge a 'new' Korea. Most South Koreans were unaware of his deeply held political convictions and policy priorities before he became president. He began his career as a human-rights lawyer and worked closely with Roh Moo-hyun. He was not at the forefront of the democratisation movement, however, and his political ascent began only when he joined the Roh administration as a senior secretary and subsequently chief of staff. At the start of his presidency, Moon identified four key priorities: to clean up the political system; to redistribute economic benefits in favour of labour; to achieve greater defence autonomy vis-à-vis the US; and to pursue a 'peace regime' between the two Koreas.

In domestic politics, he has sought to root out corruption at all levels of government and the political system. Many officials from his predecessor's administration have been brought to trial, and he has made institutional changes to investigate corruption and safeguard against it. The 2018 edition of Transparency International's Corruption Perceptions Index ranked South Korea in 45th place in a global ranking of 180 states, compared with 52nd place in 2016. However, opposition parties detect a partisan bias within the anti-corruption drive and the controls imposed on television and other media.

Figure 1: **South Korea's GDP growth, 1961–2018**

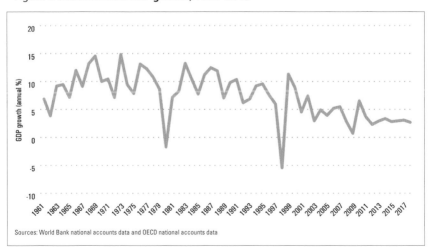

Sources: World Bank national accounts data and OECD national accounts data

In the economic sphere, he has sought to redistribute economic gains in favour of labour. To this end he has pursued pro-labour policies such as rapid increases in the minimum wage, legally binding shorter working hours and shifting temporary workers to full-time status, and pressured the chaebols (family-controlled conglomerates) to accept higher corporate taxes and pursue greater social responsibility. However, his policies on the minimum wage, real-estate taxes and surveillance of companies have contributed to a sharp downturn in economic growth. South Korea has entered a period of stagnation reminiscent of other developed economies. Under his presidency, despite his promises of jump-starting economic growth through wage increases, the economy grew at the slowest rate in six years and several economists have downgraded their growth projections for 2019 to under 2.6%. The Moon administration argues that its lacklustre economic performance is the result of decades of built-in corruption, spillovers from the US–China trade war and the maturation of the Korean economy.

In the military realm, the president has sought to 'modernise' the military alliance with the US by seeking to reduce South Korea's defence dependence on the US. His 'Defense Reform 2.0' project, announced in July 2018, emphasised shifting to a technologically superior fighting force that can meet the full spectrum of military threats; reducing the armed forces' headcount from 620,000 to 500,000 in light of falling birth rates; and cutting the number of generals from 430 to approximately 350. He seeks the requisite capabilities to fully transfer OPCON to the ROK. Current arrangements give a US general control of the US–ROK Combined Forces Command (CFC) in wartime. Every administration since 1987 has touted defence reform but failed to achieve a great deal. The Moon administration, however, plans to increase the defence budget by an average of 7.5% per annum between 2019 and 2023 – a total military investment of US$242 billion.

Diplomatically, Moon has determinedly pursued the implementation of a 'peace regime' between the two Koreas. In 2018 alone, he held three South–North summits with Kim Jong-un and signed an unprecedented military CBM accord with North Korea in September 2018. The agreement created buffer zones for land, sea and air that disallow live-fire artillery drills and major military exercises with new rules of engagement designed to foster greater military transparency. Moon has pursued detente at a breakneck pace, in tandem with Trump's own path-breaking meetings with Kim Jong-un – in June 2018 in Singapore; in February 2019 in Hanoi and the 'handshake across the 38th parallel' in Panmunjom in June 2019. Some critics fear that in the process he has been too indulgent of North Korean provocations and has downplayed the threat posed by North Korea. The 2018 Defence White Paper, for instance, departed from the established practice of directly describing North Korea as a military adversary. Instead, it praised Pyongyang for supporting efforts to reduce military tensions on the Korean Peninsula.

Figure 2: **South Korean presidential approval ratings, 1988–2019**

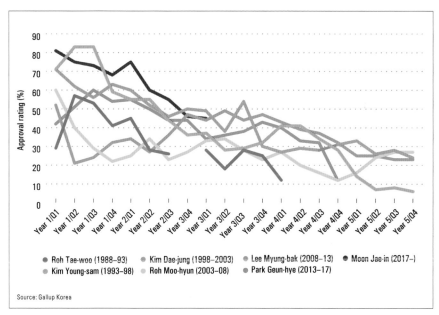

By the standards of his predecessors, Moon has been a popular president in the first half of his five-year term but he will soon face major hurdles such as much slower economic growth than expected. A July 2019 poll gave him an approval rating of 48.3% despite the anaemic economy.

The public has been broadly satisfied with his handling of South–North relations and a perceived reduction in tensions between the two Koreas. However, the third year of the term has customarily been a difficult one for South Korea's presidents and the April 2020 National Assembly election will be a key test for the ruling Democratic Party, which holds 128 seats in the 300-member parliament, while the opposition Liberal Korea Party has 114 seats and the Bareun Mirae Party (an offshoot of the conservatives) has 28. Moon's supporters aspire to emerge with a solid majority.

## The Games begin

Moon's desire to forge a permanent peace on the Korean Peninsula, and in so doing to establish his own legacy, finds some equivalence in Trump's desire to demonstrate his deal-making ability in service of achieving the goals of an 'America First' agenda. Trump inherited the North Korean nuclear problem from his predecessors. Barack Obama told Trump that North Korea was the biggest security challenge he would face, but Trump has taken every opportunity to blame Obama for the 'mess' he left on the Korean Peninsula and to say that it fell on his shoulders to bring the US back from the brink of war. In reality, he has evinced no great interest in the details of the North Korean nuclear file, nor the underpinnings of powerful geopolitical forces. His clear determination is to reach a deal with North Korea that he can present as reducing the threat to the US; he seems willing to downgrade America's long-term commitment to the defence of South Korea if that is the price of an agreement. Moon is focused on putting into place political and military measures that cannot be reversed; he is less focused on South Korea's longer-term security other than believing that by creating a peace regime, the overall threat from North Korea will decline sharply.

For Moon, South Korea's hosting of the Pyeongchang Winter Olympics in February 2018 provided a golden opportunity to set in motion direct talks between the US and North Korea, by engaging Kim and assuring Trump that the North Korean leader was ready to make a deal. By cajoling Trump and working on his showmanship, Moon offered Trump the perfect stage: the first US president to craft a breakthrough deal with North Korea and by extension, bring enduring peace to the Korean Peninsula. Given the absence of any major foreign-policy victory since he entered office in January 2017, Trump is keen to highlight his peacemaking efforts between the two Koreas and ultimately, the full normalisation of relations between the US and North Korea.

Moon publicly maintains that Kim Jong-un is serious about giving up his nuclear weapons once he receives a security guarantee from the US and attendant incentives such as the lifting of onerous sanctions. However, the North Korean leader's steps to date do little to dispel long-held suspicions that he has no intention of relinquishing them. The June 2019 US–North Korea joint declaration made after the Singapore summit noted that 'Reaffirming the April 27, 2018 Panmunjom Declaration [between the two Koreas], the DPRK commits to work toward complete denuclearization of the Korean Peninsula'. Even prior to the Singapore summit, however, North Korean officials have consistently emphasised that Pyongyang would never dismantle its nuclear weapons unless the US took reciprocal steps such as removing the US nuclear umbrella from South Korea. North Korea has long maintained that it supports nuclear disarmament so long as other nuclear powers such as the US follow suit.

In late June 2019, the *New York Times* reported that Trump might consider a nuclear 'freeze' rather than verifiable dismantlement; then-US national security advisor John Bolton firmly rebuffed the notion. A nuclear freeze would entail the partial dismantlement of key nuclear facilities such as the sites at Yongbyon and verified assurances that all work on manufacturing additional warheads or modernising them would stop. In October 1994, the US and North Korea signed the Agreed Framework whereby Pyongyang agreed to freeze work on its nuclear reactors in exchange for two proliferation-resistant light-water reactors. This accord ultimately broke down in October 2002 when North Korea admitted to a uranium-enrichment programme.

When the February 2019 Hanoi summit broke down despite high expectations in Washington and Seoul that a breakthrough was imminent, Trump stated that 'it was all about the sanctions. They wanted the sanctions lifted in their entirety and we couldn't do that.' Despite denials from his aides that Trump would consider a nuclear freeze rather than fully verified dismantlement of North Korea's nuclear arsenal, Trump may feel impelled to reach a deal with North Korea – or at least to show tangible progress towards one – before he faces the US electorate in November 2020. For Kim Jong-un, securing a deal with the US that includes sanctions relief during Trump's first term is essential, because of the (receding) risk that he might lose the 2020 presidential election. Kim fears that if a Democrat becomes US president in January 2021, all the progress he has made with Trump will be lost.

## Kim Jong-un's intentions

Throughout the remaining months of 2019 and well into 2020, Kim Jong-un will press hard to cap his foreign-policy achievements by trying to conclude a nuclear-freeze accord with Trump while also signing a permanent peace treaty formally ending the Korean War. But this depends on whether Trump will accept a watered-down nuclear-freeze agreement with a commitment to lifting the most onerous sanctions. Kim has shored up vital diplomatic and security backing from Chinese President Xi Jinping and Russian President Vladimir Putin. According to analysis by the Bank of Korea in Seoul, North Korea's GDP fell by 3.5% in 2017, with a 37.2% decline in exports in the same year. As disruptive as sanctions have been, however, so long as China continues to supply about 70% of North Korea's fuel and food aid, North Korea's economy is unlikely to collapse. Moreover, the *jangmadang* (informal markets) now comprise as much as 70% of the North Korean economy, according to a leading North Korean economic analyst in Seoul. With their impetus, North Korea's economy is likely to expand incrementally.

Kim can live with a nuclear freeze because he understands that even if the US contemplated a pre-emptive attack on North Korea to destroy his nuclear weapons, not only would South Korea be against it, there is no guarantee that such an operation would succeed. There is little evidence, if any, that Kim Jong-un is seriously contemplating giving up his nuclear arsenal. Indeed, it is the progressive government in power in Seoul that places greater weight on Kim Jong-un's promises to denuclearise.

Former South Korean president Kim Dae-jung argued vociferously that then North Korean leader Kim Jong-il had neither the intention nor the capability to make nuclear weapons. When Kim Jong-il tested his first nuclear bomb in 2006 during the Roh Moo-hyun administration, former South Korean president Kim insisted that Kim Jong-il's real intention was to use nuclear weapons as a negotiating tool with the US rather than as a key component of North Korea's military strategy. What Kim Jong-un has accomplished since 2011 is to achieve de facto acceptance by South Korea and, increasingly, the US, of North Korea as a nuclear-weapons state. Despite this achievement, Moon seems to believe that Pyongyang may be willing to give up that status if properly incentivised.

Kim is the scion of a communist dynasty that provides his core legitimacy, but some analysts infer that he intends to shift from 'traditional legitimacy' based on core revolutionary precepts to 'charismatic legitimacy' focused on economic development. If that is correct, it is possible that he might consider trading his nuclear weapons – themselves a source of legitimacy and security – in exchange for lifting sanctions. However, such a view glosses over the critical fact that Kim Jong-un's core legitimacy stems from his bloodline and has little to do with how much economic welfare he bestows on the North Korean people.

Opinions differ widely on what a nuclear deal would actually entail, but four major possibilities can be considered. Firstly, Kim might freeze operations at Yongbyon without a full declaration of nuclear-development capabilities, in return for partial sanctions relief. Secondly, he might agree to a freeze at Yongbyon in tandem with a full declaration of capabilities, in return for partial sanctions relief. Thirdly, he might make a partial declaration of capabilities and freeze activity at all facilities, in return for substantial sanctions relief. Finally, and most expansively, Kim might freeze all nuclear facilities with a full declaration of nuclear-development capabilities in return for major sanctions relief.

The fourth option is the least likely, and the chances of proceeding from there to the long-held US objective of the irreversible and permanent dismantlement of North Korea's nuclear weapons and attendant capabilities are slimmer still. A full freeze and partial declaration, in return for substantial sanctions relief, seems the most viable option from Pyongyang's perspective. Kim is probably counting on Trump being accommodating in pursuit of an agreement, but despite his desire to roll back the sanctions, Kim is unlikely to take the risk of nuclear disarmament.

## Real costs, uncertain benefits

While the prospects for denuclearisation remain highly uncertain, Moon's presidency has already introduced unwelcome complications in South Korea's relations with other Asian powers. In particular, Korean–Japanese ties have declined to their lowest point since the normalisation of relations in 1965. In November 2018, the South Korean Supreme Court ruled that certain Japanese firms that used forced Korean labourers during the Second World War must provide compensation. As expected, Japan vigorously disputed this decision and maintained that all relevant issues were settled by the Basic Treaty of 1965.

In response, Japanese Prime Minister Shinzo Abe ordered limits on the export of Japanese chemicals and other high-tech components to South Korea's vast electronics industry, citing national-security concerns. While South Korean firms may suffer in the short term, Japan will also face longer-term losses since it spurred South Korean technology giants such as Samsung Electronics, SK hynix and LG Electronics to find alternative sources for critical components and materials.

South Korea's all-important relations with China are also in the throes of major adjustments. Since the normalisation of relations in 1992, China has become South Korea's most important trading partner in addition to exerting significant influence over North Korea. While Seoul has benefited from its growing ties with Beijing, Chinese pressure on South Korea has also grown significantly. In October 2017, the Moon government agreed to mend relations with China, following the controversy generated by Park's decision to deploy US THAAD missiles in South Korea in response to North Korea's fourth nuclear test in January 2016. China continues to maintain that the THAAD system based in South Korea would denigrate its own nuclear-deterrence capabilities. China responded with economic sanctions, dissuading its tourists from visiting Korea and using regulatory measures to punish South Korean firms operating in China, such as the confectionary and retail giant the Lotte Group, which eventually quit the country. These steps encouraged conglomerates such as Samsung to relocate their manufacturing plants from China to Vietnam, and generally to accelerate their search for alternative supply chains and manufacturing hubs.

While China maintains that its fundamental opposition to THAAD is unchanged, Beijing has supported Moon's inter-Korean detente by fostering closer Sino-North Korean relations. Given the importance Moon attaches to engineering a fundamental breakthrough in South–North relations and normalising US–North Korea ties under his watch, he has been willing to accommodate China as much as politically feasible. However, a diluted ROK–US alliance and worsening Korean–Japanese ties, for example, could have the unintended consequence of shifting South Korea closer to China. If so, the biggest leverage South Korea has over China – a strong and vibrant alliance with the US and tangentially, the benefits accruing from solid US–Korea–Japan trilateral security cooperation – is bound to weaken, and that will leave South Korea in a more precarious situation vis-à-vis China.

## Risking a great deal for peace

Moon has stressed the alignment of strategic interests between the US, North Korea and China in order to accentuate the possibilities of ending the cold war on the Korean Peninsula. Yet this raises questions over whether Seoul is able simultaneously to navigate increasingly incongruous goals: maintaining a robust alliance with the US while forging ahead with unparalleled concessions to North Korea; accentuating the primacy of correcting deeply rooted historical disputes with Japan while coping with critical economic fallout and worsening US–Korea–Japan security cooperation; fending off China's multi-thronged pressures while not endangering critical economic and political ties; and continuing to accommodate North Korea while not receiving any concrete reductions in the nuclear or other asymmetrical military threats.

In a period of intensifying US–China competition above and beyond the ongoing trade wars, frayed Seoul–Tokyo and Seoul–Beijing ties, and uncertainty in North Korea, Moon's attempts to jump-start inter-Korean economic ties are likely to fall flat. Domestic considerations, including the slowing economy and the third-year challenge that has beset his predecessors, will also test his ability to stay focused on forging a lasting peace. Even if he can overcome these hurdles, Moon has placed a heavy bet on Trump and Kim reaching a deal that renders the North's nuclear arsenal a strategic irrelevance. To this end, he has already assumed costs by risking weakened ties with Japan and the US, and consequently has less room for manoeuvre with China. Whether he will succeed in creating the legacy he desires is left in the hands of his US and North Korean counterparts and importantly, Moon's ability to influence Kim or Trump is already waning.

For Moon and the progressives, gaining OPCON in wartime is seen as a key step towards opening a new era in Korea's more independent security posture. This may already have been triggered by Trump's perception of the US–ROK alliance in starkly transactional terms. However, Moon and his supporters might consider the significant opportunity costs for South Korea, such as growing Chinese influence on account of a diluted alliance with the US. This has been South Korea's biggest source of strategic leverage since the Korean War, but it is being eroded by a combination of one-sided overtures to North Korea, a breakdown in relations with Japan and limited incentives for maintaining trilateral security cooperation. The question of how South Korea will cope with these costs will persist well after Moon leaves office.

# The Foreign-policy Consequences of Southeast Asia's Slide to Illiberalism

Southeast Asia's political systems range from absolute monarchy in Brunei, to authoritarian regimes in Vietnam, Cambodia and Laos, hybrid military–civilian governments in Myanmar and Thailand, a dominant single-party democracy in Singapore, a fragile liberal democracy in Malaysia, and increasingly illiberal democracies compromised by patronage politics in Indonesia and the Philippines. Yet outside Malaysia, every government in Southeast Asia adopted or implemented illiberal measures that narrowed public space over the past year. These developments are often seen as purely domestic matters, but they have also reduced the space for debate around important foreign-policy questions such as China's role in the region, and have challenged the strength of relationships with many Western governments. The failure of several Southeast Asian governments to address concerns around human trafficking or lesbian, gay, bisexual and transgender (LGBT) rights has also strained relationships with the West in ways not applicable to relationships with Beijing. As a result, Southeast Asian countries have been pushed closer to China, and the potential influence of Western governments on their Southeast Asian counterparts has declined.

Southeast Asian governments have sought to silence opposition voices through a variety of means, some old, some new. In Cambodia, Indonesia, Laos, Myanmar, the Philippines, Singapore, Thailand and Vietnam, governments imprisoned prominent critics either explicitly for their criticisms or on unrelated charges. In Cambodia and Myanmar, leaders of major opposition parties were jailed; in Thailand, the primary opposition leader was charged with eight offences. Criticism was directed at a wide variety of government actions; but in Vietnam in particular, and to a lesser degree in Cambodia, Indonesia and the Philippines, prominent jailed critics had spoken out against closer relationships with Beijing.

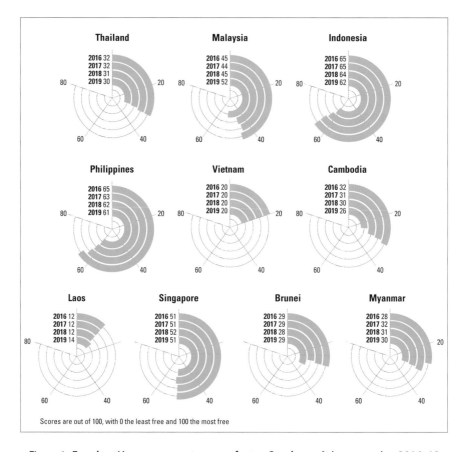

Figure 1: **Freedom House aggregate scores for ten Southeast Asian countries, 2016–19**

The 2017 imprisoning of Cambodian opposition leader Kem Sokha on charges that he was seeking to overthrow the government with American assistance is perhaps the signal example. Sokha was moved to house arrest in 2018 after a year in prison, and the leadership of his Cambodia National Rescue Party remains in jail, under house arrest or in exile. The party itself has been dissolved. The government of Cambodian Prime Minister Hun Sen is perhaps the closest to Beijing in Southeast Asia, and the Chinese presence in the country has been a source of considerable opposition. In response to the crackdown, the European Union and the United States have threatened to withdraw trade preferences granted to Cambodia, yet this would only increase the share of Cambodia's trade with China, increasing Beijing's leverage over Phnom Penh.

During the year to mid-2019, governments in the region appeared to have begun to cooperate to send exiled dissidents back to their home countries, where they had then been jailed for criticism of leaders or policies. Authorities in Cambodia, Laos, Thailand and Vietnam appeared to have exchanged fugitive activists in a quid pro quo. In some cases, exiled activists may have been disappeared or killed. Two Thai anti-monarchy activists who had fled to Laos were found dismembered on the Thai side of the Mekong River.

## Limiting dissent

Governments in the region have a variety of tools at their disposal to curtail political speech, including sedition and lese-majesty laws. Over the past decade, governments in the region have promulgated additional laws that specifically extend state control to cyberspace. In Indonesia, the Electronic Information and Transactions Law (2008) has been used to prosecute critics of the Joko Widodo (Jokowi) administration, such as the musician Ahmad Dhani. In the Philippines, the Cybercrime Prevention Act of 2012 has been used to prosecute critics of the Duterte administration such as the journalist Maria Ressa for libel. Though better known for their views on other issues, both Dhani and Ressa had been critical of their governments' relationships with China.

This legislative activity gained momentum in the year to mid-2019. In February 2019, Thailand passed a new cyber-security law allowing a new National Cybersecurity Committee to detain individuals suspected of a broad new category of 'cyber threats' and to access any electronic device without a court order. The law joins the 2016 Computer Crimes Act, which broadened the Thai junta's already considerable powers to police the internet. In Vietnam, a new cyber-security law that prohibited 'undermining national solidarity', among other actions that threaten the power of the Vietnamese Communist Party, was passed in June 2018. It sparked nationwide protests, which also drew upon hostility to Chinese investment in the form of opposition to a bill that would establish three special economic zones. Officials denied that the zones were designed specifically to accommodate Chinese investment, but the locations were popular with Chinese firms.

Southeast Asian governments also sought to intimidate or shut down independent media outlets. In Cambodia, the *Cambodia Daily* was shut down while the *Phnom Penh Post* was forced to sell to a buyer friendly to the government. These papers had been among the only media outlets critical of the government's relationship with Beijing. In the Philippines, officials filed multiple charges against the website Rappler, which had published some of the toughest coverage of both the Duterte administration's drug war and its policy of accommodating Beijing's actions in the South China Sea.

In May 2019, the Singaporean parliament passed a law allowing government ministers to order the removal or correction of 'malicious online falsehoods'. It allows the government to police the transmission of content from overseas sources on social-media networks run by large multinationals, significantly extending the government's control of cyberspace within the city-state. Though the government has promised to use the legislation in a limited way, the possibility that it will be copied by other governments in the region cannot be discounted. In other parts of Southeast Asia, such tools could be used to limit access to information about key foreign-policy issues such as ties with Beijing.

## Rejecting the promotion of Western values

Australia, the EU and the US have redoubled efforts to reduce human trafficking and modern slavery in recent years. These abuses are not directly linked to particular political systems; indeed, much human trafficking and modern slavery takes place in liberal Western democracies. But Western attempts to eliminate the practice, through scrutiny of supply chains and sanctions against governments deemed to have taken insufficient action against it, led to tensions with Southeast Asian governments and to anxiety among Western businesses regarding the ethics of investment in the region.

Changes to the American approach were particularly salient. The US operates a system of tiered sanctions for governments that fail to make progress in preventing human trafficking, but in the past had granted waivers on these sanctions for most of those cited. In November 2018, the Trump administration indicated that it would no longer grant these waivers by default, leading to a series of automatic trade and aid sanctions for several Southeast Asian countries, and the threat of more sanctions with each annual re-evaluation. Perhaps most consequentially, the White House directed international financial institutions to veto any further assistance for countries in the lowest tier, including Myanmar and Laos.

Much demand for trafficking of persons in Southeast Asia, particularly sex trafficking and for the purposes of forced marriage, comes from mainland China. Such activities occasionally create resentment in Southeast Asian societies, but for many of their leaders the absence of concerted Chinese efforts to eradicate the practice through supply-chain scrutiny or sanctions contrasts positively with the perceived sanctimony of Western governments and businesses. Likewise, Chinese businesses have taken advantage of Beijing's approach to invest in Southeast Asian economies that have become less attractive to Western businesses due to supply-chain scrutiny or sanctions. This has led to greater economic interdependence between China and the region.

Western and Southeast Asian countries have often found themselves on opposite sides of the debate over the rights of LGBT individuals. Some Southeast Asian societies, such as Thailand and Vietnam, have more permissive norms and laws with regard to same-sex relations, but these are outliers. In Indonesia, barring an extraordinary intervention by political leaders, legislators were expected to criminalise sex outside marriage by the end of September 2019 – which would, by default, criminalise sex between partners of the same gender throughout the world's most populous Muslim-majority nation for the first time. (In the westernmost province of Aceh, a 2005 peace agreement ending a long-running insurgency permitted the passage of a sharia criminal code. Same-sex relations were made illegal in 2014, and two men were caned in 2017.) In Malaysia and Myanmar, same-sex relations remain illegal with little prospect of change. In Singapore, sex between men is illegal, but no charges have been brought since 2010.

In Brunei, sharia-based, severe penalties for adultery and homo-sexual behaviour entered into force in 2018. This was the latest and most draconian step in Brunei's move towards a much more austere approach to Islam. Analysts pointed out that the most severe penalties were unlikely to be implemented, as the sultanate has not carried out a death sentence since independence in 1972 despite laws allowing capital punishment for serious crimes such as murder during that period. After a global outcry, the sultan promised a moratorium on death sentences under the new law.

While European governments in particular criticised these measures, and activists in the US boycotted businesses owned by the sultan, anti-LGBT attitudes are more in line with the conservative norms around sexuality found in mainland China. As the sultan has become more conservative and petroleum reserves have begun to dry up, Brunei's government has sought Chinese investment to develop infrastructure like the Muara Besar petrochemical facility and port. Criticism of Chinese investment in Brunei has been subject to strict censorship.

## Illiberal sympathies

Although there are many and varied reasons for increased authoritarian behaviour in Southeast Asia, with its diverse set of societies and particular histories of political development, some common causes can be discerned.

Even before the latest illiberal turn, the US and European governments had become relatively less influential in Southeast Asia as the economies of China, India and others grew. US and European diplomacy encouraging the development of strong civil societies and respect for liberal-democratic norms had a powerful effect on the conduct of Southeast Asian leaders in the immediate period following the Cold War. Moscow was in global retreat, abandoning a particularly strong presence in Vietnam, and by extension Cambodia. Beijing was inwardly focused and China's economy only 4% of its present size. Japanese politics was undergoing a period of party realignment, and Japanese trading houses – which once offered Western-style investment without Western governance concerns – were consolidating following the real-estate bust and bad-loan crisis of the 1990s.

Today, China, Japan and Russia have all at least partly recovered from their earlier setbacks, and are again playing leading roles in the region, whether as purveyors of capital, markets for goods, partners in military and defence-industrial matters, or diplomatic allies of Southeast Asian governments. They play these roles without asking too many questions about political systems or human rights. Though Japan is a liberal democracy itself, in its race to keep pace with Chinese investment it has subsidised authoritarian governments which might have once hesitated to impose illiberal measures for fear of losing Western investment.

While Beijing might demand particular external behaviour of Southeast Asian states in exchange for aid, investment or access to its markets, there is no evidence that China is today seeking to export its model of economic and political governance to the region in the way that it or the Soviet Union did during the Cold War. The US and European governments, on the other hand, often make demands related to democracy, human rights and governance in exchange for access to the same perquisites. For Southeast Asian leaders (as for most national leaders around the world) retaining power through the maintenance of political stability and economic development takes precedence over foreign policy. All other things being equal, Beijing's offers, even with strings attached, are relatively more attractive than Western offers of the same assistance.

US and European support for democratisation, moreover, has been damaged over the past two decades by the success of the Chinese model and by US and European policy in the Middle East. Some Southeast Asian public intellectuals have long pushed back on the Western argument that economic progress would not be possible without political progress; Singapore was ground zero for the Asian values debate of the 1990s. But those intellectuals' argument has been strengthened by the rise of China, an authoritarian system well on its way to becoming the world's largest economy. Meanwhile, liberal prescriptions for the Middle East – first in Iraq, then during the Arab Spring – are widely seen as having led to nothing but sectarianism, extremism, terrorism and the dislocation of millions of refugees.

Finally, authoritarian leaders and measures enjoy substantial popular support among Southeast Asian publics, support that shows no sign of diminishing. Singapore's People's Action Party is Southeast Asia's most successful political party, having never won less than 60% of the overall vote in a general election. Duterte's approval ratings are the highest for any Philippine president at this point in his or her term, despite a brutal drug war that has led to tens of thousands of extrajudicial killings. The party representing the interests of the Thai junta in the March 2019 parliamentary election captured around one-quarter of the vote. In Indonesia, supporters of Jokowi excuse his illiberal turn by arguing that it has been justified by an even more illiberal opposition. And though the authoritarian Najib Razak government lost the May 2018 parliamentary election in Malaysia, it still received substantial support, and the United Malays National Organisation that Najib led could very well return to power at the next election.

## Advantage China

The more authoritarian Southeast Asian governments become, the more likely they are to seek an economic relationship with Beijing that allows them to continue to develop without acquiescing to Western demands for liberalisation. As they become increasingly dependent upon Beijing's markets, capital and aid, these governments increasingly defer to Beijing with regard to regional-security arrangements in order to maintain control at home. Where pro-Beijing policies are unpopular, governments may crack down on opposition to them, creating a cycle of repression and dependence.

In 2020, the wheel may turn again in Thailand. Prime Minister Prayuth Chan-ocha, who led the military coup in 2014, was returned to office in 2019 through a process that stacked the 750-member electoral college with 250 of his appointees, an electoral formula that advantaged parties supportive of his continued rule, and backroom politics that featured unpopular promises of patronage in exchange for political support and threats of prosecution against those who did not go along. Nevertheless, Prayuth holds a bare majority in the lower house of parliament. The process that brought him back to power further damaged the rule of law and investor certainty, and thus threatens economic ties with the West. If he wants to prevent parliamentary deadlock, moreover, he may need to crack down even more on dissent in ways that will further estrange democratic partners.

Events in Hong Kong will also affect how Southeast Asians view these debates. As the protests intensified there in mid-2019, Southeast Asian elites voiced concerns that the demonstrations could disrupt the regional economy. However, if the Chinese Communist Party (CCP) cracks down violently on the protests, sympathies in the region could shift towards the protesters. Indeed, the longer the protests go on, the more they could have demonstration effects in authoritarian countries where other young people are frustrated with the lack of control over their own futures. Even if dissent is crushed in Hong Kong, it may succeed in parts of Southeast Asia.

# Afghanistan and its Neighbourhood After an American Withdrawal

The United States is seeking to negotiate its withdrawal from Afghanistan, 18 years after it sent forces into the country to topple the Taliban and destroy al-Qaeda. It has acceded to Taliban calls for direct talks, without a ceasefire or the presence of the Afghan government, and is seeking guarantees that Afghanistan will not host al-Qaeda or other extremist groups after Western forces leave. The prospective US departure will shake up regional relations, testing the durability of some coalitions and presenting India in particular with difficult choices.

In August 2017 the administration of President Donald Trump increased the US commitment to winning the war in Afghanistan as part of a new strategy for South Asia. Trump declared that 'conditions on the ground, not arbitrary timetables, will guide our actions from now on', and vowed that the US would 'fight to win'. More forces were ear-marked for the conflict and the rules of engagement were relaxed. In 2018, according to official reports, US military aircraft, manned and unmanned, fired 7,362 weapons in Afghanistan – the highest number for any year of the conflict. However, the Taliban also increased its military activity and by the end of the year controlled more territory than at any time since it was ousted in late 2001.

The US decision was somewhat surprising, given Trump's long-held aversion to foreign wars. After H.R. McMaster resigned as national security advisor in March 2018, the US changed course. In September 2018, the State Department appointed Zalmay Khalilzad – an Afghan-American, and former US ambassador to Afghanistan, Iraq and the United Nations – as the Special Representative for Afghanistan Reconciliation. The US also dropped one of its principal positions, namely that it would not engage in talks with the Taliban without the involvement of the Afghan government.

Between October 2018 and August 2019, the US and the Taliban held nine rounds of bilateral talks about the terms for the withdrawal of US/

# Errata

On pages 256–257, some of the opinion data are incorrect. The correct numbers are reproduced below.

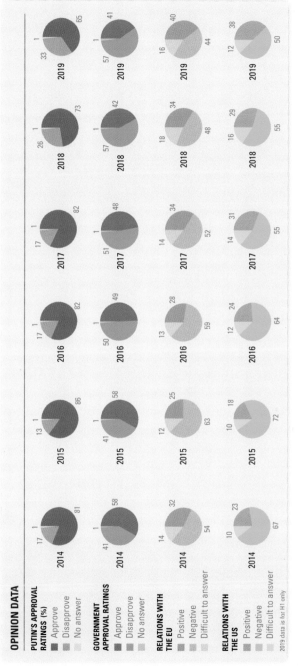

**OPINION DATA**

*(Pie charts showing Putin's Approval Ratings (%), Government Approval Ratings, Relations with the EU, and Relations with the US for years 2014, 2015, 2016, 2017, 2018, 2019)*

Sources: National Industrial Information Agency, 2019; Russian Federal State Statistics Service (Rosstat), 2019; Yuri Levada Analytical Center, 2019; Bank of Finland Institute for Economies in Transition (BOFIT), 2019. Not all polls sum to 100 because of rounding.

NATO troops from Afghanistan, in which the US sought guarantees from the Taliban that it would not harbour or support violent foreign extremist groups, and that there would be no threat to the US or its allies from Afghan territory. Speaking in Kabul in late June 2019, US Secretary of State Mike Pompeo said that he hoped to reach an agreement with the Taliban before 1 September. Analysts expected that the agreement, if achieved, would include a phased withdrawal of US forces.

The conflict in the country actually intensified while the US–Taliban peace talks were in progress. The insurgents had usually been responsible for the majority of civilian casualties, but in July 2019 the UN Assistance Mission in Afghanistan (UNAMA) reported that in the first half of 2019, for the first time since it began recording casualties ten years earlier, more civilians were killed by the Afghan and international forces (717) than by the insurgent groups (531). Both sides sought to strengthen their respective positions in the negotiations. The Afghan government in particular was eager to slow the Taliban's momentum and prevent it from acquiring more territory. In January 2019, Afghan President Ashraf Ghani said that more than 45,000 members of the Afghan security forces had been killed since he took office in late 2014; he added that 'the number of international casualties is less than 72'.

Since it entered into negotiations with the US, the Taliban has stepped up its attacks on the Islamic State, also known as ISIS or ISIL, which has for several years operated in some eastern provinces bordering Pakistan, despite repeated Afghan and Western pledges to eliminate it. Partly it did this to assert its monopoly over the insurgency. Yet it also signalled to the US, Iran, Russia and China that the Taliban does not aspire to threaten neighbouring states and will not tolerate any such group on Afghan territory.

## Obstacles to peace

The path to peace in Afghanistan is unlikely to be smooth or short, given the numerous obstacles. Firstly, the Taliban has so far refused to engage in direct talks with the government, which it regards as a US puppet. The first intra-Afghan meeting took place in Moscow in February 2019 when a delegation of Afghan politicians, former commanders and warlords, and civil-society members – led by former president Hamid Karzai – met the Taliban representatives. It was a historic meeting, bringing together adversaries who had fought each other for years. The second intra-Afghan meeting in May, also in Moscow, was even more important because it involved the Taliban's deputy chief and the head of its political office in Qatar, Mullah Abdul Ghani Baradar, as well as Afghanistan's ambassador to Russia and the head of the government's High Peace Council. The third meeting, co-hosted by Qatar and Germany, took place in Doha in early July and was attended by several current officials from the Afghan government, albeit in a personal capacity, in addition to a number of politicians and civil-society representatives. Further complicating the outlook, the Afghan government is divided. Ghani's team, and that of Chief Executive Abdullah Abdullah, formed a national unity government in 2014 but they have clashed frequently. Abdullah's faction complains that Ghani has an authoritarian streak. Other politicians have also accused Ghani of trying to monopolise the peace process and excluding them from participating in what they call a 'national process'. All this made it harder for the Afghan government and politicians to agree on an inclusive and authoritative team for negotiations with the Taliban.

Secondly, neither the format nor the agenda for talks has been agreed. The Taliban insists on first reaching a deal with the US on the timetable for troop withdrawal. It also insists that subsequent intra-Afghan talks should involve civil society and representatives of political parties, rather than simply being negotiations with Ghani's government, and that any future government and political system must adhere to Islam and sharia law. Ghani's view is very different.

Thirdly, Ghani is opposed to the large-scale withdrawal of US forces in view of his military dependency on them. The Taliban accuses him of seeking to undermine its talks with the US by prosecuting the war in ways that increase insecurity, especially for civilians, such that the US might feel compelled to remain.

Fourthly, both the Taliban and the government aspire to be the dominant political power in the country after the US withdrawal. Ghani expects that the Taliban will join his government and receive certain ministries and posts from him. However, although the Taliban has stated that it will not seek to monopolise power and has expressed a willingness 'to work with all Afghans', it is doubtful whether it would be willing to share power with Ghani, even if he was the junior partner.

Finally, the peace process will require the active support of regional states if it is to succeed. Peace in Afghanistan (and the wider region) will only be achieved through a multilateral mechanism involving the US and key regional players – China, India, Iran, Pakistan and Russia. Potentially disruptive elements inside the country, whose interests are best served by a continuation of the conflict, could also derail peace.

## Winners and losers

The clear US preference is for a negotiated withdrawal that satisfies its core objectives while also leaving Afghanistan reasonably stable. If the talks result in a political settlement, ending the longest war in US history, it will be a foreign-policy success for Trump. Most likely it will also result in the Taliban becoming an important, or indeed dominant, player within the Afghan government.

If that proves to be the case, Pakistan could be one of the principal beneficiaries. Firstly, it could achieve its long-held objective of having a sympathetic government in Kabul over which India has little or no influence. (However, Pakistan might lose leverage over the Taliban if it were to enter government.) Pakistan was one of just three governments that recognised the Taliban in the 1990s and has since been the power most sympathetic to it. Secondly, if the Taliban were legitimised by becoming part of the Afghan government, a major irritant would be removed in Pakistan's relations with the US, which is its principal foreign donor and one of its largest export markets. US officials have long accused Pakistan of supporting the Taliban, providing it with safe havens and hosting the group's leadership. Trump also accused Pakistan of lying and deceiving the US while receiving billions of dollars in foreign aid. Ending the dispute over the Taliban would not necessarily clear Pakistan of culpability for aiding terrorism in the eyes of the US, but it would go a long way towards doing so. Notably, in the wake of US–Taliban talks, US officials said that Pakistan was cooperating with the US in the Afghan peace talks.

Pakistan is not the only regional state that will be glad to witness the departure of US and other Western forces. Iran, Russia and China all supported the US-led intervention in 2001 but subsequently became suspicious about Washington's intentions in the region. They are alarmed at the inability of the US to stabilise Afghanistan and at the rise of ISIS in the country under NATO's watch. Officials in those countries wonder whether the US has either tolerated or encouraged the export of narcotics and violent extremism from Afghanistan for the purpose of destabilising rival states. (Russia, for instance, has experienced a surge in heroin addiction since 2001.)

From the US side, withdrawal would remove one bone of contention in its relations with Russia and Iran: namely the suspected support that Moscow and Tehran have provided to the Taliban in recent years, although this is denied by the Russian and Iranian governments. Unlike in the case of Pakistan, however, there is no basis for hoping that a US withdrawal from Afghanistan would greatly improve bilateral relations with the US. Iran remains in Washington's cross hairs for its regional ambitions in the Middle East, its use of proxies and its nuclear programme. Russia seeks to challenge the US in many regions of the world, and disputes over electoral meddling might soon be overtaken by tensions over nuclear-forces modernisation.

The regional state most negatively affected by a negotiated US withdrawal from Afghanistan will be India. Prime Minister Narendra Modi and his immediate predecessors have long supported the US military presence in Afghanistan as a means to stabilise the country, protect the anti-Taliban government and provide security for India's development projects in the country. India is eager to ensure that Afghanistan does not become a safe haven for militant groups intent on fighting in the Indian state of Jammu and Kashmir. In addition, India views the Taliban as overly dependent on Pakistan and does not wish to see Afghanistan revert to Taliban rule. The dilemmas created by a US-negotiated withdrawal will therefore be most acute for India. To commit substantial military forces to Afghanistan, with the aim of keeping Ghani in power, would be a bold and unprecedented step. Yet without foreign military muscle it seems unlikely that Afghanistan's government will retain its hold on power for long. The other option would be to recognise the Taliban as a major actor in Afghanistan and explore ways to blunt Pakistan's influence in Kabul after the Taliban achieves at least a share of power. That too might be uncomfortable and unrewarding for Modi. India will wait for other powers to recognise the Taliban before it will consider doing so.

Saudi Arabia and the United Arab Emirates (UAE) might also be inconvenienced by a US withdrawal. This is somewhat ironic, considering that in the late 1990s these were the only two other states, alongside Pakistan, that recognised the Taliban government. Today, the Afghan government is a supporter of Saudi Arabia and Ghani has spoken strongly in support of the Saudi-led intervention in Yemen, which was undertaken partly to check Iran's regional ambitions. The Taliban, by contrast, views Saudi Arabia and the UAE as being closely aligned with Ghani's government and the US, its principal rivals. The two Gulf monarchies also view with alarm the growth in Taliban ties with Iran and Qatar over the last few years, including the fact that Qatar has since 2013 hosted the Taliban's political commission. In short, a negotiated US withdrawal from Afghanistan that causes a change in the make-up of Afghanistan's government is likely to set off a renewed bout of competition between Saudi Arabia, the UAE, Qatar and Iran for influence in Kabul. More broadly, Pakistan would be a major beneficiary; China, Russia and Iran would have one fewer worry in the region (although they would remain exposed to Afghanistan's instability); and India would face some potentially agonising choices.

Yet it is also possible that, if the US–Taliban negotiations do not result in an agreement in late 2019 or early 2020, Trump might choose to withdraw unilaterally. The manner and timing of such a departure would matter a great deal. Even those regional states that are eager to see the back of US forces do not wish for a precipitate pull-out that would likely be destabilising. If the US forces withdraw without a peace deal, it will be a devastating blow for the morale of the Afghan armed forces. They are likely to lose more territory to the Taliban, even if they do not collapse, and their rival would be in a position to dictate the terms of a political settlement. Yet in the extended chaos it is also likely that militant groups such as al-Qaeda and ISIS would be able to persist in the country, and the number of refugees from Afghanistan would likely rise.

While much remains to be settled, it seems obvious that the Taliban has endured and will emerge victorious. It may quite possibly be the core of Afghanistan's government in the future. Given the group's hard-line ideology, and its previous experience of government, this might cause unease on the part of the international community and some neighbouring states. One major question for those considering this eventuality rests on the extent to which the Taliban has been affected by its previous experience of government and the subsequent invasion. It seems likely that the Taliban will be more cautious and open in its foreign policy in the future. It desires a basic level of relations with other states. In the 1990s its approach to the issues of women's rights, the pro-duction of opium and hosting al-Qaeda precluded this. The Taliban's attitude to heroin has since changed and it seems minded to break all ties with global jihadis. Indeed, it claims (and no contradictory evidence has been put forward) that none of its fighters have been involved in attacks outside Afghanistan for the past 18 years. If it treads more carefully on domestic questions, this may give it the space to conduct foreign policy on its return to government.

The Taliban will probably be more accommodative of other Afghans in government. It may toe a less dogmatic line on issues of women's rights and the media than in the past, although in both cases the current levels of freedom enjoyed by Afghan citizens will probably not be maintained.

# Modi's Geo-economic Challenges

In 2019 the Indian economy became the world's third largest, in purchasing power parity (PPP) terms, and sixth largest in US dollar terms, and the World Bank expects its national income to exceed US$3 trillion by the end of the year. Prime Minister Narendra Modi has set a target of US$5trn to be attained by 2024, when his second term in office ends. Such optimism should be balanced against the fact that the economy has slowed down in the past few years and the central government is severely cash-strapped as a result of a decline in the growth rate of revenues, partly because of the introduction of a nationwide goods and services tax (GST). With its fiscal ability to promote higher economic growth constrained, the Modi government hopes to trigger a 'virtuous cycle' of growth led by private investment from both foreign and domestic sources.

The narrative of a 'rising India' has been based on an annual average rate of growth of national income of 3.5% in 1950–80, 5.5% in 1980–2000 and 7.5% in 2000–12. In the five years preceding the global financial crisis of 2008–09 the Indian economy grew at a historically high rate of 8.3% per year, but economic growth has since slowed. In 2018–19 official estimates by the Indian government put the growth rate at 6.8%, though several economists have questioned such estimates – on account of both data limitations and methodological problems – and suggested that the rate may have been no higher than 5%. The Indian Ministry of Finance's annual Economic Survey states that the rate of growth in 2019–20 will be 7%. With a slowdown in domestic economic growth and the global economic environment becoming more challenging, India may find it difficult to attain the US$5trn target.

### First economic policy statement of the second Modi government

Modi's optimistic 2024 target is partly explained by the fact that he was voted back into office with an impressive mandate in May 2019, becoming the first Indian political leader since Indira Gandhi to secure a

Table 1: **Fiscal deficit and public-sector borrowing requirement (PSBR) of Indian central government (percentage of national income)\***

| Financial year (April–March) | Fiscal deficit to national income ratio | Fiscal deficit + public-sector borrowing requirement (PSBR) |
|---|---|---|
| 2004–05 | 3.9 | 4.1 |
| 2005–06 | 4.0 | 4.5 |
| 2006–07 | **3.4** | **4.1** |
| 2007–08 | **2.6** | **3.3** |
| 2008–09 | **6.1** | **7.9** |
| 2009–10 | 6.6 | 6.6 |
| 2010–11 | 4.9 | 4.9 |
| 2011–12 | 5.9 | 5.9 |
| 2012–13 | 4.9 | 4.9 |
| 2013–14 | 4.5 | 4.5 |
| 2014–15 | 4.1 | 4.1 |
| 2015–16 | 3.9 | 3.9 |
| 2016–17 | **3.5** | **4.0** |
| 2017–18 | **3.5** | **4.3** |
| 2018–19 | **3.4** | **4.7** |

Source: Ministry of Finance, Government of India
\*Note: These figures do not include provincial-government fiscal deficit. Years in which PSBR significantly exceeds fiscal deficit are highlighted in **bold**

single-party majority in parliament in two consecutive elections. Against the ruling National Democratic Alliance (NDA)'s tally of 353 members in the 545-member Lok Sabha (the lower house of parliament), the opposition United Progressive Alliance (UPA) has only 91 members. Given his impressive mandate, in his second term Modi is expected to focus on economic policy, stepping up investment in infrastructure and facilitating the ease of doing business (EODB) in India. During his first term India's position in the World Bank's EODB ranking went up from 134 (of 190 countries) in 2014 to 77 in 2019.

The rising expectations of a young electorate (India's voting age is 18) and the geo-economic and geopolitical challenge posed by China – which is more than four times larger than India, with a national income estimated by the World Bank at more than US$13trn – have both contributed to the pressure on the Modi government to drive faster economic growth. Against this background of increasing expectations at home and economic and political challenges abroad, the Modi government presented its first economic and fiscal policy statement to parliament on 5 July.

Rather than fuel higher growth through a larger deficit, Minister of Finance Nirmala Sitharaman has opted to stay the course on fiscal correction and not allow the fiscal deficit to national income ratio to exceed last year's 3.4%. The target set for the fiscal year 2019–20 is 3.3%. However, taken together with the fiscal deficit of state (provincial) governments and the public-sector borrowing requirement (PSBR), which is government-guaranteed debt, the total fiscal deficit has been estimated to be close to 9% of national income. The last time India's fiscal deficit deteriorated sharply was in the aftermath of the global financial crisis of 2008–09. While that episode was marked by high rates of inflation, in the 2018–19 fiscal year Sitharaman has been fortunate that the rate of inflation has touched a historically low level of around 3%. This has also given monetary authorities the policy space to ease interest rates.

The budgetary strategy for 2019–20 has been shaped in the context of a severe shortfall in central-government revenue. Declining domestic savings have accentuated the financial constraints imposed on government by a high fiscal deficit. India's domestic savings rate had gradually increased from less than 20% in the 1980s to 33% during the high-growth years of 2003–08 and has since declined to around 29%. A combination of higher deficits and lower savings has constrained the government's ability to push for higher economic growth based on domestic financial resources.

## External dimension of budgetary strategy

The external economic strategy of the 2019–20 budgetary policy statement has three elements. Firstly, it responds to a higher trade and current-account deficit by becoming more protectionist, with customs tariffs raised on more than 36 products and local taxes increased on oil (India imports 90% of its crude oil) and gold (another major import item). Secondly, it liberalises norms for foreign direct investment (FDI) in order to attract more foreign capital in sectors like civil aviation, insurance, single-brand retail, media and real estate. Thirdly, the government plans to issue dollar-denominated sovereign bonds to mobilise funds externally, given the fiscal constraints at home. This will open India up to closer external scrutiny while imposing constraints on its monetary and exchange-rate policies.

The decision to raise rupee resources through sovereign bonds follows the currency-swap arrangements India entered into with Japan and the United Arab Emirates (UAE) in 2018. India's rising dependence on foreign borrowing will expose it to currency risk apart from creating contending pressures on the exchange rate, with the rising trade deficit requiring rupee depreciation and dollar-denominated bonds exerting pressure in favour of exchange-rate stability, if not appreciation. The Indian government has avoided contracting sovereign debt since 1991 when it had to enter into a fiscal-stabilisation and structural-adjustment programme with the IMF and the World Bank to deal with a balance-of-payments and fiscal crisis. Hence, India is entering uncharted policy territory for Modi's nationalistic Bharatiya Janata Party (BJP).

The new wave of protectionism, introduced in 2014 as an import-substitution strategy called 'Make in India', is a response to both the virtual stagnation in growth of industrial output and exports and a sharp rise in the import bill as a result of rising crude-oil prices. India also raised tariffs on several commodities and products imported from the United States in response to US President Donald Trump's decision in 2018 to impose a 25% duty on Indian steel and a 10% duty on aluminium imports, followed by the removal of India from the list of countries benefiting from the Generalised System of Preferences (GSP). The withdrawal of GSP will impact a wide range of potential and actual Indian exports to the US, including organic chemicals, plastics, leather, stone, iron and steel, electrical machinery, automobile parts, nuclear reactors and boilers and agricultural products and handlooms. While China remains the main target of Trump's 'trade war', Trump has been vocal in his criticism of other countries that enjoy a trade surplus with the US, including Germany, India and Japan. Before travelling to Osaka for the G20 summit in late June, Trump responded to India's pre-budget tariff hikes, tweeting:

'I look forward to speaking with Prime Minister Modi about the fact that India, for years having put very high Tariffs against the United States, just recently increased tariffs even further. This is unacceptable and the Tariffs must be withdrawn!'

On returning from Osaka and after Sitharaman had presented her budget proposals to parliament, Trump upped the stakes in July, putting India on notice by tweeting 'India has long had a field day putting Tariffs on American products. No longer acceptable!' Officials from the Indian Department of Commerce and the Office of the US Trade Representative met in New Delhi in early July to resolve differences on trade policy but the two are yet to arrive at a compromise.

## Fiscal constraints on defence and diplomacy

The restraints on government expenditure imposed by weak fiscal balances have also impacted India's spending on defence and foreign aid, imposing limits on what India can do in the short term to deal with the military and diplomatic challenge posed by China's rise and the persistent threat of a border clash with Pakistan.

While many analysts have routinely looked at the share of Indian defence spending in GDP terms, the more meaningful ratio is the share of total central-government expenditure allocated to the Ministry of Defence. This is because under India's quasi-federal constitution, the central government gets only part of the total revenue raised through

Table 2: **Budget allocation to Indian Ministry of Defence as a percentage of total central-government expenditure**

| Financial year (April–March) | Percentage |
| --- | --- |
| 2014–15 | 18.6 |
| 2015–16 | 16.4 |
| 2016–17 | 17.4 |
| 2017–18 | 16.9 |
| 2018–19 (revised estimate) | 16.6 |
| 2019–20 (budget estimate) | 15.5 |

Source: Ministry of Finance, Government of India

Table 3: **Pakistan's economic size relative to India's (ratio of GDP in PPP$ terms)**

| 1985 | 1995 | 2005 | 2015 |
|---|---|---|---|
| 0.201 | 0.196 | 0.165 | 0.121 |

Source: World Bank

direct and indirect taxes, sharing gross revenue with state governments. Since defence spending is entirely undertaken by the central-government, its quantum is decided by the centre's capacity to spend.

Even though Modi's BJP is viewed as a nationalistic party with a strong determination to deal with India's many security challenges – most importantly Pakistan and terrorism – the share of defence spending in central-government expenditure declined during Modi's first term in office. Moreover, a substantial part of this expenditure is personnel costs, which has increased in recent years with a more generous pension plan, from 45% of defence spending in 2011–12 to 60% in 2019–20. With personnel costs accounting for nearly two-thirds of the budget there is little left for capital expenditure. Consequently, the modernisation of India's defence equipment has seriously suffered.

During Sitharaman's tenure as minister of defence (September 2017–May 2019), the armed forces estimated that the combined shortfall in the budget required for the three services – army, navy and air force – given all their equipment needs, is 1,320 billion rupees (US$18.6bn). In the 2019–20 fiscal year the budget proposes to fill only around 10% of the gap in required spending. Adding to the fiscal constraint, the government's inability to reform the excessively bureaucratic process of armaments acquisition and localisation of manufacture, under the Make in India and offsets programmes, has also delayed defence modernisation.

Persistently low allocations for defence also suggest that while Modi remains focused on the challenge of cross-border terrorism emanating from Pakistan, he does not see a Pakistan mired in debt, with an economy shrinking relative to India's (see Table 3), as a major military threat. Even in the fight against terrorism, India is using the Financial Action Task Force (FATF) to exert further pressure on Pakistan's economy. The FATF is an intergovernmental organisation that monitors country performance with respect to policing and penalising money laundering, terror financing and related activities. India has sought Pakistan's 'blacklisting' by the FATF for alleged financing of terrorists. If Pakistan is blacklisted for non-compliance it risks losing access to commercial and multilateral financial support. The FATF is presently examining India's case against Pakistan, with a final view likely to be taken by October 2019.

Modi has also come to recognise China's economic challenge as a bigger problem for India than its military might, particularly after the two demonstrated their diplomatic ability to deal with tricky border tensions during the Doklam stand-off in August 2017. In response to China's emergence as a major trading partner of most Asian countries, India has been pursuing a policy of 'non-reciprocal trade liberalisation' with less-developed economies in its neighbourhood, namely Bhutan, Maldives, Nepal and Sri Lanka. In January 2008 then-prime minister Manmohan Singh offered zero-duty access to exports from these four countries. The policy of non-reciprocal trade liberalisation was aimed at bringing these smaller South Asian economies closer to India through a geo-economic initiative.

Fiscal constraints have also hurt diplomacy. While the budget for the Ministry of External Affairs has increased this year, with several new embassies to be opened across Africa, India has not been able to match China's large and increasing aid programme across Asia and Africa. China's huge development-assistance budget is exerting enormous pressure on India to loosen its purse strings. Sitharaman has stated her intention to increase funding for diplomacy and aid, including the India Development and Economic Assistance Scheme (IDEAS). India plans to spend US$1.32bn overseas, on projects located mainly in its neighbourhood, in 2019–20. The major recipients of Indian development assistance this year will be Bhutan, Maldives, Mauritius and Nepal, Mauritius being a new entrant into India's aid basket. South Asian nations, excluding Pakistan, account for 58% of total aid spending, down from 86% in 2014, when Modi became prime minister. The share of African countries, including Mauritius, has gone up.

Interestingly, however, the 2018–19 and 2019–20 budgets have not provided any funds for the completion of Chabahar Port in Iran, a project considered to be of strategic importance for India given that it offers access to Afghanistan and Central Asia that has been denied because of Pakistan's unwillingness to allow Indian goods and vehicles to travel westward across its borders. India also stopped purchasing oil from Iran in May 2019, in response to US sanctions.

To place India's foreign assistance in perspective, it should be noted that foreign aid and grants accounted for a mere 0.33% of total central -government expenditure in the fiscal year 2018–19. Within the limits of fiscal constraints India is pursuing an alternative to China's Belt and Road Initiative (BRI), working mainly with Japan. India and Japan are promoting the Asia–Africa Growth Corridor as an alternative to the BRI in Africa. Both countries will invest in the development of the Port of Colombo in Sri Lanka and will jointly undertake infrastructure-development projects in South Asia and Africa.

Making Maldives his first port of call in his second term as prime minister, Modi announced that India would extend budgetary support to the Maldives government to the tune of US$1.4bn. This follows an earlier decision to extend an US$800 million credit line to fund 'people-centric, socio-economic projects', including water and sanitation, port development, fisheries, health, tourism and energy. India has also provided grants totalling US$11.5m for other programmes. This assistance to Maldives comes against the background of the voting out of a pro-China government and the election of a pro-India government in the Arabian Sea island nation. The race for influence between China and India within South Asia and the wider Indian Ocean region is on.

## Geo-economics of Indian foreign policy

Global uncertainties created by the US–China trade war and Trump's relentless campaign against the trade policies of important partner countries including Germany, Japan and India have made India's economic-growth slowdown even more challenging. But the US–China trade war and the decision of several US and European companies to reduce their dependence on China have presented India with new opportunities to promote exports and attract FDI. India has identified 151 products that the US has been selling to China that India can now sell to China. India enjoys competitive advantage over the US in the Chinese market for at least 47 of these products. Trade analysts have calculated that of 774 products that China imports from the world market, India has so far had a low share that can easily be increased given China's new willingness, in response to Trump's trade actions, to be more open to Indian exports. The potential export basket would include petroleum products, x-ray tubes, several chemicals, paper and paperboard, iron ore and rubber.

China is also expected to step up FDI in India, with several Chinese companies having already established production facilities in telecoms and related industries, although the bigger beneficiaries of the US–China trade war have been China's smaller neighbours including Bangladesh, Thailand and Vietnam. India has borrowed funds from the Beijing-based Asian Infrastructure Investment Bank (AIIB) for infrastructure development at home, even as it continues to criticise the BRI.

With the US not taking much interest in multilateral trade talks through the World Trade Organization, most Asian trading nations are keen on an early completion of negotiations towards a Regional Comprehensive Economic Partnership (RCEP). Members of the Association of Southeast Asian Nations (ASEAN), along with China and Japan, are seeking an early signing of the RCEP, while India negotiates a more balanced agreement that would liberalise not only trade in goods but also trade in services. India is also examining proposals for an India–European Union free-trade agreement.

Japan and South Korea have emerged as important economic and strategic partners for India in its search for capital and technology. India has signed a Comprehensive Economic Partnership Agreement (CEPA) with both countries, seeking both market access and investment. To meet its defence needs in the face of fiscal constraints at home, India continues to buy equipment from Russia, a lower-cost supplier than the US. Thus, despite the US threat of sanctions, India has inked an agreement with Russia to buy an S-400 missile-defence system, which it plans to pay for in euros. On the other hand, India's defence relations with the US have become stronger with both increasing Indian purchases of US defence equipment and India signing a series of protocols to facilitate inter-operability between Indian and US forces.

Modi has placed rapid economic growth at the heart of his foreign policy, with the aim of becoming a US$5trn economy within his present term, and is strengthening India's relations with all major powers. India is presently a member of a trilateral group with Russia and China, and another with the US and Japan, and remains engaged with the BRICS group (Brazil, Russia, India, China and South Africa). Modi plans to engage EU and African nations more actively, while closer to home his focus has been on the wider neighbourhood including South, West and Southeast Asia. He has also devoted time and resources to underline India's strategic presence in the Indian Ocean region. Each of these relationships is defined by India's medium-term economic goals. In pursuing strategic and economic relations with a wide range of countries, India pursues a policy of parallel engagement of all major powers and economies that has come to be defined as 'multi-alignment'.

# Sub-Saharan Africa: Drivers of Strategic Change

- The ANC government in South Africa is struggling, under a new president, to get to grips with the country's endemic domestic troubles. Voter disenchantment is rising, placing an increasing strain on the state's ability to maintain its regional security role.

- Omar al-Bashir's 30-year rule in Sudan has come to an end; the military and civilian opposition groups are ostensibly committed to power-sharing but the arrangement is unstable and competition among external powers is adding to the uncertainty.

- Nigeria has consolidated the principles of civilian governance, fair elections and the rotation of power. However, the north–south division in the country remains stark and is likely to promote a cautious approach on the part of Abuja to taking on greater responsibilities in sub-Saharan Africa.

- China has acted to curb fears that its lending plans for the region constitute a debt-for-equity trap, but it is now seeking to promote its 5G mobile networks and military equipment, as well as security cooperation, both bilaterally and through UN peacekeeping missions.

- The US is belatedly seeking to counter the influence-building activity of China and other states, and has promoted BUILD, a private-sector alternative to China's debt-financed infrastructure-development model.

## DEMOGRAPHY

POPULATION AND MEDIAN AGE
(IMF, April 2019; UN Department of Economic and Social Affairs, Population Division, 2019)

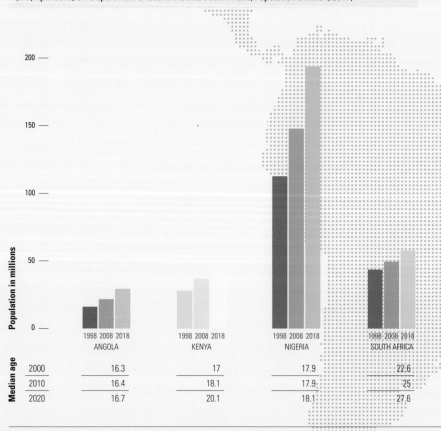

| Median age | ANGOLA | KENYA | NIGERIA | SOUTH AFRICA |
|---|---|---|---|---|
| 2000 | 16.3 | 17 | 17.9 | 22.6 |
| 2010 | 16.4 | 18.1 | 17.9 | 25 |
| 2020 | 16.7 | 20.1 | 18.1 | 27.6 |

AGE STRUCTURE
(CIA World Factbook, 2019)

| NIGERIA | |
|---|---|
| Under 25 years | 62.26% |
| 25–64 years | 34.48% |
| 64 years and older | 3.26% |

| KENYA | |
|---|---|
| Under 25 years | 58.64% |
| 25–64 years | 38.27% |
| 64 years and older | 3.08% |

| ANGOLA | |
|---|---|
| Under 25 years | 66.40% |
| 25–64 years | 31.27% |
| 64 years and older | 2.32% |

| SOUTH AFRICA | |
|---|---|
| Under 25 years | 45.42% |
| 25–64 years | 48.76% |
| 64 years and older | 5.81% |

# ECONOMICS AND DEVELOPMENT

## GDP AT PPP
Constant 2011 international dollars (IMF, April 2019)

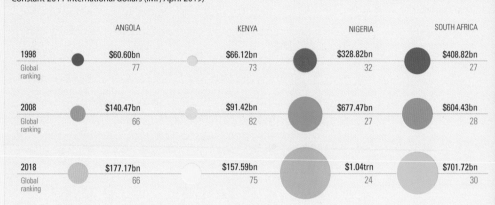

|  | ANGOLA | KENYA | NIGERIA | SOUTH AFRICA |
|---|---|---|---|---|
| **1998** | $60.60bn | $66.12bn | $328.82bn | $408.82bn |
| Global ranking | 77 | 73 | 32 | 27 |
| **2008** | $140.47bn | $91.42bn | $677.47bn | $604.43bn |
| Global ranking | 66 | 82 | 27 | 28 |
| **2018** | $177.17bn | $157.59bn | $1.04trn | $701.72bn |
| Global ranking | 66 | 75 | 24 | 30 |

## GDP PER CAPITA AT PPP
Constant 2011 international dollars (IMF, April 2019)

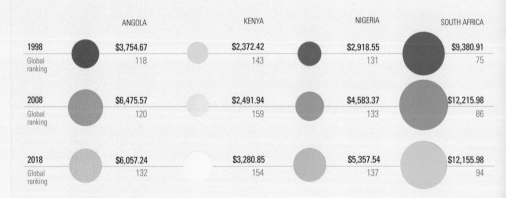

|  | ANGOLA | KENYA | NIGERIA | SOUTH AFRICA |
|---|---|---|---|---|
| **1998** | $3,754.67 | $2,372.42 | $2,918.55 | $9,380.91 |
| Global ranking | 118 | 143 | 131 | 75 |
| **2008** | $6,475.57 | $2,491.94 | $4,583.37 | $12,215.98 |
| Global ranking | 120 | 159 | 133 | 86 |
| **2018** | $6,057.24 | $3,280.85 | $5,357.54 | $12,155.98 |
| Global ranking | 132 | 154 | 137 | 94 |

## HUMAN DEVELOPMENT INDEX (HDI)
(UN Development Programme, 2019)

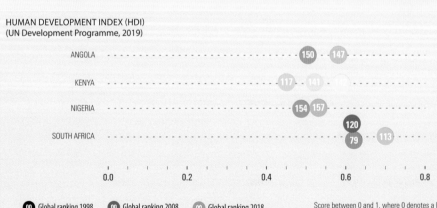

ANGOLA 150 — 147

KENYA 117 — 141 — 149

NIGERIA 154 — 157

SOUTH AFRICA 120 / 79 — 113

0.0    0.2    0.4    0.6    0.8

 Global ranking 1998     Global ranking 2008    Global ranking 2018

Score between 0 and 1, where 0 denotes a low level of development and 1 a high level of development.

# INTERNATIONAL INTEGRATION

## TRADE
Exports of goods and commercial services, constant 2010 US dollars (World Trade Organization, 2019)

## INTERNATIONAL NETWORK
Total number of diplomatic missions, 2017
Lowy Institute Global Diplomacy Index (2017)

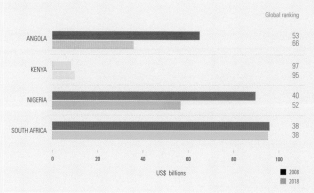

| | Missions abroad | Global ranking |
|---|---|---|
| ANGOLA | N/A | N/A |
| KENYA | N/A | N/A |
| NIGERIA | N/A | N/A |
| SOUTH AFRICA | 124 | 24 |

# DIPLOMACY AND DEFENCE

## DEFENCE BUDGET
Constant 2010 US dollars (Military Balance 1998, and Military Balance+)

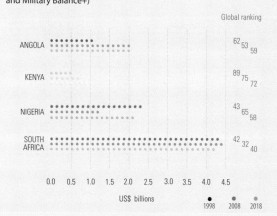

## OFFICIAL DEVELOPMENT AID
Constant 2015 US dollars (OECD, 2019)

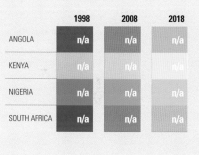

| | 1998 | 2008 | 2018 |
|---|---|---|---|
| ANGOLA | n/a | n/a | n/a |
| KENYA | n/a | n/a | n/a |
| NIGERIA | n/a | n/a | n/a |
| SOUTH AFRICA | n/a | n/a | n/a |

## POLITICAL SYSTEM
(Economist Intelligence Unit, 2008, 2018)

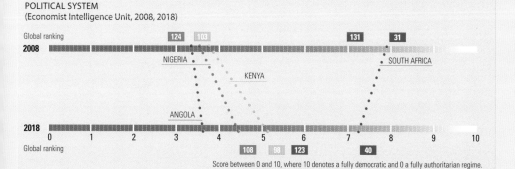

Score between 0 and 10, where 10 denotes a fully democratic and 0 a fully authoritarian regime.

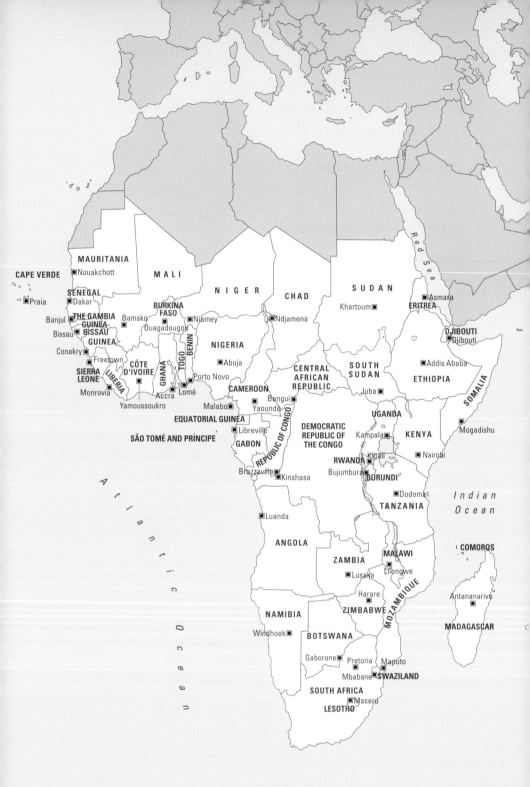

MAURITANIA
Nouakchott

CAPE VERDE

MALI

NIGER

CHAD

SUDAN
Khartoum

Red Sea

Asmara
ERITREA

SENEGAL
Dakar
Praia

BURKINA
FASO

Niamey

Ndjamena

DJIBOUTI
Djibouti

THE GAMBIA
Banjul
GUINEA-
Bissau
BISSAU
GUINEA
Conakry
Freetown
SIERRA
LEONE
Monrovia
LIBERIA

Bamako
Ouagadougou

Addis Ababa

NIGERIA
Abuja

CENTRAL
AFRICAN
REPUBLIC

SOUTH
SUDAN

Juba

ETHIOPIA

BENIN

CÔTE
D'IVOIRE
GHANA
TOGO
Porto Novo
Accra
Lomé

Yamoussoukro

CAMEROON
Bangui

SOMALIA

Malabo
Yaoundé

UGANDA
Kampala

Mogadishu

EQUATORIAL GUINEA
SÃO TOMÉ AND PRÍNCIPE

Libreville

KENYA

GABON

REPUBLIC OF CONGO

DEMOCRATIC
REPUBLIC OF
THE CONGO

Nairobi

RWANDA
Kigali

Brazzaville
Kinshasa

Bujumbura
BURUNDI

Luanda

Dodoma
TANZANIA

Indian
Ocean

ANGOLA

ZAMBIA
Lusaka

MALAWI
Lilongwe

COMOROS

Harare

Antananarivo

NAMIBIA

ZIMBABWE

MOZAMBIQUE

MADAGASCAR

Windhoek

BOTSWANA

Atlantic Ocean

Gaborone
Pretoria
Maputo
Mbabane
SWAZILAND

SOUTH AFRICA
LESOTHO
Maseru

©IISS

# Chapter 5

# Sub-Saharan Africa

## 2018–19 Review

Sub-Saharan Africa's two largest economies held elections in the first half of 2019, resulting in broad continuity in both cases. In South Africa, the ruling African National Congress (ANC) secured a sixth successive general-election victory in May 2019, albeit with its lowest-ever share of the vote in such a poll. The ruling party gained 57.5% of the vote – down from 62.1% in 2014 – to gain 230 out of the 400 parliamentary seats. This was nonetheless a solid result for the ANC, given high levels of voter dissatisfaction with alleged corruption and state capture under the previous president, Jacob Zuma. However, areas of concern persist for the ruling party, notably the improved performance of radical parties and increasing voter disengagement. The far-left Economic Freedom Fighters increased its share of the vote from 6.4% to 10.8% – close to the vote share lost by the ANC – winning 41 seats (up from 25), while the white conservative VF Plus increased its representation from four to ten seats. This slow drift to more radical parties is of potential concern given signs of growing disenchantment with the political system as a whole, as reflected in the drop in turnout from 72.4% in 2014 to 66% in 2019. Moreover, the ANC remains split between reformers (grouped around the current president, Cyril Ramaphosa) and traditionalists who are supportive of the policies adopted under Zuma. The margin of victory was insufficiently decisive to give reformers a complete mandate and tensions within the party will persist, with a potential negative impact on policymaking.

In Nigeria, incumbent President Muhammadu Buhari and his All Progressives Congress (APC) party secured victory. Buhari gained 56% of the vote, but turnout was depressed, at a mere 35% of registered voters, down from 44% in 2015. In part this was due to the last-minute rescheduling of the vote, which was delayed by a week just hours before polling stations were due to open. However, it also reflected deep divisions between the broadly APC-supporting north, and the south, traditionally a stronghold for the opposition People's Democratic Party. Turnout in some southern areas, such as Rivers State, was less than 20%. Such electoral divisions threaten to exacerbate existing religious and ethnic divisions, particularly as the government is likely to prioritise security threats in the north, intensifying disenchantment among voters in the richer southern states.

In other areas, however, there were breaks in continuity. Most notably, in Sudan the long-standing president, Omar al-Bashir, was overthrown by the armed forces in April 2019. This removal of the president, in power for more than 30 years, came some four months after the start of sustained mass nationwide protests, initially over rising inflation and general economic hardship, and subsequently over Bashir's rule more generally. Following Bashir's fall, the armed forces assumed control of the country, suspended the constitution and formed a Transitional Military Council (TMC), and in June the TMC concluded a power-sharing deal with the Declaration of Freedom and Change (DFC), a coalition of opposition groups. The two sides agreed to establish an 11-member sovereign council, with chairmanship rotating between the military and civilians during a 39-month transition period leading to democratic elections. However, the political environment in the country remains highly unstable, with the TMC in July claiming to have thwarted a coup designed to restore to power the former ruling group, the National Congress Party.

The authorities in Gabon and Ethiopia also claimed to have thwarted coup attempts. In January 2019, the self-declared Patriotic Movement of the Defence and Security Forces seized control of a national Gabonese radio station and announced the establishment of a 'national restoration council'. Although easily thwarted, the attempt underscored the political uncertainty in the country caused by lack of clarity over the health of the long-standing President Ali Bongo Ondimba, who reportedly suffered a stroke during a visit to Saudi Arabia in late 2018. In Ethiopia, meanwhile, there was an attempt to overthrow the regional government of Amhara State in which four high-ranking officials, including the Ethiopian Army's chief of staff, General Seare Mekonnen, and Amhara regional governor, Ambachew Mekonnen were killed. Although not apparently an attempt to gain national power, the coup attempt highlighted the security risks facing Ethiopia following political reforms made by Prime Minister Abiy Ahmed, who has been in power since April 2018. Reforms are strongly opposed by vested interests within the military-industrial complex, and by elements of the ruling Ethiopian People's Revolutionary Democratic Front coalition, while efforts to rebalance the country's political system of ethnic federalism have brought social and ethnic divisions into the open. Concerns about violence in the country led Ethiopia's election board to suggest in June that parliamentary elections – due to be held in 2020 – may be delayed. Any such move would likely lead to unrest.

## United States seeks to compete in soft power

The Trump administration moved away from its somewhat isolationist stance, in tacit recognition of the need to tackle near-peer influence in sub-Saharan Africa – and that of China in particular. In early 2018, the Trump administration had announced the reorientation of its official defence policy away from counter-terrorism – the previous focus of its limited African engagement – and towards efforts to compete with key geopolitical rivals such as Russia and China. It thus targeted Asia-Pacific and Europe as the main theatres of operation, while also highlighting the need to contain 'chaos' in the Middle East. Subsequently, however, US officials became increasingly critical of Chinese influence in emerging markets, and the perceived nexus of Chinese development strategies, including the Belt and Road Initiative (BRI), and efforts to expand its military influence. Notably, US officials averred that China is using the BRI as a cover for 'debt-trap diplomacy', whereby developing countries' strategic assets, including mineral deposits and – crucially – port-access rights, are targeted by creditors as collateral in development deals. US National Security Advisor John Bolton stated that China is making 'strategic use of debt to hold states in Africa captive to Beijing's wishes and demands'.

There have been examples of the handover of strategic assets: in 2017, Sri Lanka, unable to repay China for a loan used to upgrade Hambantota port, gave China a 99-year lease for its use, potentially giving the Chinese navy a strategic base in the Indian Ocean. Although sub-Saharan states such as Mozambique and Zambia are potentially vulnerable – Mozambique's debt to China at the end of 2017 accounted for 38.3% of total debt to other countries, while in December 2018 Bolton stated that China was about to take over Zambia's state power utility Zesco to recover a US$6 billion–10bn debt, although China denied this – the clear (if unstated) concern for US officials is of a similar situation arising in Djibouti, where public debt stood at around 104% of GDP at the end of 2018, and where China has its sole overseas military base. Such concerns were exacerbated in February 2018 by the Djiboutian government's termination of a 30-year concession agreement (signed in 2006) with United Arab Emirates (UAE)-based port operator DP World to manage Doraleh Container Terminal (DCT). China has already invested heavily in the Doraleh Multipurpose Port – where one of the six berths is used by the Chinese navy – and speculation persists that Chinese interests will also take over DCT.

In an effort to counter Chinese influence in this respect, in October 2018 the US Senate passed the Better Utilization of Investments Leading to Development (BUILD) Act, probably the most substantial piece of US soft-power legislation in more than a decade. BUILD aims to facilitate private-sector capital investment in developing countries, transforming the Overseas Private Investment Corporation (OPIC) – originally slated for elimination by the Trump administration – into the US International Development Finance Corporation (USIDFC), an agency with a budget of US$60bn (twice that of OPIC), and one that will be able to take equity positions in investments. The initiative is unlikely to be able to match the scale of BRI, which includes some 2,220 deals spread across 87 states, while Morgan Stanley has predicted China's overall expenses over the life of the BRI could reach US$1.2 trillion–1.3trn by 2027. However, the USIDFC is designed to offer a clear alternative to China's model of large state-to-state lending by offering a private-sector solution – with USIDFC potentially able to leverage substantial private-sector involvement – and one that is not funded primarily by debt. It will also have a clear strategic imperative, with US Secretary of State Mike Pompeo commenting that BUILD 'strengthens the US government's development finance capacity, offering a better alternative to state-directed investments and advancing our foreign policy goals'. This suggests that its funds may be targeted at those countries that are most geopolitically important to the US (and China), such as Djibouti and Ethiopia (deemed important because of its substantial population size and role as a bulwark against Islamist terrorism).

However, soft power will continue to be combined with more overt security support, notwithstanding earlier announced plans to reduce US forces in sub-Saharan Africa by around 10% from 7,200 to 6,500 personnel over a period of years, although the time frame was not specified. In March, General Thomas Waldhauser, then head of US Africa Command (AFRICOM), stated that numbers had been reduced by around 300 people, although he called into question 'whether we'll ever be directed to execute the second half [of cuts]'. There are, however, some efforts to realign US forces. Those cut thus far are counter-terrorism forces and their support personnel, and while the precise nature of the reductions has not been revealed for operational reasons, the likely focus is West Africa, since the US administration remains highly focused on North Africa – where the Libyan branch of the Islamic State (also known as ISIS or ISIL) continues to have a presence – and East Africa (al-Qaeda affiliate al-Shabaab is based in Somalia, while US forces in Djibouti are involved in operations targeting insurgents in Yemen). In addition, there are clear concerns about the ability of local security forces in North and East Africa to tackle the terrorist threat. In West Africa, however, there is a 3,000-strong French force, headquartered in Chad, tackling insurgency in the Sahel, as well as the Joint Force of the Group of Five for the Sahel (G5 Sahel), which involves 5,000 soldiers from the G5 Sahel members: Burkina Faso, Chad, Mali, Mauritania and Niger. In November 2018, the US boosted pledged financial support for the G5 Sahel Joint Force from US$60 million (made in October 2017) to around US$111m, and the following month Bolton stressed the need for sub-Saharan states to take greater responsibility for regional security, leveraging better local knowledge rather than having 'the deployment of American forces who are comparatively very well paid and well equipped'. It thus appears that in West Africa US forces will be moved away from tactical-level counter-terrorism missions and more into advisory roles, and that US forces will not necessarily be permanently deployed in the area. However, Waldhauser has stated that AFRICOM is prepared to 'push back' on such cuts, warning that if insurgency groups in West Africa grow, 'we may have to revisit these decisions'. Equally, Major General Marcus Hicks, head of US Special Operations Command Africa, warned against decreasing forces in the Sahel at this stage, saying that the US should monitor the area 'very closely' and 'continually reassess' whether or not there are enough resources applied.

## China continues to lead the field

The US was not the only major player to seek to counter Chinese influence. Similar concerns prompted the European Commission to launch its own version of the BUILD Act in September 2018 in the form of a 'connectivity strategy'. This strategy aimed to provide alternative financing options to countries and emphasised sustainable development and labour rights. However, underscoring the fact that the US and European Union are late to the international 'aid competition', in September 2018 China hosted the seventh triennial Forum on China–Africa Cooperation (FOCAC), and announced loan and investment commitments of US$60bn over the next three years. The US$60bn – the same amount as was pledged at the previous, 2015 summit – will include credit lines (US$20bn), grants, interest-free loans and concessional loans (US$15bn), projected direct investment by Chinese companies (US$10bn) and two special funds: one to deepen China–Africa relations (US$10bn) and a second to boost Chinese imports from Africa (US$5bn). As part of moves to address criticism of putative debt diplomacy, Chinese President Xi Jinping announced a partial debt write-off, centring on interest-free loans owed by least-developed countries, landlocked states and small island nations. A significant amount of the funds pledged will seek to address sub-Saharan Africa's large infrastructure deficit, according to Chinese officials – although this has a potential security aspect. Indeed, during his April confirmation hearing as head of US Africa Command, General Stephen Townsend cited Chinese telecommunications infrastructure in sub-Saharan Africa – notably plans by Huawei to build large-scale 5G networks – as the most significant long-term security threat to US interests in the area.

However, FOCAC included more overt security aspects, since China also pledged to channel funding into a China–Africa Peace and Security Fund, as well as bilateral military assistance and around 50 individual programmes focusing on issues including law and order, peacekeeping, anti-piracy and counter-terrorism. The pledge underscored the ongoing deepening of Sino-African security ties – and Chinese efforts to rebalance global alliances – as further evidenced by the holding in June–July 2018 of the first China–Africa Defence and Security Forum (CADSF). The two-week meeting, organised by China's Ministry of National Defense, focused on topics including regional security and military cooperation, and was attended by delegations from 49 African states as well as the African Union (AU). The AU's attendance was unsurprising given that in a 2015 address to the UN General Assembly, Xi offered US$100m in military assistance over five years to support the AU's peace and security architecture through initiatives such as the African Standby Force and African Capacity for Immediate Response to Crises. In fact, the Chinese authorities have yet to finalise a plan for the disbursement of such assistance, but in the interim China has continued to increase its presence in the African security sector, notably via participation in UN peacekeeping operations. As of March 2019, China was providing 2,513 personnel in regional peacekeeping missions – more than any other permanent member of the Security Council – and based on the UN's formula for assessing funding, which also considers relative wealth, China is the second-largest contributor to the peacekeeping budget.

However, CADSF marks an effort to formalise dialogue with individual African states and regional groupings, as well as promote Chinese defence equipment (via visits to People's Liberation Army, Navy and Air Force facilities, for example). As with FOCAC, CADSF was designed to leverage China's ability to convene large numbers of regional participants to build personal connections – existing bilateral relations include the deployment of military attachés and the holding of joint military exercises – while positioning China as a key and supportive security partner. According to the plan of action unveiled at FOCAC, there will be further CADSF meetings – a putative attempt to institutionalise Sino-African cooperation in the security sphere, as FOCAC has in multilateral cooperation – and increased bilateral intelligence sharing.

## Russia seeking to branch out

Russia has continued to seek to position itself as a credible alternative to both the US and China, in pursuit of new trading partners following the imposition of Western sanctions in 2014 and to bolster its geopolitical influence. This requires a rebuilding of Russia's regional political capital – which largely disappeared in the 1990s – with the Russian authorities seeking to use military exports and broader security apparatus, as well as natural-resource parastatals, to establish a presence in sub-Saharan Africa. It largely pioneered this model in Central African Republic (CAR) – Russia's highest-profile military foray in sub-Saharan Africa in decades – with the Russian authorities sending military and civilian instructors, as well as weapons and ammunition, to support the administration since the end of 2017. The two countries signed an official military-cooperation accord in August 2018, paving the way for increased Russian training of CAR's armed forces, and Russian assistance has given vital support to the government in its efforts to tackle rebel groups, to the extent that in January 2019 CAR Defence Minister

Marie-Noëlle Koyara flagged the possibility that Russia would open a full military base in the country. According to documents published in June 2019 and obtained by the Dossier Centre – a United Kingdom-based investigative unit funded by Mikhail Khodorkovsky, a high-profile and exiled critic of the Putin administration – the Russian authorities regard CAR as a 'buffer zone between the Muslim north and Christian south' that will allow Russia to expand 'across the continent', and Russian companies to garner lucrative mineral deals.

Unsurprisingly, countries with which the Soviet Union had close ties have remained a priority in terms of such expansion, with the Putin government building on existing security agreements with Angola and Mozambique. For example, Russia delivered at least six SU-30K fighter jets to Angola in the first half of 2019, and during a government visit to Russia in April, Angolan Defence Minister Salviano de Jesus Sequeira stated that Angola was interested in buying Russian S-400 air-defence systems, but had struggled because of Angola's economic challenges. However, the Russian authorities are looking further afield. Member states of the G5 Sahel have also sought Russian assistance in tackling ISIS and al-Qaeda insurgencies in the Sahel, while in January 2019 the then Sudanese president, Omar al-Bashir, used Russian private military contractors in an (unsuccessful) attempt to shore up his regime against mass protests.

This is at least partly in line with documents published by the Dossier Centre, which purport to show particularly strong Russian relations with Sudan and Madagascar, as well as CAR. Equatorial Guinea, Chad, the Democratic Republic of the Congo, Mali, South Africa, South Sudan, Uganda, Zambia and Zimbabwe are all cited as existing or potential partners, while Ethiopia is described as a state 'where cooperation is possible'. Russia has already sought to establish a presence in the Horn of Africa, holding talks with the Eritrean government to set up a port-based logistics centre. However, underscoring sensitivities in the area, Djibouti reportedly blocked Russian attempts to set up a base there, saying that it wished to avoid a proxy conflict on its territory (which already hosts bases for China, Japan, France, Italy and the US). Russia intends to foster closer regional links with the continent by holding an inaugural Russia–Africa summit, due to take place in Sochi in October 2019.

## France targets non-francophone states

Notwithstanding its partial setback in the Horn of Africa, Russia has had a measure of success in at least one of its putative aims – to act in areas previously deemed a Western sphere of influence. Notably, its activities in CAR appear to have unsettled former colonial power France – itself a major proponent of government-backed defence and industrial agreements with (and periodic intervention in) its former colonies during the 1970s and 1980s. In November 2018, French Foreign Minister Jean-Yves Le Drian pledged US$27.2m in aid and weaponry for CAR, while in March 2019 French President Emmanuel Macron announced the establishment of a regular 'strategic dialogue' between France and the AU. The first such session was held in June, with Le Drian and Moussa Faki Mahamat, chair of the AU Commission, discussing security in CAR and the Sahel, as well as the Lake Chad Basin and Somalia.

CAR and the Sahel are customary areas of influence for France, which regards the latter as of strategic importance, and France has more than 3,500 personnel in Burkina Faso, Chad, Mali, Mauritania and Niger via its *Operation Barkhane*, which is aimed at tackling the jihadi threat across the Sahel. While Le Drian warned West African states in May that French troops would not be in region 'for an eternity', this is likely designed more to encourage G5 and other states to assume a greater responsibility for security operations than any suggestion of a French withdrawal in the short to medium term.

Somalia is not in France's usual sphere, but is consistent with recent French efforts to move policy beyond traditional Francafrique. Macron's two predecessors, François Hollande and Nicolas Sarkozy, both sought to expand French relations with anglophone Africa, while Macron's three-day visit to Africa in March was designed to boost links with Ethiopia and Kenya and reinforce ties with Djibouti – all countries where China is presenting stiff competition in both geostrategic and commercial terms. During the trip, Ethiopia and France agreed their first military-cooperation accord, which provides for joint operations, training and French assistance in helping landlocked Ethiopia develop a navy. Deals signed in Kenya, meanwhile, included a €200m (US$223m) deal under which a consortium led by Airbus will provide coastal and maritime surveillance. Macron also used the visit to issue a coded warning about debt diplomacy, stating that the French authorities 'wouldn't want a new generation of international investments to encroach on our historical partners' sovereignty or weaken their economies'. However, France will continue to face strong competition from China and to a lesser extent Russia in such areas, while it will struggle to reduce its military involvement across West Africa. Indeed, it was notable that in February France carried out airstrikes in Chad in support of President Idriss Déby – an action that was well outside the mandate of *Operation Barkhane*, since it was in effect an intervention in internal Chadian affairs. Given the risk of destabilisation in the subregion, France will likely continue to take a broad view on its definition of tackling terrorism.

# Middle Eastern States' Competition in the Horn of Africa

Over the last ten years, the increased engagement of Gulf states and other Middle Eastern powers in the Horn of Africa has changed its politics, security, commerce and regional relations. Their involvement has been critical to brokering reconciliation between Ethiopia and Eritrea, as well as to improving regional states' options for cooperation on development and security. Yet the competition between rival powers has also had some destabilising impacts in the Horn of Africa, while strengthening the trend of regional states moving away from Western models of democratic governance.

The Horn of Africa has long attracted the interest of Western powers, principally the United States and the United Kingdom, and, to a lesser extent, France. Today, these states are important security partners for the region, sizeable markets for some states and the principal sources of development assistance. More recently, China has also become a security presence in the Horn of Africa, as well as a trading partner and source of foreign direct investment. Middle Eastern states such as Iran, Turkey, Saudi Arabia and the United Arab Emirates (UAE) also have a long association with the region. However, their level of engagement has risen considerably in the last decade, driven by a determination to achieve greater food security and to secure shipping lanes and a base from which to influence the war in Yemen. There is a markedly competitive element to much of this engagement, as rival powers in the Middle East seek to mould domestic politics in the Horn of Africa to their advantage.

Economic ties between Gulf states and the Horn of Africa have always been important to both regions. The Gulf countries have looked to the Horn for supplies of food, while the African states have sent their labourers to the Gulf and benefited from remittances sent back home. In this decade, however, ties have become deeper. This is partly a result of rising insecurity on both sides of the Bab el-Mandeb Strait, a critical node for global trade and a vital route connecting the Gulf states with Europe and much of Africa. The UAE in particular is a major player in seaborne transit and thus has a deep interest in the risks and opportunities the Horn presents.

The Gulf states import large volumes of food and are sensitive to global price changes. In 2008, at the end of the long commodities boom, sharp rises in prices led several Gulf states to seek land in the Horn of Africa – particularly in Sudan, which has some of the most fertile land in the region – on which to grow crops for the home market. The secession of oil-rich Southern Sudan in July 2011 underscored for Khartoum the value of its arable land. In 2016, Saudi Arabia reached an agreement with Sudan to lease just over one million acres of land in the east of the country for agriculture. Further to the west, the UAE leased 40,000 acres. Moreover, Jordan, Lebanon, Qatar, Pakistan, Syria and Yemen have all leased land close to the Nile. Ethiopia is also a target for Saudi Arabia's agricultural investment, leasing out 10,000 hectares of land in Gambella for 50 years in 2009. However, the practice of leasing land has become controversial of late, with protests in Sudan and elsewhere at the loss of land and water to foreign investors.

Security concerns are at the heart of increased Gulf engagement in the Horn. In 2015, Saudi Arabia and the UAE intervened in Yemen's civil war, and in support of this mission they have sought footholds and friends across the Horn. Prior to 2015, Iran was a significant diplomatic presence in the region. Under the presidency of Mahmoud Ahmadinejad, Iran established strong economic ties with Djibouti and was a rare source of support for Eritrea and Sudan in their shared diplomatic isolation. It also developed a religious and cultural presence in the country. Sudan had alienated its Arab allies by receiving Iranian weapons in its fight against southern separatists, and by supporting Saddam Hussein's invasion of Kuwait in 1990.

Concerns that Iran would extend its regional influence in the wake of the sanctions relief that accompanied the Joint Comprehensive Plan of Action (JCPOA, better known as the Iran nuclear deal) encouraged the Gulf states to become more active in the Horn. Saudi Arabia sought military bases and personnel for the fight against the Houthi rebels in Yemen.

## Sudan

In 2014, Sudan's relationship with Iran dramatically deteriorated as Khartoum sought more lucrative partnerships in the wake of the secession of South Sudan and its oilfields. Saudi Arabia stepped in, providing Sudan's Central Bank with at least US$1 billion in August 2015 to bolster its reserves. A Reuters investigation also found that the UAE had sent Sudan up to US$7.6bn, on the condition that President Omar al-Bashir worked to undermine Islamists within the political establishment. Towards the end of 2015, several thousand Sudanese ground troops arrived in Yemen to join the Saudi-led coalition, and a further 6,000 Rapid Support Forces (RSF) paramilitary troops joined them in April 2016.

However, Sudan is a case in point that large donations by Gulf states in exchange for assistance do not always manage to secure a compliant ally. The relationship between Sudan and Saudi Arabia was tense, and complicated by Bashir's continued links to Turkey and Qatar. Bashir had claimed neutrality in the 2017 Gulf Cooperation Council (GCC) crisis between Qatar and its erstwhile allies: as much as he needed Saudi and Emirati money, he had reason to remain on good terms with Qatar, which is an important investor in Sudan and was an important diplomatic actor in the 2011 agreement that brokered peace in Darfur between major armed groups and the Sudanese government. In 2013, when protests broke out over the lifting of fuel subsidies, Qatar deposited US$1bn in the Central Bank of Sudan to stabilise the Sudanese economy, which helped ensure the survival of Bashir's regime. In 2018, Qatar signed a deal worth US$4bn to develop a commercial port at Suakin that it claimed would be the largest container port in the Red Sea. That was a direct challenge to Emirati interests.

Bashir was also keen not to alienate Turkey, which since 2017 has been an important military, development and commercial partner. In particular, Ankara signed a deal in December 2017 to develop tourism and military facilities on Suakin Island. This alarmed Saudi Arabia and Egypt, which both feared the growing influence of a power deeply connected with Islamist politics in the region.

While the UAE and Saudi Arabia were riled by Bashir's continuing ties to Ankara and Doha, the Khartoum–Riyadh relationship was strained further by discontent on the part of Sudan's armed forces over the high death toll among Sudanese soldiers in Yemen. Trust between Riyadh and Khartoum worsened in mid-2017 when Bashir's intelligence services informed the president that his senior advisor Taha Osmal al-Hussein, who had been urging a break with Qatar, was on the Saudi payroll. When mass protests began against the Bashir regime in April 2019, his one-time backers in the Gulf started planning his replacement. Egypt, Saudi Arabia and the UAE reached out to senior military officials to promise financial support should they assume power. On 11 April, Bashir was ousted in a military coup. The Transitional Military Council (TMC) received US$3bn in aid from Saudi Arabia and the UAE shortly afterwards, and soon dispatched a further contingent of RSF troops to Yemen.

The TMC was later replaced by a transitional government comprising six civilians and five senior military officers, although the armed forces still hold sway. Elections are due to be held in 2022. The UAE and Saudi Arabia appear determined to prevent this for fear that Islamists would eventually gain the upper hand in Sudan and pose a threat to their monarchical systems. Indeed, the marginalisation of civilian political actors in Sudan has curtailed the influence of Turkey and Qatar. For Qatar, the stakes are high: in addition to its investment at Suakin, it relies heavily on Sudan for agricultural imports. The best hope for Doha and Ankara is that the TMC will give way to a civilian-led administration that might be able to restore some balance to Khartoum's foreign relations, as Bashir had managed.

## Djibouti, Eritrea and Ethiopia

Elsewhere in the Horn, Emirati and Saudi economic priorities overlap with strategic ones. Both countries see the security of the Bab el-Mandeb Strait as paramount due to their need to protect oil-export routes. For the UAE, the Horn's role in international shipping is critical, given that maritime trade is Dubai's economic cornerstone. Jebel Ali Port in Dubai is predicted to be the world's largest container port by 2030 and is already the key hub for imports and exports for Africa, a fast-growing continental market with an expanding middle class. In 2016, the UAE was the second-largest investor in Africa after China. The clearest demonstration of Abu Dhabi's commercial interest in Africa is its rapid acquisition of ports up and down the East African coastline, to ensure – among other things – that it will not lose ground to China. In the Horn, the UAE's track record of dealing with separatist movements, including in southern Yemen, may give it an advantage over China, which is a staunch supporter of state sovereignty.

At one point though, the UAE did lose. In 2015, Djibouti prevented Saudi and Emirati armed forces from launching attacks on Yemen from its territory after a disagreement with the Djiboutian Air Force. Djibouti was simultaneously taking the Emirati port-development giant DP World to court, on the grounds of corruption and mismanagement of the Doraleh Port, which DP World had been contracted in 2004 to develop over a 30-year concession. Despite winning the legal battle, DP World was fully forced out of Djibouti in February 2018 – an event that Abu Dhabi accused Chinese firms of orchestrating.

This set the UAE on a quest for new security partners in the region, and it approached Eritrea – another former Iranian ally. In exchange for significant in-kind assistance, Eritrea ended a formal cooperation agreement with Iran, allowed Emirati forces to use the port of Assab to launch amphibious attacks on southern Yemen and leased them the Hanish Islands. However, Eritrea's diplomatic isolation and arms embargo meant it would never be the transformative partner the UAE wanted, militarily or commercially. Ethiopia, Eritrea's rival, was of much greater interest.

Ethiopia also sought partners to help advance its regional hegemonic ambitions. The country was stymied by its lack of access to the sea following Eritrea's secession. Being landlocked, it was unable to leverage its low labour costs. Making a T-shirt in Ethiopia's large textile industry, for instance, costs one-third of an equivalent product in China. Yet it sells for the same price on the international market due to the increased shipping and logistics costs. Moreover, Ethiopia's overwhelming dependence on Djibouti's Doraleh Port for its imports and exports was strategically undesirable.

Ethiopia's government considered several alternatives, the most promising of which was Berbera in Somaliland. However, this presented a serious legal challenge as Somaliland is not recognised internationally, although it is de facto independent. Nevertheless, Ethiopia signed an agreement with the Somaliland government to develop the port in early 2015, although it lacked the capital and technical expertise to do so. Later that year, Ethiopian officials flew to Abu Dhabi for talks, and two developments were set in motion.

Firstly, the UAE agreed to develop Berbera Port. In May 2016, DP World signed a deal to manage and develop Berbera for 30 years, with Ethiopia getting a 30% stake in the port – a stake which will allow Addis Ababa to exercise much greater control over its shipping. While most investors would have balked at the risks of doing business in an unrecognised state, Berbera is 162 miles across the sea from Aden. The need for a new naval base after the falling out with Djibouti, coupled with Berbera's commercial potential, persuaded Abu Dhabi.

Secondly, the UAE and Saudi Arabia undertook to reconcile Ethiopia and Eritrea. In April 2018, Ethiopia's ruling coalition selected as prime minister the young reformist Abiy Ahmed, who had expressed a desire to make peace with Eritrea and liberalise Ethiopia's economy. Abu Dhabi saw a chance to leverage its good relations with Eritrea by acting as a mediator. The peace process was facilitated with US$3bn in financial aid to Ethiopia and US$1bn to Eritrea. To the amazement of regional observers, Ethiopia and Eritrea signed a joint declaration formally ending their conflict in Jeddah, Saudi Arabia, in July 2018.

Ethiopia and Eritrea are both benefiting substantially from the peace accord, as are its Gulf brokers. Ethiopia can make use of Assab Port for commercial purposes, further diversifying its maritime options; Eritrea will also benefit from new investment. The UAE intends to build an oil pipeline to export Ethiopian crude via Assab. In return, and as evidence of the good relationship between Eritrea and the UAE, the Emiratis have lobbied for the lifting of UN sanctions on Eritrea – a goal achieved in

November 2018. However, Ethiopia's increasing ethno-nationalist tensions could destabilise these profitable new partnerships, as came to fruition in the attempted coup by Amhara General Asaminew Tsige in June 2019.

## Somalia, Somaliland

Unlike its neighbour Ethiopia, competition between Gulf states for influence in the Horn has left Somalia substantially worse off. Mogadishu has found allies but has suffered a devastating blow to its already weak national authority. In 2017, Mogadishu refused an Emirati request to cut its ties with Qatar, citing Somalia's neutrality. The UAE accused Somali President Mohamed Abdullahi Mohamed (also known as Farmajo) of siding with Qatar, which had reportedly funded his 2017 election campaign and in 2019 pledged US$20m in budget support for Somalia's federal government. Farmajo has also repressed politicians accused of having ties to the UAE. Fearful of Qatar's and Turkey's growing influence in Mogadishu, the UAE focused on strengthening its ties with the federal states of Somalia and self-declared state of Somaliland. For its part, Mogadishu was incensed by the Emirati deal to develop Berbera in Somaliland, seeing it as a violation of its state sovereignty.

Farmajo banned DP World from operating in the country in April 2018 – although this has not derailed the project – and soon after, halted all military cooperation between Somalia and the UAE. The heads of the federal states then cut working relations with Mogadishu in September 2018, citing foreign-policy differences as one key reason for doing so. These events have set dangerous precedents. Firstly, foreign powers have bypassed Somalia's federal government and dealt directly with the states and Somaliland. This has cast further doubt on existing agreements for a political settlement and security transition in Somalia. The 2017 agreement to build up a Somali National Army (SNA) capable of assuming security responsibility from the AU Mission in Somalia (AMISOM) depends on cooperation between the federal government and the states, because the latter are meant to contribute their forces to the national army. This unresolved security question is all the more pressing given that AMISOM is planning to leave Somalia by 2021.

Turkey is also an important security partner in Somalia, where it operates a military base in Mogadishu. Ankara's 2005 'Open to Africa' policy combines humanitarian aid, military cooperation, and trade and investment in its engagement with African countries. It has the largest embassy in Mogadishu and trains SNA soldiers at its base in the country. Ankara is also the largest foreign investor in Somalia, and Turkish Airlines was the first major international carrier to launch flights to Mogadishu. Ankara, however, has been unable to help the federal government to extend its territorial control or bring the federal states to heel.

Somaliland, on the other hand, appears set to benefit enormously from its new partnerships with Ethiopia and the UAE. For Hargeisa, the goal is normalising its status as an independent entity and achieving international recognition. Until now, Western nations have said that it is for the African Union (AU) to decide whether to recognise its independence. However, the AU is unlikely to be the first mover on this front, given that its forerunner, the Organisation of African Unity (OAU), made the decision to maintain colonial-era boundaries. A change in this policy would energise a wave of irredentist claims elsewhere on the continent, putting several AU member states including Cameroon, Nigeria, Ethiopia, Morocco and the Democratic Republic of the Congo (DRC) in an extremely difficult position. Instead, Somaliland's government is likely to focus its efforts for independence on its investment partners. A key question here is whether Somaliland attempts to use Emirati port infrastructure to elicit recognition of its independence by the UAE.

Somalia's security in the medium term depends entirely on whether AMISOM fulfils its pledge to leave the country by 2021. While its troop-contributing countries are keen to continue fighting, a lack of donor funding has obliged them to plan to wind down operations. If this happens, al-Shabaab might rapidly regain control over swathes of southern and central Somalia, and may attempt to retake key urban centres such as Kismayo and Mogadishu. None of the Gulf states involved in Somalia want this to happen, and thus may set aside their rivalries to jointly fund AMISOM. Given their fears of Islamist governments, the UAE and Saudi Arabia are likely to be the principal investors. They would be fiercely opposed to the prospect of the Somalia government and international community entering into negotiations with al-Shabaab, although this cannot be ruled out given the weakness of the government and the militant group's territorial hold. If that happens, Qatar may see an opportunity to leverage its experience of mediating between state governments and non-state armed groups.

## A great game in the Horn?

Qatar, Saudi Arabia, Turkey and the UAE are not the only external powers seeking to exert influence in the Horn. US President Donald Trump decided at the start of his presidency to reduce the US military presence in Africa, which has generally focused on counter-terrorism. However, as China's military footprint in the Horn and East Africa grows, he may feel compelled to respond.

China is a major investor and trade partner for all regional states. For Beijing, Djibouti was a logical starting point as it plays host to a number of military bases – meaning a Chinese acquisition was relatively uncontroversial. However, as Chinese developments in the Horn of Africa associated with the Belt and Road Initiative (BRI) increase in number and scope, it may decide to expand its military infrastructure. This risks the further militarisation of the Horn as other invested countries could respond accordingly.

There have also been rumours that Russia has been negotiating for a naval base in Somaliland. Local media reported in 2018 that Russia had offered to recognise Somaliland's independence in exchange. This could prompt other external powers to follow suit. Such a move would set a difficult precedent in regard to states' handling of other secessionist claims, in Africa and beyond.

The four Middle Eastern powers have exercised considerable sway in the Horn of Africa. They have been an important source of investment and security assistance, and the Saudi–UAE initiative unexpectedly forged reconciliation between Ethiopia and Eritrea. However, some states in the subregion have been unable to turn the Middle Eastern powers' competitive engagement to their advantage, but rather have been overpowered by it. Furthermore, the emphasis on security at the expense of good governance could exacerbate domestic discontent and jeopardise hard-won political stability in some states. Somalia is a cautionary tale of the consequences of unchecked competition.

# Nigeria's Low-key Approach to Regional Leadership and Foreign Policy

Nigeria is sub-Saharan Africa's largest economy and has the third-largest defence budget in the region (after South Africa and Angola). It played a leading role in the establishment of the Economic Community of West African States (ECOWAS) regional grouping in 1975 and has been a prime proponent of an Afrocentrist approach to security and other issues in Africa. However, a focus on domestic issues – and on overt competition with South Africa – has led to underperformance relative to its ambitions in terms of both regional and global leadership (it has failed to play a dominant role in ECOWAS, the African Union (AU) and the Community of Sahel-Saharan States, for example). Rapid improvement in this area is unlikely, given the vague foreign-policy objectives of President Muhammadu Buhari, re-elected in February 2019, and a continued ambivalence towards regional economic integration, underscored by the country's long delay in signing up to – and failure thus far to ratify – the African Continental Free-Trade Area (AfCFTA) or to ECOWAS's Economic Partnership Agreement with the EU.

## Punching below its weight?

Successive Nigerian administrations have sought to portray the country as a major regional power, with the ambition and capacity to play a high-profile role in determining sub-Saharan Africa's regional trajectory and its broader global relations. As such, Nigeria played an important role in determining the final form of the Organisation of African Unity (OAU) in the 1960s – pushing for a conservative approach to continental political union – and the OAU's subsequent transmutation into the AU. Nigeria has also sought to play a larger role on the world stage, campaigning for a permanent seat on the UN Security Council. It has some of the necessary qualities for this leadership role – notably high levels of military strength relative to most of the continent (Nigeria has the fourth-largest number of active military personnel in sub-Saharan

Africa, according to IISS data). Unsurprisingly, given its focus on tackling insurgency groups, Nigeria is particularly strong in terms of land assets. In contrast, its naval power lags behind that of many of its sub-Saharan peers with maritime borders.

Nigeria has failed to fulfil its potential in several respects, however. It has made little progress in its efforts to drive reform of the UN Security Council. While Nigerian Tijjani Muhammad-Bande, elected as the next president of the UN General Assembly in June 2019, has stated that he will prioritise such reforms, there is little to suggest rapid progress on an issue that has been pending for more than a decade. In recent years Nigeria has also taken a hands-off approach to security issues beyond (and even to a certain extent within) the West African subregion. Equally, while Buhari has promised a partial rebalancing of Nigeria's hegemonic and altruistic goals, he has yet to outline a clearly defined framework for engagement in the region or globally, while domestic challenges are likely to continue to constrain the government's broader foreign-policy ambitions.

## Focus on domestic issues

The government's need to focus on multiple domestic-security issues in recent years is one of the key reasons for Nigeria's relative underperformance as a regional leader – its failure to take a lead role in regional organisations and its low-key role in addressing regional crises. This situation is unlikely to change in the short to medium term. In the north of the country the authorities need to tackle banditry in the northwest and Islamist militant group Boko Haram in the northeast. The Nigerian armed forces regularly claim to be making major breakthroughs against Boko Haram and the Islamic State–West Africa Province (ISWAP), with public statements describing the insurgents as 'remnants', but in reality Boko Haram is resurgent in the area, in part thanks to its use of new tactics (used previously in the Middle East) and more sophisticated hardware. In June 2019, for example, Islamist insurgents overran a Nigerian army base at Kareto in northeastern Borno State, some 130 kilometres from state capital Maiduguri. Buhari campaigned on a 'zero-tolerance' approach to terrorism and has strong ethno-religious ties with the northern region, suggesting that substantial federal resources and firepower will be directed towards restoring law and order in the area.

Even more challenging, but less likely to receive substantial resources, is the ongoing conflict between settled farming communities (mostly Christian) and nomadic pastoralist groups (mostly Muslim). Increasingly scarce water and land resources have pushed herders south towards Nigeria's Middle Belt, where farming communities are concentrated, although violent clashes have been reported throughout the country. Competition for resources is only likely to intensify, given the impact of climate change, and while the security impact of the clashes is relatively contained – there has been little spillover into either the administrative or commercial capitals – the economic impact, in terms of agricultural and livestock production and disruption to food supplies and thus consumer prices, is substantial. The Middle Belt will likely act as a further drain on security resources, even if it remains a lower priority than the north.

Finally, the government faces new issues in the economically important south. Nearly all the country's primary oil reserves are concentrated in and around the Niger Delta, with other resources located offshore in the Gulf of Guinea. Militancy and separatism are long-standing issues in the area – in 1967, leaders of the state of Biafra declared independence from the northern-dominated federal government, leading to a civil war that lasted until 1970. The February 2019 election underscored the alienation of Nigerians in the south, with voter turnout below 20% in some areas. In part this reflects dissatisfaction with Buhari personally, since he is perceived to be focused largely on security issues in the north. Prior to the elections, militant group the Niger Delta Avengers threatened to make the area 'ungovernable' should Buhari win a second term. While this seems unlikely – not least because the government will channel funds towards tackling militant groups – militant activity is likely to persist throughout his second term. These three domestic-security challenges will continue to dominate the Buhari government's policy agenda, and therefore skew its approach to regional issues.

## Foreign-policy agenda dominated by insurgency concerns

During his first term of office, Buhari's somewhat ill-defined foreign policy was focused on Boko Haram and other insurgent groups. Shortly after being elected in March 2015, he visited Benin, Cameroon, Chad and Niger – as well as the US and a G7 meeting in Germany – with the stated aim of raising awareness of and international cooperation against Boko Haram's operations in Nigeria and the West African subregion more generally. He also sought to revitalise the Multinational Joint Task Force (MNJTF) against Boko Haram, created as a solely Nigerian taskforce in 1994 but subsequently expanded to include units from Chad and Niger to tackle cross-border security issues in the Lake Chad region. Nigeria contributed US$21 million to the force in June 2015, and newly elected Buhari took a more positive approach to international cooperation, where previous administrations had blocked foreign forces from encroaching on national territory even in pursuit of Boko Haram. Buhari's efforts had some success: in the first half of 2016 alone, the MNJTF freed 4,690 hostages held by insurgents, dismantled 32 camps, arrested 566 Boko Haram members and 'neutralised' 675 others. However, notwithstanding cross-border cooperation, Islamic State (also known as ISIS or ISIL) and other militants have continued to carry out attacks on military bases, notably in Borno State, while well over 2m people are believed to be internally displaced as a result of violence throughout the Lake Chad Basin. Moreover, while the overwhelming focus on tackling insurgency has proved popular in northern Nigeria, it has contributed to a national (and regional) perception that Nigeria has failed to fulfil its potential.

Reflecting this, the ruling All Progressives Congress (APC) party's manifesto for the February 2019 elections pledged to adopt a more assertive foreign policy, conceding that Nigeria's international influence is well below potential and that it has 'abdicated' the responsibility of an African leadership role in recent years. It promised a 'more engaged, effective and influential' Nigeria, with Nigerian national interest the overriding factor in its regional and global policy, with this to be achieved by the following ambitious goals:

- Promoting good governance domestically and across the continent as a means of restoring the country's international reputation.
- Strengthening the efficacy of the AU.
- Engaging with South Africa and other BRICS countries (Brazil, Russia, India and China) 'on the basis of equality', while helping to develop fellow MINT (Mexico, Indonesia, Nigeria and Turkey) states as a counterbalance to BRICS (though MINT has not proved to be a promising group in this regard).
- Championing economic integration as a priority within ECOWAS so that a common tariff and currency is achieved by 2020 under Nigeria's leadership.

Buhari has taken a strong line against corruption – one of his key campaign issues – but graft remains a serious issue in Nigeria, which was ranked 144th of 180 states in Transparency International's 2018 Corruption Perceptions Index. Broader concerns about governance persist, and the conduct of the 2019 elections is unlikely to have ameliorated these – voting was postponed by a week just five hours before polling stations were due to open. This prompted some opposition groups to question the security of ballot papers and result sheets distributed prior to the postponement.

Strengthening the AU will also prove challenging given the AU's enduring institutional issues, with a lack of clear hierarchy between the authorities of the Peace and Security Council, AU Commission and Assembly of Heads of State, and a continued lack of political will to resolve disputes involving long-standing incumbents or parties. Thus, the AU has struggled to take a strong united line on questionable elections in the DRC, a 'military-assisted transition' in Zimbabwe, increased authoritarianism in Burundi and persistent instability in South Sudan, among other crises. Nigeria is not alone in pushing for reform of the AU, but enough members are committed to the principle of state sovereignty to ensure the organisation cannot impose its will upon them.

## Nigeria's role within ECOWAS

Somewhat ironically, ECOWAS – established in 1975 under an economic mandate, but with a broader peace and security element since 1993 –

has proved more effective than the AU in recent years, and been at the forefront of West African peace and security efforts. However, Nigeria has taken a less prominent role in the organisation than it did in its early stages, reflecting both public and political concerns within Nigeria about the cost of peacekeeping operations, and previous splits between franco-phone and anglophone states within ECOWAS regarding Nigeria's role in some operations. Nigeria's main roles have been in four of ECOWAS's major security-related operations.

During peacekeeping operations in Liberia (1989–2003), Nigeria financed around 80% of the cost of the ECOWAS Monitoring Group (ECOMOG) multilateral armed force deployed in Liberia, and, with Ghana, contributed most of the personnel for the operation. Nigeria spent an estimated US$250m–500m on these operations. However, deployment of a military force in Liberia led to splits between anglo-phone countries, led by Nigeria and including The Gambia, Ghana and Sierra Leone, and francophone states including Burkina Faso, Côte d'Ivoire, Mali and Togo, which argued that this violated the sovereignty of a member state.

Nigeria again played a dominant role in Sierra Leone (1991–2002), diverting forces from the Liberian operation. It spent an estimated US$1 billion a month keeping soldiers in the country, although ECOMOG failed to prevent rebel forces from taking control of the capital, Freetown, and Nigerian troops were withdrawn (or subsumed into UN peace-keeping operations). More than 1,000 Nigerian soldiers were killed in ECOMOG operations in Liberia and Sierra Leone.

Nigeria played a notably smaller role in operations in francophone states (Côte d'Ivoire: 2002–07 and 2010–11; Guinea: 2007–10; Guinea-Bissau: periodic 1998–2018), reflecting suspicions about its agenda among such countries, as well as the increasingly inward focus of succes-sive Nigerian administrations. While still providing financial support, Nigeria did not send a military contingent to peacekeeping operations in Guinea and Guinea-Bissau, while the ECOWAS forces initially deployed in Côte d'Ivoire came chiefly from other francophone nations and Ghana (reflecting its geographic proximity).

## Nigeria's Regional Weight

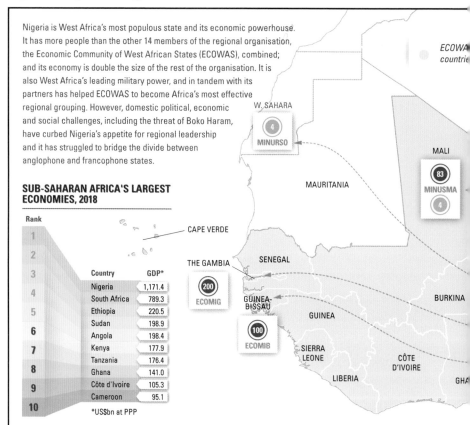

Nigeria is West Africa's most populous state and its economic powerhouse. It has more people than the other 14 members of the regional organisation, the Economic Community of West African States (ECOWAS), combined; and its economy is double the size of the rest of the organisation. It is also West Africa's leading military power, and in tandem with its partners has helped ECOWAS to become Africa's most effective regional grouping. However, domestic political, economic and social challenges, including the threat of Boko Haram, have curbed Nigeria's appetite for regional leadership and it has struggled to bridge the divide between anglophone and francophone states.

### SUB-SAHARAN AFRICA'S LARGEST ECONOMIES, 2018

| Rank | Country | GDP* |
|---|---|---|
| 1 | | |
| 2 | | |
| 3 | Nigeria | 1,171.4 |
| 4 | South Africa | 789.3 |
| 5 | Ethiopia | 220.5 |
| 6 | Sudan | 198.9 |
| | Angola | 198.4 |
| 7 | Kenya | 177.9 |
| | Tanzania | 176.4 |
| 8 | Ghana | 141.0 |
| 9 | Côte d'Ivoire | 105.3 |
| | Cameroon | 95.1 |
| 10 | | |

*US$bn at PPP

### GDP, ECOWAS COUNTRIES, 2018

| Country | GDP* | GDP per capita** | Population† |
|---|---|---|---|
| Nigeria | 1,171.4 | 5,980 | 195.8 |
| Ghana | 141.0 | 4,738 | 29.8 |
| Côte d'Ivoire | 105.3 | 4,200 | 25.1 |
| Senegal | 59.9 | 3,776 | 15.8 |
| Mali | 44.1 | 2,313 | 19.1 |
| Burkina Faso | 39.0 | 1,975 | 19.8 |
| Guinea | 32.7 | 2,630 | 12.4 |
| Benin | 27.8 | 2,420 | 11.5 |
| Niger | 23.5 | 1,049 | 22.4 |
| Togo | 13.9 | 1,761 | 7.9 |
| Sierra Leone | 12.3 | 1,603 | 7.7 |
| Liberia | 6.3 | 1,306 | 4.8 |
| The Gambia | 3.9 | 1,706 | 2.3 |
| Cape Verde | 4.1 | 7,495 | 0.5 |
| Guinea-Bissau | 3.4 | 1,796 | 1.9 |
| ECOWAS total | 1,688.6 | 44,748.0 | 376.7 |

*US$bn at PPP **US$ †millions

### FOREIGN DIRECT INVESTMENT (FDI) AND EXPORTS, ECOWAS COUNTRIES

| Country | FDI‡ | Exports†† |
|---|---|---|
| Nigeria | 4.17 | 60.67 |
| Ghana | 3.87 | 14.64 |
| Côte d'Ivoire | 0.80 | 11.26 |
| Guinea | 0.69 | 4.09 |
| Sierra Leone | 0.67 | 0.83 |
| Senegal | 0.63 | 3.52 |
| Burkina Faso | 0.58 | 3.23 |
| Niger | 0.40 | 1.43 |
| Mali | 0.32 | 2.94 |
| Liberia | 0.29 | 0.49 |
| Benin | 0.22 | 2.25 |
| Togo | 0.17 | 1.11 |
| Cape Verde | 0.13 | 0.08 |
| The Gambia | 0.10 | 0.15 |
| Guinea-Bissau | 0.02 | 0.35 |
| ECOWAS total | 13.06 | 107.02 |

‡US$bn, 2017 ††Goods US$bn, 2018

### DEFENCE BUDGETS, ECOWAS COUNTRIES, 2018

| Country | Defence budget** | % of GDP |
|---|---|---|
| Nigeria | 2,062.85 | 0.44 |
| Côte d'Ivoire | 917.73 | 2.16 |
| Mali | 628.90 | 4.22 |
| Senegal | 352.84 | 1.44 |
| Burkina Faso | 307.31 | 2.21 |
| Ghana | 244.63 | 0.33 |
| Niger | 223.07 | 2.49 |
| Guinea | 178.48 | 1.62 |
| Togo | 104.07 | 1.95 |
| Benin | 89.14 | 0.87 |
| Liberia | 13.23 | 0.49 |
| Sierra Leone | 12.19 | 0.34 |
| Cape Verde | 11.51 | 0.56 |
| The Gambia | n.k | n.k |
| Guinea-Bissau | n.k | n.k |

**Constant 2010 US$, millions

Sources: Transparency International, 2019; WTO, 2019 and IMF, 2019; African Development Group Bank (Africa Information Highway), 2019; UNHCR, 2019; Military Balance+, 2019; Nigerian National Bureau of Statistics, 2019; XE Currency Converter, 2019; WTO World Statistical Review

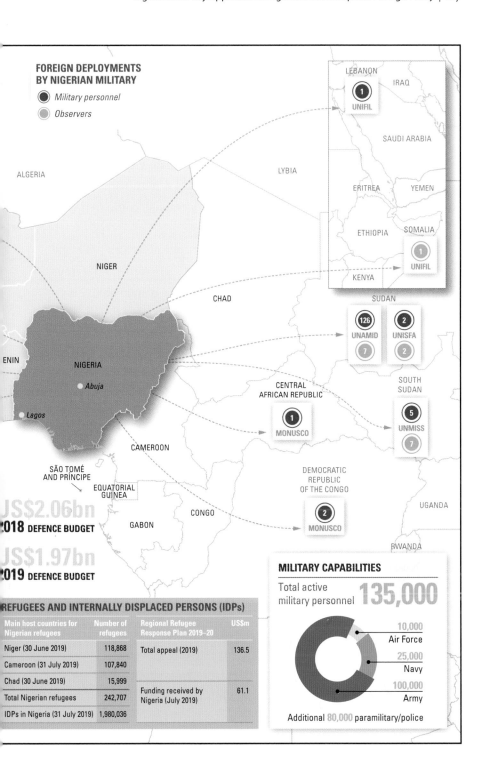

FOREIGN DEPLOYMENTS
BY NIGERIAN MILITARY
- Military personnel
- Observers

UNIFIL 1

UNIFIL 1

UNAMID 126 / 7 — UNISFA 2 / 2

MONUSCO 1

UNMISS 5 / 7

MONUSCO 2

US$2.06bn
2018 DEFENCE BUDGET

US$1.97bn
2019 DEFENCE BUDGET

## REFUGEES AND INTERNALLY DISPLACED PERSONS (IDPs)

| Main host countries for Nigerian refugees | Number of refugees | Regional Refugee Response Plan 2019–20 | US$m |
|---|---|---|---|
| Niger (30 June 2019) | 118,868 | Total appeal (2019) | 136.5 |
| Cameroon (31 July 2019) | 107,840 | | |
| Chad (30 June 2019) | 15,999 | | |
| Total Nigerian refugees | 242,707 | Funding received by Nigeria (July 2019) | 61.1 |
| IDPs in Nigeria (31 July 2019) | 1,980,036 | | |

## MILITARY CAPABILITIES

Total active military personnel **135,000**

10,000 Air Force
25,000 Navy
100,000 Army

Additional 80,000 paramilitary/police

ECOMOG's intervention in The Gambia (2017–present) after the long-standing president, Yahya Jammeh, refused to step down following the victory of Adama Barrow in the 2016 presidential elections, is probably its most successful intervention in regional affairs. Buhari co-chaired an ECOWAS negotiating team alongside presidents from Ghana, Liberia and Senegal, although this failed to persuade Jammeh to accept his clear electoral defeat. ECOWAS ultimately authorised the use of force against Jammeh, but Nigeria played a reasonably limited role in this, contributing around 750 military personnel, compared with 7,000 Senegalese troops.

In part this disparity was the result of geographical factors – Senegal entirely surrounds The Gambia's land mass – but it also reflects previous perceptions within Nigeria that it was having to take responsibility for a disproportionate amount of regional peacekeeping. It must also be seen in the context of previous resentment from other ECOWAS members that Nigeria has used its greater military and financial resources to impose an agenda on the regional grouping that has prioritised Nigerian interests over broader West African interests – meaning that it would support leaders perceived as favourable to Nigerian interests, even if they were domestically unpopular or repressive. This has even seen states such as Burkina Faso, Côte d'Ivoire, Liberia and Senegal effectively obstruct peace efforts. Without regional buy-in, and facing increasing domestic security challenges, Nigeria will likely continue to adopt a relatively low-profile approach to regional peacekeeping and intervention.

## Leading from behind

Despite its stated aim of championing economic integration within ECOWAS to achieve a common tariff and currency by 2020, Nigeria appears unlikely to take a leading role in broader regional integration efforts. It has not signed the Economic Partnership Agreement between ECOWAS and the EU, reportedly over concerns about exposing its industries to Western competition, and while it is the continent's largest economy, Nigeria only signed the ambitious AfCFTA, which offers the potential of greatly increased intra-regional trade, in July 2019 – more than a month after the agreement entered into force. Nigeria was the joint 52nd country out of 54 AU states to do so (and the remaining state, Eritrea, is unlikely to sign in the short to medium term), underscoring national perceptions that the benefits and costs of the AfCFTA are finely balanced. Buhari has previously expressed concern that Nigeria would become 'a dumping ground for finished goods', and told leaders of the Manufacturers Association of Nigeria that he would be guided by 'national interest' in his decision on AfCFTA, implying a wish to prioritise the development of Nigerian manufacturing. These issues have not been settled with the signing of AfCFTA: Nigeria has yet to ratify the deal, and this is unlikely to be a rapid process. For example, the Petroleum Industry Governance Bill, a key piece of domestic legislation dealing with reform of the vital oil sector, has yet to come into force despite being passed by the Senate in 2017. The larger Petroleum Industry Bill, of which it is theoretically the most straightforward part, was first introduced to parliament in 2001.

Although AfCFTA does not have any specific foreign-policy dimension, other than offering the potential for a more coherent negotiating position with other trading blocs, it does signal a clear intent as regards continental unity, regional integration and deeper economic ties. As such, protracted failure to ratify the agreement would suggest continued abnegation of a sub-Saharan leadership role, even if Nigeria does do more to drive integration in West Africa. This is far from guaranteed but is potentially more likely given politicians' belief that Nigeria is well placed to dominate any such grouping, as its economy is nearly seven times bigger than the next-largest economy in the region, Ghana. Even here, however, there are good reasons to expect a cautious approach by the Nigerian authorities, notably over plans to adopt a single currency by 2020. Although ECOWAS heads of state reiterated this commitment at a meeting in Abuja (Nigeria's administrative capital) on 29 June, Nigeria is poorly placed to meet a number of the benchmarks that countries need to attain before joining – including a fiscal deficit of less than 4% of GDP and single-digit inflation. Moreover, as the dominant subregional economy, Nigeria would likely end up with some responsibility for other members' debt under any fiscal and monetary union, and it is questionable whether its leadership would regard ECOWAS integration as compatible with a 'Nigeria first' approach in this regard.

## If not Nigeria, who?

In the absence of sustained Nigerian leadership efforts, there is likely to be a patchwork approach to foreign policy and security efforts within West Africa, the sub-Saharan Africa region more generally, and between the region and the rest of the world. In pure ECOWAS terms, Côte d'Ivoire and Senegal have historically made substantial efforts at regional integration, in terms of trading, movement of people, and financial and macroeconomic metrics. Given that they and six other (smaller) members of ECOWAS use a shared currency, the CFA franc, they may seek a more dominant political role in the organisation, and in relations with the EU in particular (particularly given that Brexit may give France an increased role in EU foreign policymaking).

In West Africa more broadly, however, these two countries are probably less well placed to play a dominant role: Côte d'Ivoire has around 27,000 military personnel (compared with Nigeria's 135,000), and while pro-government forces and anti-government rebels have been integrated into a single army following the 2011 civil war, the disarmament, demobilisation and reintegration programme has not been wholly successful, leading to a lack of clarity in the military chain of command. Moreover, in the short term, Ivorian politicians are likely to remain focused on the forthcoming 2020 elections. Senegal is somewhat better placed but faces rising popular tensions over high poverty rates and perceived official corruption. Its long-standing reputation for a well-entrenched democratic political culture has also been damaged somewhat by the February 2019 presidential election, since the authorities have been accused of using the judicial system to exclude rivals on dubious grounds.

Ghana appears to be seeking more of a West African leadership role and has also increasingly espoused Afrocentrism, with the president having warned against a mindset of dependency on external players such as the EU. With strong democratic credentials, Ghana is well placed to act as a strong voice for anglophone West African states. It lacks Nigeria's military resources and will be no better placed to tackle any strategic divide between anglophone and francophone states, but could certainly forge a higher profile in terms of sub-Saharan Africa's overall foreign-policy direction, joining South Africa and Kenya as perceived regional leaders.

Nigeria will remain a key interlocutor for EU states, but chiefly because, along with Ghana and Senegal, it is a major source of migrants seeking to reach Europe – which does not sit particularly well with Nigerian politicians' stated leadership ambitions, or the country's self-image as a regional powerhouse. However, there is little to suggest that the Nigerian authorities will be willing or able to overcome their inward-looking focus during Buhari's second term, meaning that Nigeria will struggle to position itself as a major world or even regional power. It therefore risks being eclipsed not just by traditional rival South Africa, but also by up-and-coming players including Ghana and even Ethiopia.

# Africa's Eternal Leaders and Parties

Democracy has advanced in sub-Saharan Africa in the last 30 years. The incidence of coups (and coup attempts) has declined significantly since the end of the Cold War, while the holding of regular elections is now the norm in many states. However, while many of these votes are genuinely competitive, there are obvious constraints. Notably, no 'liberation party' in Southern Africa has lost power, meaning that a swathe of states have been ruled by the same parties for decades. There is a similar pattern in parts of East Africa too. In recent years there have been forced or voluntary changes of leader in a number of states, including Angola, Ethiopia, Sudan and Zimbabwe. Yet in many of these cases the make-up of the elite has barely changed. Parties are more durable than presidents. There are signs, however, that some liberation parties are gradually losing their hegemony. This could have a substantial political impact in the longer term.

Democratic observance has become more entrenched in sub-Saharan Africa in a number of ways. Most obviously, the incidence of successful and attempted coups has declined significantly since the 1960s and 70s, while an increasing number of states regularly hold competitive legislative and presidential elections. This trend has been particularly apparent in West Africa, which previously had a high degree of politi-

| AFRICA'S LONGEST-SERVING RULERS | Years in power | Period in power |
|---|---|---|
| Teodoro Obiang (Equatorial Guinea) | 40 | 1979–present |
| José Eduardo dos Santos (Angola) | 38 | 1979–2017 |
| Robert Mugabe (Zimbabwe) | 37 | 1980–2017 |
| Paul Biya (Cameroon) | 37 | 1982–present |
| Yoweri Museveni (Uganda) | 33 | 1986–present |
| Omar al-Bashir (Sudan) | 30 | 1989–2019 |
| Idriss Déby (Chad) | 29 | 1990–present |
| Isaias Afwerki (Eritrea) | 26 | 1993–present |
| Denis Sassou Nguesso (ROC) | 22 | 1997–present |
| Paul Kagame (Rwanda) | 19 | 2000–present |
| Joseph Kabila (DRC) | 18 | 2001–19 |

cal instability. For example, Burkina Faso – which has experienced ten post-independence coup attempts – held its first-ever open democratic presidential election in 2015. In the same year Goodluck Jonathan became the first incumbent president to lose an election in Nigeria, which had eight coup attempts between 1966 and 1993. There has even been some improvement in Central Africa, with the 2016 presidential election in the Central African Republic ushering in the first democratically elected government in many years, and a transfer of power (of sorts) in the Democratic Republic of the Congo (DRC).

However, the holding of regular elections, and even changes of incumbent in some cases, does not by itself guarantee the creation or maintenance of a genuinely vibrant democratic space. Four of sub-Saharan Africa's longest-serving rulers have left power, voluntarily or otherwise, since 2017: Robert Mugabe (Zimbabwe), Omar al-Bashir (Sudan), José Eduardo dos Santos (Angola) and Joseph Kabila (DRC). However, many other long-serving presidents remain in power, notably in Cameroon, Chad, Equatorial Guinea, Eritrea, the Republic of the Congo (ROC), Rwanda and Uganda.

## Eternal parties

Long-serving presidents have been adept at changing constitutions to stay in power. Yet sub-Saharan Africa is also home to 'eternal parties' that have held power for decades. In East Africa, Tanzania's Chama Cha Mapinduzi (CCM) has been in power since 1977, Uganda's National Resistance Movement since 1986 and the Ethiopian People's Revolutionary Democratic Front (EPRDF) since 1991. In Southern Africa, the Movimento Popular de Libertação de Angola (MPLA) has ruled Angola and the Frente de Libertação de Moçambique (Frelimo) Mozambique since their independence from Portugal in 1975, while the Zimbabwe African National Union – Patriotic Front (ZANU-PF) has been in power since independence in 1980, and the African National Congress since the end of apartheid in South Africa in 1994.

There are a number of reasons why such parties have managed to stay in power for so long. Some of them are the political offshoots of liberation movements that played a critical role in securing independence from either colonial powers or – in the cases of Ethiopia and Uganda – dictatorial regimes. In the early years of their rule they enjoyed substantial popular support, giving them a major electoral advantage – particularly as other political parties were either underdeveloped or viewed as tainted (having operated during colonisation). A number were also able to take over existing state machinery, giving them further advantages associated with incumbency. Although the benefits conferred by being a liberation movement are not open-ended – a new generation of voters is likely to focus on current rather than historical issues – they have often

| URBAN POPULATION, SELECTED SUB-SAHARAN AFRICAN COUNTRIES, 2018 | |
| --- | --- |
| Country | Urban population (percentage of total population) |
| Djibouti | 78% |
| São Tomé and Príncipe | 73% |
| Equatorial Guinea | 72% |
| Botswana | 69% |
| Republic of the Congo | 67% |
| Angola | 66% |
| South Africa | 66% |
| Cameroon | 56% |
| Namibia | 50% |
| Nigeria | 50% |
| Democratic Republic of the Congo | 44% |
| Eritrea | 36% |
| Mozambique | 36% |
| Sudan | 35% |
| Tanzania | 34% |
| Zimbabwe | 32% |
| Burkina Faso | 29% |
| Kenya | 27% |
| Uganda | 24% |
| Chad | 23% |
| Ethiopia | 21% |
| Rwanda | 17% |
| Burundi | 13% |

Source: World Bank, 2018

been sufficient to secure two or three successive terms, after which other factors favourable to such parties tend to come into play.

One such factor is the perpetuation of an uneven playing field. Having gained access to the state machinery, ruling groups are able to maintain privileged access to state institutions, resources and the media. While the number of privately owned newspapers and radio stations has increased substantially in recent years, these tend to be focused on urban areas, and thus do not reach large numbers of voters (sub-Saharan Africa's overall urbanisation rate is 40%, but three-quarters of Uganda's population and two-thirds of Zimbabweans still live in rural areas, for example). This means ruling parties have been able to control the flow of information via state media, while using a selective version of national history to reinforce their central role in politics and preserve their hegemony.

ZANU–PF has been particularly adept at this, but leaders in Angola and Mozambique have also sought to portray their parties as a bulwark against a return to civil war. Given that the Angolan and Mozambican civil wars only ended in 2002 and 1992 respectively, this has resonated with many voters. Parties or leaders have also used Western hostility – perceived or actual – to their own advantage, using it to associate themselves with nationalism and to portray opponents as under neo-colonialist control.

Over time, the dominance of an individual party has tended to become self-perpetuating, in that ambitious and talented politicians seek to join the ruling group, since this gives them access to resources and power. This leads to a situation in which opposition groups lack strong leadership (as in Zimbabwe) or are led by long-standing leaders who have been repeatedly defeated in elections (as in Sudan and, until recently, Angola and Mozambique). Meanwhile, ruling groups often attract (or create) wealthy individuals. Given that such individuals tend to exercise control over local resources – whether land, banks or local businesses – ruling groups are further able to dispense patronage to voters and their own members, so as to retain their loyalty. Restrictions on competition, and an increasing emphasis on localisation of the economy, help perpetuate this. The business empire amassed by the family of president José Eduardo dos

Santos during his rule in Angola is an obvious example of resource control. His son Zenú founded Angola's first private investment bank, Banco Kwanza Invest, and was appointed manager of the country's US$5 billion state-owned wealth fund, while his daughter Isabel dos Santos – deemed Africa's richest woman by Forbes – chaired the state-owned oil company Sonangol and had interests in hundreds of companies in various sectors, including telecommunications, media, diamond trading, tourism and real estate in Angola, Portugal and elsewhere.

## Sudan: dropping the pilot

A number of these factors were apparent in Sudan, where Omar al-Bashir and his National Congress Party (NCP) held power from 1989 – having led a military coup against the prime minister, Sadiq al-Mahdi – until his overthrow by the armed forces in April 2019. During his 30 years in office, Bashir consolidated power with support from both the official armed forces and from a network of parallel security organisations (such as the feared National Intelligence Security Services) and armed militias, which formed a crucial part of Sudan's political system, to the extent that Bashir stayed in power by playing off the various groups against each other. The loyalty of the army and semi-formal military groups was driven by two main factors: the economic benefits available to them, and their complicity in – and fear of being held to account for – war crimes and atrocities committed by them under Bashir's leadership, in particular the genocide in Darfur in 2004.

The final catalyst for Bashir's fall was national protests beginning in December 2018, sparked by persistent economic underperformance, inflation and the lack of democratic reform. There had been similar protests in Sudan before – student demonstrations escalated into wider anti-austerity protests in 2012–13 – and similar crackdowns by the security forces, with at least 2,000 activists detained in the second half of 2012. On this occasion, however, the protesters were not deterred by such crackdowns – or by the imposition of a nationwide state of emergency in February 2019. The NCP failed because the military, which was itself divided, chose to switch its loyalty away from the Bashir regime.

This underscores another key characteristic of regime elites: ruthless-ness, and a willingness to surrender key members so as to preserve their overall interests.

This certainly appears to have succeeded in Sudan. Notwithstanding the July 2019 power-sharing arrangement between the Transitional Military Council (TMC) – broadly comprising the senior military officers who seized power from Bashir – and the opposition pro-democracy alliance, key elements of the regime are likely to remain in place. Chairmanship of the so-called sovereign council will rest with the military for the first 18–21 months of the arrangement, after which it is scheduled to move to civilian leadership for a further 18 months. Even if this handover does take place – which is far from guaranteed – the protesters' key aim of dismantling the entire system associated with the Bashir regime will not take place until 2022 at the very earliest, and more likely not at all. Experience elsewhere in sub-Saharan Africa suggests that changing the public face of the ruling elite does not necessarily lead to a transition to secure and democratic civilian rule, and risk factors are particularly high in Sudan, with its weak democratic foundations. Freedom House gives it an overall freedom score of just seven out of 100. In this environment there will be concerns about the credibility of the elections due to be held after the three-year transition period. Many Sudanese assume that they will simply mean a continuation of military/elite rule under a democratic facade.

## The party that persisted: ZANU–PF

One probable factor in Sudanese concerns is the trajectory in Zimbabwe following the removal of Robert Mugabe in a 'military-assisted transi-tion' in late 2017. As in Sudan, military and civilian ruling-elite interests became closely linked; and as in Sudan, the armed forces intervened to remove a long-standing ruler when broader elite interests were threatened – although in Zimbabwe's case it was the sitting presi-dent's putative attempt to establish a dynastic succession (with Grace Mugabe as successor) and marginalise the military-favoured candi-date, Emmerson Mnangagwa, that prompted the intervention. Unlike in Sudan, however, the military's so-called *Operation Restore Legacy* –

whose stated purpose was to remove 'criminal elements' around the president – saw the imprisonment or exiling of some of Robert Mugabe's closest allies but left most key civilian members of the ruling ZANU–PF party in their government posts. Indeed, only three of the 22 members of Mugabe's cabinet lost their portfolios. Major-General Sibusiso Moyo became foreign minister, Air Marshal Perrance Shiri became agriculture minister, and General Constantino Chiwenga, the head of the Zimbabwe Defence Forces (ZDF), was appointed vice-president. Chiwenga remains the front runner to succeed Mnangagwa as president.

Opposition to Mugabe and by extension ZANU–PF had been growing for some years: in 2008 then-opposition leader Morgan Tsvangirai won the first round of the presidential election before withdrawing from the second round amid a wave of state violence against opposition supporters. Despite this opposition, the elite remained united and ZANU–PF won a clear majority in both the presidential and the parliamentary elections held in July 2018. The voting patterns underscored the electoral advantages held by many of sub-Saharan Africa's 'eternal' political parties. Mnangagwa was heavily defeated in urban areas, with just under three-quarters of his support coming from six rural provinces, where populations remain heavily reliant on state-run radio and television services, and where traditional chiefs can exercise 'soft intimidation' (for example suggesting there might be severe consequences for failing to vote a certain way) and offer inducements. Moreover, as in other peer states, levels of recognition for the ruling party were much higher than for the opposition Movement for Democratic Change (MDC) – particularly as Tsvangirai, the MDC's long-standing leader, had died just months before the election – or even for Mnangagwa himself. Indeed, it was notable that ZANU–PF won a two-thirds majority of constituencies and around 60% of the national share, whereas Mnangagwa secured a very narrow majority of 50.8% of the national vote, only just avoiding a second-round run-off. This would seem to suggest that ZANU–PF will be able to retain its dominance for the time being, particularly as around two-thirds of the population still live in rural areas, and urbanisation is estimated to be increasing by just 2% a year.

## Fading hegemony?

In several other Southern African states the hegemony of the ruling group is already fading, with the Botswana Democratic Party (BDP) and Namibia's South West African People's Organisation (SWAPO) both facing challenges. The BDP, in power since 1965, secured just 46.5% of the vote in the 2014 legislative elections, and might see its share contract further in the election scheduled for October 2019. However, as with a number of its regional peers, the BDP has tended to benefit from splits in the opposition, as well as from the fact that, unusually, presidential terms and national elections are not aligned. This has enabled the BDP to groom new leaders, while also avoiding a situation whereby dissatisfaction with any incumbent also hits the vote for the party itself.

In Namibia, too, the dominance of SWAPO – in power since independence in 1990 – looks likely to lessen somewhat, given popular opposition to austerity and its resistance to calls for ancestral lands to be returned to tribal groups. The latter factor has seen the establishment of a new party, the Landless People's Movement, which could attract votes in the November 2019 elections. However, even if this does reduce SWAPO's margin of victory, it is unlikely to present a serious threat to the ruling group, since it secured 80% of the popular vote in the 2014 poll and has yet to see its share of the vote drop below 73.9%.

The African National Congress (ANC) in South Africa is potentially more vulnerable. While it secured a sixth successive term in May 2019 elections, obtaining 57.5% of the overall vote, its vote share was well down on the 62.2% it took in the 2014 general election; indeed, it was the first time that the ANC's vote share had slipped below 60% in national elections. Weak economic growth and voter anger over corruption under the previous head of state, Jacob Zuma, are factors in its declining popularity, but so too are potentially more sustained issues. Its credentials as a liberation movement during apartheid are not particularly important to younger voters, while more radical parties such as the Economic Freedom Fighters have eroded its young support base. Should the pace of decline in its vote share be sustained, the ANC – in power since 1994 – would win the largest share of votes but not an overall majority at the next two elections.

In the longer term the loss of hegemony for the ANC or any other long-standing ruling party is probably positive for democratic development, potentially leading to increased voter engagement and the representation of a broader range of interest groups within the legislature. In the short to medium term, however, such a development would likely have a destabilising impact. South Africa, like most Southern African states with long-dominant political parties, has almost no experience of coalition government at the national level (the National Party was hegemonic from 1948 to the end of apartheid, while the ANC has dominated since 1994, even during the 1994–97 government of national unity). At best, such governments can lead to increased compromise, with constituent parties obliged to discard their more controversial (and potentially populist) policies.

However, there are also substantial downside risks. The government of national unity in Zimbabwe (2009–13) was fragile, with political infighting leading to policymaking gridlock, while in Kenya the ruling coalition has been beset by factionalism and the two main factions have focused on raising funding in case the alliance splits before the next legislative election, scheduled for 2022. In South Africa itself, a de facto minority administration in Nelson Mandela Bay municipality was marked by infighting because of stark ideological divisions between supposed partner parties, as well as allegations of corruption (with parties seeking to buy support) and opportunism. If repeated at a national level, clientelism and corruption could actually exacerbate existing signs of voter disillusionment – prior to the May 2019 vote, Ipsos calculated that more than ten million people eligible to vote had not registered to do so, including half of those aged between 18 and 30. If unaddressed, such alienation could lead to the development of a radical, populist and extra-parliamentary movement, with a negative impact on overall stability.

If the move away from a long-standing political regimen presents a potential risk in a relatively stable country such as South Africa, where democracy is fairly well established, the threats are much higher in states where the institutional framework is weaker. In Sudan, the military authorities already claim to have faced an attempted counter-coup, while the example of Libya post-Gadhafi underscores the risk that a sudden power vacuum can lead to a new dictatorship or even civil war. This is likely to be an additional factor sustaining support for ruling groups in states such as Mozambique and Angola, which have had relatively recent experience of such conflict. In Angola under José Eduardo dos Santos, who stood down in late 2017 after 38 years in power, the ruling MPLA regularly suggested that support for opposition groups could precipitate a return to civil conflict. Such warnings – and the change of head of state – help explain why growing popular frustrations with entrenched corruption and high levels of unemployment in Angola have not led to sustained unrest, and why the MPLA's vote share, while declining, has yet to fall below 60% in national elections.

# Middle East and North Africa: Drivers of Strategic Change

- Iran faces sustained economic and political pressure from the US, after the latter withdrew from the JCPOA nuclear agreement. It seeks to calibrate a response that demonstrates defiance and imposes costs on the US and its regional allies, without triggering a war. Many regional states likewise hope to avoid conflict.

- Saudi Arabia's standing in Western capitals suffered a severe blow with the murder of an exiled Saudi journalist by Saudi state officials in Turkey. This did much to erode the goodwill and optimism engendered by Crown Prince Muhammad bin Salman Al Saud political and economic reforms, and underscored the limits and risks of an authoritarian modernisation project.

- Regional states have reluctantly embraced Syria's president, Bashar al-Assad, now that he has defied expectations and won the civil war. However, swathes of the country remain outside his control and his patrons, Iran and Russia, have neither the resources nor the inclination to fund reconstruction.

- The US has joined France and Russia in backing Khalifa Haftar's Libyan National Army (LNA) over the UN-acknowledged government in Tripoli. While diplomatically this is a boon for Haftar, his rival continues to enjoy substantial military and economic support from Qatar and Turkey.

## DEMOGRAPHY

POPULATION AND MEDIAN AGE
(IMF, April 2019; UN Department of Economic and Social Affairs, Population Division, 2019)

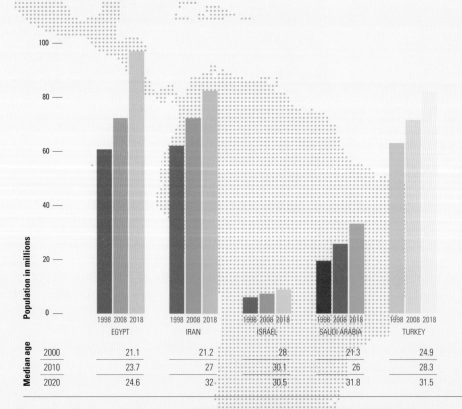

| Median age | EGYPT | IRAN | ISRAEL | SAUDI ARABIA | TURKEY |
|---|---|---|---|---|---|
| 2000 | 21.1 | 21.2 | 28 | 21.3 | 24.9 |
| 2010 | 23.7 | 27 | 30.1 | 26 | 28.3 |
| 2020 | 24.6 | 32 | 30.5 | 31.8 | 31.5 |

AGE STRUCTURE
(CIA World Factbook, 2019)

| IRAN | |
|---|---|
| Under 25 years | 38.28% |
| 25–64 years | 56.25% |
| 64 years and older | 5.48% |

| TURKEY | |
|---|---|
| Under 25 years | 40.14% |
| 25–64 years | 52.08% |
| 64 years and older | 7.79% |

| EGYPT | |
|---|---|
| Under 25 years | 52.03% |
| 25–64 years | 43.70% |
| 64 years and older | 4.28% |

| ISRAEL | |
|---|---|
| Under 25 years | 42.84% |
| 25–64 years | 45.61% |
| 64 years and older | 11.55% |

| SAUDI ARABIA | |
|---|---|
| Under 25 years | 41.32% |
| 25–64 years | 55.36% |
| 64 years and older | 3.32% |

# ECONOMICS AND DEVELOPMENT

## GDP AT PPP
Constant 2011 international dollars (IMF, April 2019)

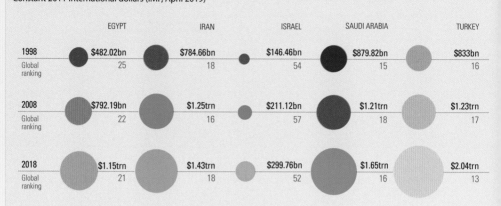

| | EGYPT | IRAN | ISRAEL | SAUDI ARABIA | TURKEY |
|---|---|---|---|---|---|
| **1998** | $482.02bn | $784.66bn | $146.46bn | $879.82bn | $833bn |
| Global ranking | 25 | 18 | 54 | 15 | 16 |
| **2008** | $792.19bn | $1.25trn | $211.12bn | $1.21trn | $1.23trn |
| Global ranking | 22 | 16 | 57 | 18 | 17 |
| **2018** | $1.15trn | $1.43trn | $299.76bn | $1.65trn | $2.04trn |
| Global ranking | 21 | 18 | 52 | 16 | 13 |

## GDP PER CAPITA AT PPP
Constant 2011 international dollars (IMF, April 2019)

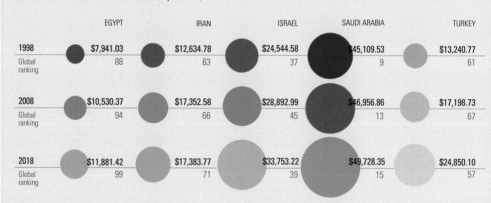

| | EGYPT | IRAN | ISRAEL | SAUDI ARABIA | TURKEY |
|---|---|---|---|---|---|
| **1998** | $7,941.03 | $12,634.78 | $24,544.58 | $45,109.53 | $13,240.77 |
| Global ranking | 88 | 63 | 37 | 9 | 61 |
| **2008** | $10,530.37 | $17,352.58 | $28,892.99 | $46,956.86 | $17,198.73 |
| Global ranking | 94 | 66 | 45 | 13 | 67 |
| **2018** | $11,881.42 | $17,383.77 | $33,753.22 | $49,728.35 | $24,850.10 |
| Global ranking | 99 | 71 | 39 | 15 | 57 |

## HUMAN DEVELOPMENT INDEX (HDI)
(UN Development Programme, 2019)

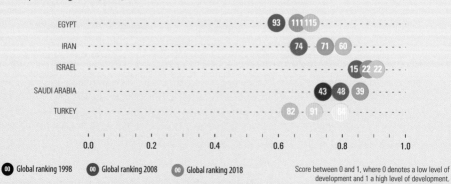

EGYPT — 93 111 115

IRAN — 74 71 60

ISRAEL — 15 22 22

SAUDI ARABIA — 43 48 39

TURKEY — 82 91 64

0.0    0.2    0.4    0.6    0.8    1.0

**00** Global ranking 1998    **00** Global ranking 2008    **00** Global ranking 2018

Score between 0 and 1, where 0 denotes a low level of development and 1 a high level of development.

# INTERNATIONAL INTEGRATION

## TRADE
Exports of goods and commercial services, constant 2010 US dollars
(World Trade Organization, 2019)

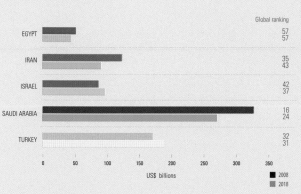

| | | Global ranking |
|---|---|---|
| EGYPT | | 57 / 57 |
| IRAN | | 35 / 43 |
| ISRAEL | | 42 / 37 |
| SAUDI ARABIA | | 16 / 24 |
| TURKEY | | 32 / 31 |

US$ billions

■ 2008
▨ 2018

## INTERNATIONAL NETWORK
Total number of diplomatic missions, 2017
Lowy Institute Global Diplomacy Index
(2017)

| | Missions abroad | | Global ranking |
|---|---|---|---|
| EGYPT | N/A | | - |
| IRAN | N/A | | - |
| ISRAEL | 104 | | 34 |
| SAUDI ARABIA | 112 | | 30 |
| TURKEY | 229 | | 6 |

# DIPLOMACY AND DEFENCE

## DEFENCE BUDGET
Constant 2010 US dollars (Military Balance 1998,
and Military Balance+)

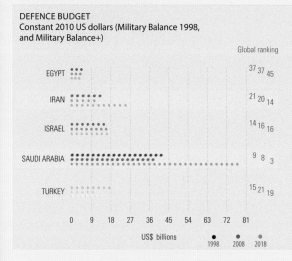

| | | Global ranking |
|---|---|---|
| EGYPT | | 37 37 45 |
| IRAN | | 21 20 14 |
| ISRAEL | | 14 16 16 |
| SAUDI ARABIA | | 9 8 3 |
| TURKEY | | 15 21 19 |

US$ billions

● 1998  ● 2008  ● 2018

## OFFICIAL DEVELOPMENT AID
Constant 2015 US dollars (OECD, 2019)

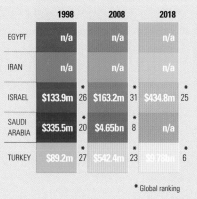

| | 1998 | | 2008 | | 2018 | |
|---|---|---|---|---|---|---|
| EGYPT | n/a | | n/a | | n/a | |
| IRAN | n/a | | n/a | | n/a | |
| ISRAEL | $133.9m | 26 | $163.2m | *31 | $434.8m | *25 |
| SAUDI ARABIA | $335.5m | *20 | $4.65bn | *8 | n/a | |
| TURKEY | $89.2m | *27 | $542.4m | *23 | $9.78bn | *6 |

\* Global ranking

## POLITICAL SYSTEM
(Economist Intelligence Unit, 2008, 2018)

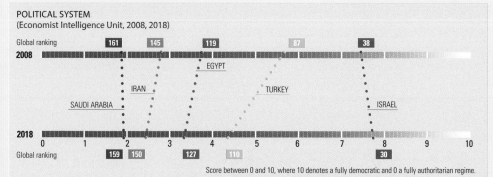

Score between 0 and 10, where 10 denotes a fully democratic and 0 a fully authoritarian regime.

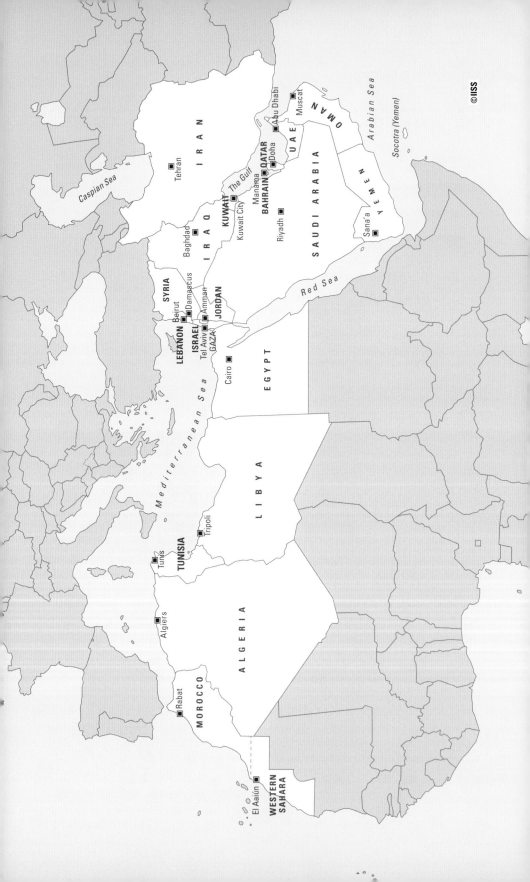

©IISS

Caspian Sea

I R A N

Tehran

Arabian Sea

Socotra (Yemen)

Muscat

O M A N

Abu Dhabi

U A E

QATAR

Doha

The Gulf

BAHRAIN

Manama

KUWAIT

S A U D I   A R A B I A

Kuwait City

Riyadh

I R A Q

Baghdad

Sana'a

Y E M E N

SYRIA

Damascus

Red Sea

JORDAN

Amman

Beirut

LEBANON

ISRAEL

Tel Aviv

GAZA

Cairo

E G Y P T

Mediterranean Sea

L I B Y A

Tripoli

TUNISIA

Tunis

A L G E R I A

Algiers

MOROCCO

Rabat

WESTERN
SAHARA

El Aaiún

# Chapter 6

# Middle East and North Africa

## 2018–19 Review

Middle Eastern security and politics remained tense and unsettled during the year to mid-2019. State weakness, hot wars, regional competition and international rivalry continued to have a potent destabilising effect on the region, as they have since 2011. It remained unclear if a new regional order could emerge from such entropy: whatever progress was achieved in fragile countries seemed domestically tenuous and vulnerable to regional dynamics. This was notably the case in Iraq, where the recent defeat of jihadi organisation the Islamic State, also known as ISIS or ISIL, and national elections created hopes for reconciliation and better governance. Intractable politics and fears that a United States–Iran war would again jeopardise its stability quickly dashed this optimism.

Regional competition featured three sets of actors and played out in complex ways. The first set consists of Saudi Arabia and the United Arab Emirates (UAE), supported by Bahrain and to a lesser extent Egypt: it has prioritised the fight against political Islam and sought to contain Iran. The second brings together Turkey and Qatar, both supporters of the Muslim Brotherhood. The third combines Iran and Syria and includes a variety of Shia militias across the region.

## Growing tensions in the Gulf

The prospect of a new conflict in the Middle East grew as the US and Iran entered a new phase of enmity. In May 2018, the US administration announced that it would withdraw from the Joint Comprehensive Plan of Action (JCPOA) in November. A strategy of maximal pressure on Iran followed, including severe sanctions on any state buying Iran's oil exports and on key economic sectors, designations of Iranian entities as terrorist groups (most notably the Islamic Revolutionary Guard Corps–IRGC) and adversarial rhetoric from Washington.

US objectives remained unclear, however: senior officials, including President Donald Trump himself, variously mentioned regime change, limited strikes, Iranian capitulation and diplomacy to reach a 'better' nuclear deal. The US escalation found few supporters beyond Israel and several Gulf states. Criticism abounded in Europe, Asia and the Middle East, with the decision seen as yet another ill-considered unilateral move that discarded a functioning agreement without realistic alternative and jeopardised a rare diplomatic success in the Middle East. Yet despite its diplomatic isolation, the US successfully deployed its coercive economic power to considerable effect. Asian countries reliant on Middle East energy imports rushed to find alternative sources in Saudi Arabia and elsewhere. India and Turkey had stated that they would continue importing Iranian oil, but ultimately complied with US pressure.

The resulting economic and political repercussions cornered Iran. The rapid decline in oil exports (from two million barrels per day (b/d) to less than 0.5m b/d) hurt Iran's budget and economy, which was expected to contract by 6% in 2019, while inflation soared. Disillusionment with diplomacy was rife and recriminations inside the Iranian system intense, but Iran had few options. Tehran faced a dilemma: its continued adherence to the terms of the nuclear deal did not deliver the expected returns, but withdrawing from the JCPOA would alienate European countries and risk a war that the leadership seemed keen to avoid. Iranian officials who had advocated diplomacy with the US in previous years found their position weakened but still hoped that strategic patience and European incentives would preserve the deal and provide some economic benefits pending a more reasonable US policy should Trump lose the 2020 election; more hardline factions in Tehran called for retaliation and withdrawal from the JCPOA. Iran counted on China (which continued to import Iranian oil) and Russia – both locked in geopolitical rivalries with the US – to push back against Washington's perceived diktats; while denouncing US policy, both largely passed on the responsibility for placating Iran to the European Union.

European powers also mobilised to avoid a confrontation. In January 2019 the EU announced the establishment by the middle of the year of a payment mechanism called the Instrument in Support of Trade Exchanges (INSTEX), designed to shelter humanitarian and other trade with Iran from US sanctions. It also displayed patience and magnanimity in the face of Iran's contraventions of the JCPOA: to signal displeasure and pressure its interlocutors, Tehran announced in June that it would enrich larger quantities of uranium at higher levels. The Europeans dismissed US calls for renewed sanctions.

This left the Middle East on edge. Potential flashpoints for US–Iran tit-for-tat included Iraq, Syria, Lebanon, Yemen, the Persian Gulf and the strategic straits of Hormuz and Bab el-Mandeb, and possible targets ranged from US forces in Syria and Iraq to maritime traffic and soft targets across the region. In May 2019, a series of incidents across the region began to illustrate the escalatory risk. Citing intelligence warnings, the US upgraded its military posture in the region and downgraded its diplomatic presence in Iraq. Soon afterwards, attacks against tankers in the UAE port of Fujairah, drone attacks against a key Saudi pipeline, the shooting down of a US drone by Iran's air defence and more attacks against tankers in the Gulf of Oman worsened an already tense environment. Washington interpreted actions that Iran saw as defensive as provocative, and vice versa. The absence of any direct channel of communication poisoned the atmosphere further: Trump communicated important decisions through provocative tweets, as did Iranian Supreme Leader Ayatollah Ali Khamenei.

Trump's apparent desire to avoid another war in the Middle East prevented further escalation: he announced in June that he had called off an airstrike designed as retaliation for the shooting down of the drone, which Iran argued had flown over Iranian territory but the US insisted had stayed in international airspace. The ostensibly calibrated and tit-for-tat nature of Iranian attacks also helped to avert a showdown: no loss of life was attributed to Iranian actions, whether at sea or during rocket attacks by Iran-backed militias in Iraq. The resistance of key regional actors to another conflict was notable. Iraq, fearful of a relapse into war, lobbied the US and Iran to practise restraint, while Qatar, Oman and Kuwait all counselled moderation out of concern that their own territory and interests would be exposed. Even Iran's most determined foes in the Gulf appeared unwilling to risk an all-out war – the UAE and Saudi investigation into the Fujairah attacks, while blaming a state actor, refrained from naming Iran. Gulf vulnerabilities to Iranian retaliation but also scepticism about Trump's commitment and strategy shaped their risk appetite. The US struggled to organise its regional response. It was undermined by Trump's announcement – later toned down – of a US withdrawal from Syria and by regional rivalries that hobbled the Middle East Security Alliance, a defence organisation that Washington had hoped would unite its Arab allies but failed to gain any momentum.

Despite the restraint all sides showed in mid-2019, the risk of war remained considerable. The deepening impact of US sanctions tested Iran's inclination to outwait the Trump administration. The US had largely exhausted its arsenal of economic sanctions and rhetorically had left itself with little room for manoeuvre. The prospects for the EU, Russia or China to broker a compromise seemed remote.

## Saudi Arabia: fallout of the Khashoggi assassination

The modernisation drive and reputation of Saudi Crown Prince Muhammad bin Salman Al Saud suffered a massive setback in October 2018, when it emerged that prominent journalist turned critic in exile Jamal Khashoggi had been murdered in the Saudi consulate in Istanbul by an assassination squad directed by senior Saudi officials. The assassination brought the Kingdom's domestic and human-rights record into the spotlight, fuelled criticism in Western countries of Saudi Arabia's intervention in Yemen and initiated a debate in Western capitals about the merits of partnership with the powerful Saudi Kingdom.

The Khashoggi crisis highlighted the dilemma of authoritarian modernisation. Just as Prince Muhammad ushered in important social and economic reforms – such as allowing women to drive and labour-market reforms to encourage Saudi employment – he gradually narrowed the political space and cracked down on dissent. A wave of repression affected female activists as well as Islamist and liberal critics of the regime, while growing numbers of Saudis sought asylum abroad.

The reputational cost of the assassination was quickly felt. Attendance at a major economic conference organised in Riyadh weeks later was low. This compounded dire economic figures: GDP growth in 2017 was negative, timidly recovering in 2018 thanks to higher oil prices, while foreign direct investment hit a low of US$1.4 billion in 2017, one-fifth of what it was in 2016. Outflows of capital remained high, indicating low confidence in the government's economic reforms or concerns among wealthy citizens after Prince Muhammad's anti-corruption campaign. Efforts at encouraging Saudi private-sector employment disrupted the Saudi economy, as foreign workers were expelled or their work permits suspended before enough Saudi substitutes became available.

In Washington, the backlash against Saudi Arabia was broad. Republican and Democratic lawmakers, including those once friendly to the Kingdom, introduced legislation to constrain US arms exports to Saudi Arabia, scrutinised more closely its nuclear-energy plans and passed bills to punish Saudi officials who played a direct role in the Khashoggi assassination. The Trump administration shielded Riyadh from the most consequential rebukes, vetoing congressional action on arms sales and calls to end US assistance to the Saudi intervention in Yemen, refraining from endorsing the US intelligence community's own findings implicating Prince Muhammad in the assassination, and continuing to deal with him despite media and political censure. It seemed likely that Saudi Arabia would feature prominently in the US presidential campaign, with most Democratic candidates pledging to review US ties to Riyadh.

Key European countries also reacted strongly. Germany announced the suspension of arms sales to Saudi Arabia, affecting the United Kingdom's own exports and servicing of the Eurofighter aircraft. In June the UK court of appeal ruled that UK arms sales to Saudi Arabia were unlawful based on its targeting practices in Yemen, constraining further sales. The Khashoggi crisis was a boon for Saudi Arabia's rivals, however. Iran and Qatar, but most importantly Turkey, used it to corner Riyadh as regional competition heated up: Saudi Arabia's deteriorating image and apparent loss of momentum benefited them in Western but also Arab capitals.

However, Western opprobrium did not spread globally. Prince Muhammad continued to find welcoming audiences elsewhere, notably in Asia, as illustrated by his visits to Japan, China, India and Pakistan, but also in Argentina at the G20 meeting. By mid-2019, it seemed that Saudi Arabia would overcome ostracisation. Saudi Aramco, the initial public offering (IPO) of which had been indefinitely postponed to the embarrassment of Prince Muhammad, managed to raise US$12bn in bonds in a massively oversubscribed round. Coincidentally, Riyadh was also gearing up to host the G20 meeting in 2020.

## Turkey: Erdogan's difficulties multiply

The Khashoggi affair offered Turkey's president, Recep Tayyip Erdogan, an opportunity to reorient the country's troubled relationship with the US. In July, Washington had imposed sanctions on Turkey's justice and interior ministers over the detention of Andrew Brunson, a US pastor and long-time resident of Turkey convicted by a Turkish court for having links to the banned Kurdistan Workers' Party (PKK) and the Gulenist movement that Erdogan blames for the mid-2016 coup attempt against him. Erdogan had tried unsuccessfully in 2017 to swap Brunson for Fethullah Gulen, an erstwhile ally of the president who now lives in the US. In October 2018, at around the time that Turkey claimed to have supplied the US authorities with secret recordings of Khashoggi's murder, Brunson was released and US sanctions against Turkey were reportedly eased. However, this did little to ease Erdogan's suspicions that the US had been involved in the coup attempt and still sought to oust him. Relations between the two states became further strained in 2019 as Turkey pressed ahead with its plans to buy S-400 air-defence systems from Russia, which the US insisted would preclude Turkey from buying the latest-generation F-35 combat aircraft as planned and could potentially trigger fresh US sanctions.

Erdogan also faced domestic difficulties. He narrowly won a second presidential term in June 2018, although at the same time his Justice and Development Party (AKP) lost its parliamentary majority despite allegations that it had sought to manipulate the vote. Thereafter the AKP relied upon the Turkish ultranationalist Nationalist Action Party (MHP) to pass legislation and Erdogan made greater use of presidential decrees, but a deterioration in the economy exacerbated his situation. Inflation rose from 15% around the time of the election to more than 25% by October, eroding consumers' buying power and forcing interest rates still higher. By March 2019, one quarter of the workforce under the age of 25 was unemployed. In local elections that month, the AKP suffered heavy losses in metropolitan areas, including the capital Ankara. The Supreme Electoral Council ordered a rerun of the mayoral election in Istanbul on the grounds that some of the election officials lacked the necessary qualifications. Yet despite extraordinary efforts by the AKP, the opposition candidate won Ankara with an increased majority.

This represented a major setback for Erdogan, who in early July dismissed Murat Cetinkaya, the governor of the nominally independent Turkish Central Bank, for failing to reduce annual inflation – then running at 15.7% – and vowed to oversee monetary policy himself. In mid-2019 the AKP and MHP together held 340 seats in the 600-member parliament, but that majority appeared vulnerable to expected defections from the AKP. However, Erdogan had little incentive to call a fresh election while the economy continued to struggle.

## Unresolved conflicts

There was no significant progress in any of the three hot wars afflicting the Middle East. In Syria, Libya and Yemen, cycles of fighting followed by lulls remained the norm, with international diplomacy struggling to keep up with local and regional dynamics.

## Syria

Having achieved its key military goals in the three previous years, the regime of Bashar al-Assad struggled to stabilise Syria on its own terms. The country remained an arena for intense regional competition. The presence on Syrian territory of five foreign militaries (Iran, Israel, Russia, Turkey and the US) created the potential for geopolitical friction but also shaped the behaviour of local actors. Pro-Assad forces split their loyalty between Iran and Russia; remnants of the Syrian rebellion coalesced around Turkey, which hoped to deploy them to constrain and possibly defeat US-backed Kurdish forces. Israel sought to preserve its air dominance and interdict Iranian shipments and infrastructure-building, conducting dozens of air raids throughout the year.

Starved of resources and politically isolated, the Syrian government restored its brutal rule without offering incentives to constituencies previously opposed to it. More than one-third of the country remained outside its reach, most notably the oil-rich but Kurdish-controlled northeast and the rebel-held province of Idlib in the northwest. The former benefited from US backing while the latter depended on Turkish assistance. This made a potential straightforward military conquest of either zone costly and risky for the Assad regime and its allies. Two attempts to retake Idlib, in September and May, illustrated the perennial weakness of regime forces.

Nevertheless, Assad benefited from a regional acknowledgement that his rule would continue and from the redrawing of regional competition. From late 2018, several countries, including Jordan, the UAE and Bahrain, began restoring relations with Damascus, and the Nassib crossing between Syria and Jordan (closed since 2015) was reopened to trade in October. Syria's re-entry into the Arab League, expected in early 2019, was however blocked by residual Arab opposition as well as Western pressure.

The question of reconstruction and the return of refugees took centre stage, in large part because of pressure from neighbouring countries struggling with the burden of hosting them. The UN and major non-governmental organisations, in addition to Western countries, assessed that a safe and fair return of refugees could not be guaranteed. Assad was not eager to welcome back refugee populations who mostly opposed his rule. Western countries, expected to foot much of the reconstruction bill – estimated by the UN to be US$400bn – argued that only a political settlement in line with UN resolutions could open the way for funding for reconstruction and the safe return of refugees. The Syrian government and its allies resisted this link. Russia was keen to secure political acknowledgement of its victory and Western financial commitments to rebuild Syria, but Iran and Assad sought neither.

In late December, contradicting stated US policy, Trump announced a full and immediate withdrawal from Syria of US forces that had supported the campaign against ISIS. The presence of a small US contingent was justified by the need to ensure a durable defeat of ISIS but also to complicate Iran's influence in Syria. Trump's decision took US partners by surprise and posed a challenge to Kurdish aspirations for autonomy, which were threatened by both the Assad regime and Turkey. Ultimately, the US lengthened its withdrawal timeline.

## Libya

The conflict in Libya between the weak UN-recognised government in Tripoli and the self-styled Libyan National Army (LNA) of Field Marshal Khalifa Haftar took a turn for the worse in early 2019, when the latter launched a massive unexpected operation to defeat the former.

Haftar's daring move came as the UN prepared to hold a national conference at the culmination of a two-year preparation process aimed at ending the conflict. After seizing large parts of the southwestern Fezzan region and garnering support from militias through financial pledges and promises of political power, Haftar set his sights on the capital, seeking complete military victory. In doing so, he undermined the UN process and alienated political players across Libya. In response, Islamist and local militias from across the country mobilised to reverse the LNA's offensive in Tripoli, succeeding in blunting its momentum. By the summer, it became clear that Haftar's blitzkrieg had failed, leaving his supply lines exposed and his position weakened.

The conflict took on a greater regional character as a result of this offensive. Haftar had sought support in Abu Dhabi and Riyadh for his campaign, obtaining Saudi funding and Emirati air support, notably drones and armaments. Their regional rivals responded, and within weeks Turkey supplied its allied militias – a loose collection of Islamist groups – with vehicles, drones and light weaponry, as well as anti-tank missiles. The provision of such supplies ran counter to a UN arms embargo, but became key to the respective factions' power.

US ambivalence contributed to these growing tensions. In May, Trump, apparently prompted by Egypt and the UAE, ended long-standing US support for the Tripoli government and the UN process by voicing support for Haftar. Other US officials attempted to temper this apparent shift. The internationalisation of the conflict affected UN Security Council deliberations. France and Russia both supported Haftar and toned down language that condemned his campaign. This infuriated the UN envoy to Libya Ghassan Salamé, who publicly blamed Haftar for the escalation. With Libyan factions unwilling to compromise and confident in the regional support they received, and a lack of international support for de-escalation and renewed talks, the conflict appeared set for a stalemate.

## Yemen

The fragmentation of Yemen only increased during the year. The survival of the Houthis, the separatist ambitions of southern politicians, complex politics in Mahrah and Ta'izz, and the weakness of the internationally recognised government of Abd Rabbo Mansour Hadi meant that even an end to the Saudi-led intervention would not end the conflict.

The Stockholm agreement of December 2018 between representatives of the Hadi government and the Houthis – for which the UN had pushed to pre-empt an announced military offensive by the UAE and partner forces to seize the port city of Hudaydah – was a reason for optimism. Hudaydah had become the main entry point for humanitarian supplies into Yemen and a key lifeline for the Houthi movement, which relied on taxation of trade and diversion of aid to fund its own operations. The

UAE argued that capturing Hudaydah would weaken the Houthi insurgency and force it to the negotiating table. This failed to sway the UN, whose officials feared a humanitarian catastrophe should aid delivery be suspended because of fighting.

The Stockholm agreement provided for a phased redeployment of the Houthis and UAE-led coalition forces, and the handing over of the port to a neutral force. Implementation of the agreement was slow and complicated, however, with UN monitors as well as the two warring sides only deeming progress sufficient after six months. This agreement postponed, possibly indefinitely, a UAE-backed attack.

While the level of violence in Hudaydah plateaued, it remained high on most of the 30 front lines elsewhere in Yemen, such as in Ta'izz, where the besieging Houthis faced several enemies. The Houthis remained defiant in the face of their isolation, conducting numerous missile and drone attacks against Saudi territory. This served to humiliate the Kingdom and to pressure it in the context of rising tensions with Iran, the Houthis' main backer.

Elite and popular discontent in Western countries with the Saudi-led intervention played a role in moderating Saudi and UAE policy. New restrictions on arms sales linked to the Yemen intervention and the sheer reputational cost, as well as frustration with Yemeni allies, prompted some rethinking in Riyadh and Abu Dhabi. The latter shifted its focus to the stabilisation of Aden, which sits along an important route linking US economic and military investments in the Horn of Africa, and counter-terrorism operations against ISIS and al-Qaeda in the Arabian Peninsula (AQAP).

## Arab uprisings continue

While a sense of revolutionary fatigue and a new authoritarian era descended on much of the Middle East, popular mobilisation against long-standing rulers remained a feature of Arab politics. In both Algeria and Sudan, large urban protests ostensibly succeeded in ending the rules of Abdelaziz Bouteflika and Omar al-Bashir, in power for 20 and 30 years respectively. However, in both cases, as in prior Arab uprisings, divisions within the elite and the role of the military were the decisive factors in removing the president and shaping the transition. The uprisings in Sudan and Algeria illustrated the enduring complexity of political change in the Arab world, where protest movements had to contend with powerful security structures able to discard a ruler to preserve the system.

In Algeria, the immediate trigger for Bouteflika's undoing was his decision to run for another term despite having suffered a stroke in 2012 and being absent from the public eye for years. It was widely believed that a small circle of advisers, including his brother and prominent businessmen, manipulated him. The protest movement brought together urban professionals, the middle class and workers, leading to massive and relentless demonstrations over the winter and spring. Street pressure fuelled divisions within the armed forces, elements of which were at odds with the presidential counsellors. In April, following weeks of protests, the military command succeeded in obtaining the resignation of Bouteflika and senior intelligence officials. The army, led by General Gaid Salah, became the self-appointed steward of the country's transition, to the outrage of civilian groups and opposition political parties that feared it would hijack the transition. Indeed, it rapidly became clear that the army intended to set the terms of the transition, to protect its own interests as well as those of the bureaucratic and business elite that became the focus of the protesters' ire. The tension between the military and the protest movement threatened to escalate, with the latter making bold demands for free elections and democratic rule while the military pushed for a quick and superficial transition and early elections. Importantly, however, the military refrained from using violence to quell the movement, showing restraint that prevented a showdown in a country still traumatised by its civil war in the 1990s.

Bashir's fate echoed that of Bouteflika. Bashir's own base of power had frayed in recent years. His rule endured thanks to an uneasy coalition of Islamists and military officers whose economic interests and regional patronage increasingly diverged. Indeed, Bashir's alliance with the Muslim Brotherhood put him at odds with regional heavyweights such as Egypt, Saudi Arabia and the UAE. His attempt to attract Turkish and Qatari support failed to deliver the economic benefits he expected, despite Sudan leasing the important island of Suakin in the Red Sea to the Turkish military. Bashir's downfall was rooted in an economic downturn and bad governance that brought the Sudanese middle classes to the streets, and enacted by senior military and intelligence officers who assessed that his continued rule was more damaging to their interests than his departure. His senior commanders forced him to resign and offered him immunity, only to renege on this promise. Yet the Sudanese military leadership refused to hand him to the International Criminal Court, which had indicted him for war crimes in Darfur.

The Sudanese uprising was marred by considerable violence before and after Bashir's ouster. There were clear splits within the security apparatus between the military, the main intelligence agency and the tribal-based paramilitary force. The Rapid Support Forces (RSF), composed of fighters who had fought in Darfur, conducted attacks against the large civilian protest camp outside the defence ministry's compound in Khartoum, leading the African Union to suspend Sudan's membership. Violence failed to break civilian resolve, however, and the fear that the country could slide into civil strife mobilised regional action. Ethiopia, backed by key Western, Arab and African countries, played a leading role in brokering talks between activist groups and the military. Negotiations between civilian activist bodies and military commanders inside the Transitional Military Council (TMC) – established after Bashir was ousted – ultimately led to an agreement over elections and the transfer of power, though a timeline for implementation of this remained uncertain.

# Turkey: Towards the End of the Erdogan Era

Turkish President Recep Tayyip Erdogan has profoundly changed the country in the years since his Justice and Development Party (AKP) first took office in November 2002. The prosperity and promise of the early years of his rule have given way to economic turbulence, domestic divisions and a decline in legal and media freedoms, as the political system tilted in an authoritarian direction. A failed coup attempt in mid-2016 exacerbated these trends, alienating Erdogan from Turkey's Western allies. His second presidential term is due to end in 2023, yet there is no certainty over how long he will stay in office, or whether any succession plan is in place.

## A double electoral defeat

The defeat of the AKP in the rerun of the Istanbul mayoral election on 23 June 2019 was one of the worst setbacks Erdogan has suffered since the AKP took office. It reinforced the impression among his opponents both inside and outside the AKP that his popularity had entered an irreversible decline. His decision to force a rerun after the AKP had narrowly lost the original election on 31 March was the latest in a growing number of mistakes and miscalculations, suggesting that his once formidable political instincts had deserted him.

In the local elections on 31 March, the AKP lost control of a string of metropolitan areas, including the capital Ankara. In Istanbul, the provisional result suggested that Ekrem Imamoglu, the candidate for the main opposition Republican People's Party (CHP), had defeated former AKP prime minister Binali Yildirim by 0.2% or 13,000 votes. For Erdogan, Istanbul is a personal matter, being his birthplace and where he rose to national prominence as mayor in the 1990s. In addition, its population of 16 million, massive municipal budget and role as Turkey's commercial heart mean that it has offered considerable opportunities for political patronage and had come to play a key role in the network of businesses and non-governmental organisations that underpinned the AKP's domination of the Turkish political landscape.

Under pressure from Erdogan, the country's Supreme Electoral Council (YSK) ordered a rerun of the mayoral election in Istanbul on the grounds that some of the election officials lacked the necessary qualifications. It did not, however, order reruns for the district-council elections in Istanbul on the same day, which were overseen by the same officials and which had been mostly won by the AKP.

In the weeks leading up to the rerun, Erdogan mobilised the government-dominated Turkish media in support of Yildirim, while AKP workers went door to door exhorting AKP supporters who had not gone to the polls on 31 March to vote for him. Extraordinarily, Erdogan even enlisted the support of Abdullah Ocalan, the founder of the militant Kurdistan Workers' Party (PKK) who has been incarcerated on the prison island of Imrali since 1999, publishing a letter by Ocalan calling on Kurds not to vote for Imamoglu. All these strategies failed. Not only did Imamoglu win the rerun by a margin of 800,000 votes but, despite a higher turnout than in March, support for Yildirim fell by 200,000 votes.

Thereafter, Erdogan considered using his control over the Turkish judicial system to remove Imamoglu from office, before backtracking and opting for a sustained campaign of attrition – passing presidential decrees to limit Imamoglu's powers and starving the municipality of funds.

## A long decline?

On 16 April 2017, in a constitutional referendum marred by numerous allegations of irregularities, Turkish voters narrowly approved a transition from the country's decades-old parliamentary system to one in which all political power is concentrated in the presidency, with the changes to take effect after the next elections.

Through late 2017 and into early 2018, opinion polls suggested that support for both Erdogan and the AKP was weakening. Although it had yet to impact voters' daily lives, signs that the Turkish economy was heading for a sharp downturn were already emerging. The presidential and parliamentary elections on 24 June 2018 were again overshadowed by allegations of fraud and the results, particularly in more isolated areas where there was less oversight, were littered with statistical anomalies. Nevertheless, Erdogan narrowly won a second term as president but the AKP lost its majority in parliament, forcing it to rely on support from the Turkish ultranationalist Nationalist Action Party (MHP). But the transition to the presidential system – which abolished the post of prime minister, transferred the right to choose cabinet ministers to the president, and enabled Erdogan to bypass parliament and promulgate laws by issuing presidential decrees – reduced the impact of this loss.

In the run-up to the nationwide local elections on 31 March 2019 – and the rerun of the mayoral election in Istanbul in June – Erdogan again utilised his formal powers and informal influence to restrict the activities of opposition parties and try to boost support for the AKP. This included using his control of the Turkish media, television channels in particular, which are the main source of news for most Turkish voters.

The opposition parties, however, had learned from previous experience. On election day, they deployed hundreds of thousands of volunteers to monitor the voting. In the metropolises in western Turkey, the result was a sharp drop in the number of allegations of electoral fraud. But in the predominantly Kurdish southeast of the country, where the security forces restricted the activities of election observers, the number of allegations and statistical anomalies rose. In the mayoral elections for nine local councils, the YSK dismissed the successful candidates from the pro-Kurdish Peoples' Democratic Party (HDP) on the grounds that they were ineligible to hold public office, even though it had previously ruled that they were eligible to stand as candidates.

But in the west of the country, the AKP's losses reinvigorated Erdogan's opponents and revitalised their previously fading hopes of realising change through the political process. They also galvanised the growing number of dissidents within the AKP. On 8 July 2019, former deputy prime minister Ali Babacan, who had overseen the AKP's economic policies as minister of economic affairs in 2002–07 but had been sidelined as Erdogan tightened his grip on power, resigned from the AKP in order to form his own political party. The former academic Ahmet Davutoglu, who as foreign minister and then prime minister was the main architect of the AKP's increased engagement in Africa and the

Middle East from 2009 onwards, also indicated his intention to resign and establish another breakaway party.

## A rearguard action?

Babacan's and Davutoglu's new parties were expected to be formally announced in autumn 2019. Even though both threatened to make inroads into the AKP's vote, neither appeared likely to replace it as the most popular party in the country. Babacan's record as economy minister had made him a favourite of the Turkish and foreign business communities, but he lacked Erdogan's raw charismatic appeal to the urban and rural poor who make up the majority of the AKP's support base. The failure of attempts to create a sphere of Turkish influence in the Middle East had severely damaged Davutoglu's credibility.

However, Erdogan appeared to have no prospect of compensating for the decline in the AKP's vote by attracting support from other parties. Indeed, since summer 2013, when what have become known as the Gezi Park protests swept across Turkey, he had sought to deepen rather than broaden his support base, including by railing against the 'Western conspirators' and their domestic collaborators, who he claimed were constantly trying to undermine him and prevent Turkey's inexorable rise to global pre-eminence under his leadership.

Demographics were also working against Erdogan. During the AKP's first years in power, he famously declared that one of his main goals was to raise a 'pious generation' of young Turks. Since taking office, the AKP has opened thousands of new mosques and overhauled the school curriculum to increase the number of compulsory lessons in Sunni Islam. But by July 2019, opinion polls suggested that levels of religious observance were lower than they had been a decade previously, particularly among young people, many of whom had grown up knowing only AKP governments and who had also been the hardest hit by the economic downturn. In March 2019 unemployment among those under 25 stood at 25.2%, up from 17.7% in March 2018. In a country where almost half of the population was under the age of 30, support for Erdogan was lower among 18–24-year-olds than any other demographic.

One year into his second term, no new elections were scheduled until June 2023, when simultaneous general and presidential elections are due to be held. The Turkish constitution states that no one can serve more than two five-year terms as president. However, a loophole allows an incumbent president to stand for a third term if 360 of the 600 members of parliament call early elections during their second term. After he won a second term in June 2018, Erdogan had been expected to wait until 2022 before instructing the AKP–MHP deputies to call early elections, confident that they would be supported by opposition deputies.

In mid-2019 the AKP and MHP combined had 340 seats in parliament, yet up to 50 or 60 of them were regarded as potential defectors to Babacan's and Davutoglu's new parties. Moreover, there appeared little prospect of the AKP's opponents helping them reach the 360 seats necessary to force early elections. Although the new system allows the president to promulgate laws by decree, the Turkish parliament has retained its legislative functions. If there were more than 40 defections from the AKP, the AKP–MHP would lose its parliamentary majority, thus raising the possibility of deadlock as parliament and Erdogan passed laws that cancelled each other out – leaving Erdogan with little choice but to call early elections. However, Erdogan appeared likely to try to delay any new elections, not least in the hope of the economy returning to sustained growth.

## De-institutionalisation and shifting centres of domestic power

In August 2014, after he was first elected president, Erdogan relocated from his office in the prime ministry in the centre of Ankara to a sprawling new palace he had built for himself on the outskirts of the city. The increased physical distance from the rest of the apparatus of state appeared to exacerbate Erdogan's already growing disengagement from its accumulated experience and expertise. Instead of consulting with members of the relevant branches, he increasingly relied on his own conversations with a small circle of deferential advisers.

The transition to a presidential system had been expected to be followed by a re-institutionalisation of decision-making processes. In summer 2018, Erdogan created several Presidential Councils, each responsible for a policy area and chaired by himself. But they rarely met. Despite the deepening economic recession, in July 2019 the Council for Economic Policy had not convened since October 2018.

As Erdogan grew in power domestically, he also became more confident about following his own convictions in foreign policy, not so much re-orientating Turkey from membership of one strategic alliance to another but seeking to establish it as a global power in its own right. But the de-institutionalisation of policymaking meant that his understanding of the world became shaped and nurtured by his inner circle, rather than by information and expertise from the rest of the apparatus of state.

In 2013, the decision to award a contract for Turkey's proposed T-LORAMIDS air-defence system to China Precision Machinery Import and Export Corporation (CPMIEC) was based on a report drawn up by technocrats from the Undersecretariat for Defence Industries, who had been asked to evaluate the various proposals on their technical merits and prices. The contract was cancelled in 2015 following opposition from NATO, backed by expressions of concern by members of the Turkish Ministry of Foreign Affairs (MFA) and the Turkish General Staff. In contrast, the decision to buy the Russian S-400 air-defence system in 2017 was made by Erdogan and his inner circle after a meeting with Russian President Vladimir Putin, without any input from the MFA, General Staff or Undersecretariat for Defence Industries. Throughout the first half of 2019, Erdogan repeatedly dismissed warnings from Washington that taking delivery of the S-400s would result in Turkey's expulsion from the F-35 *Lightning* II programme and trigger measures under the Countering America's Adversaries Through Sanctions Act (CAATSA), publicly insisting that he would talk with US President Donald Trump to ensure that no sanctions would be applied. The government-controlled Turkish media pointedly noted that in Syria the US had formed an alliance with the Syrian Democratic Forces (SDF), a primary component of which is the military wing of the Democratic Union Party (PYD), which is closely affiliated with the PKK. The S-400s duly began arriving in Turkey on 12 July 2019.

Turkey's own active military involvement in Syria – through *Operation Euphrates Shield* in 2016–17 and *Operation Olive Branch* in 2018 – was a by-product of the de-institutionalisation of decision-making and the eradication of any lingering influence of the General Staff over policy decisions. This influence had already begun to fade when the AKP first took office in 2002. But it was not until 2007, when the AKP successfully defied an attempt by the General Staff to prevent it from appointing then-foreign minister Abdullah Gul to the presidency, that Erdogan began to realise that he no longer needed to fear the country's generals. Nevertheless, in June 2015, the General Staff still retained sufficient influence to defy an order from Erdogan to stage an incursion into Syria to strike at the PYD, on the grounds that it would leave Turkey mired in an unwinnable war.

Yet even this influence evaporated after the coup attempt of 15–16 July 2016, which Erdogan blamed on followers of his former ally, the exiled Islamic preacher Fethullah Gulen. Erdogan's subsequent purges of the officer corps – which were ongoing in July 2019 – have depressed morale, disrupted chains of command and left the Turkish Armed Forces weaker both militarily and institutionally. When Erdogan ordered the launch of *Operation Euphrates Shield* in August 2016, the General Staff made no attempt to resist.

By mid-2019 there were also signs that Erdogan's reliance on one-to-one contacts with other heads of state was exacerbating the decline in the level of expert input in decision-making. For example, until spring 2019, Turkey's growing footprint in Sudan had been almost exclusively based on the personal ties between Erdogan and then Sudanese president Omar al-Bashir. In contrast, between late 2018 and early 2019, Saudi Arabia and the United Arab Emirates (UAE) – Turkey's main rivals for influence in East Africa – cultivated multiple contacts among Sudan's ruling elite, especially in the country's armed forces, and were well placed to strengthen their influence at Turkey's expense when Bashir was overthrown by a military coup in April 2019.

Erdogan's reliance on one-to-one contacts has further complicated Turkey's taut relations with the EU, where he does not have a single interlocutor. During the AKP's early years in office, Erdogan vigorously espoused support for Turkey's accession to the EU, not least because he saw that closer ties would reduce his vulnerability to the Turkish military. But he was selective in the reforms he introduced in order to secure the opening of accession negotiations. Once he was confident of his grip on domestic power, the reform process rapidly lost momentum. Nevertheless, Erdogan appears likely to remain reluctant to unilaterally abrogate Turkey's accession process or annul its March 2016 refugee agreement with the EU – not least because of concerns about the impact on the Turkish economy of any rupture in relations.

## Erdogan's endgame

Although many AKP voters genuinely believe that only Erdogan stands between them and the Western-led conspirators he maintains are constantly plotting to destroy Turkey, there has long been discontent within the party. Some were alienated by Erdogan's predilection for issuing instructions and appointing favourites to positions in the party's organisational hierarchy from the isolation of his presidential palace, rather than consulting with its members. Others, not least in the conservative wing of the party, were uncomfortable with Erdogan's belligerence and the widespread corruption in his inner circle. But most chose to mute any public expression of unease – partly out of fear of Erdogan himself and the prospect of losing the benefits that accrue from inclusion in the AKP's clientelist networks, and partly because of concerns that, if Erdogan ever lost power, the new administration would seek revenge by subjecting AKP members to the same treatment as Erdogan has meted out to the party's opponents. Through the first half of 2019, as the doubts about Erdogan's political longevity began to intensify, the dissent within the AKP became more public.

In mid-2019, some of the dissenters – like Babacan and Davutoglu – had already left or were about to leave the AKP. But even those who were planning to remain were aware that there was no clear successor to Erdogan within the party – or at least not one who could preserve, much less increase, its electoral support. Erdogan's son-in-law Berat Albayrak, who entered parliament in 2015 and was appointed minister of finance and treasury in July 2018, was widely regarded as having presidential ambitions. But his record in office had been poor and he was resented within the AKP for having been parachuted into power as a result of his marriage to Erdogan's eldest daughter.

Despite these troubles, there was no indication either that Erdogan's departure from office was imminent or that he saw any need to change his policies, let alone relax his authoritarianism. Instead, he sought to blame the decline in his and the AKP's popularity on the failings of others and to tighten still further his control over policy. On 6 July, he dismissed Murat Cetinkaya, the governor of the nominally independent Turkish Central Bank, for failing to reduce annual inflation – then running at 15.7% – and vowed to oversee monetary policy himself. There were also concerns that, beset by setbacks at home and abroad, Erdogan would attempt to rally the country behind him by provoking an international incident, such as in the Eastern Mediterranean where Turkish ships had already begun exploratory drilling for natural gas in waters claimed by Cyprus and Greece as part of their exclusive economic zones (EEZs).

Yet there was a palpable sense that, even if it was not imminent, the Erdogan era was approaching its end. There was no doubt that, when he eventually left office, Erdogan would leave behind a changed Turkey – whether physically through his massive infrastructure projects and the construction boom that had engulfed the country's cities, his overseeing of the departure of the military from politics, his de-institutionalisation, his destruction of Turkey's once-diverse and vibrant media or his erosion of public faith in the rule of law. But he had failed either to deliver sustained prosperity or to significantly Islamicise Turkish society. Although Erdogan continued to portray himself as serving a *dava* or 'cause', in as much as it meant anything at all, 'Erdoganism' had become associated with methodology rather than ideology, a way of governing rather than a set of values.

Ironically, Erdogan appeared to have been directly responsible for the failure of some of his most cherished goals. In July 2019, one year after the introduction of the presidential system, opinion polls suggested not only that a majority of Turks favoured a return to a parliamentary system, but that their number was rising. Similarly, after a dip in support when the Turkish economy was booming and Turkey was being hailed in the West as a rising power and a model for other Muslim countries to follow, a clear majority once against supported Turkish membership of the EU, not least because it was seen as a means of safeguarding human rights and the rule of law.

# Iran After Khamenei

Since the 1979 Iranian Revolution, only two people have held the office of supreme leader: the charismatic Ayatollah Ruhollah Khomeini (1979–89) and the current leader Ayatollah Ali Khamenei (1989–). Khamenei turned 80 in April 2019, an age that very few of his countrymen reach. In March 2015, Khamenei stated that the fifth Assembly of Experts (AoE), elected in 2016 for an eight-year term, would likely select his successor. A special committee of the AoE, reporting directly to Khamenei, has been established to vet candidates.

The transition of power to a new supreme leader will mark a new chapter in Iranian politics. Whether it results in further solidification of the Islamic Republic's power or weakens the state, a period of internal political turbulence is likely. The struggle among various power centres is expected to intensify. Given the current role of the supreme leader and the balance of institutional power, the new leadership is most likely to follow in Khamenei's footsteps in both policy and process. As US–Iran tensions escalate, hard-core factions such as the Islamic Revolutionary Guard Corps (IRGC) will probably have the upper hand in choosing and directing the next leader. Since no potential candidate has both political and religious legitimacy or general public support, the IRGC and other hardline factions will be highly influential in the early post-Khamenei years.

## The evolving role of supreme leader

Khomeini was a charismatic, religious revolutionary leader who governed in that manner, rather than as the head of an authoritative political establishment. Popular with the public and respected by Qom's great *marjas* (high-ranking Shia clerics), Khomeini was a figure of political and religious authority. He made little effort to build political institutions because he had no need for them.

When he died in 1989 and the AoE gathered to choose his successor, it faced a nearly impossible task. From the religious standpoint, the supreme leader's role as guardian jurist (*vali-e-faqih*) was to oversee governance, law and politics. The Islamic Republic's constitution held that the supreme leader must be a *marja*. Yet the religious leaders were not politically fit, while top political figures lacked appropriate religious credentials.

To break the stalemate, Hashemi Rafsanjani, the speaker of parliament who had a lot of influence over the AoE, made a bold move. In his will, Khomeini had insisted that statements attributed to him should only be considered authentic if they were written down or broadcast. Ignoring this injunction, Rafsanjani cited a conversation he had had with the late leader, in which Khomeini had suggested that then-president Khamenei was fit for leadership. Khamenei was popular with politicians and the public, had close ties to military commanders and was considered a moderate. While he had a proven track record as a politician, he was only a mid-level religious figure. Rafsanjani's intervention helped to minimise objections from the influential religious leadership.

According to the Iranian constitution, the supreme leader symbolises divine governance of the Islamic Republic, establishing Iran as a Muslim state. As Khomeini conceived the role, the leader's powers are not limited to the traditional framework of Islamic law. The leader's authority as absolute guardian can be used to veto any action contradicting state interests, even if the leader's decision conflicts with religious principles.

The supreme leader is both an individual and, through his various offices and representatives, an institution. With his power of veto, he sits at the apex of Iran's system of intragovernmental bargaining. Institutions compete to get closer to the leader. He influences the representative apparatus, is commander-in-chief of the armed forces, and settles arguments with final and binding proclamations, although he does not always get his way. Through networks of political institutions such as the Guardian Council, which qualifies candidates for elections, the supreme leader can determine the make-up of Iran's democratic institutions and ensure the support of other organisations and informal power centres. Almost all critical decisions, however, are shaped through the political process and there is extensive lobbying to secure the support of the leader.

When Khamenei became supreme leader, the public assumed that the kingmaker, Rafsanjani, was the power behind the throne, having been Khomeini's right-hand man. For years, Khamenei struggled to pursue his agenda and consolidate his authority as Rafsanjani overshadowed his leadership, pursuing his own agenda to reshape the state. As Khamenei and Rafsanjani began to diverge on a range of issues from foreign policy to economic development, Khamenei was eventually able to consolidate his leadership. In the past 30 years he has reshaped the Iranian power apparatus to create his own support base and network of influence. The three critical pillars of this power base are the IRGC, the Office of the Supreme Leader and its associated networks, and religious institutions, principally the Association of Teachers of the Qom Theological Seminary and the Imam Khomeini Institute.

## The IRGC

When Khamenei came to power, he vetoed Rafsanjani's proposed merger of the IRGC and the military, ostensibly on the basis that the two forces had distinct responsibilities. It is more likely, however, that Khamenei simply needed the IRGC to solidify his authority. Khamenei exploited tensions between high-ranking IRGC commanders and Rafsanjani dating back to the Iran–Iraq War (1980–88) to build his support base. A reform movement that began in 1999 with Mohammad Khatami's election as president subsequently strengthened the IRGC. Khamenei regarded the movement's pro-Western foreign policy as a threat to his own power and boosted the IRGC's influence and political backing to support his anti-Western stance. The IRGC thus came to wield significant influence over Iran's foreign policy and economic decision-making.

Khamenei also gave the IRGC's Quds Force its present shape. The force manages Iran's extraterritorial activities in the region and many Iranian ambassadors are members. Although formally it is a branch of the IRGC, its commander reports directly to the supreme leader. Its arc of influence extends from Beirut to Sana'a and it is pivotal to the security of the Islamic Republic. Its commander, Qasem Soleimani, is therefore one of Iran's most powerful figures and will have considerable influence in the selection of the next leader.

The IRGC has effectively become a business conglomerate, controlling 25–35% of Iran's economy by 2015, according to some estimates – a reward for the unconditional support and loyalty it offers the supreme leader. It initially rebuilt infrastructure destroyed during the Iran–Iraq War, but IRGC-affiliated entities are now active in almost every sector of the economy, including banking, shipping, manufacturing and consumer imports. The justification is that the IRGC takes on projects that are too challenging for the private sector.

The IRGC has also benefited hugely from a process begun by Khamenei with the purported aim of accelerating economic growth by reviving the private sector. In practice, however, it empowered an oligarchic semi-public sector with the resources and authority to take over privatised businesses. This now controls approximately 40% of the economy. In 2018, the value of investment by Khatam-al-Anbia – an IRGC-owned industrial conglomerate – in various oil and gas and infrastructure projects alone was about 7% of Iran's total money supply. The company is Iran's largest contractor in industrial and development projects – the equivalent of General Electric and the US Army Corps of Engineers combined.

Besides these official activities, the IRGC controls a vast proportion of Iran's black-market economy. The IRGC's illicit economic activities have benefited from decades of sanctions and significantly expanded in scale and value. A 2007 estimate by an Iranian MP of the IRGC's smuggling operations suggested annual revenues of US$12 billion. According to Iran's anti-smuggling agency, more than US$7bn-worth of refinery products was smuggled out of the country at the height of international sanctions in 2014.

## Office of the Supreme Leader

From the modest legacy left by Khomeini, Khamenei has created an extensive bureaucracy with more than 4,000 employees. The revamped institution allows him to micromanage domestic political and economic issues. More importantly, the supreme leader oversees many businesses and directly appoints the heads of many of Iran's largest *bonyads*, the charitable foundations that have a considerable share of the economy. This network of interconnected businesses provides the supreme leader with financial resources independent of the government and is indispensable for hardline factions close to the leader.

Hardliners are eager to ensure that they will control important power centres at the time of Khamenei's death or departure. Astan Quds Razavi (AQR), perhaps the largest *bonyad*, is reportedly worth billions of dollars, with interests in almost every sector of the economy including construction, heavy manufacturing, oil, gas, transportation, financial services, information technology, sugar and yeast production. Until 2015, Ayatollah Tabasi, a prominent and influential cleric with close ties to Rafsanjani, headed AQR. After Tabasi's death, Khamenei appointed Ebrahim Raisi, who is closer to the leader and the hardliners. In March 2019, Khamenei made Raisi the head of the judiciary and appointed Ahmad Marvi, who had served in the Office of the Supreme Leader for 30 years, as the new custodian of AQR.

The Office of the Supreme Leader runs its own economic empire through the Headquarters for Executing the Order of the Imam (better known as 'Setad'). According to a comprehensive Reuters investigation in 2013, Setad was originally a temporary organisation created by Khomeini 'to manage and sell properties abandoned in the chaotic years after the 1979 Islamic Revolution'. Under Khamenei, however, 'it has morphed into a business juggernaut that now holds stakes in nearly every sector of Iranian industry, including finance, oil and telecommunications'. Setad is worth between US$100bn and US$200bn. Like any large bureaucracy, the Office of the Supreme Leader is likely to resist major changes and Khamenei's successor will be bound to follow his path for years.

### Religious educational organisations

The religious establishment did not regard Khamenei warmly in the early years of his rule. By the mid-1990s, however, many of the *marjas* from that period had died. Khamenei then made a concerted effort to win over the religious leaders in Qom. After the death of the last pre-revolution great *marja*, Ayatollah Muhammad Ali Araki, in November 1994, the Seminary Teachers Association, a pro-government clerical entity, listed Khamenei among seven people qualified to be a *marja* while excluding Ayatollah Ali al-Sistani and Ayatollah Hussein Ali Montazeri.

Through extensive sponsorship of religious institutes and promotion of leaders and parties that support the supreme leader, Khamenei has expanded his network of influence among religious factions while limiting their independence in the process. This sponsorship is funded through the state budget, slush funds and the transfer of public assets. The list of sponsored institutions is vast, and includes the Dar al-Hadith Institute (run by former intelligence minister Mohammad Reyshahri), the Asra Institute (run by Abdollah Javadi Amoli), the Imam Khomeini Institute (run by Mohammad-Taqi Mesbah-Yazdi), the Imam Sadeq Institute (run by Jafar Sobhani) and Al-Mustafa International University. These institutions received more than US$500 million from the government in 2010. The supreme leader also supported the creation of the Supreme Council of the Seminaries in 1995, which oversees religious education and prevents 'the penetration of foreigners in seminaries and protects clerics against the influence of deviant currents'. In fact, it has bureaucratised the previously independent religious-education institutions to ensure support for the theory of guardianship of the ruling jurist in general and the leader in particular.

All this aims at buying the support of high-ranking religious figures and orienting a younger generation of clerics in the leader's favour. These efforts are so extensive that recently some religious figures have expressed concerns about the reduced status of the *marjaiya* and the level of dependency of the religious establishment on the government. Some even called for non-revolutionary *Huwza*, an independent clerical system that has a long history in Shiism and is showcased by Sistani's leadership in Iraq. Khamenei rejected the call as unacceptable.

In short, Khamenei has been the architect of the revolutionary establishment. Its institutions have allowed him to solidify his power, institutionally and personally. Hardliners accept his decisions to avoid compromising their own interests, but the next leader cannot expect similar acquiescence. The apparatus of institutional and personal power is too vast and intricate to be passed smoothly to a successor. Iran's next supreme leader must win the support of more diverse and much more powerful players within government as well as the military and economic spheres, and it is more likely that these players will exert influence on the next leader for their own ends. The system that Khamenei built and managed is likely to manage his successor – this dynamic is key to understanding the impending transition.

## Countervailing dynamics

Although the supreme leader and his institutions dominate, they lack the support of the general public – the middle classes and youth in particular. The strength and influence of moderates and reformists has waxed and waned during Khamenei's leadership. In 2005, after two terms of reformist government under Khatami's popular presidency, hardliners sought to manipulate the election to ensure the electoral victory of Mahmoud Ahmadinejad, who stood very close to the leader. He provided his political supporters with lavish compensation. Yet his re-election in 2009 (also allegedly manipulated) led to a decline in popular support for the establishment, as a result of vast crackdowns on protesters across the country.

Moreover, many reformists and moderates were forced to temporarily resign from domestic politics following the failure of the Green Movement in 2009. The Guardian Council even disqualified Rafsanjani from entering the 2013 election, a major shock to the public. As the economy worsened under international sanctions, moderates found that their time had come again. The election of President Hassan Rouhani in 2013 epitomised their ascent. His marginal victory came with the support of Khatami, who mobilised the middle classes and more secular public and youth. Rouhani restarted talks with the P5+1 to resolve Iran's nuclear issue, resulting in the signing in 2015 of the Joint Comprehensive Plan of Action (JCPOA), for which the moderates took credit.

In 2016, after the nuclear deal was signed, moderates won major elections for both parliament and the AoE, despite the fact that the Guardian

Council disqualified many of their key figures. The moderates' agenda for the AoE election was to prevent the so-called 'JYM triangle' – Ahmad Jannati, Mohammad Yazdi and Mohammad-Taqi Mesbah-Yazdi, all hardline clerics – from entering the assembly, since the current AoE will most likely appoint the next leader. Despite their efforts, and the fact that Rafsanjani garnered the most public votes, however, Jannati was elected AoE chairman. His victory was the supreme leader's way of showing Iranians that he retained his grip on power.

Hardliners are once again on the rise. With the escalation of the US–Iran conflict and the shadow of war hovering above the region, they can justify seeking greater control: desperate times require desperate measures. This dynamic is strengthening the IRGC's role in Iranian politics, economy and diplomacy. Simultaneously, the threat of war is justifying even more suppression of reformists and activists. Rafsanjani's death in 2017 has also allowed Khamenei to further expand his network of influence and authority. He recently assigned new commanders to key positions in the armed forces, in the IRGC in particular. His motivations are unclear, but one thing is certain: these actions could have an impact beyond his reign.

## Potential successors

Since the signing of the JCPOA, moderates have speculated that Rouhani or Hassan Khomeini, the ayatollah's grandson, could be potential successors to Khamenei. However, Hashemi Shahroudi, a religious figure close to Khamenei accepted by politicians, was a more realistic option. All three were moderately popular with the public and were possibly acceptable to some key religious figures, but they could hardly have won the support of key players such as the IRGC, the supreme leader's office and his hardline elite supporters. These players would most likely have tried to prevent moderates from influencing someone like Shahroudi once in power. In any case, Shahroudi died in December 2018.

As things stand, hardliners have marginalised moderates, who have less to offer to the public than ever, and who cannot expect to significantly influence the selection of the next leader. The maximum-pressure campaign by US President Donald Trump has further undermined the moderates by severely affecting the economy. Rouhani is barely meeting promises made during his re-election campaign. The moderate camp is under substantial pressure from both hardliners and the public who feel tricked by seemingly powerless reformists. Nonetheless, public support still favours the moderates. Should the next leader face social unrest, he might need moderates to help unite the nation and ease public tension.

Other potential names have emerged from the hardline camp. First is the supreme leader's second son, Mojtaba Khamenei, who supposedly has great influence over his father and close ties to intelligence and military commanders of the IRGC. Reformists have accused him of rigging Ahmadinejad's election and taking part in the suppression of the 2009 uprisings. Although the IRGC and the bureaucratic apparatus may accept him, Mojtaba lacks religious and public credentials. He is a cleric, but his religious status is even weaker than his father's when he became supreme leader. The public views him as a 'mystery man' who exerts influence behind the scenes. More importantly, if he were to succeed his father, it would create a hereditary monarchy – an absolute contradiction of Islamic revolutionary ideals.

The second figure is former AQR head Raisi, a high-ranking member of the judiciary who is close to hardliners. Raisi has more religious prestige with clerics in Qom but has a negative public image. He was a member of a special committee that sentenced many Mujahedin-e-Khalq (MEK) members to death in a mass execution in 1988. On the 28th anniversary of that incident, the office of the late Ayatollah Hussein Ali Montazeri leaked an audio recording of a conversation between Montazeri and the committee in which the cleric strongly objected to the executions. The leak rekindled public debate and damaged Raisi's reputation. Given the timing of the leak, some believed it was a move by the moderate camp to compromise another hardline candidate for the supreme leadership.

In the 2017 presidential campaign, once it became clear that Rouhani would be re-elected, hardliners tried to rehabilitate Raisi through an extensive publicity campaign. All other conservative and hardline candidates stepped down in support of Raisi, and he won 40% of the popular vote. Farid Hadad, the brother-in-law of Mojtaba Khamenei, was involved in his campaign, suggesting that hardliners have long-term plans for Raisi. Recently, in an unprecedented move, the supreme leader's website ran an exclusive interview with Raisi as the new head of Iran's judicial system, implying that he has Khamenei's support.

Many moderates have embraced Raisi's new appointment as their influence has waned. This might suggest that the moderate camp is investing in Raisi to secure at least a modicum of influence in the post-Khamenei era. Moderates may consider Raisi's leadership as a best-case scenario under current circumstances. In such a scenario, moderates could preserve their status quo in Iran's political arena and await an opportunity to reinvigorate their agenda when the pendulum swings again.

## The selection process

Given unpredictable domestic and international developments, current speculation about the identity of the next supreme leader may be wide of the mark. The timing of the transition might be of critical importance. Had Khamenei died after the JCPOA was signed or while Rafsanjani was still alive, the succession would probably have unfolded differently to the present expectation. Yet since Rafsanjani's death, it appears that the only real kingmaker is Khamenei himself. He can command the key players, most importantly the IRGC, and has undermined the influence of religious leaders.

To become a strong supreme leader with established authority, any aspirant must pass three tests: perceived legitimacy from a religious perspective, public support, and personal acceptance by all key players from a political perspective. The successful candidate must be legitimate in the eyes of a swathe of the establishment, from military commanders to religious leaders and among hardliners and moderates. Moreover, the new leader must be sufficiently close to elite circles that most key players will accept his authority.

It is unlikely that any candidate could initially enjoy such status. Any new leader must first consolidate power. Before that happens there will be a transition period during which key players may influence the leader and secure their future share of power. The precise balance of power prevailing at the time of the succession is critical to the question of who will assume leadership and to the position of every other power player.

Given existing formal and informal political and military institutions and structures, any new leader is unlikely to cause a major foreign-policy shift in Iran for some time. Even if moderates won an election, they would struggle to arrest the drift of state policy away from the West and closer to Russia and China. Khamenei's power base, moreover, makes it likely that his successor will have to lead the country in a similar fashion. There will be one major difference, however. Khamenei and his political, military and economic networks, particularly the IRGC, are now so intertwined and interdependent that they rely heavily on one another for support. The new supreme leader will be highly dependent on the network and the IRGC in particular, and will thus have little authority or influence over them.

# Gas and Geopolitics in the Eastern Mediterranean

Major offshore gas deposits were discovered in the Eastern Mediterranean between 2009 and 2011. The US Geological Survey published a report in 2010 suggesting that the Levant basin, encompassing waters off Israel, Lebanon, Syria and Cyprus, contained 3.4 trillion cubic metres of recoverable reserves of natural gas. Given the rising global demand for gas and higher prices, this encouraged hopes of a bonanza in the region that might encourage states to work together. Yet there were also fears that it might aggravate existing conflicts or spark new ones. The Arab–Israeli conflict, the simmering tensions between Israel and Iran, the Cyprus dispute, and the political rivalry between Egypt and Turkey all had an important bearing on the prospects for developing the natural-gas deposits in the Eastern Mediterranean. A decade later, the anticipated bonanza has not happened, partly because of market realities: the only significant market for this gas is Egypt. The geopolitical impacts, too, have been less marked than some predicted.

The potential of the East Mediterranean as a natural-gas zone first became apparent in the late 1980s after the Egyptian government took steps to encourage exploration in this area. Its success motivated neighbouring countries to investigate how far into the Mediterranean the gas-bearing structures off the Nile Delta stretched. Natural gas became an increasingly attractive investment proposition in comparison with the other main energy sources as it became perceived as a potential 'bridge-fuel' to a carbon-neutral future, owing to its lower emissions as compared with coal and oil (although this claim is now being contested by those seeking more radical measures to mitigate climate change). Between the mid-1980s and 2018, global consumption of natural gas rose by 134%, compared with 56% for oil and 81% for coal; use of natural gas for power generation increased more than fourfold during this period, compared with two-and-a-half times for coal and a one-third contraction for oil.

Egypt took advantage of the rising natural-gas consumption for a brief period in the late 2000s, as its exports climbed to a peak of almost 20 billion cubic metres (bcm) in 2009. The speedy development of the Damietta and Idku terminals enabled Egypt to climb to seventh place, just behind Australia, among global liquefied natural gas (LNG) exporters in 2009. However, within a few years it had to resort to importing LNG as its production went into decline. The post-2011 political turbulence was partly to blame for this reversal in its energy fortunes, but there were other factors, including the build-up of arrears on payments due to international oil companies from Egyptian utilities, as well as unattractive investment terms, notably a cap of US$2.65/million British thermal units (mmBtu) on the price of the gas sold by the operators to the government.

## Seismic shifts in the natural-gas market

The world gas market has been transformed in the past decade. The most important developments have been the twin surges of US production and Chinese demand, together with the rise of Australia to challenge Qatar for the top position in the world ranking of LNG exporters. China has accounted for roughly one-fifth of the increase in the volume of world gas demand since 2008, while one-third of the increase in global supply has come from the US. Gas production in the US rose by 85 bcm in 2018 alone – a volume that is greater than the combined output of Egypt and Israel during that year (59 bcm and 10 bcm, respectively). In the meantime, Australia's LNG production has quadrupled in the past decade to more than 70m tonnes per year, which is roughly equivalent to 95 bcm, and the US is poised to move into third place, behind Australia and Qatar, among global LNG exporters. Among other actual and potential rivals to the Eastern Mediterranean, Russia has forged ahead with expansion of its export outlets, through both new pipelines and investment in LNG plants, and several African countries (notably Mauritania, Mozambique and Senegal) are looking to join the ranks of major exporters, while Iran remains a land of missed opportunity, having failed to capitalise on its huge reserves of natural gas.

Nevertheless, the Eastern Mediterranean has some advantages as an aspiring player in the global gas market. These include the infrastructure that has already been developed in Egypt; the region's location, with established shipping routes to both Europe and Asia; and the prospect of discovering more gas fields on the scale of Israel's Leviathan and Egypt's Zohr (discovered in 2010 and 2015 respectively). The vision presented at the launch of the Egypt-based Eastern Mediterranean Gas Forum in early 2018 – involving Cyprus, Egypt, Greece, Israel, Italy, Jordan and the Palestinian Authority – entailed the creation of a hub that would pool the region's gas resources for the benefit of both consumers and producers, while fostering prosperity in countries that are the source of unmanaged migration to Europe, and helping Europe to diversify its sources of supply and reduce reliance on Russia. One of the keys to realising that vision will be whether Egypt can maintain the recent momentum of its gas-industry development.

The revival of the Egyptian gas industry started in late 2013 when the government took steps to address the lack of adequate incentives for international oil companies to invest. The price cap was lifted on a case-by-case basis, payment arrears were whittled down and commercial terms were made more flexible. The effectiveness of this approach was reflected in the speed with which the Zohr field, the discovery of which was announced by oil and gas company Eni in mid-2015, was developed, with the first gas flowing towards the end of 2017. It had a similar impact on BP's West Nile Delta project, which had been marking time since the late 2000s. The final phases are now set to come on stream by the end of 2019. Egypt's production bottomed out at 40 bcm in 2016, before climbing to almost 60 bcm in 2018. It is likely to reach at least 70 bcm in 2019.

Egypt's gas exports – LNG and by pipeline to Jordan – are starting to increase, but there is a risk that the volumes available for export will be eroded by a combination of field depletion and rising consumption. The rate of depletion is particularly high in the fields in shallow water off the central and western Nile Delta. Prospects for the Zohr field are more positive, but the period of plateau production could be shortened if the government insists on raising output to about 32 bcm per year from an initial target of 27 bcm per year. The recent rapid expansion in Egypt's gas-fired power-generating capacity has pushed up consumption, but the rate of increase should slow in the early 2020s as more solar and wind capacity comes on stream. One way in which the surplus can be maintained is through new discoveries, to compensate for depletion. Exploration activity in Egypt remains at a healthy level, but there have recently been disappointments, notably with the discovery of the Noor field off the north coast of Sinai, which was initially touted as a Zohr-scale find, but has recently been downgraded.

## The Egyptian hub scenario

Assuming that Egypt will at best maintain a rough equilibrium between production and consumption in the medium term, exports from the Eastern Mediterranean can still be sustained through the addition of gas from neighbouring countries to the mix.

The first such addition is supposed to come from Israel. The Tamar field largely covers domestic demand, so in net terms the output from the Leviathan field (with reserves of 620 bcm) is available for export. Production from Leviathan has been subject to delays, but it is hoped that it could begin in late 2019 and soon reach 12 bcm per year. Agreements are in place for some of this gas to be delivered to Jordan. Another market is Egypt. In 2018 the main stakeholders in the Tamar and Leviathan fields agreed to sell 7 bcm of gas a year to an Egyptian company, to be delivered through the Eastern Mediterranean Gas (EMG) pipeline. The EMG was built in the mid-2000s to transport Egyptian gas to Israel, although it was shut down in 2011 because of explosions on a feeder line and declining Egyptian output. Delivery of Leviathan gas to Egypt via the EMG pipeline will boost the overall supply in Egypt, thereby enabling operators such as Eni, BP and Shell to export more gas through the Idku and Damietta LNG terminals. However, the start of these supplies has been repeatedly delayed, amid reports of regulatory issues to be resolved in Israel, and of a lack of capacity in the internal Israeli pipeline system. Furthermore, little information has been divulged on the price of the gas.

The planned start-up has coincided with a sharp fall in prices in the main global markets – the Title Transfer Facility (TTF) in Europe, Henry Hub in the US and the Japan/Korea Marker (JKM) for spot LNG trades in Asia. The TTF price is the most likely to be used as a benchmark for the price for the Israeli gas sales, but in mid-2019 it was questionable whether this price would cover the costs of production and transportation. The economics of the Israeli pipeline deal could change if gas prices were to recover, but with demand growth easing in Asia and higher volumes of US LNG on the way, a significant price rally seems unlikely. Another option for operators in Israel is to link their fields directly by sub-sea pipelines to the Egyptian offshore infrastructure. However, for the time being, the Israeli operators appear to have committed to the EMG pipeline, which could be expanded in the future if necessary.

A direct tie-in to Egypt across the maritime border is also one of the most attractive options for the three large fields recently discovered in Cypriot waters to the north of Zohr: Aphrodite (2011), Calypso (2018) and Glaucus-1 (2019). The Egyptian and Cypriot governments have already signed natural-gas cooperation agreements that would allow the construction of cross-border infrastructure to transport the gas to the Idku and Damietta plants for export. The commercial feasibility of such a deal is helped by the fact that Shell (the majority stakeholder in Idku) has a stake in the Aphrodite field, and that Eni, which is the operator of Zohr and holds a stake in the Damietta LNG plant, is the operator of the Calypso field. Altogether, the three Cypriot fields could eventually supply 15–20 bcm per year to the Egyptian LNG plants. With the addition of supplies from Israel, this could entail up to 30 bcm per year being added to the Egyptian gas mix, potentially justifying the construction of additional LNG trains at Idku and Damietta. Such a scenario is relatively optimistic, but factors in the likelihood of delays and other operational setbacks.

## International political challenges

Political factors are a critical consideration. Within Egypt, cooperation with Israel remains controversial because of the long legacy of conflict and strong popular sympathy with the Palestinians. However, during

## Gas in the Eastern Mediterranean

In the last ten years, major gas finds in the Eastern Mediterranean raised the prospect of a change in patterns of regional cooperation and rivalry. However, disputed exclusive economic zones (EEZs) along with the highly volatile security landscape and abundance of domestic conflicts pose major challenges to large-scale gas production in this region. The biggest potential gas-trading partners in the region, notably the EU and Turkey, remain unconvinced about fully developing gas projects, despite the plentiful presence of gas fields.

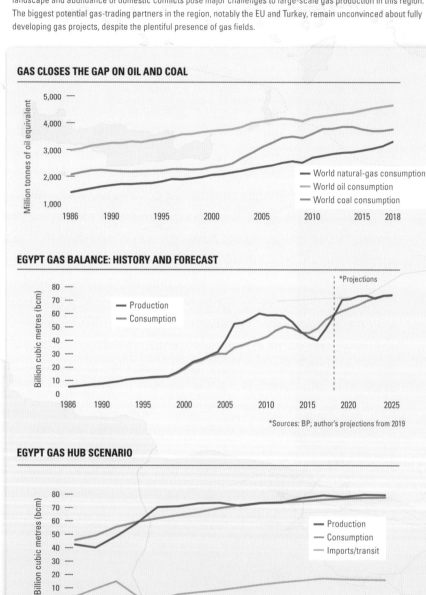

### GAS CLOSES THE GAP ON OIL AND COAL

— World natural-gas consumption
— World oil consumption
— World coal consumption

### EGYPT GAS BALANCE: HISTORY AND FORECAST

— Production
— Consumption

*Projections

*Sources: BP; author's projections from 2019

### EGYPT GAS HUB SCENARIO

— Production
— Consumption
— Imports/transit

Sources: Author projections; Bloomberg; BP Statistical Review of World Energy, 2019; European Network of Transmission Systems Operators for Gas (ENTSOG); TEKMOR Monitor

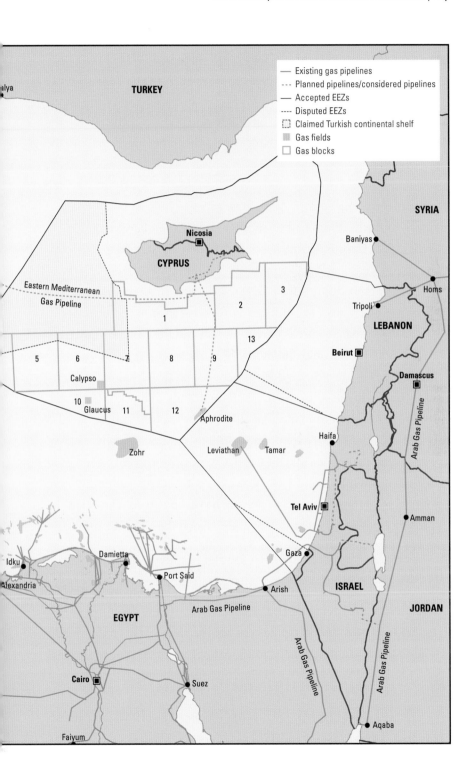

the era of President Abdel Fattah Al-Sisi, military cooperation with Israel has developed strongly in the context of the north Sinai insurgency, and the gas-pipeline project is conceived as a strategic connection, in which, on the Egyptian side, many of the stakeholders have ties to the military and intelligence establishment. In any political settlement to the Palestinian issue, the Gaza Marine gas field could be integrated into the Israel–Egypt network.

More broadly, European and US policymakers have conceived the development of an Eastern Mediterranean gas hub as being complementary to the development of security cooperation between the main stakeholders – Cyprus, Egypt, Israel and, potentially, Greece – as a counterweight to Russia and an increasingly troublesome Turkey. However, the notion of embedding such a strategic alliance in a pipeline from the Eastern Mediterranean to southern Europe is fanciful: the volumes of gas available for such a project are too small and the costs are much too high to render it a feasible option for the European market.

Turkey has made clear its dissatisfaction with the Cypriot gas operations by deploying its navy to impede Eni's drilling in Block 3 (bordering Lebanon's exclusive economic zone–EEZ) in early 2018. Turkey has also declared its intention to commence drilling off the western coast of Cyprus. It has maintained that the Greek Cypriot government had no right to declare its own EEZ and to seek to exploit resources within it before a political resolution of the Cyprus issue has been agreed. However, the Cyprus EEZ has been recognised by the UN, and the Greek Cypriot government has given assurances that any political settlement would respect the rights of Turkish Cypriots to any benefits accruing from natural-gas resources. Turkey, for its part, has thus far refused to sign up to the UN Convention on the Law of the Sea, and has not made any definitive moves to establish its own EEZ in the Eastern Mediterranean. Given the weight of international support for Cyprus's natural-gas endeavours, Turkish opposition is unlikely to deter further progress, although Turkey could seek to exploit the issue for leverage elsewhere.

The other principal territorial dispute affecting Eastern Mediterranean gas is that between Israel and Lebanon over their maritime boundary.

Israel's version of the boundary is based on charting a line from the land border on the coast to the points where its sea border with Cyprus joins the maritime border agreed by Cyprus with Lebanon. The furthest point out to sea lies about 17 kilometres to the north of the line that Lebanon calculates as being correct. This means that a narrow wedge of about 856 square kilometres is in dispute. Block 9, one of two exploration permits issued by the Lebanese government in 2018 to a consortium of Total, Eni and Novatek, includes about 145 sq. km of the disputed zone, account-ing for 8% of the block's total area. Failure to resolve the dispute would not prevent the consortium from proceeding with its drilling plans, but it could affect future development if a gas discovery was made stretching into the contested area, or indeed over the border. The US has mediated between Israel and Lebanon on this issue since 2012. In mid-2019 the Israeli and Lebanese governments indicated that they were prepared to take the issue to international arbitration, with the US acting as an observer. This has prompted comments that the common inter-est of Israel and Lebanon in developing offshore gas resources could help to reduce military tensions between Israel and the Iranian-backed Hizbullah, which is the most powerful force on the Lebanese political scene. Such a trade-off is unlikely while Israel and Iran continue to view each other as strategic threats, and as long as Iran remains committed to reinforcing its strategic allies in Lebanon and Syria.

The Syrian government has taken steps to assess prospects for natural gas in its Mediterranean waters. Its initial seismic surveys in the mid-2000s were not sufficiently attractive to garner interest in an offer of exploration acreage, but a block was awarded to Russia's Soyuzneftegaz in 2011 in a second-bid round. The company withdrew on the eve of Russia's military intervention in Syria in 2015, but the government has recently said that exploration activity will soon recommence. Any major discovery would be welcomed by the Syrian authorities, but it is doubtful whether they could mobilise sufficient investment to develop it unless a comprehensive political settlement is achieved.

The high point in expectations for Eastern Mediterranean gas came with the Leviathan and Zohr discoveries, which gave substance to the

230 | Middle East and North Africa

assessment of this region as a world-class gas basin that could transform the European energy market. It has since become clear that the identification of actual and potential reserves is no guarantee of commercial success. The companies that are engaged in offshore gas exploration and development in Israel and Cyprus have a reasonable chance of finding a worthwhile market in Egypt or via Egyptian LNG plants, but the returns are unlikely to be spectacular unless the global surplus of supply over demand eases and prices stage a significant recovery. Some cargoes of LNG from the Eastern Mediterranean will reach the European market, but they will be competing with LNG from the US, Russia and Qatar, as well as with Russian (and, to a small extent, Azerbaijani) gas delivered by pipeline. The relatively modest financial return that can realistically be garnered from Eastern Mediterranean gas means that this resource has limited scope to help resolve conflicts, or to ignite or exacerbate conflicts.

# Russia and Eurasia: Drivers of Strategic Change

- In Russia, President Vladimir Putin has taken further steps to insulate the country from external pressure, including the establishment of a 'sovereign internet'. Protests increased in the context of economic stagnation and a decline in Putin's approval rating; the challenge was primarily to Putin's authority, rather than his hold on power.

- Ukrainian politics continued to surprise, with the election by a huge margin of a political novice, the actor Volodymyr Zelensky, as president in April 2019. His election underscored the continuing hunger in Ukrainian society for a change from the oligarchic system of politics, although effecting such change is a formidable task.

- While the conflict in Donbas remained in stalemate, Russia and Ukraine clashed in the Sea of Azov as Russia opened a bridge over the Kerch Strait and sought to turn Azov, where Ukraine had opened a naval base, into a Russian lake. Russia seeks to use the conflict to destabilise Ukraine and frustrate Ukrainian efforts to achieve political and economic consolidation, or westernisation.

- In Kazakhstan, Nursultan Nazarbayev brought his 30-year presidency to an end, handing the post to the speaker of the Senate. The transition occurred peacefully, although Nazarbayev retains extensive powers and the full test of any transition may not come until he dies.

## DEMOGRAPHY

POPULATION AND MEDIAN AGE
(IMF, April 2019; UN Department of Economic and Social Affairs, Population Division, 2019)

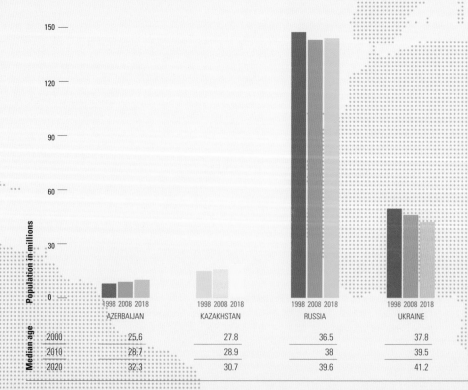

| Median age | AZERBAIJAN | KAZAKHSTAN | RUSSIA | UKRAINE |
|---|---|---|---|---|
| 2000 | 25.6 | 27.8 | 36.5 | 37.8 |
| 2010 | 28.7 | 28.9 | 38 | 39.5 |
| 2020 | 32.3 | 30.7 | 39.6 | 41.2 |

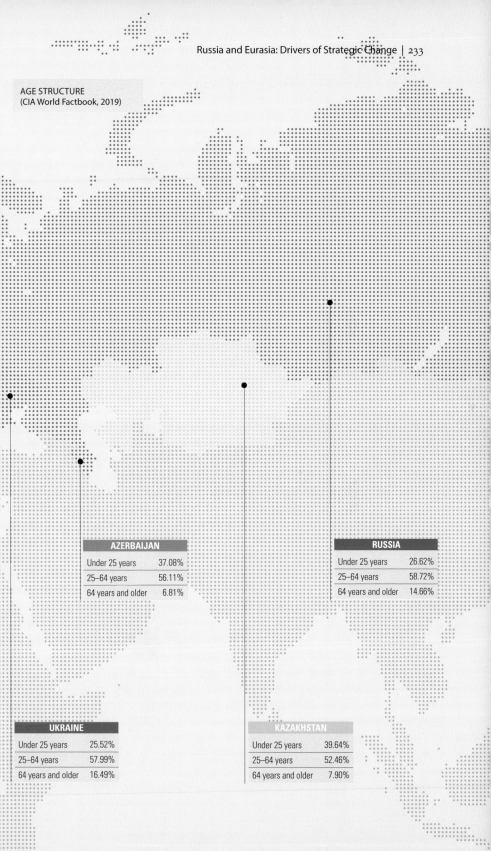

AGE STRUCTURE
(CIA World Factbook, 2019)

**AZERBAIJAN**

| Under 25 years | 37.08% |
|---|---|
| 25–64 years | 56.11% |
| 64 years and older | 6.81% |

**RUSSIA**

| Under 25 years | 26.62% |
|---|---|
| 25–64 years | 58.72% |
| 64 years and older | 14.66% |

**UKRAINE**

| Under 25 years | 25.52% |
|---|---|
| 25–64 years | 57.99% |
| 64 years and older | 16.49% |

**KAZAKHSTAN**

| Under 25 years | 39.64% |
|---|---|
| 25–64 years | 52.46% |
| 64 years and older | 7.90% |

# ECONOMICS AND DEVELOPMENT

## GDP AT PPP
Constant 2011 international dollars (IMF, April 2019)

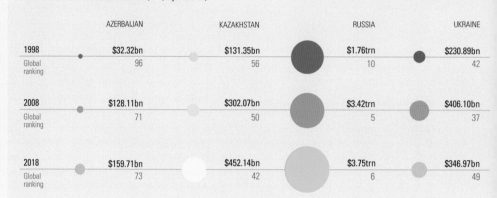

| | AZERBAIJAN | KAZAKHSTAN | RUSSIA | UKRAINE |
|---|---|---|---|---|
| **1998** | $32.32bn | $131.35bn | $1.76trn | $230.89bn |
| Global ranking | 96 | 56 | 10 | 42 |
| **2008** | $128.11bn | $302.07bn | $3.42trn | $406.10bn |
| Global ranking | 71 | 50 | 5 | 37 |
| **2018** | $159.71bn | $452.14bn | $3.75trn | $346.97bn |
| Global ranking | 73 | 42 | 6 | 49 |

## GDP PER CAPITA AT PPP
Constant 2011 international dollars (IMF, April 2019)

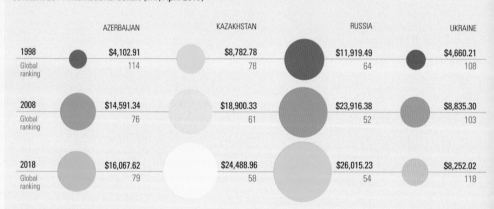

| | AZERBAIJAN | KAZAKHSTAN | RUSSIA | UKRAINE |
|---|---|---|---|---|
| **1998** | $4,102.91 | $8,782.78 | $11,919.49 | $4,660.21 |
| Global ranking | 114 | 78 | 64 | 108 |
| **2008** | $14,591.34 | $18,900.33 | $23,916.38 | $8,835.30 |
| Global ranking | 76 | 61 | 52 | 103 |
| **2018** | $16,067.62 | $24,488.96 | $26,015.23 | $8,252.02 |
| Global ranking | 79 | 58 | 54 | 118 |

## HUMAN DEVELOPMENT INDEX (HDI)
(UN Development Programme, 2019)

| | Global ranking 1998 | Global ranking 2008 | Global ranking 2018 |
|---|---|---|---|
| AZERBAIJAN | 86 | 84 | 80 |
| KAZAKHSTAN | 62 | 63 | 61 |
| RUSSIA | 55 | 56 | 49 |
| UKRAINE | 70 | 78 | 88 |

Scale: 0.0 0.2 0.4 0.6 0.8 1.0

 Global ranking 1998  Global ranking 2008 Global ranking 2018

Score between 0 and 1, where 0 denotes a low level of development and 1 a high level of development.

# INTERNATIONAL INTEGRATION

## TRADE
Exports of goods and commercial services, constant 2010 US dollars
(World Trade Organization, 2019)

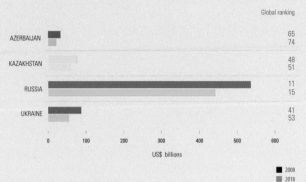

Global ranking

| | |
|---|---|
| AZERBAIJAN | 65 / 74 |
| KAZAKHSTAN | 48 / 51 |
| RUSSIA | 11 / 15 |
| UKRAINE | 41 / 53 |

US$ billions

■ 2008
■ 2018

## INTERNATIONAL NETWORK
Total number of diplomatic missions, 2017
Lowy Institute Global Diplomacy Index
(2017)

| | Missions abroad | | Global ranking |
|---|---|---|---|
| AZERBAIJAN | n/a | | |
| KAZAKHSTAN | n/a | | |
| RUSSIA | 242 | ✳ | 4 |
| UKRAINE | n/a | | |

# DIPLOMACY AND DEFENCE

## DEFENCE BUDGET
Constant 2010 US dollars (Military Balance 1998,
and Military Balance+)

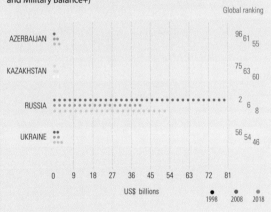

Global ranking

| | |
|---|---|
| AZERBAIJAN | 96 / 61 / 55 |
| KAZAKHSTAN | 75 / 63 / 60 |
| RUSSIA | 2 / 6 / 8 |
| UKRAINE | 56 / 54 / 46 |

US$ billions

● 1998   ● 2008   ● 2018

## OFFICIAL DEVELOPMENT AID
Constant 2015 US dollars (OECD, 2019)

| | 1998 | 2008 | 2018 |
|---|---|---|---|
| AZERBAIJAN | n/a | n/a | n/a |
| KAZAKHSTAN | n/a | n/a | n/a |
| RUSSIA | n/a | n/a | n/a[a] |
| UKRAINE | n/a | n/a | n/a |

[a]in 2017, Russia's foreign-aid budget was $1.189bn

## POLITICAL SYSTEM
(Economist Intelligence Unit, 2008, 2018)

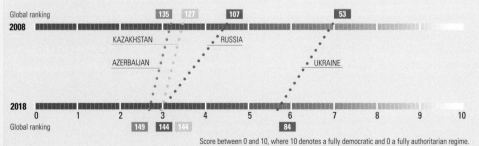

Global ranking
**2008**

| 135 | 127 | 107 | 53 |

KAZAKHSTAN   RUSSIA

AZERBAIJAN   UKRAINE

**2018**

0  1  2  3  4  5  6  7  8  9  10

Global ranking

| 149 | 144 | 144 | 84 |

Score between 0 and 10, where 10 denotes a fully democratic and 0 a fully authoritarian regime.

©IISS

Bering Sea

*Arctic Ocean*

*Pacific Ocean*

Novosibirskiye Ostrova

Severnaya Zemlya

Zemlya Frantsa Iosifa

Novaya Zemlya

RUSSIAN FEDERATION

KAZAKHSTAN

Astana

■ Moscow

Bishkek ■
KYRGYZSTAN

Tashkent ■
UZBEKISTAN

TAJIKISTAN
■ Dushanbe

TURKMENISTAN
Ashgabat ■

Baku ■
Tbilisi ■
GEORGIA
Yerevan ■
ARMENIA
AZERBAIJAN

Minsk ■
BELARUS

Kiev ■
UKRAINE
Chisinau ■
MOLDOVA

Kaliningrad
(Russia)

# Chapter 7

# Russia and Eurasia

## 2018–19 Review

The security situation in Eastern Europe deteriorated further in the year to mid-2019 as the five-year conflict between Russia and Ukraine spilled over into direct naval clashes in the Sea of Azov. Russia's relations with the United States and European Union remained highly adversarial and by mid-2019 the conditions for a new dispute over gas supply to Europe were crystallising. The system of US–Russia arms control and confidence-building measures was further weakened following the collapse of the Intermediate-Range Nuclear Forces (INF) Treaty, raising the risk of a new arms race. Russia's domestic policy continued to focus on insulating the country from Western pressure and tightening social controls, amid signs that public support for President Vladimir Putin, and the regime as a whole, had fallen significantly.

### The conflict in Ukraine

The conflict in the eastern Ukrainian region of Donbas continued at a low intensity, although the OSCE Special Monitoring Mission reported a decline in armed violence and a reduction in ceasefire violations in 2018 compared with the previous year. The Line of Contact between the Ukrainian army and Russian-backed paramilitaries has remained largely static since early 2015, when the second Minsk ceasefire agreement was signed, and armed forces are engaged largely in artillery and gunfire exchanges from well-embedded positions.

While the conflict on land has remained in stalemate, tensions have been rising off the Donbas coast in the Sea of Azov, linked to the Black Sea to the south by the narrow Kerch Strait and bounded by Ukraine, Russia and the contested Crimean Peninsula. The annexation of Crimea in 2014 gave Russia control of both sides of the Kerch Strait. In May 2018, Russia completed a bridge over the strait, breaking Ukraine's overland blockade of the Crimean Peninsula and creating impediments to Ukrainian shipping. The Kerch Bridge is just 33 metres high, preventing large container ships from passing through the Strait. At the same time, Russia stepped up inspections of Ukrainian and third-country vessels, causing major losses for Ukrainian exporters and disrupting access to the eastern ports of Mariupol and Berdiansk. The ports handle around 6% of Ukraine's exports and are critical to the operations of the remaining major industry on both sides of the contested Donbas region.

Both Russia and Ukraine increased their military presence in the region. Russia redeployed several ships from the Caspian to the Sea of Azov via inland waterways. In September 2018, the Ukrainian government announced the opening of a new naval base in Berdiansk and sailed two naval vessels through the Kerch Strait, its first deployment in the Sea of Azov since the annexation of Crimea. In November 2018, rising tensions spilled into open conflict when Russian border guards opened fire on two Ukrainian gun boats and a tug as they passed through the Kerch Strait, capturing the vessels and detaining 24 Ukrainian sailors. The incident marked a dangerous escalation of the conflict in eastern Ukraine. This was the first time that the Russian armed forces, which denies it is a party to the war in Donbas, has openly attacked Ukrainian forces. Petro Poroshenko, then Ukrainian president, responded by declaring martial law for a period of 30 days in ten regions bordering Russia, the Black Sea and the breakaway territory of Transdniestria in Moldova, where Russian troops are also deployed.

The clash in the Sea of Azov represents an intensification of Russia's conflict with Ukraine, but Russia's broader strategy remains unchanged. This is to use the conflict as a pressure point to disrupt Ukraine's politics, weaken its economy and prevent the consolidation of a pro-Western state that could conceivably seek EU or NATO membership. Russia's strategic interest is not currently served by a full-scale war with Ukraine or the full recognition of the breakaway 'republics' in Donbas. However, the latter option remains open and Russia has been gradually enhancing its formal engagement with the territories. In April 2019, the Russian government announced that it would provide passports to residents of the Donbas and Luhansk People's Republics on humanitarian grounds. The naval clash in the Sea of Azov underlines Russia's determination to maintain military dominance of the entire eastern Black Sea region. From Russia's perspective, Ukraine's blockade of the Crimean Peninsula and its proposals to develop military infrastructure in the Sea of Azov represent a serious strategic threat. If Ukraine were to make substantive progress towards NATO membership, Russia might seek to take full control of the Azov seaboard to secure its access to the Crimean Peninsula from the Russian mainland.

## More of the same from Ukraine's new president?

Poroshenko's decision to declare martial law was motivated in part by domestic political considerations ahead of the presidential elections in March 2019. Over the past five years, Poroshenko's administration has made significant progress in macroeconomic stabilisation. However, this has been achieved through a punishing series of utility-price rises and sharp cuts in public spending, while investment and economic growth have remained weak.

With little domestic record to run on, Poroshenko sought to revive his flagging ratings by adopting an increasingly nationalist line, pushing forward efforts to unpick all diplomatic, economic and cultural ties with Russia. In mid-September, Ukraine abrogated the 1997 Treaty on Friendship, Cooperation and Partnership, which could complicate efforts to challenge the contravention of Ukrainian sovereignty by Russia in international courts. His administration scored a major diplomatic victory in November 2018, when Patriarch Bartholomew, the Ecumenical Patriarch of Constantinople, granted autocephaly to the Ukrainian Church. This allowed for the creation of a newly constituted Ukrainian Orthodox Church that will be independent of the Russian Orthodox Church.

Despite this diplomatic coup, Poroshenko suffered a heavy defeat in the presidential election, losing by a 50-percentage-point margin in the second round to Volodymyr Zelensky, a comedian and actor with no political experience. Zelensky's unexpected and rapid rise to the presidency, which benefited from strong support from media controlled by the controversial tycoon Ihor Kolomoisky, is indicative of the deep public disillusionment with the failure of the Poroshenko administration to tackle corruption and institutional dysfunction and deliver an improvement in living standards. In common with other populists, Zelensky has pledged to purge the state of elite corruption. However, several key appointments, such as Andriy Bohdan, the new head of the presidential administration, have close ties to Kolomoisky, calling into question the new president's commitment to breaking the deep ties between business and the state that have hollowed out Ukraine's institutions.

Early indications suggest Zelensky's presidential style will be less unconventional than his election campaign, and there is unlikely to be any major shift in relations with Russia. Zelensky took a more pragmatic line on Russia during the campaign, suggesting that he would do more to reach out to residents of the breakaway territories in Donbas. Since assuming office, he has stressed continuity in foreign policy, underlining the government's commitment to transatlantic integration and maintaining a tough line on Russia. Ukraine remains heavily dependent on external financing and the support of its Western allies. In October, the government agreed a new 14-month standby financial agreement with the International Monetary Fund. Debt service in 2019 is set to account for more than a third of the central budget. In late June, a month after Zelensky's inauguration, Ukraine withdrew from the Parliamentary Assembly of the Council of Europe after the council voted to lift restrictions on Russia's participation, imposed after the annexation of Crimea.

The first major diplomatic test for Zelensky is likely to be reaching a new gas-transit agreement with Russia when the current ten-year deal expires at the end of 2019. Negotiations are complicated by several factors. Russia is seeking to increase its transit capacity, bypassing Ukraine through the construction of Nord Stream II, a gas pipeline to Germany under the Baltic Sea, and TurkStream, which runs to Turkey and southern Europe under the Black Sea. In the first half of 2019, it became evident that Nord Stream II would not be completed before 2020, in part because of delays in the issuance of licences by the Danish authorities. At trilateral talks in January 2019, Ukraine pushed for a long-term deal, but with a substantial increase in transit capacity due to come online in the early 2020s, the Russian side is seeking only a framework contract that can be prolonged each season, allowing it to substantially reduce transit volumes through Ukraine in the future. This could render Ukraine's extensive gas-transit system unprofitable and lower its leverage in future energy negotiations. Trust between the parties is very low, owing to both the broader diplomatic context and an ongoing dispute over the existing gas-transit deal, which was put to international arbitration in 2018. There is therefore a risk of another gas-transit dispute in early 2020 similar to that of 2009, when Gazprom temporarily cut off supplies to Ukraine, leading to shortages across much of the EU.

## A rare case of cooperation

While Russia and the West remain fundamentally opposed over Ukraine, the political crisis in Moldova provided a rare alliance of interests between Russia and the EU. Parliamentary elections in February delivered an inconclusive result, with the vote split between the pro-Russian Socialists, aligned with President Igor Dodon; the ACUM bloc, an alliance of pro-European parties; and the incumbent Democratic Party (PDM), headed by Vladimir Plahotniuc, Moldova's most powerful businessman who has wielded control over large parts of the state.

For several years, Plahotniuc had succeeded in securing Western support by positioning himself in opposition to Russia and Dodon's presidency. After months of uncertainty, ACUM and the Socialists entered an unexpected coalition in early June to form a new government with the backing of both Dmitry Kozak, the Russian special representative to Moldova, and Johannes Khan, the EU Commissioner for European Neighbourhood Policy and Enlargement. Apparently acting under the direction of Plahotniuc's allies, the Constitutional Court ruled that the government had been formed after the three-month deadline and temporarily relieved Dodon, who had approved the new government, of his duties. However, following domestic protests and under strong pressure from Russia, the EU and the US – all of which recognised the legitimacy of the new government – the PDM was forced to resign on 14 June, allowing the new government to be confirmed.

## Russia's relations with the West remain adversarial

Despite the brief alignment of interests in Moldova, Russia's relations with the West remained highly adversarial over the year to June 2019. In August 2018, US senators introduced a new sanctions bill to punish Russia for interference in the 2016 US presidential elections, including measures to limit the operations of Russian state banks and a ban on the sale and trade in Russian sovereign debt. The threat of new sanctions put Russian markets and the rouble under pressure, forcing the Russian Ministry of Finance to pause its monthly purchases of foreign assets to support the currency. Despite weak domestic demand, the central bank raised interest rates twice in the second half of 2018. At the St Petersburg International Economic Forum in June, Putin attacked US measures against Nord Stream and China's Huawei and warned that the fragmentation of the global economy could lead to 'endless conflict, trade wars, and maybe not just trade wars'.

On 1 February, the US announced that it would begin the process of withdrawing from the INF Treaty with Russia, which bans the use of land-based short- and intermediate-range ballistic and cruise missiles, and launchers. US officials have indicated for several years that they believe Russia is in violation of the treaty owing to the deployment of the 9M729 cruise missile – known by NATO as the SSC-8 – which is believed to have a range within the 500–5,500-kilometre spectrum proscribed by the INF Treaty.

The demise of the INF Treaty raises several security issues. From Russia's perspective, the deployment by the US of intermediate-range missiles in Europe would present a major threat, although the US is yet to deploy or test such weapons. In December 2018, Russian Chief of the General Staff General Valery Gerasimov warned that European countries hosting US intermediate-range missiles would be the target of Russian responsive measures. The abrogation of the INF Treaty increases the risk that the US and Russia will not renew the New Strategic Arms Reduction Treaty (New START), which limits the number of long-range nuclear warheads, when the current treaty expires in 2021. Following a meeting with Putin in mid-May in Sochi, US Secretary of State Mike Pompeo said that the two countries had agreed to establish an expert group to discuss an extension. There is no certainty that a deal will be reached given the low level of trust between the two sides, the Trump administration's sceptical view of international arms control and Russian anxieties over developments in US conventional weaponry, which it believes could compromise its nuclear deterrent.

Geopolitical competition with the West is shaping Russia's economic and social agenda in far-reaching ways. Over the past year the government continued to pursue a comprehensive strategy to insulate the country from external pressure. At the start of May, Putin signed into law a bill to create a 'sovereign internet', aimed at ensuring that Russian websites can function independently of the rest of the global infrastructure. The legislation is part of a comprehensive strategy to further insulate the country from Western pressure and increase social control. This reflected both the regime's deep sense of technological vulnerability and long-standing anxieties over social stability. The most notable domestic political development of the past year was the sustained decline in reported public support for Putin, which has now fallen below the levels recorded before 2014, suggesting that the mobilisation effect from the annexation of Crimea has now dissipated.

Faced with the threat of further sanctions, the Russian government also developed a strategy to further 'de-dollarise' its economy and develop new channels for international transactions that avoid expo-

244 | Russia and Eurasia

sure to the US financial system. Responding to the threat of expanded US sanctions, the Bank of Russia substantially reduced its dollar assets, while increasing holdings of euros, gold and yuan. The impact of this strategy has to date been limited – over 75% of its trade with China was in dollars in 2018 – but it may gain in salience in the coming years given that both the eurozone countries and China are seeking to increase the international role of their currencies.

## Russia's delicate balance in the Middle East

Over the past year, Russia further consolidated its position as a key regional power broker in the Middle East, boosted by the US announcement in December of a drawdown of troops from Syria. Russia is seeking to advance its role in Syria from stabilising the regime of Bashar al-Assad to post-conflict state-building and reconstruction. Russia has proven adept at maintaining functional or even positive relations with all states in the region, but its support for Assad's brutal military operations limits its credibility as mediator for large parts of the opposition. In January, Russia hosted the Congress of Syrian National Dialogue in Sochi, but the event did not include many armed Syrian opposition and Kurdish groups.

The interests of the state parties to the conflict will also continue to pose major challenges for Russian diplomacy. It remains unclear how the Kremlin can balance Iran's long-term presence in Syria with Israeli demands for a complete Iranian withdrawal. This dilemma was thrown into sharp relief in September, when a Syrian anti-aircraft system accidentally downed a Russian Il-20 after being triggered by Israeli airstrikes on Iranian and Syrian forces. This is the second time that a Russian military plane has been downed by a neighbouring state in Syria after Turkish fighter pilots fired on a Sukhoi Su-24 in 2015, and underlines the complexity and dangers of a conflict involving so many external powers. The rising risk of an outright military conflict between Iran and Israel or the US also poses a major challenge to Russia's carefully balanced regional diplomacy.

Russia's relations with Turkey continued to recover over the past year from the crisis of 2015. In June, President Recep Tayyip Erdogan confirmed plans to purchase Russia's advanced S-400 anti-aircraft system, despite warnings from the US that it could be excluded from the F-35 fighter-jet programme. Nevertheless, major differences remain over the role of Kurdish forces along the border with Turkey, and the future status of Idlib province, and adjoining parts of northern Hama and western Aleppo, which is the last bastion of the opposition and includes the largest city outside government control. In mid-September 2018, Turkey and Russia reached an agreement to establish a new de-escalation zone patrolled by Russian and Turkish military police. In exchange for Russia restraining Syrian government forces, Turkey would force extremist groups, in particular Hayat Tahrir al-Sham (HTS), out of the region. The agreement has been poorly observed, and Russia has complained that Turkey has done too little to manage the extremist threat. The Sochi deal has likely only temporarily delayed a full-scale operation to take Idlib, which would lead to high civilian casualties and deepen the refugee crisis.

## Another authoritarian transition in Central Asia

In March 2019, Kazakhstan, which has hosted several rounds of Russian-led negotiations on Syria, began a process of political transition when Nursultan Nazarbayev unexpectedly stepped down as president after 30 years in power. He was replaced by Kassym-Jomart Tokayev, the Senate speaker, whose position was confirmed by a snap election in June. The transition was carefully managed to allow Nazarbayev to retain influence over the political system and ensure elite stability. Nazarbayev retains a special constitutional status as Elbasy, or leader of the nation, and lifelong chairmanship of the national-security council. He has retained a prominent role in national politics in the early months of Tokayev's presidency, including attending a summit of the Eurasian Economic Union (EEU) in May. To date, there has been little evidence of major elite turnover or a redivision of major assets. Regardless of how much real power Tokayev currently holds – and this could change over time – the presidential succession is unlikely to lead to major changes in foreign policy, over which there is widespread elite consensus.

As in Uzbekistan in 2016, the regime in Kazakhstan appears to have confounded assumptions that a change of leadership represents a moment of high political risk for the autocratic and personalised regimes in Eurasia. Some analysts have suggested that Nazarbayev's side-step from the presidency could offer a model for Putin when his current term ends in 2024. A new constitutional position for Putin could allow him to pass on the presidency to a chosen successor while retaining influence and protecting his family and networks. One pretext for constitutional change would be to appoint Putin as head of a reformatted 'Union State' between Russia and Belarus. The supranational union of the two states has existed on paper since 1997 but has had limited practical significance. This would be strongly resisted by the Belarusian elite. Moreover, the experience of Dmitry Medvedev's brief presidential stint, during which Putin occupied the prime minister's office, suggests that even a partial division of executive power could prove to be destabilising.

The Kazakhstan model may also not provide comprehensive proof of concept. Tokayev is unlikely to command the same level of popular support and elite loyalty as his predecessor, and his accession already appears to have emboldened public opposition. The presidential election in June 2019, where Tokayev faced no meaningful competition, provoked unexpectedly large protests.

# Putin's Russia: Consolidation and Manoeuvre

The Russian state sees more challenges than opportunities both at home and abroad. Domestically, the Kremlin faces a stagnant economy, a disaffected population and a nervous elite, at a time when the electoral calendar makes reform an unpalatable proposition. Internationally, despite enhanced strength and confidence, Moscow finds itself increasingly locked into conflict both locally and globally, and without the resources to pursue major new policy initiatives.

Despite the evident turbulence, however, policy circles in Moscow are remarkably self-assured. Taken individually, at least, all the challenges they face are problems they have seen before, so panic has not set in. Instead, policymakers have set about widening Moscow's room for manoeuvre, re-establishing its advantages and hedging against uncertainty.

## The domestic environment

For all the crises allegedly afflicting the Kremlin's grip on the country, all three of the challenges facing President Vladimir Putin by mid-2019 were, in one way or another, familiar. Firstly, the president's approval ratings – while much diminished from the period following the annexation of Crimea – were not appreciably below their mid-2013 level, when the situation seemed stable enough and territorial acquisition was not on the agenda. Secondly, the machinations and internecine jockeying for position ahead of the 2024 presidential elections, when Putin's rule runs into a constitutional roadblock, are difficult to distinguish from the run-up to the 2008 elections, the last time Putin faced term limits. And thirdly, the country's nearly stagnant economy creates problems not unlike those Putin and then-president Dmitry Medvedev faced in 2009–11 in the aftermath of the global financial crisis. The problem is that the confluence of these challenges has created an unprecedented situation for Putin and the system of governance he has engendered.

One of the peculiarities of modern authoritarianism is that autocrats want to be popular, for multiple reasons. Most modern authoritarian states hold multiparty elections, even if the electoral field is heavily tilted towards the incumbent authorities or – as in Russia – the state exerts control over all the political parties that matter, along with television stations and electoral commissions. George Washington University political scientist Henry E. Hale argues that authoritarian regimes – particularly in the post-Soviet space – are most likely to falter around the time of an election. They are then hardest pressed to demonstrate to their clients in the economic and political elite that they can maintain control and protect elite interests; when elites are unconvinced of the regime's capacity, they tend to defect.

Authoritarian leaders also recognise the importance of maintaining public legitimacy between electoral cycles, because elections are not really the way in which such regimes come by their power. The Kremlin therefore invests tremendous resources in running opinion polls and focus groups, as well as in managing the messaging Russian citizens receive through the media, political parties and public officials on all levels. The results of these efforts, however, are mixed. As the scholars Samuel Greene and Graeme Robertson argue, the Kremlin is most successful at convincing ordinary Russians of the lack of a viable alternative, and of the futility of public politics more broadly. Rarely is it able to instil any genuine enthusiasm for Putin himself, whom most Russians see as vaguely corrupt and primarily governing in the interests of oligarchs, according to polls by the independent Levada-Center.

In this context, the 'rally around the flag' effect that emerged after the annexation of Crimea – boosting Putin's approval ratings from 61% in November 2013 to 86% in June 2014 and a peak of 89% a year later, according to Levada-Center data – was an aberration. This significant jump temporarily reversed the fatigue that had gradually eroded Putin's popularity during his first 12 years in power. Most rallies around the flag, such as those enjoyed by Margaret Thatcher after the Falklands War or George W. Bush after 9/11, are short-lived. Putin's lasted until February 2018, when his approval ratings dipped below 80% for the first time since March 2014. His numbers went back up briefly, reinforced by his presidential re-election campaign and Russia's successful hosting of the FIFA World Cup, but promptly fell to a post-Crimea low of 64% by January 2019.

While Putin would certainly be happy to be more popular, he and his team have faced and survived such levels of support before. Even the protests of 2018–19 that seemed to roil the country – involving everything from municipal elections in Moscow and St Petersburg to waste-disposal projects in the Arctic and church construction in the Urals – are not particularly new. Russia has always had a degree of localised protest, and wherever the issues at hand can be safely divorced from national-level policy, the government is as likely as not to back down. No part of the public-opinion landscape in Russia at the time of writing appears to fall significantly outside the Kremlin's comfort zone.

The same, broadly speaking, appears to be true of the elite landscape, despite two interlocking challenges: the '2024 question' and the stagnant economy, both of which raise the stakes of competition. In 2024, Putin will come to the end of his second consecutive presidential term, at which point he will be constitutionally required to leave office. In 2008, the last time he faced this problem, he tapped Medvedev to stand in as president, while Putin became prime minister; four years later, they swapped roles. (Prior to 2012, Russian presidents served four-year terms. A constitutional amendment lengthened terms to six years just as Putin returned to office.) While this was not seen as a wholly positive experience – under Medvedev's rule a moderately anti-Putin group emerged within the ruling elite, while Putin's return provoked a large wave of street protests beginning in December 2011 and continuing until his inauguration in May 2018 – it allowed for the system of power to be preserved without risking the domestic and international legitimacy that flows from the country's nominally democratic constitution.

More importantly, however, what became known as the 2008–12 'tandem' prevented the fracturing of the Russian political and economic elite around competing visions of the country's future. For most of Putin's second term (2004–08), various business and bureaucratic interests attempted to position themselves to benefit from – or, failing that, to counteract – whatever post-Putin arrangement might have emerged. These groups, including ministers and regional power brokers, bankers and oilmen, plus the military and intelligence services, constantly form fluid coalitions to take advantage of opportunities for rent-seeking. As political turning points approach, however, they tend to become more skittish, worrying that an unfortunate shift in the power structure could leave them permanently locked out. By keeping the elite guessing about his intentions until some six months before the March 2008 election, and then by maintaining that uncertainty right up until he announced his impending return in September 2011, Putin avoided becoming a lame duck.

The same tactic is at work now. Putin is maintaining maximum ambiguity about his post-2024 plans, a stance in which he is expected to remain until late 2023. Any attempt to predict his intentions before then will be inherently futile. Ensuring the continuity of the system, however, will not assuage all elite anxieties. In 2007, such anxieties led to the outbreak of conflict between various parts of the security establishment, including the Federal Security Service (FSB) and the anti-narcotics service, most prominently. Twelve years later, the situation is complicated by a less liquid economy. With less money to go around, the stakes of elite competition are raised, and the Kremlin itself has fewer resources for firefighting. In part as a result, intra-regime conflict has increased, whether in the form of prosecutions or even armed robbery. The arrests of former open government minister Mikhail Abyzov and Volgograd Investigative Committee chief Mikhail Murzaev – and even Baring Vostok investor Michael Calvey – can be read in this context.

Absent another highly successful foreign adventure, neither mass nor elite sentiment can be significantly improved without an uptick in the economy. Ordinary Russian citizens are now in their fifth year of declining or flat real disposable incomes, as years of belt-tightening cut ever deeper into social welfare and consumers increasingly turn to debt, including from unscrupulous payday lenders, to make ends meet. What little economic growth there is – the IMF is predicting an anaemic 1.6% GDP growth in 2019, despite strong prices for Russia's commodity exports – tends to settle at the upper echelons of the economy, padding the profits of exporters who earn in dollars and spend in roubles. More domestically focused areas of the economy, including banks, retailers and homebuilders, continue to suffer and are increasingly either concentrated in a few hands, dominated by state ownership, or both. And what wealth is being generated for ordinary Russians and genuinely private businesses tends to settle in the larger cities – Moscow and St Petersburg in particular – that have more dynamic economies and easier access to capital for investment. The result is a widening of inequalities along multiple dividing lines.

As a result, Russian elites and ordinary citizens alike are badly in need of a new vision for the country's economic future – at precisely the time when the Kremlin is least inclined to provide one. Embarking on the kind of structural reform that would reduce corruption, increase competition and potentially boost production and wages would inevitably create new groups of winners and losers among the elite. Moreover, the elite (and perhaps also citizens) would interpret such moves as a strong signal of what is to come after 2024, thus provoking exactly the kind of political competition the Kremlin hopes to avoid.

If structural reform is off the table, two other options remain. One is to increase liquidity by borrowing more internationally, tapping into the sovereign reserves and/or loosening monetary policy. Indeed, Russia has returned to international debt markets, and even financial hawks like former finance minister and current Audit Chamber chair Alexei Kudrin have begun arguing for more fiscal stimulus. Thus far, however, the Kremlin has been extremely reluctant to go too far down this path, feeling that financial solvency is key to the country's sovereignty.

The last option – and perhaps the easiest – is to continue to squeeze the real economy. Although Putin promised to reverse cuts to social welfare as part of his re-election campaign, the general trend towards seeking efficiencies through moves such as closing and merging schools and hospitals and reducing university places continues. At the same time, the government has gradually sought to increase tax burdens. Given continued spending on major infrastructure projects, many of

252 | Russia and Eurasia

which are contracted to government-linked interests, this amounts to redistribution from the bottom to the top of the economy. That, in turn, suggests that the Kremlin is more confident in its ability to ride out mass opinion than to manage elite conflicts.

## The international environment

Given Russia's domestic political and economic challenges, the international agenda almost inevitably takes a back seat (barring an unforeseen crisis). That does not mean, however, that Moscow is likely to become significantly less active on the global stage. Rather, Russian foreign policy will be crafted and pursued in the service of domestic interests even more than usual.

Despite the flagging of the post-Crimea public-opinion rally and a growing public demand for the government to focus on domestic issues, foreign policy remains an integral part of the Kremlin's political-legitimation strategy. Polling data suggests that, while generally disaffected with the quality of governance at home, many Russians remain proud of Putin's international achievements, insist on maintaining control over Crimea, and support the ongoing wars in Ukraine and Syria. While most Russians would like to see a better relationship with the West – and with Europe in particular – there does not appear to be any support for unilateral Russian concessions. Rather, most Russians firmly believe that their country is in the right. As a result, the Kremlin will be reluctant to seek a significant improvement of its relations with Washington, Brussels, Berlin and London, even if such an improvement would reduce sanctions. Putin's political advisers seem to fear that diminished tensions could further undermine Russians' emotional attachment to their president, as well as possibly lead to uncomfortable questions about the initial premise of the conflict itself.

Further conflict to improve public opinion does not appear to be an option. While the wars in Syria and the Donbas are supported, they are not sources of additional support for Putin, nor were they in their initial phases. That 'work' was done by Crimea, which presented a unique set of circumstances: a historically and emotionally resonant territory, easy military access, an unprepared adversary and extremely limited loss of life. No other target presents a comparable opportunity.

That said, there are at least two other drivers of Russia's involvement in conflicts around the world. The first is the Kremlin's traditional affinity for collecting places at negotiating tables and bargaining chips, reinforced now by an increased confidence in its ability to project force. Moscow's insertion into hotspots from Libya to Venezuela – or Syria before that – complicates US and European actions in those regions and thus creates opportunities for deal-making; the repeated and evidently uncomfortable conversations over Venezuela that Washington has been forced to have with Moscow are but one example.

Increasingly, meanwhile, non-state interests are also driving participation in foreign conflicts. Research by Columbia University political scientist Kimberly Marten shows that private military companies such as Wagner – in addition to being contracted by the Russian Ministry of Defence for war fighting in Syria and Ukraine – often engage on their own behalf or in the interest of private clients. Thus, in theatres including the Central African Republic, Sudan and Nigeria, such private interests use their military capacity to open up avenues for rent-seeking – an activity to which the Kremlin accedes, given the paucity of rent sources available at home. This can, in turn, draw the Russian state into these conflicts by extension.

All this international activity – which is considerably greater in complexity and breadth than at any point since the break-up of the Soviet Union – is enabled by a combination of increased confidence in Moscow and decreased confidence in Western capitals. It does not, however, reflect a structural shift in Russia's position in the world: while Moscow can create short-term outcomes in a variety of situations, it does not have the institutional strength to create long-term outcomes or maintain the durable affiliation and allegiance of friends without renewed inducements or a prolonged military presence, as in Syria. In order to compete with more institutionally robust adversaries, including the US, the EU and China, Moscow therefore traditionally relies on its ability to manufacture and manipulate uncertainty. Much as in domestic politics, the

Kremlin's ability to keep its international interlocutors guessing as to its intentions means that rivals cannot settle on an effective strategy, thus maximising Moscow's own room for manoeuvre.

In this context, it is important for Moscow to maintain first-mover advantage, so that the Kremlin can calculate risks and rewards before its adversaries do, even when the adversary is weaker. Thus, after the election of Volodymyr Zelensky in Ukraine on a platform of ending the war in Donbas, Moscow quickly moved to box Kiev in, offering Russian passports to residents of the occupied territories, ramping up hostilities along the ceasefire line and refusing overtures for dialogue. The clear implication is that any change to the nature of the conflict will occur on Moscow's timescale, not Kiev's.

Globally, however, Moscow's approach to managed uncertainty relies on relatively predictable behaviour on the part of the other major powers. Consequently, Moscow has been reasonably happy to engage in institutional formats – whether the World Trade Organization or various strategic arms-control deals – where it was certain that the US and the EU would stick more or less to the rules. American unilateralism, while a problem for Moscow's strategy under George W. Bush, has increased exponentially under Donald Trump. Meanwhile, structural challenges in Europe, including but not limited to Brexit, mean that the future of strategic political and economic engagement on the continent is fraught. Thus, when Moscow approaches a negotiating table with any of its Western partners, there is now ambiguity on both sides.

This is not, unfortunately, a problem with a positive solution set. Russian foreign-policy circles – and even relatively liberal economic circles – increasingly see American and European behaviour as systemic. Moscow believes that Washington and Brussels are structurally committed to conflict with Russia. Most interests in Moscow have concluded that conflict with Russia is now firmly entrenched in American foreign policy for a generation or more, and that European policy will broadly follow suit. Attempts to break up the transatlantic relationship have, by and large, led only to frustration, and while it is possible that Trump could induce a rift himself, it is far from certain that this would redound to

Moscow's benefit. Instead, as a hedge against this uncertainty, Moscow can be expected to redouble its efforts to maintain strategic flexibility, while opportunistically collecting bargaining chips in conflict zones around the world.

Consequently, domestic and external factors are prompting Russia to halt the expansion seen in recent years. Russia has actively extended its strategic reach, testing its ability to fight multiple wars, project force beyond its immediate region, and carry out covert influence and other operations. It now seems poised to embark on a phase of consolidation. This should not be mistaken for retreat or retrenchment. The forward position Moscow has taken around the world has proved sustainable and profitable, bringing both financial and political dividends. The impetus for further experimentation, however, is much diminished and is likely to remain so for the next few years.

The reason for this reduced emphasis on foreign policy is the re-emergent primacy of domestic politics. The challenges posed by faltering public opinion, a stagnant economy and a restless elite – compounded by the looming (if distant) challenge of 2024 and the end of Putin's presidential term – are far from insurmountable. Taken together, however, they are considerable and will occupy an increasing measure of the Kremlin's attention. Above all, addressing these challenges requires flexibility, a traditional lynchpin of Russian domestic and foreign policymaking, but one that is proving increasingly difficult to maintain.

## Political and Economic Stagnation in Putin's Russia

The annexation of Crimea gave a huge boost to the popularity of Russian President Vladimir Putin early in his third term, which sustained him for several years. Polls show that he still has the support of a majority of the population, although his government is less popular and so too the direction the country is taking. In contrast to its experience of previous recessions, the economy has struggled to bounce back from the 2014 downturn. Slow economic growth and rising income disparities between Moscow and St Petersburg on one hand, and the rest of the country on the other hand, may have contributed to popular discontent.

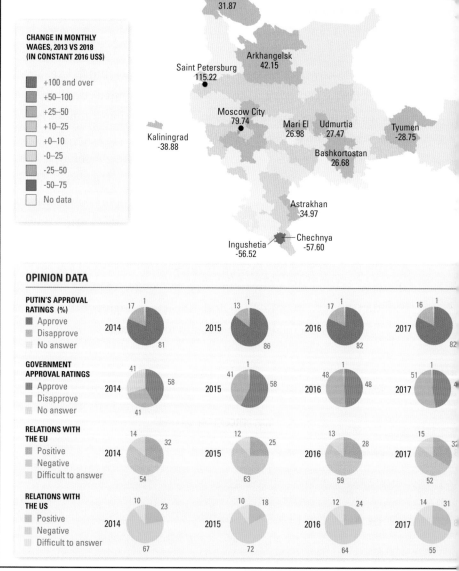

Sources: National Industrial Information Agency, 2019; Russian Federal State Statistics Service (Rosstat), 2019; Yuri Levada Analytical Center, 2019; B of Finland Institute for Economies in Transition (BOFIT), 2019

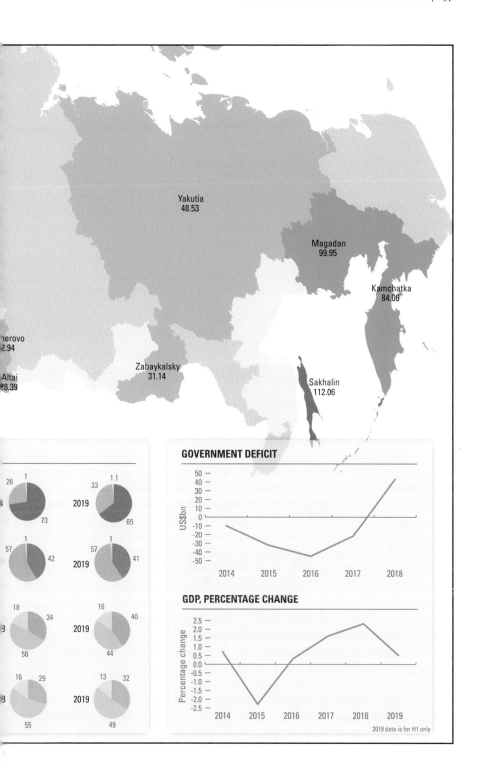

Yakutia
48.53

Magadan
99.95

Kamchatka
84.06

ierovo
2.94

Altai
8.39

Zabaykalsky
31.14

Sakhalin
112.06

26 — 1
73

2019 — 33 — 1.1
65

57 — 1
42

2019 — 57 — 1
41

18 — 34
58

2019 — 16 — 40
44

16 — 29
55

2019 — 13 — 32
49

**GOVERNMENT DEFICIT**

US$bn
50 —
40 —
30 —
20 —
10 —
0 —
-10 —
-20 —
-30 —
-40 —
-50 —

2014    2015    2016    2017    2018

**GDP, PERCENTAGE CHANGE**

Percentage change
2.5 —
2.0 —
1.5 —
1.0 —
0.5 —
0.0 —
-0.5 —
-1.0 —
-1.5 —
-2.0 —
-2.5 —

2014    2015    2016    2017    2018    2019

2019 data is for H1 only

# ...

# Ukraine: Five Years After Euromaidan

Ukraine demonstrated impressive resilience after Russia's annexation of Crimea and the establishment of separatist regimes in Donbas following the 2014 Euromaidan Revolution. Four factors made this possible: a strengthening of nationhood in response to Russian aggression; civil society's ability to plug gaps left by a dysfunctional government; support from Western countries; and the start of long-overdue economic reforms.

Five years on, the optimism of the Euromaidan is a faded memory. Many of the initial reforms remain incomplete. Meanwhile, the country is undergoing a major political realignment after the extraordinary victory in this year's presidential election of Volodymyr Zelensky, a political novice with a background in show business. His triumph is testimony to society's weariness with the established political class and its frustration with the slow pace of change manifested by slow economic growth and incomes that are still among the lowest in Europe. However, it is unclear whether the new parliament elected in July will have a stable majority able to appoint a government committed to a second wave of reforms.

At the same time, the external fundamentals have not changed. Ukraine is at the centre of Russia's confrontation with European Union and NATO countries over the principles of European security. Western countries continue to support Ukraine's sovereignty and remain invested in its reform agenda. Russia continues to deploy a range of instruments to pressure Ukraine into staying in its zone of influence. In addition, Western sectoral sanctions against Russia remain in force against the background of a smouldering conflict in Donbas.

With its decisive rejection of Russia's embrace and with a stronger sense of nationhood than at any time in its history, Ukraine also continues to enjoy unprecedented levels of support from the EU and other Western countries. As a result, it has arguably never had a better chance over the long term to anchor itself in Europe as a genuinely independent country that embodies Western values of freedom, democracy and rule of law. Yet it is still unclear to what extent either Ukrainians themselves or their Western backers believe that such a transformation is realistically achievable.

Such caution is justified: Ukraine has a system of governance much more resistant to change than the ones faced by reformers in Central Europe after 1989, where nationhood rested on stronger foundations, political traditions were different and counter-elites stronger. Moreover, the new political class in those countries was united in its determination to re-join the West at a time when Western institutions were in a far better condition to accommodate them.

Ukraine is a latecomer to the process of seeking its place in an expanded Europe. In view of its history as a troubled borderland between Russia and Europe, it is not surprising that it lacks a vision of the role it can play as a member of the European family and how such a Europe would look. Beset by internal problems and enlargement fatigue, the EU has scaled back its ambitions of a wider Europe. It is similarly vague about the possibilities for integrating a country the size of Ukraine that borders Russia and presents so many economic and security challenges. Nevertheless, the past five years have shown that Ukraine is changing and that its society is culturally different from Russia's, with greater openness to European values and much more developed civil-society organisations. Ukrainians also aspire to establish institutions that can hold their leaders to account. These qualities suggest that Ukraine has the potential to embed itself in Europe in a way that it has never previously achieved.

## Progress since 2014

It is easy to forget the seriousness of the situation faced by Ukraine's new leaders in the aftermath of the collapse of the Yanukovych regime in 2014. Having lost control of Crimea and with insurrections aimed at counter-revolution under way in southeastern Ukraine, the authorities in Kiev also faced severe economic problems: the hryvnia was in freefall and foreign-exchange reserves had plummeted to perilously low levels. At the same time, much of the armed forces and security services were unusable. The previous leadership had hollowed them out and in some cases allowed them to work for Moscow.

In extraordinarily challenging conditions, the first government under the leadership of Arseniy Yatsenyuk succeeded in stabilising the economy. A US$17-billion IMF bailout played a key role. However, it could not stop a dramatic recession as output contracted 7% in 2014 and a further 10% in 2015.

Elected president in May 2014, Petro Poroshenko made a vital contribution to the overall stabilisation effort. He coordinated an unexpected level of military resistance in Donbas, albeit with the help of 'volunteer battalions' that were funded by donations, including from oligarchs and other business people. Civil society rallied to the cause to keep front-line forces clothed and fed.

Poroshenko was also able to build alliances with EU countries and the United States that were the basis for Western sanctions against Russia initially imposed in the summer of 2014. He maintained this international support after the signing in Minsk of the peace agreements by exposing Russia as the main obstacle to their implementation. Western countries accepted his logic that elections in the breakaway territories could only take place once the security provisions of the agreements had been fulfilled and not the other way round, as Moscow insisted.

In so doing, Poroshenko stymied the implementation of a peace plan on Russian terms which threatened to limit Ukraine's choice of allies and emasculate its foreign policy. Moscow's goal was to force Ukraine to reintegrate the separatist-held territories giving them extensive autonomy and veto power over Ukraine's potential membership of the EU and NATO.

Since the Obama administration showed no appetite for involvement in Ukraine, the diplomatic burden of managing the situation and deterring further Russian aggression fell on the EU. To the surprise of many, Germany led from the front, shunning the route of accommodation with Moscow and spearheading a European policy based on non-recognition of Crimea's incorporation into Russia and a broad range of sanctions measures to support peacebuilding in Donbas.

The EU later tied these sanctions directly to Russia's implementation of the Minsk agreements. A combination of sanctions, a drop in the oil price and the diplomatic isolation of Moscow almost certainly helped to constrain Russian military action in Ukraine and create a situation of 'neither war nor peace' that holds today.

Predictably, Poroshenko turned out to be only a partial reformer. He had established himself in the system of oligarchic capitalism that took shape in the 1990s and had no interest in changing its substance. Contrary to the spirit of the Euromaidan, radical measures to introduce political and economic competition at the expense of oligarchic interests did not materialise and the new administration delayed or watered down much of the revolution's anti-corruption agenda.

Nevertheless, there were important achievements. The national gas company Naftogaz underwent significant reform as part of an effort to wean industry and households off cheap gas that had made Ukraine unnecessarily dependent on Russian gas supplies and lined the pockets of a select few. The Central Bank started a clean-up of the banking sector, culminating in the nationalisation of PrivatBank in December 2016 after an audit showed a US$5.5bn hole in its balance sheet. The Ministry of Finance also put an end to some of the most egregious abuses of the tax system.

In addition, the government began an ambitious decentralisation reform to devolve decision-making to the local level while important measures were introduced to limit traditional opportunities for corruption in the state procurement system. However, the new anti-corruption bodies were unable to prosecute any senior officials because of a tacit agreement between the authorities and a superficially reformed judiciary that no one of rank should go to jail. This continuing culture of impunity angered voters who had placed their hopes in the possibility of real change after Euromaidan; it was one of the principal reasons for Poroshenko's dramatic loss of support.

At the same time, there were no tangible improvements in corruption black spots such as customs, defence procurement, the railways and the regulation of the energy market.

The Association Agreement that Ukraine signed with the EU in 2014 contains a Deep and Comprehensive Free Trade Area designed to align

Ukraine's regulatory systems with those of the EU. Although progress in this direction remains slow because of Ukraine's limited capacity to adopt new rules, there are clear signs that trade with the EU is on the increase. In 2018, the EU's share of Ukraine's exports grew to nearly 40%, up from 26% in 2013. However, this was not enough to offset the collapse of trade with Russia, which is estimated to have more than halved since 2014.

Poroshenko could justifiably claim that Ukraine reformed more under his rule than it had between 1991 and 2014. He argued less convincingly that Ukraine could not focus more on reform because it was at war. While Western governments were reluctant to push Poroshenko harder, voters judged him on his domestic-reform record that in their view failed to honour the Euromaidan's mandate for change. Notable achievements of his time in office, including visa-free travel to the EU and the separation of the Ukrainian Orthodox Church from Moscow, counted for little.

Instead, the electorate's focus was firmly on declining living standards and slow forecast growth rates. The World Bank estimated in 2019 that on existing projections, Ukraine would take 50 years to catch up with income levels in Poland. In 1991, the two countries had similar levels of per capita income.

## Scale of the challenge

Zelensky's victory in the presidential election demonstrated that Ukrainian voters preferred an untested figure from outside the elite to an established politician with a record of having stood up to Russia after the Euromaidan. It also showed that online campaigning techniques could appeal to young voters and reach across Ukraine's traditional voting lines based on cultural and linguistic differences.

This shift in public attitudes suggests that Ukraine may be developing a stronger national consensus around its identity and path of development. If this is the case, it is likely to sustain Ukraine's resistance to Russian pressure and strengthen the readiness of Western countries to maintain their assistance to Ukraine.

However, the new president's fresh rhetoric and his professed commitment to tackling corruption are difficult to reconcile with his well-publicised connections with the oligarch Ihor Kolomoisky. To maintain his credibility as an untainted political outsider, he will be under pressure to distance himself from oligarch influence. Inevitably, the old system will try to either co-opt him or use other means to limit his reformist instincts. While it is unrealistic to expect a neophyte politician elected president to transform the current system, he may nevertheless disrupt it to a degree that none of his predecessors has managed over the past 15 years.

Zelensky's party won an outright majority in parliamentary elections in July. The extent to which he will succeed or fail will depend largely on his ability to pass legislation for reforms; the oligarchic system of patronage has weakened since 2014, but it is likely to retain a strong voice in the new parliament.

The scope of the reform agenda remains overwhelming. For incomes to increase, Ukraine urgently needs to attract foreign direct investment and improve labour productivity, which has been stagnant for decades. Not surprisingly, property rights, poor infrastructure and the conflict in Donbas make boardrooms nervous about exposure to Ukraine despite an abundance of cheap, well-qualified labour and the demonstrable success of industries such as IT outsourcing that continue to grow rapidly.

Judicial reform has yet to improve the functioning of the commercial courts and to address the perception that Ukrainian judges do not provide independent and binding interpretations of the law. Progress in this area will not come quickly because Ukrainians have never known such a culture. To create it will require establishing entirely new judicial-appointment bodies with rigorous procedures for vetting judges and effective judicial-oversight mechanisms. The establishment in April 2019 of the High Anti-Corruption Court is an important first step in this direction.

Since 2014, there has been only modest progress on deregulation. Like many countries with limited economic competition and weak rule of law, Ukraine has a superabundance of regulations that allow officials to exercise arbitrary control of business and provide mechanisms of extortion.

Other priorities are privatisation of the bloated state sector (more than 3,000 enterprises) as well as reform of the security service (SBU) and law enforcement, in particular the Prosecutor General's Office (PGO). The SBU retains powers to investigate economic crimes, but these powers are routinely abused for commercial gain either by interests willing to pay for the service or by parts of the SBU itself. The PGO is widely regarded as a political tool that serves vested interests connected with the president, who is responsible for nominating the prosecutor general.

Further reform of the energy sector is a critical priority since Ukraine urgently needs to increase domestic production of gas in order to reduce its dependence on imported supplies. Transit of Russian gas via Ukraine is set to fall over the coming years as the Nord Stream II and TurkStream pipelines come into operation. Since 2016, Ukraine has met its import requirement by buying gas from companies in east-central Europe. The method for doing so has been to take an agreed proportion of the gas transiting Ukraine in a westerly direction. If Ukraine were no longer to provide Russia with gas-transit services, this arrangement could not continue. Losses from gas transit could therefore be much greater than the forfeited transit fees, worth around US$3bn annually (over 2% of GDP).

Against this background, there is the vexed question of what to do about the separatist-held territories in Donbas, where an estimated 3.8m people still live. There is no consensus in Kiev on the issue. The choice is either to play the long game and encourage their populations to move away and enjoy better socio-economic opportunities in government-administered Ukraine (leaving Russia to foot the bill for maintaining what is left); or to seek faster reintegration of the territories based on Ukraine's interpretation of the Minsk agreements. So far, the government has shown little interest in treating the people still living in these areas as citizens of Ukraine.

Understandably, there is weariness in society with the fighting in Donbas that has cost close to 13,000 lives together with as many as 30,000 wounded and 2m internally displaced persons. Zelensky has vowed to end the conflict but it is unclear how he can achieve this aim without Kiev or Moscow giving ground. There is no indication that Ukrainians are ready to yield to Moscow's agenda and accept a peaceful reintegration of these territories at the cost of weakening their independence by opening a path to the country's federalisation. Equally, Russia shows no signs of wanting to retreat from Donbas in the absence of other means to pursue its goal of preventing Ukraine from consolidating its pro-Western orientation.

While Moscow has the capability to destabilise Ukraine rapidly, it has chosen the path of gradual pressure using political, economic, military and information tools. In Georgia and Moldova, Russia has built up considerable experience of supporting separatist regimes and using them to weaken states from within. Its trade restrictions are proving costly for the Ukrainian economy, while its actions to restrict Ukraine's room for manoeuvre in the Sea of Azov are part of a broader effort to strangle Ukraine's economic development and show the limits of its alliances with the West. NATO has indicated that it is not willing to police access to the Sea of Azov on behalf of Ukraine.

At the same time, Moscow appears to understand that renewed efforts to achieve counter-revolution, as in 2014, would entail risks not only of further international sanctions and isolation but also of popular discontent within Russia. The popular euphoria of Crimea's 'return' to Russia has evaporated after five years of falling incomes, and there appears to be little appetite in Russian society at present for further foreign adventures, let alone fighting with a nation so culturally and ethnically close to Russia.

## Relations with Western countries

The EU remains firm on the principles behind its policy of support for Ukraine and is providing valuable technical assistance, particularly in the areas of public-administration reform and decentralisation. EU assistance is now worth more than €200m (approximately US$219.6m) annually, with the total number of grants to Ukraine since 1991 set to reach €4.8bn by 2020. In per capita terms, however, this is far less than the pre-accession assistance provided to Central and Eastern Europe between 1990 and 2006. For example, the per capita amount for the three Baltic states averaged over €320 while the amount for Ukraine between 1991 and 2020 is forecast at €100.

While EU sanctions related to Crimea will continue indefinitely as long as Russia retains control of the territory, sectoral sanctions are likely to be less sustainable as Angela Merkel's premiership draws to a close amid growing calls in Germany and several other EU countries to turn over a new page in relations with Russia. The Council of Europe's decision in June to return voting rights to Russia despite non-fulfilment of its sanctions conditions is an indication of a changing mood in Europe that may evolve more quickly post-Brexit. The UK has been one of the strongest supporters of a firm line in response to Russian behaviour in Ukraine.

Washington currently shows little interest in Ukraine, viewing it as a matter for Europe. Nevertheless, there is strong bipartisan support for Ukraine in Congress and it is striking that the Trump administration has supplied Ukraine with *Javelin* anti-tank missiles, a step that the Obama White House declined to take. Speculation that US President Donald Trump and Russian President Vladimir Putin might resolve the stand-off in Donbas through a wider realignment of US–Russia ties has so far proved wide of the mark, for the simple reason that there has been no serious effort by the two sides to improve relations. Not surprisingly, Ukrainians fear that they would be the losers in any 'reset' between the US and Russia.

NATO continues to express strong support for Ukraine's territorial integrity and sovereignty but seeks to distance itself from the conflict. Its focus instead is on developing the capacity of Ukraine's armed forces, a process supported by several member states through bilateral-cooperation programmes. Although Ukraine's parliament confirmed membership of NATO as a security-policy objective in 2017, there is no sign of Ukraine receiving a membership action plan. NATO allies have no interest in further inflaming relations with Russia and putting Ukraine's security at risk. They learned a hard lesson in 2008 after issuing an ill-judged communiqué at the Bucharest Summit that stated that 'Georgia and Ukraine will become members of NATO'. Barely three months later, Russian armed forces invaded Georgia.

Zelensky takes a more cautious view of NATO membership than his predecessor and proposes holding a referendum to decide the issue. Even though there is currently majority support among the Ukrainian public for joining NATO, a referendum could prove divisive and politically damaging. The country's best option for now is to follow the examples of Finland and Sweden, keeping the issue off the political agenda while quietly expanding its defence capabilities by pursuing inter-operability with NATO.

## Uncertain prospects

Ukraine's future defies easy prediction. The reform process is likely to remain slower and less substantial than its Western partners would hope. Ukraine will continue to lack the human capacity to manage the scale of the reform agenda and the old system will continue to try to delay the reforms and limit their scope. There is a danger of muddling through, since the old Ukrainian elites know that Western countries will not abandon Ukraine as long as Russia continues to pose a security threat to the EU and NATO by forcing Ukraine to abandon its independent foreign policy. On the other hand, there is increasing pressure from society for genuine reforms that is likely to gain greater strength at both regional and national levels and demand greater political and economic competition. Such a development could be the basis for a more vigorous reform effort.

The current leadership in Moscow cannot countenance Ukraine developing independently of Russia because of Ukraine's strategic significance as part of a buffer zone that Moscow regards as essential for maintaining national security. At the same time, Moscow views Ukrainian independence as artificial and unsustainable. However, despite the deep and enduring cultural, historical and personal links between the two countries, the extent to which the Kremlin has already alienated Ukrainians makes the return to a close bilateral relationship impossible in the short to medium term.

This is, of course, not Moscow's conclusion. Over the past 15 years, the Russian leadership has repeatedly misjudged Ukraine. With the Putin system facing increasing problems of legitimacy at home, it may be tempted again to unite the country around fighting Western interests in its self-defined zone of 'privileged interests' that includes Ukraine. This would not necessarily involve deploying large numbers of military units to Ukraine. Expanded 'hybrid' warfare, together with stronger economic pressure, could destabilise Ukraine's reform effort and test the will of its Western allies to continue their support.

Yet Ukraine is also showing signs of developing the capacity to influence Russia. Zelensky's election victory has resonated in Russian society, which is increasingly frustrated by lack of change and would like to hear its leaders speak in similar new language. The decisive test is whether the new president and government can turn rhetoric into reality and persuade Russians that life in Ukraine is better than they imagined and that Russia needs to follow the example of Ukraine's reforms. Such an outcome would be the best guarantee of Ukraine's security.

# Turkmenistan's Mismanaged Decline

Turkmenistan belongs to a small group of highly repressive regimes that defy the logic of globalisation. Almost three decades after the collapse of the Soviet Union, it remains isolated and impenetrable to foreign observers. Entry to the country is strictly limited and even basic information about the state of its economy and society are unavailable or unverifiable.

The Caspian state is landlocked, located far from its export markets and dependent on exports of a single commodity, natural gas. It faces security risks emanating from northern Afghanistan; in recent years, its armed forces have been engaged in regular cross-border hostilities with jihadist groups. Despite its geographical challenges, the Turkmen regime remains wedded to a policy of semi-isolation in economic and diplomatic affairs. Drawing on the concept of 'positive neutrality' developed by Saparmurat Niyazov, who ruled the country from the collapse of the USSR in 1991 until 2006, Turkmenistan has avoided engagement in all regional economic and security alliances. His successor, Gurbanguli Berdymukhamedov, has increased the level of engagement with foreign powers, but Turkmenistan's approach to international relations has remained fundamentally unchanged. It is the only Central Asian state that does not participate in either the Russian-led Collective Security Treaty Organization (CSTO) or the Shanghai Cooperation Organisation (SCO).

Turkmenistan is a rentier state that cannot maximise its rents. It has the theoretical capacity to become one of the largest energy exporters in the world. A geological survey conducted by international consultants in 2011 indicated that Turkmenistan possesses the world's fourth-largest gas reserves (behind Russia, Iran and Qatar), the majority of which are located onshore and relatively easily accessible. However, the challenging geopolitical environment and tight constraints the government places on international investment have seriously impeded the potential exploitation of its gas reserves. Gas production has consistently missed official government targets and remains around 25% lower than that recorded in the final years of the Soviet Union.

Turkmenistan's economy has undergone the least restructuring of any post-Soviet state and private enterprise remains highly restricted. Currency controls constrict cross-border transactions and almost all foreign investment is mediated by the regime. This has led to the collapse of much of the country's Soviet-era productive capacity and widespread poverty, with analysts estimating the unemployment rate at 60% or higher. The economic decline has been compounded by the departure of a sizeable part of the country's non-ethnic-Turkmen population, in particular ethnic Russians, for whom Turkmenistan has become an increasingly hostile environment. In the early 2000s, Russian officials estimated that 300,000 of their citizens were in Turkmenistan, one-third of whom also held Turkmen citizenship. However, in 2008 Turkmenistan placed restrictions on dual citizenship and the authorities continue to make life uncomfortable for those people.

**Economic crisis**

Since 2014, a severe fiscal squeeze has called into question the sustainability of Turkmenistan's economic and foreign-policy model. The fall in oil prices that year led to a sharp decline in the value of its gas contracts, which make up more than 80% of its exports and are believed to account for a similar share of government revenue. The Oxford Institute for Energy Studies (OIES) estimates that the price at Turkmenistan's border for gas exported to China fell by almost half between 2014 and 2016, from just over US$300 per 1,000 cubic metres to a price of US$165. It recovered slightly to US$185 per 1,000 cubic metres in 2017. In mid-2016, the IMF estimated that Turkmenistan's total hydrocarbon revenues had fallen by over half during the previous three years. Budget data for Turkmenistan is sparse and unreliable, but an indicator of the strain is apparent in the country's current-account deficit, which averaged below 8% of GDP per year in 2000–13 but widened to almost 20% of GDP in 2016, before narrowing sharply in 2017–18 as domestic consumption collapsed.

The fall in export earnings has exacerbated an already dire situation in the broader economy. The authorities have resisted a full revaluation of currency (the manat) in response to the decline in the country's terms of trade. The official exchange rate of the manat fell by just over 20% to 3.5 to the dollar in 2015 but no further adjustments have followed. The black-market rate for the manat depreciated from seven to the dollar in late 2016 to 24–25 to the dollar in 2018. Currency controls and the sharp fall in the black-market rate of the manat have given regime insiders vast scope for rent-seeking at the expense of a rebalancing of the economy. Reports by opposition and foreign media suggest that these controls have led to widespread shortages of basic foodstuffs. This has coincided with the withdrawal of government subsidies of electricity, water and natural gas, which were once considered a mainstay of the social contract, accounting for a significant share of GDP. In the 1990s, citizens received free gas, electricity and water, as well as subsidised flour, sugar and cooking oil. During a public address soon after he became president in 2007, Berdymukhamedov promised that these would never be withdrawn. Yet in 2017, the government capped the volume of free utilities and in September 2018 scrapped them entirely. Allowances for subsidised flour also contracted by two-thirds and in 2017 it was reported that the price of a sack of flour had doubled from 50 manats to 100.

Turkmen companies, including in the gas sector, have cut staff numbers and imposed wage arrears, raising questions about the long-term sustainability of gas production. In 2015, a restructuring at Turkmengaz, the state gas producer, led to an undisclosed number of redundancies, and Turkmengeologiya, the state exploration and field-development company, cut its staff by 30%.

The implications of the fall in export revenue for the solvency of the Turkmen state are unclear as the government distorts and restricts data on social and economic trends. At the request of the Turkmen government, the report of the latest IMF Article IV consultation on Turkmenistan's macroeconomic and fiscal position was not publicly released. Importers and foreign firms operating in the country have reported that contract payments have been delayed or not honoured, suggesting that the government is encountering financing problems, although the state has a history of delaying payment to subcontractors.

Default nevertheless seems unlikely. Declared sovereign liabilities are low, consistent with the regime's policy of insulating itself from foreign dependence. Currency controls are likely to have depressed imports and brought the current-account deficit under control. The regime is believed to have accumulated large foreign-currency reserves in offshore accounts: data from the Bank for International Settlements (BIS) indicates that offshore funds of Turkmen residents amounted to more than US$26 billion at the end of 2018, most of which is likely to be earnings from gas exports. Almost no information is available, however, on how these funds are administered, or whether they can be meaningfully considered sovereign assets that could be mobilised to support the economy or fund investment in the gas sector. In 2008, Berdymukhamedov announced the creation of a Stabilisation Fund under the supervision of the Ministry of Finance, but almost no information on the sovereign wealth fund has since been released. In late 2018, Berdymukhamedov said that it held 'sufficient funds' without elaborating further.

## Energy policy – trapped in a low equilibrium

Despite the economic crisis, the regime has so far made no moves to adjust its approach to development of the country's vast gas reserves, which has held back production volumes and the construction of new transit routes. Turkmenistan's proven gas reserves, according to the *BP Statistical Review of World Energy 2019*, are estimated at 19.5 trillion cubic metres. However, gas exports in 2018 totalled just 35 billion cubic metres (bcm), compared with 248 bcm from Russia and 137 bcm from Qatar.

Development of Turkmenistan's gas fields has been constrained both by a lack of export options and by the Turkmen government's refusal to grant production-sharing agreements (PSAs) to major international energy companies to develop onshore fields. As a result, production has consistently failed to meet official targets. In 2018, Turkmenistan produced just over 60 bcm of natural gas, the same volume as a decade earlier and below the level reached in the last years of the Soviet Union. The China National Petroleum Corporation (CNPC) is the only foreign company that has secured a PSA for an onshore project, in 2006 when it signed a framework agreement with then-president Niyazov, which remained in place after Berdymukhamedov came to power. In 2007 the company obtained a licence to explore and produce in the Bagtyyarlyk area in the Lebap region in the northeast of the country, the output of which now feeds into the Central Asia–China pipeline. A consortium headed by CNPC also holds a US$10bn PSA for the development of Galkynysh field (also known as South Yolotan–Osman, the world's second-largest gas field), which also contributes to the gas volumes delivered to China.

The China–Turkmenistan framework agreement also led to the construction of a new 1,800-kilometre pipeline linking Turkmenistan's onshore gas fields to western China via Uzbekistan and Kazakhstan. The first string of the pipeline was completed in 2009, with two further phases completed in 2010 and 2014, increasing transit capacity to China from Central Asia to 55 bcm per year. Until the completion of the Central Asia–China pipeline, Turkmenistan had been almost entirely reliant on Russia and Ukraine as export markets, with Iran accounting for only a small share of exports. Russia's Gazprom had exploited its monopsony position and high European prices in the mid-2000s to capture a large share of sales revenue.

While the new pipeline broke Russia's grip on Turkmenistan's export infrastructure, it has not increased Turkmenistan's bargaining power or resulted in a significant rise in export volumes. Completion of the Central Asia–China pipeline coincided with a slump in Russian and European gas demand. Following an explosion on one of the main gas-export arteries to Russia in April 2009, Gazprom suspended and then permanently reduced its gas imports from Turkmenistan. The Turkmen government has therefore effectively exchanged one set of dependencies for another, as falling Russian demand has offset the increased exports to China. Moreover, in the short term at least, Turkmenistan's export rents have been further depressed by the requirement to repay soft loans issued by China for the construction of the new pipeline infrastructure.

The European Union has long been interested in developing transit routes from the Caspian Sea to southern Europe to reduce its dependence on Russian gas. Under the Southern Gas Corridor projects, parts of the infrastructure are already in place: the Trans-Anatolian Pipeline (TANAP), carrying Azerbaijani gas through Turkey to the Greek border, was completed in mid-2018, although its initial capacity of 16 bcm per year is a fraction of total European and Turkish gas imports. The Trans-Adriatic Pipeline (TAP), which will carry Caspian gas on to Greece and Italy, is under construction. However, there is a capacity problem in Azerbaijan. The South Caucasus Pipeline (SCP), which connects to TANAP, is currently handling 8 bcm per year, though plans are in place to raise its capacity above 20 bcm per year to accommodate increased output from Azerbaijan's Shah Deniz field. The SCP can be expanded to 31 bcm per year, but Azerbaijan would likely take up most of the additional capacity. Creating capacity to transport substantial volumes of Turkmen gas to Europe will therefore require either a second string of the SCP or a whole new pipeline across the Caspian or northern Iran. Western efforts to diversify European pipeline gas supplies have fallen far short of the rhetoric, despite the crisis in relations between Russia and the West. The Southern Gas Corridor is set to provide no more than 2% of European gas imports by the early 2020s, far below the 10–20% originally planned.

At present it appears unlikely that Turkmenistan will be able to strengthen its bargaining position by further diversifying its export options. Two pipeline projects have been under discussion for many years, with minimal progress made on either: a western route, the Trans-Caspian Pipeline (TCP), running along the Caspian Sea bed to Azerbaijan, Turkey and Europe; and a southern route, TAPI, from Turkmenistan to Afghanistan, Pakistan and the Indian border.

Recent geopolitical developments have removed some potential impediments to the construction of the TCP. In August 2018 the Caspian littoral states (Azerbaijan, Iran, Kazakhstan, Russia and Turkmenistan) signed a landmark convention to delimit the Caspian Sea. The agreement forbids military vessels of non-littoral states from accessing Caspian waters, reaffirming Russia's dominance of the sea (foreign naval vessels can only enter the Caspian via the Volga–Don Canal). This is in line with its more active role in the Middle East, and its military engagement in Syria: Russia has experimented with power projection from the Caspian, firing rockets at targets in Syria from its Caspian fleet. A new naval base on the Caspian, in Kaspiysk, Dagestan, is set to be completed by 2020. At the same time, the convention allows the signatories to build pipelines along the floor of the Caspian Sea if they comply with environmental standards, removing potential legal obstacles to the construction of a gas pipeline linking Turkmenistan to Azerbaijan. The agreement marks a positional shift for Russia, which had long been assumed to have an interest in keeping the legal status of the sea unresolved to constrain the development of offshore fields by other states.

But while the convention on delimitation has removed the formal legal barriers to the construction of the TCP, Russia could still exercise diplomatic pressure to discourage its construction or seek to block the project on environmental grounds. If the TCP looked close to being realised, Gazprom could reopen its pipeline system to supply Turkmen gas to Europe, further undercutting the project's economic rationale.

Regardless of the geopolitics, the economics of the TCP remain uncertain. The cost of construction is around US$2bn, compared with US$8.6bn for TANAP, but Western investors continue to be deterred by the Turkmen government's refusal to allow foreign companies to take an operational role in upstream development of fields that would supply the pipeline. Even if uncertainties over supply could be resolved, analysis by the OIES suggests that after the cost of transit is considered, Turkmen gas would struggle to be competitive in Turkey and would be prohibitively expensive for export to Europe.

On paper the TAPI project is further advanced than the TCP, but major security and financing constraints remain. The proposed pipeline, with a planned initial capacity of 33 bcm, would run 1,700 km from the Galkynysh field through Herat and Kandahar in Afghanistan, Quetta and Multan in Pakistan, to the city of Fazilka on the Indian border. The pipeline would be a landmark in the broader economic orientation of the Central Asian region, where Indian investment, outside Kazakhstan's steel sector, has to date been modest. India's Oil and Natural Gas

Corporation (ONGC) attempted to gain a foothold in Caspian energy resources by buying a share in the giant Kashagan offshore field, but the stake was acquired by CNPC.

In 2015, Turkmengaz was confirmed as the leader of a consortium (also including Afghan Gas Enterprise, Pakistan's Inter State Gas Systems and GAIL of India) and a ground-breaking ceremony was held in December in the Turkmen city of Mary. Since then, Turkmenistan has regularly reported progress, but the project remains shrouded in mystery and there is little hard evidence of construction. However, developments reported to the May 2019 Turkmenistan Gas Congress suggest that some progress has been made. Saudi interests are reported to have provided US$740m in financing, with Kuwait and the Islamic Development Bank together contributing some US$150m. Key to their involvement is securing in 2020 roughly US$5bn of guarantees from European export-credit agencies for Turkmen sovereign debt for the project. With those guarantees, banks will extend credit to enable construction into Afghanistan. Phase 1 envisages deliveries of 11 bcm annually into Afghanistan, with the revenue generated to provide finance for Phase 2. However, Afghanistan has little gas infrastructure and will struggle to pay for gas. It is possible that TAPI will expand to Herat and no further.

If financing concerns are a mammoth obstacle to the realisation of TAPI, security concerns are scarcely less daunting. During the 1990s, the Turkmen government successfully maintained equal working relations with both the Taliban and the opposition United Islamic Front for the Salvation of Afghanistan, and regularly offered to act as an international mediator. Turkmenistan is already a significant exporter of electricity to northern Afghanistan, and the Turkmen regime, which is believed to be deeply integrated into drug-smuggling routes, has retained strong informal ties with the Taliban. But since 2014, the security situation on the Turkmen–Afghan border has deteriorated and Turkmenistan's armed forces have been engaged in regular hostilities with militant and jihadist groups. The Afghan government has pledged 7,000 soldiers to protect the pipeline, some of which could be built below ground; nevertheless, the risk of sabotage in both northern Afghanistan and Pakistan's Balochistan region is high and possibly insurmountable. Even if security concerns can be resolved, the pipeline faces the same dilemma as the TCP: the Turkmen government's refusal to allow international energy companies to develop the onshore Galkynysh field makes it highly unlikely that the required US$10bn–16bn financing for the project can be secured, despite the enduring interest of the Asian Development Bank and Japanese investors in the project.

## Little prospect of change

Turkmenistan's economic and foreign-policy model has led the country to crisis and has likely locked it into a long-term dependence on China. Reports of food shortages, unacknowledged mass unemployment and the removal of government subsidies for utilities raise basic questions about human security. These strains, reportedly far worse in the countryside than in the capital Ashgabat, are likely to grow more acute as climate change places further pressure on scarce water resources and depresses crop yields. The opacity of the system makes it impossible to gauge public opinion and the risk of social unrest, but there have been anecdotal reports of social disturbances, including strikes by workers in the gas sector.

Turkmenistan's isolationist foreign policy contradicts the logic of its location and its economic structure. The resistance of the government to change this model may in part be because the elite, by contrast, is well-integrated into the global financial system. A report by the NGO Global Witness in 2007 indicated that US$8bn in earnings from gas exports were held in offshore funds in Western bank accounts personally controlled by the president.

The exceptionalism of Turkmenistan's system has been thrown into stark relief by the shift in economic and foreign policy in neighbouring Uzbekistan. In 2016, president Islam Karimov, who had ruled the country since independence, was replaced by Shavkat Mirziyoyev, creating an opening for economic restructuring. The new president has pursued an unexpectedly far-reaching policy of structural reform in line with the dogmas of international financial institutions. The government has lifted currency controls, opened state monopolies to private competition, and pursued increased integration into the global financial system. Mirziyoyev has ended years of tensions with Uzbekistan's neighbours, which included threats of war over water management. Foreign-policy detente and economic liberalisation have led to rapid growth in cross-border exchange. Trade between Kazakhstan and Uzbekistan grew by almost 50% in 2018 and Uzbekistan's trade with Russia rose by more than 20% in the same period.

Despite the fiscal and economic crisis of the past five years, at present there is little indication that the Turkmen government is considering a similar process of 'authoritarian upgrading' to expand its revenue base. The regime's only structural response to the economic crisis has been the removal of the system of subsidies, which points to an even greater reliance on coercion. But the government's room for manoeuvre should not be overstated.

Turkmenistan's pipeline deal with China, placed alongside the failure of the TCP, is a striking example of the power dynamics and geopolitical asymmetries at play in Central Asia as China pursues its Belt and Road Initiative (BRI). China has succeeded where Western international oil companies have consistently failed and secured the right to develop Turkmenistan's onshore resources. This may in part be due to its greater willingness to play by local rules, providing substantial informal payments to secure regime buy-in. In the interests of long-term security of supply, CNPC appears to have been willing to suffer short-term losses on the deal, as domestic Chinese prices do not currently cover the cost of extraction and transit. China has prevailed over the EU by spending large sums via its state-controlled companies. While regional relations have improved markedly since the change of president in Uzbekistan, the construction of the first Central Asia–China pipeline bucked the regional trend towards the decoupling of cross-border energy and railway infrastructure.

The BRI has delivered new investment and infrastructure to Turkmenistan and the broader region, but as academic Luca Anceschi notes, it has also created a new framework of dependency. Few if any local companies were involved in the project's development and in the short term, repayments to cover the US$10bn cost of the pipeline have cut the government's revenues from gas sales. In practice, the project has not led to a diversification of Turkmenistan's export options: changes in European gas markets and an increase in Russia's domestic production have virtually eliminated Gazprom's demand for Turkmenistan's gas, and its economy is now as reliant on China as it was on Russia prior to 2009. Budgetary pressures have prompted Turkmenistan to close institutions providing training for oil and gas specialists. Turkmenistan will in future send its engineering students to China for training, leading to a long-term human-capital dependency.

Chinese markets alone are unlikely to enable Turkmenistan to substantially increase its gas exports, despite its huge reserves. As of mid-2019, it appeared likely that a fourth string of the Central Asia–China pipeline would be built, via a different route through Tajikistan and Kyrgyzstan, taking its total export capacity to 80 bcm per year. If Turkmenistan could raise output to mostly fill that expanded pipeline, it may generate enough revenue to ease the government's financial concerns. This may spare the Turkmen authorities from making a difficult decision about changing the way they have ruled the country until now.

If Ashgabat had made different decisions in the 1990s, it could now be a well-established supplier of gas to Europe as well as China and possibly Russia. The international energy majors were interested in significant upstream investment in the country and would, in that case, have put their commercial, financial and political heft behind the TCP. Those same companies might also have given TAPI a fighting chance. Instead, Turkmenistan is now heavily reliant on China. Beijing is unlikely to increase its purchases of Central Asian gas much beyond the mooted 80 bcm per year to avoid becoming too reliant on a single source. Even sales at that level cannot be taken for granted. Russia's 'turn to the East' means that Gazprom is now competing with Central Asian producers for market share in China.

# Europe: Drivers of Strategic Change

- German Chancellor Angela Merkel's last term is coming to a conclusion, but her nominated successor as leader of the CDU has performed in a lacklustre fashion and her party is struggling to hold off the challenge from far-right and liberal parties. Despite slowing economic growth, there is little sign that Merkel is prepared to countenance a more expansionary fiscal policy.

- In France, President Emmanuel Macron's plans for radical transformation were challenged by mass protests. Escalating violence prompted the authorities to step back from confrontation and reverse planned reforms, casting doubt on the future trajectory. Still, Macron remains a driving force within Europe and a standard-bearer for those seeking to stem the rise of nativist politics.

- The UK missed a deadline to leave the EU, as parties in Parliament failed to form a majority over the terms of departure and the model for a new partnership. The imperatives to avoid a hard border in Ireland and to pursue an independent trade policy seemed impossible to reconcile. Brexit, which had barely registered among voters' main concerns prior to 2015, may become the new dividing line in UK politics.

- EU–US relations turned more tense as European states sought to preserve the Iran nuclear deal while the US used its economic leverage to force European companies to uphold a trade and financial embargo. European states have also failed to take action sufficient to silence the complaints of the US administration that the US bears a disproportionate share of NATO's spending burden.

- European tensions with Turkey moderated somewhat, despite Turkey's authoritarian turn of recent years, with the two sides cooperating on migration despite the failure to advance relations in other areas including EU accession talks, trade relations and visas. Relations with Russia were little changed: the EU upheld sanctions despite a desire on the part of southern states to revisit the issue.

## DEMOGRAPHY

POPULATION AND MEDIAN AGE
(IMF, April 2019; UN Department of Economic and Social Affairs, Population Division, 2019)

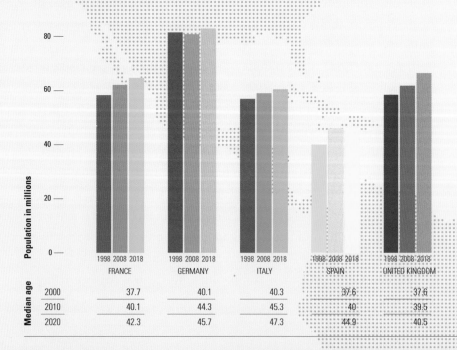

| Median age | FRANCE | GERMANY | ITALY | SPAIN | UNITED KINGDOM |
|---|---|---|---|---|---|
| 2000 | 37.7 | 40.1 | 40.3 | 37.6 | 37.6 |
| 2010 | 40.1 | 44.3 | 45.3 | 40 | 39.5 |
| 2020 | 42.3 | 45.7 | 47.3 | 44.9 | 40.5 |

**AGE STRUCTURE**
(CIA World Factbook, 2019)

| UNITED KINGDOM | |
|---|---|
| Under 25 years | 30.28% |
| 25–64 years | 49.90% |
| 64 years and older | 19.82% |

| GERMANY | |
|---|---|
| Under 25 years | 22.81% |
| 25–64 years | 54.83% |
| 64 years and older | 22.36% |

| ITALY | |
|---|---|
| Under 25 years | 23.21% |
| 25–64 years | 55.11% |
| 64 years and older | 21.69% |

| FRANCE | |
|---|---|
| Under 25 years | 30.28% |
| 25–64 years | 49.90% |
| 64 years and older | 19.82% |

| SPAIN | |
|---|---|
| Under 25 years | 24.94% |
| 25–64 years | 56.92% |
| 64 years and older | 18.15% |

# ECONOMICS AND DEVELOPMENT

## GDP AT PPP
Constant 2011 international dollars (IMF, April 2019)

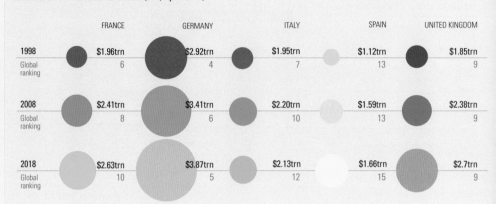

| | FRANCE | GERMANY | ITALY | SPAIN | UNITED KINGDOM |
|---|---|---|---|---|---|
| **1998** | $1.96trn | $2.92trn | $1.95trn | $1.12trn | $1.85trn |
| Global ranking | 6 | 4 | 7 | 13 | 9 |
| **2008** | $2.41trn | $3.41trn | $2.20trn | $1.59trn | $2.38trn |
| Global ranking | 8 | 6 | 10 | 13 | 9 |
| **2018** | $2.63trn | $3.87trn | $2.13trn | $1.66trn | $2.7trn |
| Global ranking | 10 | 5 | 12 | 15 | 9 |

## GDP PER CAPITA AT PPP
Constant 2011 international dollars (IMF, April 2019)

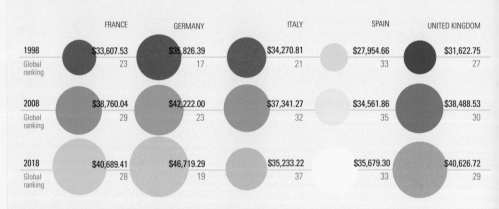

| | FRANCE | GERMANY | ITALY | SPAIN | UNITED KINGDOM |
|---|---|---|---|---|---|
| **1998** | $33,607.53 | $35,826.39 | $34,270.81 | $27,954.66 | $31,622.75 |
| Global ranking | 23 | 17 | 21 | 33 | 27 |
| **2008** | $38,760.04 | $42,222.00 | $37,341.27 | $34,561.86 | $38,488.53 |
| Global ranking | 29 | 23 | 32 | 35 | 30 |
| **2018** | $40,689.41 | $46,719.29 | $35,233.22 | $35,679.30 | $40,626.72 |
| Global ranking | 28 | 19 | 37 | 33 | 29 |

## HUMAN DEVELOPMENT INDEX (HDI)
(UN Development Programme, 2019)

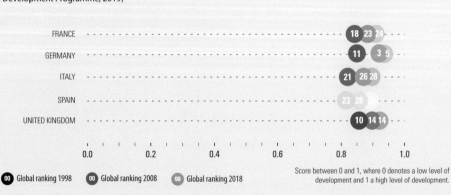

FRANCE — 18 23 24

GERMANY — 11 3 5

ITALY — 21 26 28

SPAIN — 23 28

UNITED KINGDOM — 10 14 14

0.0   0.2   0.4   0.6   0.8   1.0

- (00) Global ranking 1998
- (00) Global ranking 2008
- (00) Global ranking 2018

Score between 0 and 1, where 0 denotes a low level of development and 1 a high level of development.

# INTERNATIONAL INTEGRATION

## TRADE
Exports of goods and commercial services, constant 2010 US dollars
(World Trade Organization, 2019)

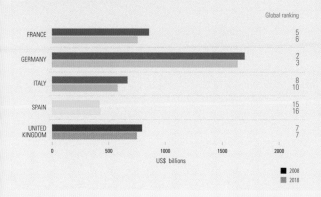

Global ranking

| | |
|---|---|
| FRANCE | 5 / 6 |
| GERMANY | 2 / 3 |
| ITALY | 8 / 10 |
| SPAIN | 15 / 16 |
| UNITED KINGDOM | 7 / 7 |

0    500    1000    1500    2000

US$ billions

■ 2008
■ 2018

## INTERNATIONAL NETWORK
Total number of diplomatic missions, 2017
Lowy Institute Global Diplomacy Index
(2017)

| | Missions abroad | | Global ranking |
|---|---|---|---|
| FRANCE | 266 |  | 3 |
| GERMANY | 224 | | 8 |
| ITALY | 205 | | 11 |
| SPAIN | 215 | | 10 |
| UNITED KINGDOM | 225 | | 7 |

# DIPLOMACY AND DEFENCE

## DEFENCE BUDGET
Constant 2010 US dollars (Military Balance 1998,
and Military Balance+)

Global ranking

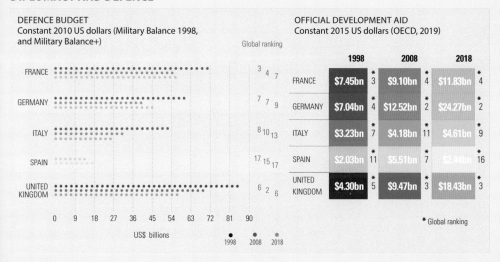

| | |
|---|---|
| FRANCE | 3  4  7 |
| GERMANY | 7  7  9 |
| ITALY | 8  10  13 |
| SPAIN | 17  15  17 |
| UNITED KINGDOM | 6  2  6 |

0   9   18   27   36   45   54   63   72   81   90

US$ billions

● 1998    ● 2008    ● 2018

## OFFICIAL DEVELOPMENT AID
Constant 2015 US dollars (OECD, 2019)

| | 1998 | | 2008 | | 2018 | |
|---|---|---|---|---|---|---|
| FRANCE | $7.45bn | *3 | $9.10bn | *4 | $11.83bn | *4 |
| GERMANY | $7.04bn | *4 | $12.52bn | *2 | $24.27bn | *2 |
| ITALY | $3.23bn | *7 | $4.18bn | *11 | $4.61bn | *9 |
| SPAIN | $2.03bn | *11 | $5.51bn | *7 | $2.44bn | *16 |
| UNITED KINGDOM | $4.30bn | *5 | $9.47bn | *3 | $18.43bn | *3 |

* Global ranking

## POLITICAL SYSTEM
(Economist Intelligence Unit, 2008, 2018)

Global ranking

**2008**

29   24   21   15   13

FRANCE ● ● ●     ● ● GERMANY
ITALY ●
SPAIN ● ●     ● UNITED KINGDOM

**2018**

0    1    2    3    4    5    6    7    8    9    10

Global ranking

33   29   19   14   13

Score between 0 and 10, where 10 denotes a fully democratic and 0 a fully authoritarian regime.

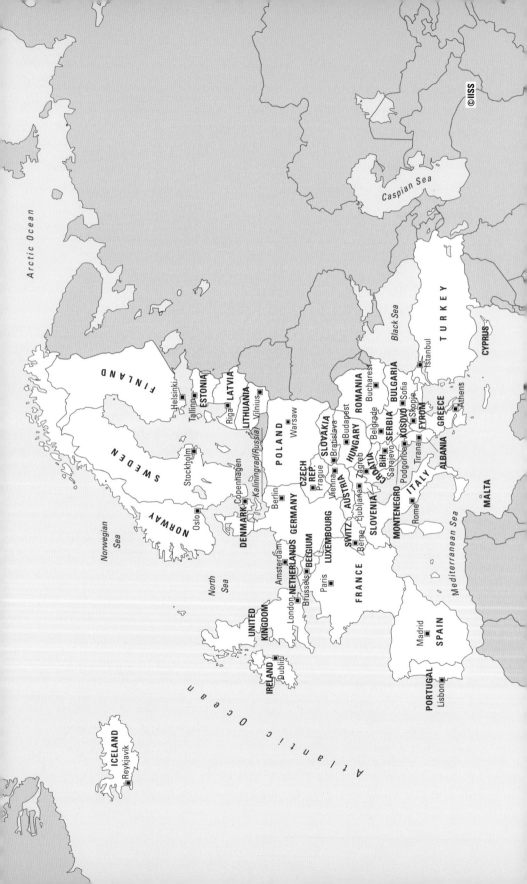

Arctic Ocean

Norwegian Sea

North Sea

Atlantic Ocean

Caspian Sea

Black Sea

Mediterranean Sea

©IISS

ICELAND
Reykjavik

IRELAND
Dublin

UNITED KINGDOM
London

PORTUGAL
Lisbon

SPAIN
Madrid

FRANCE
Paris

NORWAY
Oslo

SWEDEN
Stockholm

FINLAND
Helsinki

DENMARK
Copenhagen

NETHERLANDS
Amsterdam

BELGIUM
Brussels

LUXEMBOURG

GERMANY
Berlin

SWITZ.
Bern

ESTONIA
Tallinn

LATVIA
Riga

LITHUANIA
Vilnius

Kaliningrad/Russia

POLAND
Warsaw

CZECH REP.
Prague

SLOVAKIA
Bratislava

AUSTRIA
Vienna

HUNGARY
Budapest

SLOVENIA
Ljubljana

CROATIA
Zagreb

BiH
Sarajevo

MONTENEGRO
Podgorica

SERBIA
Belgrade

ROMANIA
Bucharest

BULGARIA
Sofia

KOSOVO

FYROM
Skopje

ALBANIA
Tirana

ITALY
Rome

GREECE
Athens

TURKEY
Istanbul

CYPRUS

MALTA

# Chapter 8

# Europe

## 2018–19 Review

Against a backdrop of growing populism, an increased likelihood of a messy Brexit, threats to cyber security, global tensions over trade and technology, and a faltering economic recovery, there were several significant developments in Europe in the year to mid-2019, including the European Parliament elections in May in the 28 member states of the European Union (including the United Kingdom). Reflecting increasingly divergent regional and national political priorities, the EU looked even more divided internally than before, threatening to undermine further the effectiveness of its leadership in the region and on the global stage at a time of growing United States unilateralism.

In December 2018, German Chancellor Angela Merkel stepped down as leader of her party, the Christian Democratic Union (CDU), following poor results by the CDU and its sister party, the Christian Social Union (CSU), in regional elections in October. The performance of her successor, Annegret Kramp-Karrenbauer, was lacklustre and gaffe-prone: despite her shift to the right, she failed to halt the rise of the far-right nationalist Alternative for Germany (AfD). AfD's share of the vote in the May European Parliament elections rose to 11%, up four percentage points compared with the 2014 European elections, while the CDU/CSU saw its support decline by six percentage points to 29%, although this was small compared with the centre-left Social Democratic Party (SPD), the junior partner in the governing coalition, which won only 16% of the vote (down from 27% in 2014), which could increase the likelihood of a pre-term federal election. Compounding the government's problems, the German economy slowed sharply in the second half of 2018, almost falling into recession as external demand weakened. In July–September, German real GDP contracted by 0.2% quarter on quarter and was flat in the final three months of the year before returning to growth of 0.4% in the first quarter of 2019.

In France, President Emmanuel Macron came under intense pressure from the *'gilets jaunes'* (yellow vests) demonstrations held across the country in late 2018 and early 2019 to protest against issues of economic injustice. Having initially adopted a hardline security response towards the protests, which frequently turned violent, Macron eventually had to step back from the confrontation, offering an apology for the treatment of the protesters, tax cuts for low- and middle-income workers and a 'great debate', a nationwide consultation of citizens on how to fix France's problems. However, he vowed to continue with his economic 'transformation' programme to liberalise the French economy and overhaul France's welfare system. Campaigning on a pro-EU reform agenda in the European Parliament elections, Macron's centrist Republic on the Move party (LRM) came second, albeit by a narrow margin, behind the far-right National Rally (RN, previously the Front National) led by Marine Le Pen.

The UK's planned departure from the EU, which was originally scheduled for 29 March 2019, remained in political deadlock. The British Parliament was given two extensions to provide more time to approve the withdrawal agreement reached in late 2018 between then-UK prime minister Theresa May and the EU, but on both occasions the withdrawal agreement failed to win the required majority of votes. The next deadline for the UK to leave the bloc was 31 October 2019. The delay forced the UK to hold European Parliament elections in May, which inflicted heavy defeats on the country's two mainstream parties, the Conservatives and Labour, by the Brexit Party and the pro-Remain Liberal Democrats and Green Party. May resigned as the Conservative Party leader and prime minister in June, as agreed with her party, triggering a Tory leadership contest, the winner of which would take over as prime minister and determine the next steps to take regarding Brexit. The overwhelming favourite was Boris Johnson, a former mayor of London and leader of the Leave referendum campaign in 2016. There was little prospect of the UK leaving with a deal by the end of October, increasing the risk of a no-deal Brexit, which would be extremely disruptive to the UK and EU economies. However, failure to leave the EU in October threatened to trigger a general election in the UK, in which the Conservatives and Labour would be likely to suffer heavy losses again.

Despite May's attempts to persuade individual member states to soften their positions on Brexit, the bloc of 27 EU countries maintained its unified stance regarding the withdrawal agreement, sending a strong political message to Eurosceptic parties that leaving the bloc cannot be easy, and that any deal must ultimately be less favourable than EU membership. The 'Irish backstop' – a mechanism intended to prevent the return of a hard border between the Republic of Ireland and Northern Ireland – had been the biggest stumbling block to winning the approval of the UK Parliament for May's withdrawal agreement. In the event of a no-deal Brexit, however, the onus would fall on the government of the Republic to establish a border with Northern Ireland in order to ensure its own continued participation in the EU's single market.

While the UK's planned departure from the EU posed the biggest challenge to the bloc's unity in recent years, several other member states continued to push back against EU and eurozone rules. In particular, the Italian government formed in June 2018 by the anti-establishment Five Star Movement (M5S) and the far-right League party was a disruptive force in the EU, despite having formally dropped its objective of leaving the euro. In addition to repeated clashes with some of its EU partners over Italy's hardline response to illegal immigration, in the second half of 2018 a dispute erupted with the European Commission over Italy's

2019 budget plan. After several months of brinkmanship, an unconvincing compromise was reached in December, allowing Italy to avoid the opening of an excessive deficit procedure (EDP) over its high and rising debt. However, the reprieve was only temporary and the stand-off resumed in June 2019 when the Commission issued a recommendation to the Council to open an EDP against Italy for its failure to comply with debt-reduction obligations under the EU's Stability and Growth Pact. Italy's ruling coalition was increasingly divided, making the negotiation of a solution extremely challenging. Seeking to take advantage of its strong performance in the European Parliament elections, the League adopted a hardline stance against the EU, which threatened to trigger a political crisis, possibly over the 2020 budget, and an early general election. In a snap election the League was likely to emerge as the single-largest party, allowing Matteo Salvini, the League leader, to ditch the M5S for a broad centre-right alliance.

The nationalist, socially conservative governments in Hungary and Poland also clashed repeatedly with the EU, exacerbating the perception that an East–West divide between old and new member states was emerging in the bloc. The main sources of tension were Poland and Hungary's refusal to take their allocation of refugees under the EU's refugee-relocation policy, as well as their attempts to curb judicial independence, control public-service media and place restrictions on civil-society organisations. These anti-democratic tendencies prompted the European Commission and the European Parliament to invoke procedures under Article 7 of the treaty of the EU, first against Poland in December 2017 and subsequently against Hungary in September 2018. The process could theoretically result in the two countries losing their voting rights in the EU, but it made little progress in either case as it requires the unanimous support of all other member states in the European Council, and Hungary and Poland made clear that they would support each other in the event of such a vote. However, in a landmark ruling in late June 2019 the European Court of Justice (ECJ) deemed that the overhaul of Poland's supreme court had broken EU law, even though the Polish government amended the reform in December 2018, after the case was brought. The ruling created a binding precedent that should help to strengthen the EU's protection of judicial independence and the rule of law. In the European Parliament elections, the ruling Law and Justice (PiS) party won 45% of the vote in Poland, putting it in a strong position to be re-elected for a second term at the national parliamentary election, due by November 2019. Hungary's governing party, Fidesz, won 52% of the vote in the European elections, which was likely to galvanise Prime Minister Viktor Orbán in future clashes with the EU.

Rising populist nationalism and increased political fragmentation also destabilised national politics in several EU member states in the year to June 2019, leading to early elections, protracted government-formation negotiations and unstable executives, as well as harsher anti-immigrant rhetoric and more restrictive national migration policies. These trends were particularly evident in Spain, despite the country's strong economic performance since the Spanish banking crisis in 2012. After decades of domination by two main parties – the conservative nationalist People's Party (PP) and the leftist Spanish Socialist Workers' Party (PSOE) – the political system has undergone upheaval since the eurozone crisis with the emergence of several new parties, notably the anti-austerity populist Podemos (We Can) and the centrist, liberal Citizens party, which came to the fore during the crisis, as well as Vox, the right-wing anti-immigrant offshoot of the PP, support for which surged after the Catalonia crisis in 2018. In April 2019, Spain held its third general election since December 2015, following the collapse of the minority PSOE government led by Pedro Sánchez, which only in June 2018 had replaced the PP government led by Mariano Rajoy brought down by a no-confidence vote in parliament. Sánchez's PSOE won the election with almost 29% of the vote, up from 22.6% in 2016, but this was insufficient to obtain a majority of seats in parliament. Vox entered the Spanish parliament for the first time as its support surged to 10.3%, from 0.2% in 2016. Support for the centre-right liberal Citizens also increased, rising to about 16% from 13% in 2016. By contrast, support for the PP halved to 16.7%, from 33%. Hampered by internal divisions, support for leftist Unidas Podemos (United We

Can, UP, an alliance of Podemos and other left-wing parties) dropped to 14.3% from 21.1% in 2016. Government-formation negotiations between Sánchez and UP have been difficult, making a repeat minority PSOE government or a snap election the two most likely outcomes. The PSOE made further gains at the expense of UP at the European Parliament elections, while support for the PP recovered partially after taking votes from Vox and the Citizens party.

Following the victory of the centre-right New Democracy (ND) in the European Parliament, regional and municipal elections held on 26 May 2019, then Greek prime minister Alexis Tsipras, of the ruling Coalition of the Radical Left (Syriza), called a snap general election held on 7 July, just a few months before the end of the parliamentary term. Tsipras's popular support has declined sharply since he was elected in 2015, despite taking Greece out of the EU-backed economic and adjustment programme (EAP) in August 2018, concluding eight years of austerity and unpopular reforms under three EAPs. In early January 2019 Tsipras lost his majority in parliament, following the withdrawal of the small, right-wing, nationalist Independent Greeks from the ruling coalition in protest against the ratification of the government's agreement with Macedonia to change that country's name to North Macedonia. Fiscal handouts as well as promises of tax cuts and public-spending increases failed to revive support for the party in the European Parliament elections in May, in which the more business-friendly ND led by Kyriakos Mitsotakis maintained a lead of almost ten percentage points over Syriza. At the general election, ND won 39.9% of the vote and 158 seats in the 300-seat national parliament compared with Syriza's 31.5% and 86 seats. Although the Mitsotakis government will be the first single-party government since the start of the Greek crisis almost ten years ago, it will face multiple challenges, including dealing with the consequences of fiscal loosening by Syriza in 2019. ND could also find itself at loggerheads with Greece's international partners in the EU and NATO, if Mitsotakis seeks to maintain his promise to renegotiate the Macedonia name-change deal, which is widely unpopular in Greece.

## European Parliament elections

The European Parliament elections held across the bloc on 23–26 May 2019 produced an even more fragmented political landscape than in the outgoing parliament. The pro-European centre-right European People's Party (EPP) and the centre-left Progressive Alliance of Socialists and Democrats (S&D) remained the two largest parliamentary groups, but they lost ground as well as their combined majority. The pro-European liberal, centrist Alliance of Liberals and Democrats for Europe (ALDE) and Greens/European Free Alliance (Greens–EFA), made significant gains, as did nationalist, populist and Eurosceptic parties (most notably the newly formed Brexit Party in the UK and the League in Italy).

This inconclusive outcome complicated the appointment process to renew for another five years the leadership of the EU's key institutions – the European Parliament, the European Commission, the European Council and the European Central Bank (ECB) – as well as the High Representative of the Union for Foreign Affairs and Security Policy. In particular, it resulted in the jettisoning of the modicum of transparency and democratic legitimacy that came with the Spitzenkandidaten process used in previous appointment rounds whereby the Commission presidency went to the candidate of the largest group in the European Parliament. It was also likely to hamper efforts to get beyond recent crises driven by Brexit and migration in order to revitalise the bloc's reform agenda, including strengthening the respect of rule of law within the EU, reinforcing the institutions underpinning the European single currency, tackling climate change and enhancing the EU's external-relations policy. At the same time, the member states must negotiate the next multiannual financial framework (MFF) package for 2021–27, the EU's long-term budget, a task that has become more challenging without the UK's net contribution of about €13 billion (US$14.7bn) per year.

With the European economy at a delicate juncture as the recovery from the global and eurozone crises showed signs of stuttering, and many European banks were still struggling to clean up their balance sheets, replacing Mario Draghi, the president of the ECB, posed a particularly difficult challenge. The ECB's actions under Draghi, which

included the adoption of some new and some unorthodox policies, prevented the collapse of the single currency at the height of the eurozone
crisis in late 2011 and underpinned the economic recovery that followed.
Largely to ensure the continuity of these policies, EU leaders nominated
Christine Lagarde, the managing director of the International Monetary
Fund, as Draghi's successor. In the second half of 2018, the ECB signalled
strongly that it was on track to follow the process of monetary-policy
normalisation that the Federal Reserve (the US central bank) had begun
several years earlier. However, just a few months after the ECB ended
its asset-purchasing programme (quantitative easing) in December 2018,
weakening economic activity in the eurozone, disrupted by escalating
global trade tensions and a falling inflation outlook, prompted an abrupt
volte-face. In June 2019, Draghi indicated that the ECB would keep interest rates low for longer and possibly cut rates further, and also announced
the pricing of a third round of targeted longer-term refinancing operations (TLTROs). This change of direction followed a similar change of
course in the US in late 2018, when the Federal Reserve signalled a shift
to an easing bias, despite still relatively solid economic data.

**External relations remain tense**
EU–US relations have deteriorated significantly since Donald Trump won
the US presidential election in 2016 – with Trump seeking re-election in
2020, it was unlikely that transatlantic tensions would ease in the coming
year. The main areas of disagreement have been on global trade; NATO
and low defence spending in Europe; and the United States' withdrawal
from the 2015 Iran nuclear deal and the Paris agreement to address
climate change reached in the same year. In the area of trade, Trump's
main focus since the beginning of 2019 was predominantly on pressuring
China with hefty and wider-ranging tariffs to obtain further concessions
in trade negotiations. With the EU, the issue was in abeyance following
an agreement reached in July 2018 between Trump and then-European
Commission president Jean-Claude Juncker, which averted the US president's plan to introduce a 25% tariff on automotive imports from the EU
while the two sides conducted wider negotiations to improve trade ties.

In the meantime, the wider negotiations have not even begun, making the imposition of a wave of US tariffs on EU goods increasingly likely after the new European Commission (led by Ursula von der Leyen) comes into office in November 2019, unless significant progress can be achieved.

The EU's external relations with its two largest neighbours, Russia and Turkey, remained strained in the year to June 2019. However, there was no perceptible escalation of the level of tension, despite Russia's continued weaponisation of information, cyberspace and corruption to destabilise Western democracies and the continued erosion of democracy in Turkey under President Recep Tayyip Erdogan. This relative stability probably reflected the EU's focus on its internal divisions and possibly a perception of greater threats from elsewhere, notably deteriorating relations with the US and the rise of China.

The sanctions on Russia – imposed by the EU in 2014 in response to Russia's support for separatists in eastern Ukraine and the annexation of Crimea – remained in place. Despite the reservations repeatedly expressed by some member states, particularly Italy under the M5S–League government, EU member states have unanimously agreed since mid-2015 to roll over the sanctions every six months, most recently in June 2019, because of the lack of progress on the implementation of the Minsk agreements, to which the sanctions are linked. In March 2019, the EU, along with the US and Canada, imposed additional sanctions for Russia's attack on two Ukrainian gunboats and a tug in the Sea of Azov in November 2018. But in June 2019 a majority of the Parliamentary Assembly of the Council of Europe, the continent's leading human-rights organisation, gave in to Russian pressure and voted to end Russia's suspension from the assembly, much to the dismay of, among others, Ukraine, the Baltic states, Poland and the UK.

Tensions between the EU and Turkey simmered at a perceptibly lower level than in previous years, when the EU and particular EU member states, notably Germany and the Netherlands, were the targets of some of Erdogan's harshest anti-Western rhetoric. Cooperation between the EU and Turkey under the joint action on migration continued, despite the lack of progress on Turkey's EU accession negotiations and the promised lifting of visa requirements for Turkish citizens visiting the EU or negotiations to update Turkey's customs-union agreement with the EU. A growing source of instability in the region, however, was increased gas exploration in the Eastern Mediterranean. In response to drilling by international companies awarded licences by Cyprus, Turkey sent in navy ships to harass Cyprus-contracted ships and began to increase its own drilling activity, usually accompanied by Turkish navy vessels. Turkey does not recognise Cyprus's exclusive economic zone (EEZ) agreements with Egypt, Lebanon and Israel, and argued that until Greek and Turkish Cypriots reach a settlement regarding the division of the island, Cyprus's gas exploration in Cypriot waters violates Turkish Cypriots' rights. In mid-June 2019, Turkey warned the EU not to interfere after the EU threatened sanctions against Turkey if it continued its 'illegal' exploration activities in Cyprus's territorial waters.

By comparison, Turkey's relations with the US continued to deteriorate over issues ranging from the widespread popular perception in Turkey, which the Turkish government and government-controlled media has encouraged, that the US was involved in or supported the 2016 attempted coup by parts of the Turkish Armed Forces, to US military support for Syrian Kurdish groups affiliated with Turkey's outlawed Kurdistan Workers' Party (PKK). After a protracted stand-off over Erdogan's purchase of Russia's S-400 missile system – which Erdogan insisted he will not reverse – the US threatened to impose sanctions against Turkey if it took delivery of the S-400s, due in July 2019. The US administration argued that the S-400s would compromise the security of its new F-35 fighter jet, which Turkey was helping to develop. With the Turkish economy on the brink of a crisis since mid-2018, heavy sanctions would risk destabilising the economy further. This would further weaken popular support for Erdogan's ruling People's Alliance, particularly in urban areas — the opposition won all the major cities in Turkey in the local elections on 31 March 2019, including Ankara, the capital, and Istanbul (twice, owing to a rerun demanded by the People's Alliance). However, Erdogan could not afford to be seen to back down under US pressure, having built strong nationalist support among Turks through the perception that he has stood up to Turkey's unsupportive traditional allies in the West.

Enlargement fatigue – as well as the difficult challenges of negotiating Brexit and trying to reform the EU to prevent rising Euroscepticism and anti-immigrant sentiment – weakened the EU's stabilising role in the strategically important Western Balkans comprising Albania, Bosnia-Herzegovina, Kosovo, North Macedonia, Montenegro and Serbia. In mid-2018, the EU indicated that it would decide in mid-2019 about whether to open accession negotiations with North Macedonia, which had just signed the name-change deal with Greece, and with Albania. The one-year delay was hardly encouraging at the time, but the decision was pushed back again to October 2019, despite a recommendation from the European Commission in late May to open talks with both countries.

# The Challenge of Populist Politics in Europe

Populism has been a recurrent issue in European politics since 2002, when Pim Fortuyn emerged in the Netherlands and Jean-Marie Le Pen made it into the second round of the French presidential elections. Almost 20 years later, populism is now at the centre of the narrative. The May 2019 European elections were dominated by two themes. Before the voting took place, the story focused on the rise of right-wing populism. After the votes were counted, the storyline shifted to focus on the surprising success of the European Green Party, a pan-European alliance of political parties that espouse green policies. For journalists, this shift provided a compelling narrative arc — from deepening concern to refreshing optimism. For analysts with a deeper sense of history, however, these developments were less reassuring. Right-wing populism is not new in Europe, even if we ignore the interwar period. The Greens are even older. Moreover, and in important ways, the two political movements point in the same direction.

The two very different movements are connected ideologically in their rejection of mainstream, representative democracy. The Greens have a long tradition of favouring both grassroots participation and direct democracy; the new radical right has adopted many of the same themes. They are connected historically because when grassroots movements and Green parties created divisions within the traditional left in the early to mid-1970s, they created opportunities for traditional conservative parties to move to the centre. This created a vacuum even further to the right, which in the 1980s led to the sudden re-emergence of political groups such as the French National Front, the Austrian Freedom Party and the Italian National Alliance. In turn, these new right-wing challenger parties sparked a splintering on the right that brought the mainstream left-wing parties back toward the centre.

By implication, while the European elections signalled a hopeful shift from nativism to environmentalism, they also revealed both the fragmentation and the volatility of the European electorate. In this sense, the important point is not that voters moved from right to left. Rather it is that voters were looking in ever greater numbers for anything that lies outside the political mainstream and that promises fundamental change in how European representative democracy functions. There are many good reasons for European voters to engage in that search. Mainstream politicians have failed in many ways to adapt to the challenges of technological innovation, globalisation, mass migration and climate change. No matter how justified this hunt for alternatives may be, however, it has serious strategic implications for both Europe and NATO.

## Disaffection with traditional democratic parties

The simple answer to the question of where this disaffection comes from lies in what political scientists refer to as a blocked 'circulation of elites'. The concept was developed at the end of the nineteenth century around the origins of mass democracy and it connects the idea of policy failure to patterns of representation. Whenever there are significant changes in society or in the economy that cause pain for large parts of the population, traditional elites struggle and often fail to respond. The electorate may vote out the elites, but then the fixed menu of parties to choose from becomes the problem. Hence the next step is for the leaders of disenchanted groups to look for ways to broaden the reach of the party system to include groups that are under-represented or to change the way political elites and voters are connected. The choices are not exclusive; usually would-be political leaders opt for both at the same time.

One prominent example of this change to the party menu was the rise of the Christian Democrats and the Socialists (later Communists) at the start of the twentieth century, both populist outsiders who came to dominate the Italian political system. These parties promised to break the stranglehold of the Liberals over the political process and to represent the working classes and rural communities. Likewise, when the Green Party emerged in Germany in 1980, it offered an issue it believed that mainstream elites failed to address (the environment), a new party to add into the competition and a different way of tying that party to the electorate (through direct democracy and grassroots mobilisation).

The emergence of the Greens was a symptom of a broader trend of political foment, when, in addition to the environment, civil rights, gender equality and nuclear weapons also began to attract attention. The Greens were only part of the larger fracturing of the left that took place alongside the emergence of new social movements in the 1970s and early 1980s.

The left was not alone in being affected. The traditional conservative parties also had problems holding onto their vote share. They could shore up their positions, however, by pulling some of the more traditional constituencies located on the centre-left who felt disoriented by the many new dimensions of political conflict. This was easier for Christian Democratic parties in places such as Italy, Germany or the Low Countries, where the Christian Democrats always had strong connections to the working classes, but Margaret Thatcher in the United Kingdom showed that it was possible to draw traditional left-wing supporters by weakening their organisational supports by attacking the trade unions and then changing the voters' self-interests by privatising public housing. France would appear to be the exception in this pattern because the Socialists came to power in the early 1980s, but what is instructive about the French case is what happened under that left-wing government.

As soon as then-president of France François Mitterrand recognised the failure of his experiment to practise Keynesianism in one country in 1982–83, he moved in 1984 to change the electoral law from a two-round, first-past-the-post system (which encouraged the voters to cluster around the major groups of centre-right and centre-left), to a proportional system that would make it easier for the far-right National Front to challenge Mitterrand's centre-right opposition. Jacques Chirac was able to win a parliamentary majority in the centre in 1986, but he still had to wrestle with Jean-Marie Le Pen's National Front in the parliament to his right. Le Pen then built on his new-found legitimacy to run for the presidency in 1988. Chirac reversed Mitterrand's changes to the electoral law in 1987, but he never managed to put Le Pen back into the box again. Redesigning electoral systems cannot prevent the emergence of political alternatives.

## What can be done?

Mainstream strategies for dealing with both left- and right-wing challenger movements have been largely unsuccessful. Trying to hold challenger parties outside government with 'grand' coalitions or minority governments only makes the left- and right-wing populist movements stronger, as demonstrated by the rise of the Freedom Party in Austria and the Flemish Interest and New Flemish Alliance in Belgium.

In Austria, the mainstream Social Democratic Party and the People's Party kept the Freedom Party out of power at the national level in the 1980s and 1990s by forming grand coalitions, although the Freedom Party was allowed to enter government at the regional level. In the end, however, this strategy backfired. The Freedom Party campaigned aggressively against the two-party condominium (and the sharing of public appointments that went along with it) to capture just under 27% of the vote in the 1999 national parliamentary elections, narrowly edging out the People's Party, which came in third place overall. Although the Social Democratic Party won the most votes, the People's Party was able to return to power by forming a coalition with the Freedom Party. The principle of exclusion reached its limits when Wolfgang Schüssel, leader of the People's Party, realised he had to choose between another weakening grand coalition with the Social Democrats or the alternative of using the Freedom Party to maintain his party's participation in government.

The situation in Belgium was slightly different, insofar as the exclusion of the Flemish Bloc and later Flemish Interest was more consistent at all levels of government. That held the party at bay, but not the demand for representation of Flemish cultural and political identity. When the New Flemish Alliance emerged to tap into Flemish discontentment in 2001, it immediately attracted attention within the electorate. The Flemish Christian Democrats tried to harness that attention to their own political movement but could not contain the demand for a fundamental shake-up of Belgium's political institutions on the part of many Flemish voters. Once the New Flemish Alliance broke free from the Christian Democrats in 2008, it quickly established itself as the largest political movement in Flanders and – by extension – in

Belgium. Over the following decade, the New Flemish Alliance became increasingly mainstream, participating in the federal government, although this evolution has involved tempering many of the party's reform demands. This has not satisfied many of the party's supporters, who shifted back to the Flemish Interest in the May 2019 national elections that coincided with the vote for the European Parliament. The New Flemish Alliance is still the country's largest party, but the Flemish Interest now comes in second.

The stories of exclusion end in Austria and Belgium with efforts to bring the challenger parties into government; the stories of inclusion reveal that challenger parties often struggle once in positions of power. In the Austrian case, the Freedom Party quickly fractured under the strain of governing responsibility; in the Belgian case, the New Flemish Alliance learned to shoulder the responsibilities but then had to wrestle with the conflicting demands of its constituents, some of whom have drifted away. Neither of these consequences is surprising, and neither are they limited to the centre right. The left-liberal D66 party in the Netherlands entered government in 1994 with a strong political-reform agenda, only to fracture after the strain of two terms in office; the Green Party in Germany did not fracture as a result of its experience in government in 1998–2005, but it did struggle to hold onto its support base; the Liberal Democrats in the UK suffered much more dramatically after forming a coalition with the Conservative Party in 2010.

What is interesting in all these cases is that the impact of governing responsibility is often short-lived. Supporters drift away to alternative groups when the challenger parties on the left or the right are in office and being obliged to make compromises with the political mainstream, but they tend to drift back once the parties return to opposition. Anyone who expected the Austrian Freedom Party to collapse after its leader Jörg Haider left and split the movement was quickly disappointed. The New Flemish Alliance has proved remarkably resilient, as has D66. Now the Green Party is resurgent, and the Liberal Democrats have won the support of many voters who are disillusioned with the government's approach to Brexit, among other issues.

Similarly, few populist movements are seriously dented by scandal or hypocrisy. The leaders may disappear and whole organisations may vanish, but the spirit of the movement is more tenacious. Pim Fortuyn emerged as a political force in the Netherlands very quickly between 2001 and 2002, first as the spokesperson for a left-leaning grassroots politics movement and then as the leader of his own eponymous movement that many analysts characterise as right-wing because of his strong views on immigration and Islam. Within the Netherlands, however, that ideological placement was always more ambiguous. Hence when Fortuyn was assassinated and his group collapsed, putative heirs to his legacy quickly emerged on both the right (Geert Wilders) and the left (Jan Marijnissen).

The story about Umberto Bossi in Italy is even more dramatic. Bossi ran the Northern League (Lega Nord) from the end of the 1980s through the first decade of the twenty-first century. The theme of the party centred primarily on the corruption of Italy's ruling class and the comparative virtues of northern Italy. Support for the Lega Nord collapsed, however, when Bossi was caught misappropriating funds both for himself and for his family, with the party owing approximately €50 million (US$58m) to the Italian state. Matteo Salvini took over the party in 2013. Since then, he has not only transformed the party from a regionalist movement into a truly national political force (called Lega without the Nord) with a rapidly increasing support base across the country. Although the cloud of scandal still hangs over Bossi, and the Lega's finances remain precarious, Salvini has gone from strength to strength – first by surpassing Silvio Berlusconi on the right of the political spectrum in the March 2018 parliamentary elections and then overtaking the Five Star Movement (M5S) in the elections to the European Parliament as Italy's largest political party.

## A perilous alternative

Trying to socialise the newcomers by giving them the discipline of responsibility is problematic as well. The German Greens, the New Flemish Democrats, the Dutch D66 and the Liberal Democrats in the UK may be the exceptions that prove the rule, all being groups that sacrificed their reform agendas in the interests of holding together a national coalition. Often politicians that come from outside the mainstream look for ways to hold onto power once they get into office. Similar tendencies were evident in Tony Blair's efforts to re-engineer the British Labour Party in the 1990s and Jeremy Corbyn's efforts to re-engineer the same party today. Efforts to gerrymander electoral districts fall much in the same vein.

The situation becomes more complicated, however, when the re-engineering takes on a constitutional dimension, as illustrated by Matteo Renzi's attempt at constitutional reform in Italy. Renzi came from outside the Democratic Party elite and campaigned openly on the idea of tossing Italy's traditional political class onto the junk heap. As prime minister, he proposed to transform the electoral system to reduce its proportionality and to eliminate Italy's balanced bicameral legislative system. Voters across the Italian political spectrum expressed concern that Renzi would transform Italy into a constitutional dictatorship by undermining the careful checks and balances in the Italian constitution. Renzi retorted that these reforms were necessary to make government more effective, but public-opinion polling showed that a significant plurality of the Italian electorate would rather sacrifice effectiveness in order to protect representativeness. The voters overwhelmingly rejected Renzi's constitutional-reform agenda in a popular referendum.

Renzi's reforms failed, but some constitutional-reform efforts are more enduring. The Fidesz party in Hungary, the Law and Justice party in Poland and the Justice and Development party in Turkey have all emerged from outside the political mainstream and engaged in sweeping constitutional-reform efforts in order to consolidate their position by challenging the independence of the highest courts, re-engineering the electoral laws and strengthening the power of the executive. The goal with this comparison is not to make Renzi a moral equivalent to Hungary's Viktor Orbán, Poland's Jarosław Kaczyński or Turkey's Recep Tayyip Erdogan. That said, it is worth considering what would have happened if Renzi had succeeded in his referendum and Salvini's Lega had risen to dominate Italy's newly reformed institutions.

French President Emmanuel Macron pursues another method to consolidate influence. Macron's strategy is to shatter any legitimate opposition to his own movement. So far, he has fractured both the traditional centre-left Socialist Party and the centre-right Republicans. By weakening the Socialists and Republicans as potential challengers, Macron is very unlikely to face a mainstream contender in the second round of the next presidential elections. This is how he could come in second in the European elections to Marine Le Pen's National Rally party and yet still emerge strengthened in his control over the French presidency (and, by extension, the National Assembly). The only challenge now is for Macron to weaken the political influence of the Senate. Like Renzi, Macron hopes to make the institutions of the French Republic more effective in pursuing what he believes to be a necessary reform agenda. The open question is whether he makes those institutions more vulnerable at the same time. Macron dominates French politics now but that tells us very little about who may come next.

## Impact on Europe and the Atlantic Alliance

This analysis of the main European political developments points to three areas of influence for populist politics and parties. A first area of influence is the progressive splintering or fragmentation of national parliaments and the resulting weakness of national administrations, rendering domestic politics dysfunctional. Here the best illustration is Belgium, which has already gone through one 550-day period without a national government thanks to the demands made by the New Flemish Alliance after the June 2010 national elections and appears to face an even more intractable situation with the New Flemish Alliance and the Flemish Interest. The Dutch national parliament is also deeply divided, although still able to form effective governments. The British Parliament shows worrying signs of fragmentation as well. Whether those divisions will deepen or diminish after Brexit is an open question.

The second area of influence has to do with the changing architecture of Europe. The European project has traditionally rested on the commitment of mainstream political elites. Now that these elites are more clearly focused on retaining their hold over domestic politics, or they have been replaced by challenger parties without the same historical ties to Europe, the ability of national governments to cooperate at the European level is more limited. Again, this is not the first time we have seen this consequence. The 1970s was a decade of European pessimism and sclerosis in many respects, even if there were moments of dynamism as well. Nevertheless, the changes this time around may be more significant. The UK's decision to leave the European Union is probably the most dramatic example. The challenge to the rule of law in Hungary, Poland and Turkey could also have lasting consequences. But all of this would recede into the background should Italy decide or be forced to leave the euro, although this seems an unlikely prospect.

Thirdly, populist parties and politics drive the increasingly idiosyncratic nature of political discourse at the European level. The European People's Party (EPP) and the Socialists and Democrats (S&D) were not always the most coherent groups, but their members had more in common than groups that lie outside those ideological traditions. The political families were supposed to strengthen identification with Europe at the popular level; now they tend to generate confusion. The links between those political families and the deals made in the European Council are also hard to untangle. The difference in approach between Macron and Salvini to pan-European alliances is one illustration; the on-again, off-again relationship between the EPP and Orbán's Fidesz party is another.

The increasingly divided, fractious and incoherent European politics also poses a serious challenge for NATO. Firstly, the incentive for national governments to invest in NATO is diminished as national politicians focus increasingly on domestic concerns. 'Europe' may face strategic adversaries but countries such as Belgium, the Netherlands and Spain do not. Secondly, the significance of strategic differences across NATO partners increases. Russia means something very different to Italy and Germany than it does to the Baltic states; Turkey means something very different to Greece and Cyprus than it does to France. Of course, these differences have always existed, but now they are more palpable because domestic politics in the countries involved is more fraught. Thirdly, the ability of European NATO partners to act in unison declines even where they share a strategic vision – largely because of an absence of institutions for coordinating action. Here the best illustration is trade policy. The new pattern of trade negotiations involves issues related to product regulation and production processes beyond tariffs and quotas, for which the existing institutional machinery is ill-equipped to manage. This could be seen not only in the difficult ratification of the EU–Canada Comprehensive Economic and Trade Agreement (CETA), but also in the political mobilisation that took place across Europe in reaction to the Transatlantic Trade and Investment Partnership.

## The way ahead

The relative rise of the Greens and underperformance of the far right in the May 2019 European elections is a silver lining to the trend of rising populism. Of those parties that have arisen outside the political mainstream to challenge the patterns of representative democracy in Europe, the Greens have been the quickest to socialise around the norms of democratic governance, as illustrated by the career of the leading Green politician Joschka Fischer. Having attacked the police during public protests in Germany in the 1970s, Fischer led Germany to participate in the bombing of Serbia and Kosovo on behalf of NATO in the late 1990s.

The point to recall, however, is that support for the Greens has been volatile – nothing like the sustained support the mainstream European political parties enjoyed in the 1950s and 1960s – and the Green resurgence may turn out to be short-lived. The increasing volatility of European electorates, by contrast, is likely to prove more enduring. Europeans are searching for political alternatives. The Greens are only one choice on the menu; many of the other choices available are potentially more destabilising for the functioning of European democracy, for the coherence and effectiveness of European foreign policy and for solidarity within the Atlantic Alliance. Moreover, what is true for Europe is also true for the US. The changes in that country may prove to be even more consequential.

# Germany's Foreign and Security Policy 30 Years After the Fall of the Wall

Germany's international security environment has changed considerably in the 30 years that have passed since a mass breach of the Berlin Wall on the night of 9–10 November 1989 triggered a series of events leading to the country's unification, the collapse of the Soviet bloc and a fundamental reframing of the global balance of power. On the other hand, Germany's foreign and security policy over this time frame is characterised more by consistency than change. New developments are now forcing new responses, albeit slowly, reactively and insufficiently.

In the years that followed the fall of the wall, Germany learnt to see itself as a country 'encircled by friends'; the ambition for a 'common European home', as set out by Soviet president Mikhail Gorbachev in June 1989, was widely held to be achievable. The country's total rejection of its militarist past had already ensured its focus on the development of civilian power; any utility for military means was confined to issues of territorial and collective defence. Now, with the arc of history turned towards liberal democracy and free markets, Germany saw its future global role in areas such as humanitarian action and peacekeeping. Defence spending shrank accordingly. This laid the groundwork for Germany to slip into what German foreign minister Guido Westerwelle would, in 2011, describe as a 'culture of restraint'. Many foreign observers adopted more critical characterisations, perceiving instead a country that was shirking its international responsibilities.

In 2019, Germany's security environment stands as testament to the continuing importance of hard power and the return of great-power competition. Within Germany, a populist right-wing party, Alternative for Germany (AfD), challenges the country's traditional pro-European Union orientation. Meanwhile, the EU has been buffeted by existential crisis after crisis. On the world stage, the old threat of Russia has been re-established, the new challenge of China is crystallising and an unexpected challenge from the continent's transatlantic ally has emerged. The threats to multilateralism are multiplying. Despite this, to quote German diplomat Thomas Bagger, 'multilateralism is all there is in the German mainstream today'. The task ahead for Berlin is to rethink what German leadership on foreign and security policy looks like, and to establish what areas the country wishes to prioritise.

## The three phases of Germany's foreign and security policies

In the first 20 years after the fall of the wall, there were some incremental changes in Germany's foreign- and security-policy engagements, but in a context of overwhelming continuity. The country's default position was to find modest ways to express alliance solidarity while remaining on the sidelines of strategic action and decision-making. Germany's chief contribution to the First Gulf War was confined to chequebook diplomacy, even as nods at alliance solidarity were made with the deployment of minesweepers to the Mediterranean between August 1990 and September 1991, and then, once the war was over, to the Persian Gulf. The country's contributions to the ending of the Yugoslav wars were similarly modest at best, although efforts again became more significant once the mission shifted from war fighting to one of post-conflict stabilisation. By the tenth anniversary of the fall of the wall, the Bundeswehr was not only contributing to a war-fighting mission, NATO's *Operation Allied Force* against Yugoslavia, but one that was not based on a mandate from the United Nations Security Council. There was still little willingness to risk German casualties, but Germany was at least beginning to show up. A similar pattern could be seen in engagements in Afghanistan that followed the attacks of 11 September 2001. Germany's understated engagement with *Operation Enduring Freedom* (that nevertheless included the deployment of its special forces in combat operations) was followed up with more-meaningful contributions to what became the NATO-led International Security Assistance Force.

For these 20 years, at least in the spheres of defence and security policy, Germany broadly remained a highly cautious follower. The notable exception was the country's opposition to the US-led invasion of Iraq in 2003. Yet in some areas Germany was starting to prove itself willing to take on more of a role in diplomatic leadership. From June 2003 onwards, Germany worked closely with France and the United Kingdom as part of the E3 in pursuit of an Iranian nuclear deal. Germany also proved itself a reliable, committed and effective advocate of both NATO and EU enlargement.

From 2009, and the 20th anniversary of the fall of the Berlin Wall, the developing crisis in the eurozone brought German economic leadership to the fore. This in turn marked the beginning of the second phase of the country's post-unification foreign and security policy. By 2013, the fashion for ascribing constraining adjectives to Germany's hegemonic credentials was already well established; an *Economist* front cover, for example, depicted Germany as 'The Reluctant Hegemon'. As Germany saw itself as left with no choice but to take on greater responsibility in the management of the EU's economic affairs, so the same rhetoric on responsibility began to infuse discussions on foreign and security policy.

In Afghanistan, the Bundeswehr's dangerous combat experiences helped develop the expertise and self-esteem of the German armed forces, even as the country's domestic debate on its armed forces continued to lag behind the reality of these military advances. However, the limitations of change within Germany's domestic discourse were highlighted in March 2011 with Germany's controversial abstention on UN Security Council Resolution 1973, which prepared the ground for military intervention in Libya. This saw Germany position itself alongside China and Russia, leaving its allies abandoned. Such a failure to show solidarity with allies who were prepared to risk the lives of their soldiers in defence of freedom and human rights temporarily left the country marginalised. Anne Marie Slaughter, two months departed from the Obama administration as State Department director of policy planning, told German readers in a *Die Zeit* editorial that their country had 'failed the test' of leadership.

Nevertheless, fuelled in part by the fallout from Germany's Libya vote, Berlin's determination to prove itself a reliable and substantive ally was solidifying. The rhetoric of 'more power, more responsibility' entered the mainstream of Germany's foreign- and security-policy elite. By the time of the Munich Security Conference of February 2014, German politicians lined up to echo their president's call for the country to make 'a more substantive contribution' in foreign and security policy, and to make it 'earlier and more decisively'.

These claims of greater political will were soon put to the test; within six weeks of the Munich consensus, Russia had annexed Crimea and begun its destabilisation of eastern Ukraine. This marked the start of a third phase, in which Germany's new-found rhetoric of responsibility now had to contend with difficult realities. The Ukraine crisis cemented the status of President Vladimir Putin's Russia as both a strategic competitor and a military threat; any hopes for 'modernisation partnerships' lay in tatters. Chancellor Angela Merkel was, from the outset, laudably and consistently clear in her critique. Standing next to Putin in May 2015, Merkel spoke of the implications of Russia's actions in Ukraine on the bilateral relationship: 'The criminal and illegal annexation of Crimea and the warfare in Eastern Ukraine has led to a serious setback for this cooperation.'

The Normandy format – a diplomatic grouping of senior representatives from France, Germany, Russia and Ukraine convened to address the war in eastern Ukraine – offered a first glimpse of the changing paradigms of German engagement in foreign- and security-policy concerns. Germany would lead on issues of its choosing, albeit alongside partners (in this instance, France). It would be more pragmatic in its selection of formats as it did so, focused more on achieving results and less on ideological expressions of allegiance to the formal institutions of the EU. It would use extensive diplomatic outreach and engagement with the smaller states of the EU to counter their instinctive suspicions of big-power diplomacy. Finally, it would have the confidence and authority to lead the rest of the EU not just into agreeing sanctions but, in this instance, into then explicitly tying them to the fulfilment of Russia's obligations under the Minsk II agreements that Germany had led the way in negotiating in 2015.

Russia's illegal actions also had consequences for Germany's military posture. Amongst other developments, on 1 January 2019, Germany became the lead nation of NATO's Very High Readiness Joint Task Force (supported by additional capabilities provided by the Netherlands and Norway and additional forces provided by Belgium, the Czech Republic, France, Latvia, Lithuania and Luxembourg). Germany also took charge of one of the four new multinational battlegroups under NATO's Enhanced Forward Presence (EFP), contributing 540 of the approximate 1,055 soldiers based in Rukla, Lithuania.

The country found itself confronted with other uncomfortable realities, from the migration crisis of 2015–16 to the EU membership crisis that the UK's vote to leave the union threatened to precipitate. Nevertheless, it was with the election of a US president who was apparently ideologically hostile to the EU and ambivalent about the transatlantic relationship that Germany, to quote Bagger again, 'lost its moorings'. A new US National Security Strategy in 2017 shut the door on notions of a 'global community', announcing a new era of 'great power competition'.

However, for all of Germany's protestations of concern at the 'America first' outlook of its ally, it too could show itself more than capable of putting its interests first when required. Germany's persistent support for the controversial Nord Stream II pipeline stands in testament to its government's willingness to prioritise what it believes to be its own interests over the strategic interests and expressed wishes of its like-minded neighbours and partners.

## Leadership in a time of strategic confusion

As its approach to Nord Stream II suggests, Germany's record in responding to these new realities and the challenges they pose has been patchy at best.

The country has played a leading role in selective diplomatic negotiations, most notably in the Normandy format and in its efforts, as part of the E3, to protect the Joint Comprehensive Plan of Action with Iran following the United States' unilateral withdrawal in May 2018. These efforts have included the design of a special purpose vehicle – the Instrument in Support of Trade Exchanges, or INSTEX – to shelter trade with Iran from US sanctions. Even should it prove unable to live up to

Iranian requirements, this proffers a serious long-term conceptual challenge to US sanctions policies. Germany has sought and attained a seat on the UN Security Council for 2019–20. Meanwhile, in January 2019, it concluded a somewhat underwhelming Aachen Treaty with France, which included a commitment to 'deepen their cooperation in foreign policy and internal and external defence'.

Germany has also shown a greater willingness to engage at the sharp end of crisis-management operations, although under considerable diplomatic pressure from France in particular. In 2019, with up to 1,100 soldiers and 20 police officers, Germany's largest military deployment was within the framework of the UN's most dangerous mission – the Multidimensional Integrated Stabilization Mission in Mali (MINUSMA). Germany is also the second-largest troop contributor to the EU Training Mission in Mali. Additionally, it is sending police officers to the civilian Common Security and Defence Policy mission and the EU Capacity Building Mission in Mali, and working closely with France to step up political and, where appropriate, military cooperation with the governments of the Sahel. The need to fight illegal migration, radicalisation, terrorism and organised crime in the G5 Sahel region (Burkina Faso, Chad, Mali, Mauritania and Niger) is one that will remain for the foreseeable future. Indeed, German military commitments in the region are more likely to grow than to fade, as recognised by the country's establishment of a military base in Niamey, Niger, in late 2018. Meanwhile, the country is now the second-largest troop contributor to NATO's *Resolute Support* mission in Afghanistan.

Yet Germany's international security environment is deteriorating more rapidly than such incremental positive changes. On critical questions of cash and capabilities, the country's leaders, encouraged by a still wary and complacent population, have been falling short. German defence spending may have increased by more than 36% during Ursula von der Leyen's tenure as defence minister, but there are credible doubts as to whether Germany can meet even the target of 1.5% of GDP on defence spending by 2024 that it has set for itself. Soon after her appointment as defence minister in July 2019, Annegret Kramp-Karrenbauer committed herself to pushing for her country to meet the 2% target, but there remains little evidence that the domestic political environment in which she operates is prepared to authorise such measures. Meanwhile, the January 2019 annual report into the readiness of the German armed forces continued to record chronic shortages in equipment and recruits.

## What next?

In the immediate years ahead, the picture will remain a confused one. The story of Germany's development of greater strategic engagement in foreign and security affairs is likely to be both incremental, and one that develops within the context of partnerships with European allies. Regardless, Germany is setting new ambitions and creating paths to their potential fulfilment. For example, it has committed to raising, by 2032, three divisions collectively boasting eight to ten armoured brigades as part of NATO's EFP. Such a development would make Germany a leading power, at least within this ambit, with as many as 19 smaller NATO countries providing elements of their capabilities to the Bundeswehr under the Framework Nations Concept. The latter facilitates smaller armies in plugging their capabilities into a larger 'framework' of nations, as part of a small but still significant step towards greater burden sharing.

As von der Leyen takes over as president of the European Commission in November 2019, she is likely to take particular interest in fleshing out her long-held support for a European Defence Union. Within the context of the EU, the impact of some heavily German-influenced initiatives – most notably the Permanent Structured Cooperation (PESCO) – risks being underwhelming, unless serious political attention and a proactive approach can be sustained. In any case, Germany will continue to help lead the push for the EU's central institutions to take on expanded roles in both security and defence. Its presidency of the EU Council in the second half of 2020 is likely to develop this trend further. Berlin will, however, need to start putting empirical evidence behind its repeated intimations that, if German defence spending can be framed within a context of furthering European integration and EU capacity-building, the sums available for it can be raised more readily.

For all the focus on the increasing role of the EU's central institutions, Germany's most meaningful defence relationships will continue to lie at the bilateral level. The prospect of Brexit (the UK's withdrawal from the EU) has heightened the political imperative for close Franco-German defence cooperation. Nevertheless, the limitations of this cooperation have been highlighted by tensions over differing national arms-export policies, in particular following the murder in Turkey of the exiled Saudi journalist Jamal Khashoggi and with regards to the ongoing war in Yemen. Franco-German commitments in the Aachen Treaty to develop a common arms-export policy, at least for joint programmes, are more easily offered than realised. Meanwhile, the prospects for a genuinely common and effective EU arms-export regime remain distant.

Despite concerns over the future of the Atlantic Alliance, Germany's ambition is to reaffirm, and not challenge, its relevance. This will require more than displays of 'effective multilateralism'. It will mean committing to hard investments, making domestically contentious choices, and showing resilience of political will as the country works to project stability and promote its interests in a more contested world.

## Recognising the constraints

Despite some modest establishment efforts in recent years to promote public debate on the country's future responsibilities in foreign and security policy, Germany's domestic environment remains a constraining factor for the government. A survey of German public opinion in late 2018 showed that 32% of respondents continued to think that having a close relationship with Russia was more important than a close relationship with the US. While 41% of Germans thought that their country should become more involved in international crises, 55% preferred restraint. These constraints were on clear display in April 2018 as Merkel fashioned her response to US-, UK- and French-led military strikes on Syria in the aftermath of the Syrian government's chemical-weapons attack on Douma. These strikes were, Merkel declared, both 'necessary and appropriate'. However, with polling showing a clear majority against Germany's involvement, support for the actions of allies was once again confined to the rhetorical.

Even as German politicians have shifted to engage more with foreign and security policy, the public lags far behind. Their interest is largely focused on non-military means. A survey commissioned for the 2019 Munich Security Conference reported that some 59% of German respondents believed that their country should be 'internationally neutral'. While 70% of German respondents thought that their country 'should pursue an active foreign policy and a significant role in solving international problems, crises and conflicts', only 32% thought that Germany should 'if necessary, pursue military intervention in conflicts'. Such attitudes present a fundamental structural obstacle hindering more rapid and meaningful change.

The Social Democratic Party (SPD) has been a difficult partner for Merkel's Christian Democratic Union (CDU) on defence spending and engagement. This will continue for as long as the coalition lasts. Although the next German government – at least, if it involves a partnership between the CDU/Christian Social Union in Bavaria (CSU) and Alliance 90/The Greens as the basis for government – will find itself freed from the comparatively pacifist influences of the SPD, the speed of any shift is likely to continue to frustrate European partners and undermine transatlantic relations. In the unlikely scenario that the CDU is removed from office in favour of a left-of-centre coalition, tensions will only increase further.

Meanwhile, any German government regardless of its make-up is unlikely to start treating its defence industry as a strategic asset any time soon. As an IISS report on the fostering of the defence-industrial base for Europe argued, strong defence industries strengthen the deterrent effect of armed forces. The defence-technological industrial base is a core element of defence and deterrence, including because of its contribution to the security of supply. Yet popular pacifist instincts help ensure that active support for the country's world-class defence industry remains a taboo issue for German politicians. The debate on the relationship between German defence policy, German defence industry and German industrial policy remains stunted at best.

## Priorities for leadership

The demands for greater German leadership are manifold, but four areas stand out as requiring German foreign- and security-policy leadership sooner rather than later.

Firstly, despite Berlin's understandable protestations to the contrary, Germany is already the quiet coordinator behind the supervision of the EU's Brexit management. The implications of even an orderly Brexit for the EU's foreign- and security-policy credentials are considerable; a disorderly Brexit would be notably worse. Berlin has a key role to play in pushing back against loose talk of 'no deal', and in guiding serious and substantive negotiations that successfully ensure, to mutual benefit, ongoing close cooperation between the EU and the UK on issues of foreign and security policy.

Secondly, and tied to this, Berlin has a key role to play in ongoing deliberations over European strategic autonomy. While Paris veers towards more exclusive definitions, Berlin will need to show vision and leadership in overseeing the development of a more flexible and inclusive formulation, in particular with regard to third-party engagement in key defence and security initiatives. This means ensuring that there are docking points into the EU's evolving defence and security structures that will keep a post-Brexit UK working in close cooperation with its European partners. It also means developing frameworks for discussions of European strategic autonomy that do not seem to US counterparts either dismissive of their contributions, or worse, hostile to them.

Thirdly, as the defence and security challenges to Germany and the EU are becoming more diffuse, areas of potential greater German leadership are emerging that do not come into contact so immediately with the ongoing constrictions of the country's domestic authorising environment. The world of hybrid warfare offers one example. This is an area in which Berlin will have greater domestic licence to engage, fashioning effective responses at the nexus of EU–NATO cooperation. Leadership in this field will include working with the EU's central institutions to shape an increasing number of credible and networked responses, whether to threats of disinformation targeted at areas of priority strategic concern, such as the Western Balkans, or to threats of malign foreign investment in strategic sectors, and the boosted screening and monitoring mechanisms such concerns demand. It is also an area that brings Germany face to face with the challenges posed by the authoritarian powers of Russia and China, socialising its domestic public to these threats, and all while allowing Germany to work squarely and (largely) without controversy alongside the US.

The last priority area for action lies in Germany's successful rebuilding of the Bundeswehr in line with its NATO commitments. In September 2018, Germany's defence ministry outlined a new 'capability profile', with significant funding implications designed to develop for the Bundeswehr a set of capabilities that might allow it both to do its part on collective defence and to contribute to out-of-area operations. This involves considerable growth in funding, military hardware and human resources for the army, the air force and the navy. The formation in late 2019 of a sixth tank battalion will mark the first growth of the Bundeswehr since the end of the Cold War. Effective implementation of this planned overhaul will be critical not just for Germany but also for Europe. The scale of this task, within the context of past chronic under-investment, makes Germany a pivotal player in the development of new European defence capabilities in the years ahead.

The range of demands is such that, if Germany is to be a hegemon of any sort in foreign and security policy, it will be a selective one. In some areas (as evidenced by France's European Intervention Initiative and Germany's operations in Mali) Germany will continue to prefer to follow. That is to be expected and does not negate the possibility and indeed probability of its leadership in other areas where Germany will choose to lead, as seen in the examples of the Normandy format, the E3 Iran negotiations and PESCO. That it will lead in partnership is not a weakness but a strength that will underpin Germany's legitimacy. Ultimately, a more networked approach to consultation and partnership of the sort Germany appears to be edging towards may not produce speedy responses to international security threats, but it is likely to produce more effective and sustainable ones.

# Europe's Capability Challenge and Transatlantic Relations

Defence planners in Europe have an unenviable task. Following two decades of structural underfunding and downsizing, they must devise ways to close self-inflicted capability shortfalls and rebuild military strength. At the same time they need to consider how to prepare their armed forces for the digital age and future opponents. The challenge has become more urgent because of developments in the United States, Europe's core defence partner. On the one hand, President Donald Trump has questioned the value of NATO and has repeatedly suggested Europeans are free-riding on the coat-tails of American defence. On the other hand, current US strategy and defence planning are based on the assumption that China is the pacing military threat for the US and hence American policymakers have begun to ask Europeans to think about the contributions they could make to help Washington with defence contingencies in the Asia-Pacific. Two sets of interlinked challenges thus emerge: deterring a militarily capable and assertive Russia, possibly without the US; and helping the US to contain a rising China that is modernising its armed forces and wants to be able to fight and win wars anywhere in the world by 2049. The former challenge has achieved considerable attention; discussion of the latter has barely begun.

## Deterring Russia

Debates about European defence autonomy are almost as old as the Atlantic Alliance, which marked its 70th anniversary in April 2019. Recently they have been given impetus by a deteriorating security environment in Europe's periphery and further afield, as well as public comments by Trump that question the value of NATO and suggest that his commitment to European security is conditional on increased European capability. Several governments in the EU and NATO have begun to ask how the defence of Europe would look if the US were not involved.

One approach is to consider a scenario in which NATO, after a hypothetical US withdrawal from the organisation, would be obliged to defend its territory against a state-level military attack in the near-term future. Would European NATO states be able to successfully repel an attack on an eastern member?

A recent IISS study gauged their readiness against a scenario in which tensions between Russia on one hand, and Poland and Lithuania on the other, lead to fighting that results in Russian forces controlling Lithuania and a 30-kilometre-deep security zone running the length of Poland's border with the Kaliningrad region. In response, the North Atlantic Council (NAC) invokes Article 5, requiring all NATO nations to contribute to an initial defensive response. It directs the Supreme Allied Commander Europe (SACEUR) to plan operations to reassure Poland, Estonia, Latvia and other front-line NATO member states by deterring further Russian aggression, and to plan for and assemble forces for a military operation to restore Polish and Lithuanian government control over their territories. The land component would represent the main effort of NATO's campaign, intended to close with and defeat Russian forces in Lithuania and occupied Poland in order to eject them and liberate the territory of NATO member states. Simultaneously, in order to ensure the timely flow of logistical support to the front line, it would have to devote resources to securing rear areas against Russian sabotage and air and missile attacks.

Russia has developed a formidable arsenal of long-range missile and rocket artillery in the past decade, as well as modernising its armour and artillery platforms and recruiting large numbers of contract personnel. All of this has served to effectively close the qualitative gap between Russian ground forces and their European equivalents. Russia has also modernised a substantial array of electronic-warfare systems, and NATO forces can expect to face a substantial contest across the electromagnetic spectrum. Given the Russian capabilities and forces likely to be deployed in such a scenario, the IISS assessed that the NATO land component would have to be equivalent in size to a Major Joint Operation 'Plus' (MJO+), comprising multiple manoeuvre corps, all with sufficient combat support and combat service-support assets. A reasonable degree of confidence in a favourable outcome of operations for NATO in this scenario would require four corps, each with a headcount of roughly 60,000.

Currently, the NATO Response Force is sized to produce a land-combat division, while the NATO Readiness Initiative agreed at the 2018 Brussels summit (the 'Four 30s' plan) would produce a roughly corps-sized force in battalion terms, presumably from 2020 onwards. Even if combined, these structures would therefore prove insufficient to generate the force size required in this scenario. In addition, the bulk of the NATO force would need to be composed of armoured or heavy mechanised brigades equipped with modern main battle tanks and infantry fighting vehicles in order to meet the Russians on a relatively even playing field.

Without the US, and assuming significant Polish combat losses during the Russian incursion, the remaining European members of NATO and Canada currently only have around 20 brigades that would meet these criteria. About one-third of this total comprises formations primarily equipped with lighter, wheeled, armoured vehicles. Assuming that, on average, 50% of these formations would be able to deploy within the 90 days given, the overall force available to NATO would be equivalent only to ten brigades or a single corps. In a similar vein, the numbers of modern artillery, particularly long-range systems, are currently insufficient. To adequately address the requirement it would therefore be necessary to significantly increase the size of both capabilities through a combination of greater overall force pools, improving the equipment level of existing European heavy brigades and raising readiness levels.

Russia's ability to threaten targets in Poland with its long-range missile capabilities, and the challenges posed to NATO air forces by Russia's improved air force and integrated air-defence capabilities, mean that the land component also has a sizeable requirement for air and missile defence, both mobile short-range and long-range area coverage. Although some member states are planning to rebuild capability in this area, there is currently little or no modern mobile short-range air defence available. The limited amount of available longer-range air and missile defence would be just sufficient to cover the necessary front-line air bases for NATO, but there would be no excess to protect the land component itself or to protect critical military-infrastructure sites such as rear-area headquarters and logistics. Given the overall shortage of assets in this critical area, a substantial increase in overall force size would be essential.

NATO needs to address shortfalls in niche land-combat enabler areas, particularly combat bridging and medium uninhabited aerial vehicles (UAVs) for intelligence, surveillance and reconnaissance (ISR) missions, as well as the need for formation headquarters to control such capabilities. In general, other combat support and aviation assets are available in sufficient quantities for a three-corps-sized force. However, in order to generate a four-corps-sized force, a slight uplift in the overall numbers of combat engineers and modern attack helicopters would be required.

Finally, reserve stocks of ammunition and spares would need to be substantially increased. Even successful high-intensity operations could potentially last for weeks and very quickly consume ammunition stocks for direct- and indirect-fire weapons. With Cold War stocks run down, war-reserve stocks in many European countries may only be sufficient for a few days of operations at best, and could take months to replenish.

The air element of the campaign is tasked with gaining air superiority, protecting land assets, and providing close air support and ISR. Airborne early warning (AEW) and air-to-air refuelling (AAR) are critical enabling roles. The Russian Aerospace Forces have increased long-range aviation training exercises, including with Tu-160M *Blackjack*, Tu-95MS *Bear* and Tu-22M3 *Backfire*. The *Blackjack* and *Bear* aircraft have been regularly intercepted while skirting UK airspace, while *Backfire* and Su-34 *Fullback* aircraft have been deployed to Crimea and Syria and exercised along the Mediterranean. The threat of air-launched land-attack cruise missiles, combined with Russia's increased ability to use sea-launched land-attack cruise missiles, requires significant national air defence among the allies. This is compounded by some countries retaining comparatively few primary air bases, such that they have acquired near-strategic targeting value.

Given these demands, the force that European NATO member states and Canada could generate from their air forces would be highly unlikely to deliver a generally favourable outcome in offensive operations to retake territory in support of Article 5. All other things being near equal, platform numbers around parity strongly favour the defender. A force structure 50% larger than what is currently deployable would offer an uncertain outcome, while a deployed force double that size would provide a generally favourable outcome, at least in the air domain.

Areas of shortfall include the latest generations of fighter ground-attack aircraft, and associated types of weapons that are deemed just as important – both in terms of class and with regard to depth or arsenals. Air-launched weapons inventories among NATO nations – excepting the US – are nowhere near sufficient to conduct a high-intensity peer-on-peer campaign. Again barring the US, the NATO states that participated in the 2011 air operation in Libya depleted their stocks of air-to-surface weapons in the course of the intervention. The rate of weapon utilisation would be far higher in a peer-on-peer war in Europe – indeed, it is conceivable that some of today's holdings could be exhausted within the first 48 hours.

Given the importance of degrading Russian ground-based air defences, there is a lack of aircraft and weapons dedicated to suppression of enemy air defence/destruction of enemy air defence (SEAD/DEAD) in the inventory. There are also shortfalls in AAR and anti-submarine warfare (ASW) aircraft. Survivable ISR also presents a challenge. The small number of medium and large ISR UAVs in the inventory were not designed to operate in contested airspace. The use of such systems would, in all probability, result in unacceptably high attrition rates, even at far greater inventory levels. Instead, a low-observable UAV (notionally in the class of the RQ-180 or the *Avenger*), of which some 50 airframes would be required, could provide the necessary capability.

European space-based ISR and communications satellite infrastructure is deemed adequate by the IISS. However, this assumes no hard-kill anti-satellite (ASAT) activity on the part of Russia. Were Moscow to degrade this capability, then some rapid-access launch system combined with a constellation of small, ready-to-launch ISR satellites would be required. Alternatively, spare satellites – extraneous to the present systems – could be built up, though these would remain more vulnerable to attack when placed in orbit.

The maritime domain presents a particular challenge in terms of operating in the narrowly defined main area of operations. Moreover, Russia's navy would likely seek to interdict and pin NATO forces in the broader arena, particularly in the northeast Atlantic and the Mediterranean and Black seas. On the assumption of no US support, transatlantic resupply and convoying requirements would not be on the scale assumed by previous, and particularly Cold War, contingency planning. Nevertheless, some resupply from the US and Canada would be necessary. Likewise, the prospective NATO Europe force posture is unlikely to assume the level of offensive action or 'holding Russian strategic assets at risk' strategy as in a classic 'NATO with US' context. Yet the threats to, or vulnerability of, key maritime infrastructure and trade routes in and around northwestern Europe and the Mediterranean and Black seas, as well as potential interdiction of forces, mean that offensive action at a certain level in the maritime arena is likely to be required at some stage in order to bring operations to a conclusion.

The deployment on the scale anticipated of submarine and surface units from the Russian Northern and Black Sea fleets would represent a significant challenge to NATO maritime forces, because of both their stand-off anti-ship capabilities and their potential precision land-attack capabilities. These include 3M45 *Granit* (SS-N-19 *Shipwreck*), 3M54K (SS-N-27 *Sizzler*), 3M24 (SS-N-25 *Switchblade*) and 3M14 (SS-N-30 *Kalibr*) missiles. Threats within the Baltic Sea itself also include the *Bastion*-P (SSC-5 *Stooge*) large coastal anti-ship missile. Maritime forces further face a significant potential threat from Russian long-range missile-armed aviation.

Beyond the command and control requirements, NATO would need a surface-action group, submarine force and mine countermeasure vessel (MCMV) capability directly for the Baltic. To support operations in the Baltic and around Norway, it would need a littoral manoeuvre/amphibious group with a large screening escort force. NATO would also need a carrier-centred sea-control and ASW screening force for the North Atlantic to counter the Russian interdiction threat, as well as some support for NATO land-based tactical aviation. There would also be a requirement for an ASW force in the English Channel and a screening submarine force for the Atlantic. In addition, for the southern area of operations, a deterrent force for the western and eastern Mediterranean and the Black Sea would be needed, comprising one combined carrier-centred (CVS) sea control/littoral manoeuvre group; one surface-action group for the Black Sea; and submarine screening and general MCMV forces.

The above data and assessed naval-platform shortfalls, and the associated mission requirements, also suggest significant major weapons-system shortfalls, most notably two squadrons (12 aircraft each) of F-35B *Lightning* combat aircraft or equivalent to equip the assessed carrier deficit; 500–1,000 local-area air-defence missiles; 500–750 anti-ship missiles; and 250 heavyweight torpedoes.

## Time and money

With the capability shortfalls identified, it is possible to estimate procurement costs on the basis of US, UK and French official data plus company reports, defence media outlets and IISS assessments. The total cost for the equipment required to fill the capability shortfalls ranges between a low estimate of US$281 billion and a high estimate of US$347bn, in 2019 US dollars. Roughly half of this pertains to the land domain (US$141.4bn low; US$184.7bn high), with the aerospace requirement ranging between US$71.7bn and US$83bn, and the maritime component assessed at between US$68.2bn and US$79.5bn.

The most expensive capability shortfalls by far are air-defence platforms, with costs based on examples of *Patriot*-system acquisitions. Table 1 lists the ten most expensive capability shortfalls in this scenario. The air-defence systems required for the protection of forces and critical military infrastructure together account for 30% of the total. Recapitalisation in terms of main battle tanks, air-defence destroyers and fighter aircraft would be the next most costly procurements: each represents 10–11% of total costs.

Table 1: **Deterring Russia: most expensive European equipment shortfalls**

| Platform type | Example | Requirement | US$bn 2019, low | US$bn 2019, high |
|---|---|---|---|---|
| Long-range surface-to-air missile (force protection) | *Patriot*; SAMP/T | 72–90 batteries (24–30 battalions) | 62.15 | 77.69 |
| Main battle tank | *Leopard 2A6/2A7*; M1 *Abrams* | 2,500–3,750 (100–150 battalions) | 25.00 | 37.50 |
| Destroyer/with anti-ship missile/with hangar/with surface-to-air missile (air defence) | UK Type-45; France/Italy *Horizon* | 16 | 30.96 | 33.21 |
| Fighter aircraft | *Typhoon*; *Rafale* | 264 | 24.72 | 30.90 |
| Long-range surface-to-air missile (critical military infrastructure) | *Patriot* | 30 batteries (10 battalions) | 25.90 | 25.90 |
| Infantry fighting vehicle | CV90; *Puma*; VBCI | 2,500–3,750 | 12.88 | 19.31 |
| Short-range air defence (SHORAD) | CAMM; *Land Ceptor* | 162–216 batteries (54–72 battalions) | 10.15 | 13.54 |
| Destroyer/with anti-ship missile/with hangar/with surface-to-air missile (anti-submarine warfare/general purpose) | France/Italy FREMM; UK Type-26 | 7 | 8.55 | 13.45 |
| Air-to-air missile (radio frequency) | *Meteor* missile | 2,112 | 9.61 | 9.82 |
| Anti-submarine warfare aircraft | P-8 class | 27 | 8.99 | 8.99 |

The equipment estimates do not fully reflect the costs of raising capabilities to required levels. For instance, the acquisition of 264 fighter aircraft would require the recruitment and training of 396 pilots, as well as spending on the running costs of the additional squadrons. This would add just over US$8bn to the cost of the new aircraft.

Closing the identified capability shortfalls needed for an Article 5 operation would provide Europe with stronger deterrence against a wide range of actors and would enable Europeans to tackle a greater variety of military operations, be that in the context of NATO or the EU. It is a political decision for governments to employ the military instrument in line with their national interests.

To achieve strategic autonomy, European states would do well to focus on the capabilities needed to tackle threats to European security, rather than on vision statements. The challenge is daunting but not unachievable. In 2018, NATO's European member states spent some US$264bn on defence, according to IISS data, which is certainly a significant sum. It would of course be the responsibility of all those countries, not just one or two of them, to bridge the identified capability shortfalls. And, realistically, that would take one or two decades to achieve. In 2018, it is notable that if all European NATO member states had been prepared to spend in accordance with the benchmark of 2% of GDP, an extra US$102bn would have been available in addition to the US$264bn they did spend.

The timelines for the recapitalisation across the military domains are complex. For example, equipment procurement for the identified land shortfalls, if it were to start immediately in 2019, would probably take between eight and 12 years due to the quantities involved and the limited number of available suppliers. Training units to full operational-capability standard on new equipment would add to this. Closing the identified gaps in the air domain, likewise, would take at least a decade, given aircraft and systems-production capacity, procurement decisions and production times, recruitment and training demands, and the time it takes for new units to reach an operational capability. In the maritime domain, due to the scale of the overall additional requirement, the complexity of construction of some of the capital ships and submarines, and the limited industrial base in Europe to undertake the work, it is estimated that it would take 15–20 years to fulfil the entire requirement. The other major challenge would be to deliver the large number of high-end surface combatants that are deemed necessary. Lower-end capabilities (e.g., ocean-patrol vessels) could be delivered over a shorter period of approximately ten years.

The task of closing the capability gaps is huge because NATO member states in Europe have largely dismantled their capability to tackle a serious territorial-defence challenge. Force structures have shrunk, equipment holdings have dwindled and readiness has in some cases collapsed. Furthermore, after years of out-of-area operations against asymmetric adversaries, military planning and training has only recently refocused on territorial contingencies with a peer challenger.

European shortfalls underline the enduring importance of the US in military terms for the defence of Europe. As a NATO member, the US provides a significant reservoir of capabilities on which US and NATO commanders can and would draw in a crisis. Some of those capabilities, including logistics and sustainment for land forces, may be relatively straightforward if not cheap to replace. Others, however, are almost unique to the US, so it would be difficult to substitute European capabilities.

## Helping to contain China

For most European members of NATO, Russia is understandably the most significant military security challenge they face. The perceived threat from Moscow is geographically close, and for some European countries it is existential and immediate. The US, however, has already asked allies to weigh up what they could offer in case of conflict with China. There is no evidence at this stage that European allies have coherent answers to this challenge. Aside from the question of whether Europeans see a role for themselves in the security of the Indo-Pacific, China is already coming to Europe. The People's Liberation Army (PLA) Navy has conducted exercises in the Mediterranean and the Baltic. Chinese medical units have exercised in Germany, a first on NATO territory. At the very least it is now necessary for NATO member states in Europe to think about what China's growing military presence and prowess means for them, not least because the US will ask this question.

The key factor driving China's development of its military capability is the need to protect its interests from destabilisation by neighbouring states and from US intervention. Its near-term goal is the mechanisation of its armed forces, but as PLA modernisation progresses the balance will slowly shift to a more ambitious power-projection outlook. The Chinese government has stated that by the mid-2030s it wants to be able to project power across its region and replace the US as the pre-eminent military power there.

Against this backdrop, some observers and practitioners in Europe have begun to argue that long-term transformation rather than short- to medium-term capability renewal should drive defence policy. This would see NATO member states embrace the digitisation of their armed forces and boost efforts to leverage advanced and emerging technologies for defence purposes. Key elements of such a transformational approach would include a focus on capabilities that enable decisive influence from range, including long-range precision weapons and military cyber capabilities. Conventional platforms would be much less crucial than, for example, missiles in attacking formations and infrastructure or in creating flexible anti-access/area-denial (A2AD) screens. Technology investment would focus on undersea warfare, counter-space capability, hypersonic weapons and directed-energy weapons. Unlike the task of rebuilding the capability that has been lost in the last two decades, long-term transformation would require the design of new systems.

Even in the most favourable of circumstances European defence spending will still be limited, and there will simply not be enough money to do all that is necessary or desirable, so defence planners will have to consider how to achieve a robust posture: what are the investment priorities that would deliver the minimum capability mix to make both short- to medium-term rebuilding and long-term transformation credible options? Europeans do not need to rebuild capabilities akin to those maintained during the Cold War, but only those that would demonstrate to Moscow that it could not win a short war in Europe. European NATO members could, for example, begin a serious effort to boost air and missile defence, ASW, cyber capabilities and their capacity to restore the balance in the hybrid space, as well as in those combat enablers where the US currently provides the weight of NATO capability. Doing so would tackle areas where NATO states' lack of recent investment has allowed Russia to build an edge that might make limited incursions tempting from Moscow's point of view.

The long-term challenge for European states would then be not only to build capabilities enabling them to more effectively defend the continent, but also to use those investments as a way of demonstrating to the US the value of European defence. Building Europe's capabilities, for instance in enabling capabilities and in command and control, would not only enable better defence but also allow the US to act more globally, perhaps in tandem with more global European operations. There is a risk that doing so might lead to an unconscious decoupling of the US from Europe. However, it seems much more plausible that a new transatlantic bargain might have to be built on the basis that Europeans operate globally to help the US with its various contingencies in exchange for a reconfirmed US commitment to European security through NATO.

Both rebuilding and transforming will require decisions about spending, manpower, acquisitions, readiness, strategy and burden-sharing that are far from easy. Vulnerabilities will persist for the next decade. Unity and resolve will be needed among Europeans and across the Atlantic. A lack of internal cohesion is perhaps the greatest challenge for NATO as the Alliance limbers up for its December 2019 leaders' meeting in London. It is unlikely that many decisions will be taken at the leaders' meeting itself, but foreign and defence ministers, meeting in the run-up to the December event, will probably agree a set of measures that heads of state and government can endorse. They are likely to concern burden-sharing, the implications for NATO of disruptive technologies, the repercussions of the collapse of the Intermediate-Range Nuclear Forces (INF) Treaty, and the beginnings of a NATO-wide conversation on China as a security challenge.

The April 2019 IISS report 'Defending Europe: scenario-based capability requirements for NATO's European members' can be accessed at https://www.iiss.org/blogs/research-paper/2019/05/defending-europe.

# Latin America: Drivers of Strategic Change

- In Brazil, the right-wing populist Jair Bolsonaro, a former army officer who has spoken warmly of the 1964–85 military dictatorship, won the presidency in October 2018. He quickly distanced the country from Cuba and Venezuela in favour of closer ties with right-wing governments. However, his plans for pension and economic reforms are dependent on a fragmented Congress in which he lacks a majority.

- Mexico departed from more than a decade of centre-right rule when the leftist populist Andrés Manuel López Obrador became president in December 2018. With Congress under his control, the main impediment to his plans for a radical domestic transformation lies in the potential for upheaval caused by disputes with the US over migration and the trading regime.

- Venezuela's economic and political crisis has deepened further, with inflation reaching one million percent and more than four million people having left the country. Repairing this damage will take decades, and can only begin once President Nicolás Maduro leaves power.

- The risk of Argentina reverting to populist politics has risen sharply, as a currency crisis undermined support for President Mauricio Macri. He will struggle to defeat his Peronist opponent in the October 2019 presidential election.

- The US administration cut financial assistance to El Salvador, Guatemala and Honduras in March 2019 to punish those states for failing to arrest the tide of migrants heading to the US. Washington also reversed elements of its rapprochement with Cuba, reinstating restrictions on commerce and travel.

## DEMOGRAPHY

POPULATION AND MEDIAN AGE
(IMF, April 2019; UN Department of Economic and Social Affairs, Population Division, 2019)

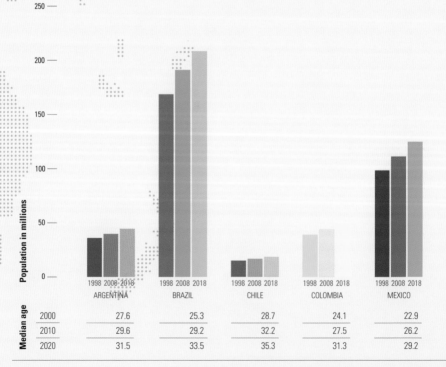

| Median age | ARGENTINA | BRAZIL | CHILE | COLOMBIA | MEXICO |
|---|---|---|---|---|---|
| 2000 | 27.6 | 25.3 | 28.7 | 24.1 | 22.9 |
| 2010 | 29.6 | 29.2 | 32.2 | 27.5 | 26.2 |
| 2020 | 31.5 | 33.5 | 35.3 | 31.3 | 29.2 |

**AGE STRUCTURE**
(CIA World Factbook, 2019)

| MEXICO | |
|---|---|
| Under 25 years | 43.96% |
| 25–64 years | 48.78% |
| 64 years and older | 7.26% |

| COLOMBIA | |
|---|---|
| Under 25 years | 40.85% |
| 25–64 years | 51.42% |
| 64 years and older | 7.73% |

| BRAZIL | |
|---|---|
| Under 25 years | 38.18% |
| 25–64 years | 53.21% |
| 64 years and older | 8.61% |

| CHILE | |
|---|---|
| Under 25 years | 34.61% |
| 25–64 years | 54.26% |
| 64 years and older | 11.13% |

| ARGENTINA | |
|---|---|
| Under 25 years | 39.64% |
| 25–64 years | 48.58% |
| 64 years and older | 11.79% |

# ECONOMICS AND DEVELOPMENT

## GDP AT PPP
Constant 2011 international dollars (IMF, April 2019)

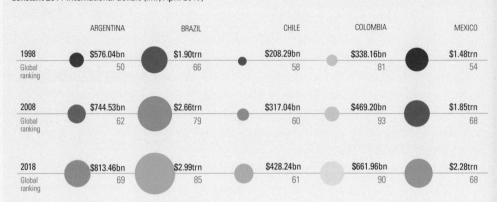

|  | ARGENTINA | BRAZIL | CHILE | COLOMBIA | MEXICO |
|---|---|---|---|---|---|
| **1998** | $576.04bn | $1.90trn | $208.29bn | $338.16bn | $1.48trn |
| Global ranking | 50 | 66 | 58 | 81 | 54 |
| **2008** | $744.53bn | $2.66trn | $317.04bn | $469.20bn | $1.85trn |
| Global ranking | 62 | 79 | 60 | 93 | 68 |
| **2018** | $813.46bn | $2.99trn | $428.24bn | $661.96bn | $2.28trn |
| Global ranking | 69 | 85 | 61 | 90 | 68 |

## GDP PER CAPITA AT PPP
Constant 2011 international dollars (IMF, April 2019)

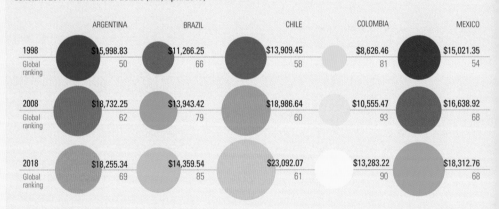

|  | ARGENTINA | BRAZIL | CHILE | COLOMBIA | MEXICO |
|---|---|---|---|---|---|
| **1998** | $15,998.83 | $11,266.25 | $13,909.45 | $8,626.46 | $15,021.35 |
| Global ranking | 50 | 66 | 58 | 81 | 54 |
| **2008** | $18,732.25 | $13,943.42 | $18,986.64 | $10,555.47 | $16,638.92 |
| Global ranking | 62 | 79 | 60 | 93 | 68 |
| **2018** | $18,255.34 | $14,359.54 | $23,092.07 | $13,283.22 | $18,312.76 |
| Global ranking | 69 | 85 | 61 | 90 | 68 |

## HUMAN DEVELOPMENT INDEX (HDI)
(UN Development Programme, 2019)

ARGENTINA · · · · · · · · · · · · · · · · · · · · · · · · · · · · · · · · · · · 41 46 47 · · · ·

BRAZIL · · · · · · · · · · · · · · · · · · · · · · · · · · · · · · 66 87 79 · · · · · · ·

CHILE · · · · · · · · · · · · · · · · · · · · · · · · · · · · · · · · · 42 43 44 · · · · · ·

COLOMBIA · · · · · · · · · · · · · · · · · · · · · · · · · · 76 91 90 · · · · · · · · ·

MEXICO · · · · · · · · · · · · · · · · · · · · · · · · · · · · · 59 70 74 · · · · · · ·

0.0          0.2          0.4          0.6          0.8          1.0

 Global ranking 1998     Global ranking 2008    00 Global ranking 2018

Score between 0 and 1, where 0 denotes a low level of development and 1 a high level of development.

# INTERNATIONAL INTEGRATION

## TRADE
Exports of goods and commercial services, constant 2010 US dollars
(World Trade Organization, 2019)

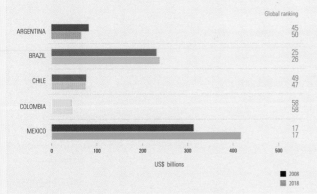

Global ranking

| | 2008 | 2018 |
|---|---|---|
| ARGENTINA | 45 | 50 |
| BRAZIL | 25 | 26 |
| CHILE | 49 | 47 |
| COLOMBIA | 58 | 58 |
| MEXICO | 17 | 17 |

US$ billions (0, 100, 200, 300, 400, 500)

■ 2008
■ 2018

## INTERNATIONAL NETWORK
Total number of diplomatic missions, 2017
Lowy Institute Global Diplomacy Index
(2017)

| | Missions abroad | | Global ranking |
|---|---|---|---|
| ARGENTINA | 155 |  | 15 |
| BRAZIL | 221 | | 9 |
| CHILE | 128 | | 22 |
| COLOMBIA | n/a | | n/a |
| MEXICO | 156 | | 14 |

---

# DIPLOMACY AND DEFENCE

## DEFENCE BUDGET
Constant 2010 US dollars (Military Balance 1998,
and Military Balance+)

Global ranking

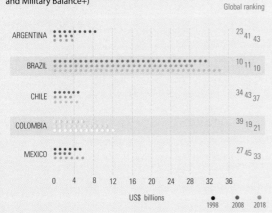

| | 1998 | 2008 | 2018 |
|---|---|---|---|
| ARGENTINA | 23 | 41 | 43 |
| BRAZIL | 10 | 11 | 10 |
| CHILE | 34 | 43 | 37 |
| COLOMBIA | 39 | 19 | 21 |
| MEXICO | 27 | 45 | 33 |

US$ billions (0, 4, 8, 12, 16, 20, 24, 28, 32, 36)

● 1998   ● 2008   ● 2018

## OFFICIAL DEVELOPMENT AID
Constant 2015 US dollars (OECD, 2019)

| | 1998 | 2008 | 2018 |
|---|---|---|---|
| ARGENTINA | n/a | n/a | n/a |
| BRAZIL | n/a | n/a | n/a |
| CHILE | n/a | n/a | n/a |
| COLOMBIA | n/a | n/a | n/a |
| MEXICO | n/a | n/a | n/a |

---

## POLITICAL SYSTEM
(Economist Intelligence Unit, 2008, 2018)

Global ranking
2008:  60  56  55  41  32

ARGENTINA   CHILE
MEXICO   BRAZIL
COLOMBIA

2018 (0, 1, 2, 3, 4, 5, 6, 7, 8, 9, 10)
Global ranking:  71  50  51  47  23

Score between 0 and 10, where 10 denotes a fully democratic and 0 a fully authoritarian regime.

MEXICO

Havana

THE BAHAMAS

CUBA

DOMINICAN
REPUBLIC

Mexico City

BELIZE

HAITI

Santo Domingo

JAMAICA

Belmopan

Kingston

Port-au-
Prince

GUATEMALA

Tegucigalpa

Guatemala City

HONDURAS

EL SALVADOR

NICARAGUA

TRINIDAD & TOBAGO

San Salvador

COSTA RICA

Georgetown

Managua

Caracas

Paramaribo

San José

Panama
City

VENEZUELA

Cayenne

PANAMA

Bogotá

GUYANA

SURINAME

FRENCH GUYANA

COLOMBIA

Quito

ECUADOR

PERU

B R A Z I L

Lima

La Paz

Brasília

BOLIVIA

PARAGUAY

Asunción

CHILE

URUGUAY

Santiago

Buenos Aires

Montevideo

ARGENTINA

©IISS

Atlantic Ocean

Pacific Ocean

Falkland Islands (UK)

South Georgia (

# Chapter 9

# Latin America

## 2018–19 Review

In the year to June 2019, Latin America saw a major shake-up of the political status quo with the rise to power of new anti-establishment, populist presidents in the region's two economic powerhouses, Mexico and Brazil, with one new leader on the left and the other on the right of the political spectrum. Argentina, the region's third-largest economy, was hit with renewed economic troubles that threatened the previously promising re-election prospects of the centre-right president and could trigger a swing back to a leftist government in October 2019 elections. Venezuela's economic and political turmoil deepened and exacerbated an exodus of refugees that made headlines around the world but had its worst repercussions for neighbouring countries.

Regionwide, relations with the United States, still Latin America's main commercial partner, chilled as the administration of US President Donald Trump ratcheted up its anti-immigrant and protectionist policies. Tensions over immigration and tariffs worsened, particularly with Mexico and the Central American countries. In March 2019, Trump cut off financial assistance to Guatemala, Honduras and El Salvador (the sources of most of the recent migrants), but the loss of US financial aid will only exacerbate the conditions driving migrants out of their homelands.

Hostility between the US and the leftist governments in Venezuela and Cuba also heightened as the Trump administration increased sanctions on both countries in a bid to spark regime change.

On the global level, conditions grew more worrisome for Latin America. The bilateral trade war between the US and China, the world's two largest economies, contributed to slowing global commerce and economic growth, as well as lower commodity prices. In June 2019, the World Bank reduced its previous forecast (made in January) for global GDP growth in 2019 from 2.9% to 2.6%, reflecting weaker-than-expected international trade and investment at the start of the year. This is a deceleration from 3% growth in 2018 and 3.1% in 2017. For its part, the International Monetary Fund warned that tariffs could weaken global growth by 0.5% in 2020. This debilitated external environment has dampened Latin America's prospects and increased policy dilemmas for many of the region's major economies. Volatile commodity prices are proving most detrimental for investment in countries such as Chile, Colombia and Peru. After a poor performance in 2018, when regional GDP grew by a mere 1%, according to IMF estimates, economic activity looked poised for a mild upturn in 2019. Instead, it stagnated or contracted quarter on quarter in all of the seven largest economies in January–March, suggesting that Latin America was heading for another year of lacklustre economic growth. This is amplifying the political uncertainty and economic challenges that are already manifest in the region.

## López Obrador comes to power in Mexico

In Mexico, after decades of centre-right rule, there was a historic swing to the left when Andrés Manuel López Obrador, of the National Regeneration Movement (MORENA), took office in December 2018. He promised to radically upend politics, expand social spending and combat corruption. López Obrador, who was elected on a populist, nationalist agenda, enjoys both strong personal appeal and majorities in both houses of Congress, giving him significant political clout. His election was also historic because it relegated Mexico's traditionally dominant political party, the Institutional Revolutionary Party (PRI) –

which had continuously ruled the country from 1929 to 2000 and again in 2012–18 – to third place in Congress, behind the National Action Party (PAN).

López Obrador promised to be a transformational president, with an agenda focused on addressing Mexico's long-standing domestic ills, including inequality, impunity and high levels of violence. He introduced a 16% hike to the minimum wage, expanded labour rights, reduced government salaries (including his own) and oversaw the creation of a new national guard to combat drug trafficking. He began a scholarship for young people, introduced income support for the disabled and expanded the pension programme for the elderly. His governing style is more personalistic, transparent and participatory than those of his predecessors. He holds a daily early-morning press briefing that can last for hours, and has submitted to two popular referendums several controversial proposals, including the building of a new refinery and of a thermoelectric plant.

However, several months into his term, López Obrador was struggling to match the expectations that his election had generated. By May, López Obrador's approval rating, while still high, had slipped to an average of 60%, down from 67% in February, according to Mitofsky, a polling firm. In part, this reflects a weakening economy: GDP contracted in the first quarter (quarter on quarter) of the year by 0.2%. On 9 April, the IMF lowered its forecast for Mexican GDP growth in full-year 2019 from 2.1% to 1.6%, but even this modest projection is optimistic. According to surveys conducted by the central bank, consumer and business confidence fell in May for the third straight month.

Besides concerns over domestic policy, investor sentiment soured owing to worries surrounding relations with the US. The Trump administration's threat on 30 May to impose tariffs on Mexico, starting at 5% and rising progressively to 25%, if Mexico did not act to stem the flow of migrants from Central America through its territory sent the peso into a slump and further exposed Mexico's extreme vulnerability to US policies. This forced the López Obrador administration to shift attention away from domestic priorities towards resolving the dispute with the US. Although an agreement was reached in June, whereby Mexico would enhance its border-enforcement capabilities and hold migrants in Mexico pending their application for asylum in the US, the Trump administration gave it just 45 days to show meaningful results or tariffs could still be imposed. Regardless of whether they are, or how quickly they might be removed, uncertainty will persist, probably through the run-up to the US presidential election in November 2020.

The dispute also exacerbated concerns surrounding the US–Mexico–Canada Agreement (USMCA), the trade deal that was signed in 2018 to update the North American Free Trade Agreement (NAFTA), the cornerstone of US–Mexico economic relations since 1994. Mexico's Congress ratified the agreement in June, but as of June it was uncertain when the US Congress would take up the bill to pass the USMCA, and any lengthy delays could have an adverse impact on investor sentiment towards Mexico.

## Brazil moves sharply to the right

As in Mexico, corruption scandals, rising crime and growing discontent over a weak economy were behind the seismic shift in Brazilian politics, with the election of a populist outsider, Jair Bolsonaro, in October 2018. In Brazil, however, the political swing was to the far right. A congressional deputy and retired military officer, Bolsonaro, of the small Social Liberal Party (PSL), took office in January 2019. He had long expressed approval of Brazil's period of military dictatorship between 1964 and 1985 and promised strong leadership, pledging to implement law and order and take Brazil away from a tradition of political patronage.

The rise to power of a relatively marginal politician without a strong political party or political machinery was a major break with the recent past: politics had been dominated during most of the previous 15 years by the leftist Workers' Party (PT). Bolsonaro's election attested to Brazilians' disgust with the political status quo, having come amid an ongoing, massive investigation, called *Operation Car Wash* (*Operação Lava Jato*), that probed corruption, kickbacks and illegal campaign financing. That investigation led to the conviction of numerous business bosses and high-level politicians, including the former president, Luiz Inácio Lula da Silva of the PT, who was sent to prison in 2018.

Yet six months after taking office in January, Bolsonaro's election was not yet proving to be the panacea he promised. He was enduring turbulent times amid political infighting in his government, strained relations with parties in Congress and still-weak economic performance. His popularity declined sharply after his election: at the end of March it stood at 32%, the lowest of any president after a first quarter in his first term since Brazil's return to democracy in 1989, according to pollster Datafolha. The economy remained feeble after several years of poor performance; GDP shrank mildly in the first quarter, after low growth of 1.1% in 2018. Although the IMF earlier in 2019 projected growth of 2.1% this year, by mid-year this forecast seemed optimistic.

Bolsonaro's ability to steer much-needed pension and other liberalising reforms – which would lift Brazil's economic-growth rates – through a highly fragmented Congress is complicated by his lack of a congressional majority. In contrast to López Obrador's party in Mexico, Bolsonaro's ruling PSL has only 10% of the seats in the lower house, making him reliant on other parties to pass reforms. His justice minister, Sérgio Moro (the main judge behind the *Operation Car Wash* corruption cases), faces pushback from politicians for his signature anti-crime and anti-corruption policies. In a recent development, Moro's anti-corruption efforts were tainted in June by revelations in the media of leaked text messages that called into question the integrity of his investigation. They suggested that Moro had improperly guided prosecutors in the case.

Tension between the political right and the left will present a challenge throughout Bolsonaro's term, particularly since his party and the PT are the largest parties in Congress. The president will only be effective if he is popular enough with voters to retain support from some of the myriad (30) parties in Congress for his reform agenda. However, with his popularity already waning just months after taking office, prospects for securing all his ambitious structural reforms, boosting economic performance and amending Brazil's complex political system appeared faint.

On the foreign-policy front, Bolsonaro has also taken Brazil on a different path compared with prior administrations. Whereas the PT governments of 2003–16 had close ties with ideologically similar, leftist governments in Latin America and favoured alliances with other developing countries, Bolsonaro has distanced Brazil from Cuba and Venezuela (he joined other nations in no longer recognising Nicolás Maduro as Venezuela's legitimate president) and has built closer ties with other right-wing governments in the region. He has also established a warmer relationship with the US, reflecting his similar, anti-globalist world view to that of Donald Trump. This new relationship was firmed up during a state visit to the US in March 2019.

## Argentina's centre-right government under threat

Rather than corruption scandals or rising crime, a beleaguered economy is the main challenge that afflicted Argentinian President Mauricio Macri of the centre-right Republican Proposal (PRO) party in the last year. He came into office in 2015 on a pledge to end the economic distortions that had long plunged Argentina into repeated boom–bust cycles. However, in 2018 he found himself pressured by a renewed crisis that was marked by severe currency weakening, runaway inflation and sky-high interest rates. This forced the government to introduce strict austerity measures (which induced a recession), and to secure a new IMF lending agreement to ease market concerns over the country's fiscal and external imbalances. Economic activity again shrank in the first quarter of 2019, and the economy did not yet appear to be on the path to recovery.

The 2018 crisis hurt Macri's popularity and bolstered that of the former president, Cristina Fernández de Kirchner (2007–15), a left-leaning populist whose heterodox and interventionist policies are blamed for the economic mess that Macri inherited in 2015. Fernández announced in May that she would run for office again, this time as the vice-presidential running mate to her former cabinet chief, Alberto Fernández (no relation) – an arrangement that many believe would make her the power behind the throne. However, she and high-ranking officials of her government are involved in a corruption scandal, accused of accepting bribes from construction firms in exchange for lucrative government contracts while in power. Her trial began days after she revealed her election plans. Even if the trial prevents her from running, or if her ticket does not arm a sufficient challenge to beat Macri in October, another candidate might be able to do so.

To avoid this, Macri needs to convince voters that he can return the country to economic stability and prosperity. This task was further complicated by a huge nationwide blackout – which also affected all of Uruguay – on 16 June, wiping out power for 48 million people. The incident highlighted insufficient investment in the electricity grid, a problem Macri had promised to address when he was elected.

Faced with the 2018 crisis and the threat to his re-election, Macri has put his structural-reform agenda on the back burner. Many of the reforms needed to correct Argentina's woes – to labour markets, the judiciary and others to enhance investor confidence in institutions and contract rights – could start to lay the groundwork for more solid long-term growth rates. However, these will have to wait until after the elections. Prospects for such reforms will dim if a left-leaning government comes to power.

## Venezuelan crisis nears a tipping point

Venezuela's economic meltdown and political turbulence deepened in 2018 and the first half of 2019, posing a challenge to US and regional policymakers. The crisis resulted from years of authoritarian rule, economic mismanagement and corruption, and in 2018 produced hyperinflation, a further sharp contraction of the economy and a massive humanitarian crisis. Added to this was a repression of protesters by the government of President Nicolás Maduro, enforced by the national guard and pro-government street gangs knows as *colectivos*.

Political tensions, already high, spiked after the presidential election of May 2018, which was widely deemed to be unfair and was condemned at home and abroad. On the basis that the elections were fraudulent, the head of the opposition-controlled National Assembly, Juan Guaidó, swore himself in as legitimate president in January 2019 (just after Maduro took office for a second term). This was the most significant challenge to Maduro's regime since he became president in 2013 and plunged the country deeper into political turmoil.

More than 50 countries worldwide, including most in Latin America, recognised Guaidó as president. The US and Canada had previously imposed sanctions against key figures of the regime, but in January the Trump administration augmented the sanctions by denying Caracas access to the revenue generated by sales of oil to the US. This de facto ban on US imports of Venezuelan oil was a huge blow to the already struggling state oil company, PDVSA, and the Venezuelan economy, since oil accounts for 95% of total exports and the US is PDVSA's main customer. PDVSA diverted some exports to faraway markets in Asia and Russia, yet its oil output plummeted by 35% between January and June, according to estimates by the Institute of International Finance.

Venezuela's economy has been shrinking for several years, while inflation has hit absurd heights. According to newly released data from the central bank, Banco Central de Venezuela, GDP plummeted in real terms by 30% between 2015 and 2017. The IMF estimated that GDP shrank by 18% in 2018 and has forecast an additional decline of 25% this year. Annual inflation in 2018, according to the IMF, hit close to 1m per cent, and could reach 10m per cent in 2019.

Sanctions, combined with promises of aid and amnesty, were intended to prompt members of the military to abandon the regime and support Guaidó. However, despite massive opposition protests – culminating in one in April that was expected to spark a military uprising – the armed forces continued to back Maduro. As of June, two rounds of negotiations had been held in Norway between representatives of the government and the opposition, but were not yet fruitful.

Venezuela's crisis has sparked a human exodus unprecedented for a country not at war. In June 2019, the UN High Commissioner for Refugees (UNHCR) estimated that 4m Venezuelans had abandoned the country in recent years, making them one of the single-largest displaced groups in the world. They have been pushed by shortages of food and basic goods, chronic electricity blackouts, a collapse of medical services and rising levels of crime and violence. The UNHCR estimates that another 1m may leave by the end of 2019.

For its neighbours, Venezuela's strife has presented serious difficulties. Colombia has received the largest number of refugees (1.3m), creating challenges for the new government of Iván Duque, itself struggling to implement the peace accords signed in 2016 with the leftist FARC group and reintegrate thousands of former guerrillas. Other countries have seen an influx, including Peru (768,000), Chile (288,000), Ecuador (263,000), Brazil (168,000) and Argentina (130,000). The migrants have strained local communities and the capacity of recipient governments to provide housing, health services and other humanitarian relief. The situation has also generated new security concerns, both within Venezuela and outside, as criminal organisations have mushroomed and often moved across borders.

In the early months of 2019 there were signs, including further declines in PDVSA's output and a set of massive nationwide power blackouts, that the sanctions imposed by the US had started to bite. Yet despite economic collapse and domestic and international political pressure, by mid-2019 Maduro's departure still appeared distant. With the April opposition protests having failed to dislodge him, it was difficult to predict when and how regime change would occur. What did seem clear was that the status quo was untenable, and that some form of transitional/unity government, probably composed of pragmatist members of the opposition, the current regime and the armed forces, would have to eventually emerge.

## Increasing tensions between US and Cuba and Nicaragua

Besides its focus on immigration, the Trump administration set in its cross hairs not only Venezuela, but also Cuba and Nicaragua – the three countries dubbed Latin America's 'troika of tyranny' by members of the administration. Trump has progressively reversed elements of the rapprochement between Cuba and the previous Obama administration, reinstating some restrictions on trade and investment. In 2019, the administration ratcheted up sanctions, including further limiting US travel to Cuba, banning the arrival of US cruise ships and restricting remittances to the island, ostensibly to discourage Cuban support for the Maduro government in Venezuela. However, the measures seemed equally designed to undermine the Cuban government of Miguel Diáz-Canel, president since April 2018. US policy further damaged Cuba's economy, already reeling from reduced trade and financial aid from Venezuela, Cuba's main commercial partner.

With regards to Nicaragua, in June US Secretary of State Mike Pompeo was to present a report, due under the 2018 Nicaraguan Investment Conditionality Act, to the US Congress that would assess the steps the government of Daniel Ortega had taken to restore democracy. The US was expected to keep up the pressure on Nicaragua and possibly increase sanctions on key officials, but to avoid the type of broad punishment applied to Venezuela.

With the Trump administration focused on migration from Mexico and Central America and on pressuring for regime change in the leftist governments in the region, US policy has not produced dramatically different bilateral trade, finance or investment relations with much of the rest of Latin America. Nonetheless, the impact of the policies that it is aggressively pursuing look likely to have some spillover effects across the region.

# Mexico's New/Old Foreign Policy

Mexico has traditionally prioritised domestic affairs over engagement with the wider world, a policy shaped by its proximity to the United States. Much of its history has been dominated by the 'power next door', to the extent that some historians argue that the very notion of 'Mexicaness' emerged from the US invasion in 1847, which resulted in the loss of half the country's territory. This created a mindset of victimhood that, in foreign policy, translated into an indefatigable support for the underdog, while Mexico permanently avoided potentially risky encounters with the US. Mexico does not see itself as a regional power, even though its presence is paramount in Central America. Although similar to Brazil in many respects, Mexico tends to punch below its weight: while the Brazilians see themselves as an emerging power, Mexicans would rather avoid any foreign entanglement.

While Mexico's politics experienced profound change after the Institutional Revolutionary Party (PRI) was defeated in 2000 and the three successive administrations began to engage in a more proactive foreign policy, the substance of the new approach was not radically different. Mexico joined the UN Security Council twice (only to find itself entangled with the US in the decision to invade Iraq) and later became an active supporter of democracy in Venezuela, but the approach to foreign policy remained inward-looking and timid, often concerned not to be seen as aligned with the US. With the election in 2018 of Andrés Manuel López Obrador – who in many ways epitomises the 'old' PRI, having begun his political career with that party in 1985 – the country's foreign policy has once again reverted to its former principles. All the while, the enormous complexity of the Mexico–US bilateral relationship has continued to define and challenge the country's broader economic and social dynamics.

## A principled foreign policy

After the Mexican Revolution (1910–17) and the creation of the National Revolutionary Party, the PRI's antecedent, Mexico developed a series of principles to guide its foreign policy. The Estrada Doctrine, conceived of by then-secretary of foreign affairs Genaro Estrada in 1930, established the principle that Mexico should not judge the governments or changes in government of other states, as such an action would imply a breach of state sovereignty. Its core principles were non-intervention, peaceful resolution of disputes and self-determination of all nations. These principles were both a guide to the country's actions in the world arena as well as a defensive mechanism to avert criticism of the country's ways.

Although not always applied in an absolute fashion, these principles guided the country's policy for decades after the revolution. Some exceptions were the decision not to recognise the regime of General Francisco Franco in Spain (1939–75) and to formally complain about Italian dictator Benito Mussolini's invasion of Abyssinia in 1935.

During the PRI era (1928–2000), there were few forays into an active foreign policy, the rationale of which was mostly protective and inward-looking. There were, however, some exceptions – such as Mexico formally joining the Allies at the very end of the Second World War in 1945 by sending the 201st Fighter Squadron to the Philippines – but most were related to domestic political needs. Mexico became a staunch defender of Cuba's revolution and harboured the Castro entourage before it launched its assault on the island, yet Mexico's stance was always aimed at domestic constituencies for whom a socialist revolution was an important objective. In addition, supporting a revolution outside the country's borders helped preserve the legitimacy of the semi-authoritarian regime that resulted from the Mexican Revolution. (The US understood the Mexican government's objective and never saw it as a threat; in fact, Mexico became a useful means to the US both as it provided frequent flights into the island nation as well as through the telephone hook-up that was established at the Yucatán Peninsula.) More controversially, in the 1980s, Mexico launched the Contadora process, a policy aimed at neutralising the United States' policy in Central America in the context of the Iran–Contra affair, with a view to helping stabilise the region and to settle the military conflicts that had plagued it. Although the process did not produce a break-through, it paved the way for future efforts, and did not result in any lasting tension with the US (which was caught up in a political scandal over the affair).

The main challenge to Mexico's foreign policy has lain in managing its highly complex relationship with the US. From the mid-1800s to the 1980s, Mexico defined its economic policy in defensive terms and did everything possible to minimise contact with (and interference from) the rapidly growing power to the north. However, a series of financial crises during the 1970s and the 1980s led Mexico to rethink its perspective. In the 1980s, as Mexico began a series of reforms aimed at liberalising and deregulating its economy, it found the need to create institutional anchors that would serve to attract foreign investment. For the first time in its history, Mexico made the extraordinary volte-face of looking at the US as a source of institutional certainty. For Mexico, the North American Free Trade Agreement (NAFTA) – which came into force in 1994 – was much more than a set of trade and investment rules: it was a factor of certainty for domestic purposes.

Mexico wedded its economy to that of the US in order to advance its own development, and foreign policy inexorably followed. The US advanced its own national-security considerations in the 1980s, shaped by the exigencies of the Cold War, when both nations agreed to compart-mentalise their disagreements, a process that eventually led to NAFTA. The trade agreement was a means to help Mexico become prosperous, therefore advancing a key US national-security objective in the form of a strong border that would reduce the risks of instability coming from the south. In the 1990s, Mexico assumed it could maintain its 'independent' (i.e., not aligned) foreign policy, but it soon found itself in permanent contradiction, partly because its objective to attract investment clashed with its position on Cuba, but mostly because the Cubans themselves saw the change in Mexico as an affront. Thus NAFTA inaugurated an era of close US–Mexico ties, tight coordination and an ever-more complex bilateral relationship largely dominated by economic and, especially, border issues.

## Breaking the mould

In 2000, Mexican voters decided to replace the PRI. By electing Vicente
Fox of the centre-right National Action Party (PAN), the country entered
into a new era in domestic and foreign policy. While the PRI regime had
enjoyed wide internal legitimacy for many decades, the era of financial
crises, followed by disputed electoral results from 1988 onwards, eroded
its credibility and further entrenched its domestic-leaning approach.
Liberated from the issue of lack of legitimacy that had plagued previous
PRI administrations, Fox launched a series of initiatives vis-à-vis the
US and Cuba. With the former, it attempted to advance towards something more akin to the European Union, with open borders for goods,
services and people, an attempt that fell by the wayside in the heightened national-security environment in the wake of the 9/11 attacks on
the US. With Cuba, it abandoned the policy of cleaving to the fiction
that Cuba was a democracy and supporting Havana in forums such as
the UN Human Rights Council, which had been a Mexican staple since
1962. Mexico became a fierce critic of the Castro regime in forums such
as the Organization of American States (OAS), and, later, of Venezuela.
Mexico also became an active participant of the G20 (created in 1999)
where it has played a minor role, focusing on the environment but,
overall, much more on being an open trading economy than on major
foreign-policy issues.

During the 2000s, Mexico also began to take a much more active role
in defending Mexican migrants inside the US. Up to 2000, Mexico's governments had seen, and portrayed, migrants to the US as people who
had abandoned the nation. After 2000, Mexico began to reach out to
the migrant communities in the US and attempted to establish ties with
them. It instituted a series of initiatives such as three-way programmes
to help the communities that migrants had left in Mexico, whereby the
federal government, the local municipal administration and the successful Mexican migrants each supplied a third of the funds needed to
finance a series of infrastructure programmes. Although very successful in their own right, the key to such projects was the fact that there
was cooperation across the border, thus diminishing the (well-founded)

suspicion by the migrants that the Mexican government merely aimed at exploiting the migrants in the US for its own purposes.

Fox's initiatives were pursued by the next two presidents, Felipe Calderón (PAN) and Enrique Peña Nieto (PRI). All three broke from the old PRI tradition of shying away from engagement in the international arena and, as the regime of Hugo Chávez deteriorated, took an ever more active and critical stance towards Venezuela. The most interesting element in that era was the fact that the Peña Nieto administration, heir to the old PRI tradition in its nature and core beliefs, did not revert to the foreign policy of the past. In fact, Peña Nieto became a central actor in the Lima Group, founded in 2017 by 12 nations to help advance a peaceful transition of power in Caracas, particularly after the much-criticised presidential election of 2018 with which Maduro attempted to consolidate his power.

Throughout the post-2000 era, Mexico and the US experienced ever-deepening political ties, following the understanding that George H.W. Bush and Carlos Salinas had reached in 1988, which set the foundation for the eventual negotiation of NAFTA. Although not always seeing eye to eye, the relationship focused on solving problems, mostly those derived from the extraordinarily complex border, encompassing legal and illegal crossings, sewers and water, bridges and drugs, violence and trade, agriculture and plagues. After NAFTA came into being, the relationship ceased to be essentially driven by foreign policy, as each other's issues became deeply domestic. For example, migration became a major political issue in the US while the de facto guarantee that the US provided to investors through NAFTA responded to Mexican political dynamics. This complex foreign–domestic dynamic came to be referred to as 'intermestic', implying a politically complex cohabitation that, in retrospect, could not last forever. Trump's election in November 2016 ended the era of compartmentalisation.

## Turning back the clock

This increased engagement with the international arena came to an abrupt end with the election of Andrés Manuel López Obrador, who reverted to the old PRI traditions upon assuming the presidency in

December 2018. López Obrador believes that Mexico's current ills are the result of the market and democratic reforms that were launched in the 1980s and 1990s. From the day of his election, he has changed the country's course in both domestic as well as foreign policy, having long argued that 'the best foreign policy is domestic policy'. He has de facto returned to the core principles established by the Estrada Doctrine, overturning his immediate predecessors' policies on Cuba and Venezuela and moving towards a far more isolationist position than even the PRI governments in which he made his early career. Under his leadership, Mexico has quit the Lima Group and has been supportive – or in López Obrador's words, respectful – of the Maduro administration. He has also put the presidential plane up for sale, both for symbolic purposes (i.e., to show his austere nature) and due to his conviction that a Mexican president needs to concentrate on domestic affairs and does not need to be present at international meetings. (López Obrador did not attend the G20 summit in Osaka in June 2019, nor did he participate in the Pacific Alliance meeting in Costa Rica in the same month.)

To support his ambitious domestic agenda, López Obrador has cut budgetary allocations to all programmes that are not part of it, including those related to foreign policy. He has curtailed his finance minister's trips abroad and aims at gradually reducing the country's ties with the rest of the world, especially with the US, believing that such relationships are not in Mexico's long-term interests. These actions will impact both Mexico's foreign presence as well as domestic politics. On the one hand, ministries such as economy (which deals with trade issues), tourism and agriculture have seen their international presence curtailed and those responsibilities being transferred to the ministry of foreign affairs, which is not getting a larger budgetary allocation for its expanded remit. On the other hand, Mexico's footprint in general will diminish as budgetary decisions, now driven by a brand new 'austerity law', require specific authorisation by a central authority at the ministry of finance even for academic travel of state universities.

The only foreign-policy initiative that López Obrador has launched relates to migration from Central American nations, particularly those of the Northern Triangle (Guatemala, Honduras and El Salvador). Although migrant flows from Central America have been a constant over the past few years, and an irritant between the Obama and Peña Nieto administrations, López Obrador decided to grant working and transit visas to migrants, thus providing an incentive for ever-larger migrant caravans to move into and through Mexican territory. (López Obrador, and Mexicans in general, regard migration to the US as an inalienable right.)

However, ever-growing numbers of migrants soon began to saturate Mexican border communities as they awaited access to the US, creating havoc on the Mexican side and providing the perfect picture-ready images for Trump to exploit. Trump used the migrant caravans during the midterm elections of 2018 but, in May 2019, went much further to demand that Mexico control all flows of migrants, otherwise he would impose a tariff on Mexico's exports to the US. Although clearly in violation of existing trade agreements – including the United States–Mexico–Canada Agreement (USMCA), the replacement for NAFTA which López Obrador had been instrumental in completing – López Obrador had to accept Trump's terms in order to stave off the risk of hindering Mexican exports.

## Historical ideals versus modern reality

López Obrador represents an extreme position within the typical Mexican foreign-policy positions of the twentieth century but is clearly within that tradition. However, his attempt to recreate a bygone era – both domestically and in the foreign arena – at a time in which global issues such as trade, investment, finance and exports (Mexico's foremost engine of growth) are fundamental to the welfare of his own country has led to accusations that he fails to grasp (or deliberately ignores) the complex economic mechanisms of the modern world. He sees Pemex's dependence on foreign financing as ill-conceived, for example, even though the national oil company is the most highly indebted oil entity in the world. Preferences and realities clash permanently in the López Obrador view of the world, but the fact is that Mexico cannot distance itself from the rest of the world. A nation can quit a variety of international forums, but it cannot walk away from the sources of its welfare, as López Obrador has found in the case of Trump's tariffs. The same goes for the financial sector, where portfolio investments have become critical in maintaining exchange-rate stability in Mexico, a variable López Obrador follows day in and day out. Since the 1980s, Mexico has become inextricably linked to the rest of the world both in the 'real' economy (i.e., exports and imports of goods and services), as well as in the financial arena, which is key to the growth of the economy.

López Obrador has three clear-cut priorities: economic growth, poverty and inequality. He has built his political platform and government programme on the notion that only a strong government that controls all the variables can deal with these issues successfully. In this, he is following the 1960s textbook to the letter. Ultimately, however, López Obrador misunderstands Mexico's ills, as well as its strengths and weaknesses. There is no better example of this than the feeble rate of growth that the economy has shown for over three decades: at 2% average growth, the economy has been performing well below its needs to satisfy a growing population. However, the average rate of growth hides more than it reveals: parts of Mexico grow at Asian-like rates, while others have stagnated, evidencing contrasting political circumstances. Special interests have been able to preserve their strongholds of power and income in some areas of the country, especially the southern states of Chiapas, Oaxaca and Guerrero, while no such hindrances to growth remain in most of the north. By conceiving the whole of the country as one and the same, López Obrador runs the risk of endangering the sources of successful growth without fixing the stagnant regions.

In the late 1980s and early 1990s, Mexico made the crucial decision to abandon its long-time economic (and foreign-policy) strategy of inward-looking development (characterised mainly by substitution of imports), and replace it with an open trading regime that would allow it to integrate itself into the global economy by becoming a manufacturing hub. That decision eventually led to NAFTA, for one very specific reason: despite Mexico having reformed its legal framework and adopted market-friendly economic policies, investors (mindful of a long history of expropriations and constant shifts in the rules of the game) were not willing to invest in the country. NAFTA was therefore sought as a means to grant credibility to Mexico, but López Obrador does not recognise the issue of trust in investors' decisions. Despite his pragmatic intervention to conclude the USMCA negotiation, he allowed Chapter 11, the dispute-settlement mechanism that was the key to NAFTA for Mexico, to wither away under Trump's pressure. In sum, López Obrador does not accept the very premise of NAFTA, but the agreement was conceived precisely for somebody like him arriving at the presidency. Unfortunately, nobody ever thought that the problem of sustaining NAFTA would come from the US side.

Overall, López Obrador's strategy is contradictory on several levels. Firstly, he has proceeded to swiftly eliminate or neutralise some of the key reforms that were undertaken in the previous three decades. Energy is the most obvious example, where he is not cancelling the reform, but no longer advancing it. However, his perception that oil should be Mexico's foremost engine of growth in the future, and should therefore be controlled by the government, runs counter to the financial capacity of the government. Secondly, he firmly believes that the government should run a tight ship financially, thus limiting the investment requirements that his energy and social programmes demand. Thirdly, he does not recognise that, in the era of globalisation, private firms, both domestic and foreign, are indistinguishable and can invest anywhere in the world. He has vowed to subordinate economic decisions to political priorities, but that clashes with the very nature of an integrated global arena where tens of big Mexican companies are successful players.

López Obrador has a political strategy – to centralise power and recreate the old, all-powerful Mexican presidency – but not a strategy for economic development. His objectives are clear and obvious and he has shown a very well-honed pragmatic streak when there are no alternatives (as with the USMCA and Trump's migration policy). However, his view of the world is largely incompatible with the realities of a rapidly changing twenty-first century. Coming to terms with that reality will be painful.

# Venezuela's Crisis and the Challenge of Reconstruction

In the space of a decade Venezuela has gone from being a confident regional actor to a beleaguered country that depends on external protectors for the survival of its *Chavista* regime. Internally, it is a deeply divided polity in which the authorities and opposition both claim to be the legitimate government. The economy has undergone a shocking deterioration: oil output has slumped, hyperinflation has taken hold and there is a shortage of basic goods. Crime is rampant and millions of Venezuelans have fled the country. External and domestic efforts to unseat President Nicolás Maduro intensified in early 2019. Although he weathered the storm, economic and social conditions continued to deteriorate. When eventually the Maduro government falls, the cost of stabilising the country and re-establishing conditions approaching those that it enjoyed at the turn of the century will be enormous.

Venezuela's vast oil wealth – its proven reserves of more than 300 billion barrels are the largest in the world – made it the richest country in Latin America in most years from the early 1950s onwards. Today, however, it is one of the poorest of the major economies in the region. The effects of years of economic mismanagement under Maduro, who has been in office since 2013, and his predecessor Hugo Chávez, were exacerbated after 2014 by a fall in global oil prices. GDP shrank by 37% in real terms between 2014 and 2017. The IMF estimates that GDP contracted by another 18% in 2018 and will have shrunk a further 25% by the end of 2019. Inflation reached close to 1m per cent in 2018, according to the IMF. The deterioration of social conditions – including a lack of fuel, food and medicines – has sharply increased poverty, malnutrition, disease and criminality. While around 48% of Venezuelans lived in poverty in 2014, according to the United Nations Economic Commission for Latin America and the Caribbean, the figure is now 90%. Caracas has become the third-most violent city in the world, with 100 homicides per 100,000 inhabitants in 2018, according to the

Citizens' Council for Public Security and Criminal Justice, a Mexican non-governmental organisation.

Political repression by the authoritarian regime has provoked even greater discontent. More than 4m Venezuelans – around 12% of the population – have fled the country since 2015, according to estimates published by the UN High Commissioner for Refugees (UNHCR) in June 2019. This is one of the largest mass displacements ever to have occurred in a country not at war, and it shows no sign of slowing down.

Profound damage has been done to Venezuela's physical infrastructure, the health and education of its population, the functioning of public services, and trust in its legal and political system. The crisis has also exacted a toll on the country's South American neighbours. Colombia has received the largest number of refugees so far (1.3m), according to the UNHCR, followed by Peru (768,000), Chile (288,000), Ecuador (263,000), Brazil (168,000) and Argentina (130,000). Infectious diseases such as malaria and measles are spreading from Venezuela to its neighbours, some of which are struggling to provide housing, health services and other relief to the migrants.

In Colombia, for instance, the influx of 1.3m Venezuelans has disrupted the labour market and put enormous strain on public services. In March 2019, Colombia's finance ministry altered its fiscal targets to allow for a wider deficit, having been obliged to increase spending on health, education and other public services. It estimated that the cost of supporting migrants from Venezuela during 2019 would be US$1.5 billion (or 0.5% of its GDP), with similar projections for each of the next three years. The Colombian labour market has been distorted too, with increased competition for jobs, a rise in underemployment levels and growth in informal working.

Venezuela's woes have also generated new security threats, both within the country and outside, as crime has spiked, migrants have been recruited into criminal gangs, and drug-trafficking organisations have mushroomed and moved cross-border. According to an investigation by CNN that cited an unnamed US official, the number of flights carrying illegal drugs out of Venezuela (largely destined for the US) tripled between 2017 and 2018, often with the complicity of high-ranking state officials. Venezuela has also become an ever-more important haven for illicit Colombian armed groups including the leftist guerrillas of the National Liberation Army (ELN).

## Political disarray

Venezuela's political turmoil had been building for years as Maduro moved to consolidate power and dismantle democratic institutions, but it reached an alarming level in early 2019. In January he was sworn in for a second term after having been declared the winner of the May 2018 election, which was widely regarded as rigged. Also in January, Juan Guaidó, leader of the National Assembly, declared himself president. This was the greatest challenge to Maduro's authority since he took office in 2013. The US recognised Guaidó and imposed new sanctions against the oil industry, depriving the state and the economy of important revenue (oil accounts for more than 90% of exports). This – added to Venezuela's increased isolation within Latin America, growing condemnation from abroad, massive economic distortions and the refugee exodus – seemed to render Maduro's position untenable. By mid-2019, some 50 countries had recognised Guaidó as Venezuela's president.

However, a planned civil–military rebellion (known as *Operation Liberty*) in April – led by Guaidó and encouraged by the US – failed to spark the intended overthrow of Maduro, as the armed forces remained loyal. This put the opposition on the back foot. The regime then renewed its repression of dissidents and arrested some opposition leaders.

Maduro was also able to draw upon support from allies in the face of US pressure. Russia, which was already a major creditor and energy partner, stepped up its military support for Venezuela by dispatching arms and military advisers to Caracas. This followed reported sales of arms worth US$10bn since the mid-2000s, facilitated by energy deals and billions of dollars of lending. In late 2017, Russia restructured more than US$3bn in Venezuelan debt to put state finances on a more stable footing. The Russian state oil company, Rosneft, has investments in Venezuela's energy sector and owns 49.9% of CITGO, the US oil-refining subsidiary that belongs to PDVSA, Venezuela's state oil company. In the wake of US sanctions on PDVSA in January 2019, Rosneft helped Venezuela to find Asian markets for its crude oil.

China has also been a major creditor (estimates of Venezuela's debt to China range from US$13bn to US$70bn) in connection with its purchases of Venezuelan oil. Yet as PDVSA's output has fallen, China's appetite for exposure to Venezuela has shrunk and Beijing's ideological attachment to Maduro seems weaker than Moscow's. Cuba, on the other hand, is fully committed to the Venezuelan government, although its resources are a fraction of those that Russia and China can mobilise. Cuban support is directed mostly through Venezuela's military and intelligence services, to which it provides security advice and personnel.

In the first half of 2019, though Maduro retained the support of key allies at home and abroad, Venezuela's economic situation continued to deteriorate as US sanctions curbed oil exports and foreign-currency earnings. There was also the possibility that the US, exploiting its dominance of the dollar-based global financial system, might intensify the sanctions regime. This rendered the outlook for the Maduro regime even more uncertain. It had demonstrated an ability to withstand internal and external shocks, but there were indications that its principal creditors, Russia and China, were not willing to increase their exposure to the country. Russian banks and grain exporters evinced less enthusiasm for doing business with Venezuela and the Russian government reportedly refused to grant new credit lines or write off existing debt.

Despite the US sanctions and somewhat reduced enthusiasm from its allies, the Maduro regime continued to govern even as Venezuela's privations deepened – indeed, depopulation made the country somewhat more manageable. Nonetheless, it seemed that the gathering crisis might cause the regime to splinter, or even that a complete breakdown in the country's social, economic and security fabric could prompt an external military intervention. For the international community the preferred solution was a negotiated transition, and there have been some signs in 2019 that China and perhaps Russia might be willing to countenance the possibility. Since 2017 the 14-member Lima Group, made up mostly of

Latin American countries, has sought to mediate a peaceful exit from the crisis. An International Contact Group (ICG) on Venezuela, consisting of eight EU and five Latin American countries, was formed in February 2019 to gain the agreement of Maduro and Guaidó to hold free and fair elections, to be supervised by international observers. Norway's government and Michelle Bachelet, the UN High Commissioner for Human Rights and a former Chilean president, have also tried to facilitate dialogue between the government and opposition. If the military were to turn its back on Maduro, he could be ushered into exile and a unity government established in order to prepare for elections.

## The costs of stabilisation and reconstruction

While US sanctions remain in place and Venezuela's turmoil continues, the country's macroeconomic and fiscal situation is set to deteriorate further. China and Russia are increasingly reluctant to underwrite the Maduro government. The US will only lift sanctions once Maduro leaves office and Venezuela has a government that Washington is prepared to recognise. Moreover, Venezuela desperately needs a financial package that can only be mobilised by the international community and the major lending institutions. That too requires a change of government.

Regardless of how a political transition eventually occurs, in a post-Maduro climate the economic and social challenges will be overwhelming. Domestic and international attention will have to quickly shift to reviving the devastated economy. This will require not only the lifting of sanctions but also emergency adjustment measures and a substantial macroeconomic stabilisation package, backed by foreign aid and multilateral financing, most likely an IMF loan agreement, and debt restructuring.

The most urgent need will be for humanitarian assistance in the form of both food and medical aid. Food production has fallen sharply since 2012, leading to a surge in imports. In the last few years, imports have contracted but domestic production has not risen. Healthcare is also in crisis, with a resurgence of vector-borne infections such as malaria (which has reached epidemic proportions), dengue fever, Chagas disease, chikungunya and Zika. Humanitarian relief will have to come not only from governments and private sources but also from multilaterals such as UN agencies with experience of responding to humanitarian emergencies. There are no precise estimates of Venezuela's total humanitarian needs, but the financial aid offered by governments thus far provides some initial indication. Following a meeting of members of the Organization of American States in February 2019, 25 countries pledged US$100m in humanitarian aid to Venezuela, and European governments have also provided millions of dollars in assistance. Since fiscal year 2017 the US has earmarked US$213m for countries hosting Venezuelan migrants and to help fund the regional crisis response. However, the amounts allocated to date are likely to be dwarfed by the requirements once Maduro leaves office.

Economic stabilisation will require vast sums of multilateral finance. Comparisons are sometimes drawn with Argentina, the recipient in 2018 of the IMF's largest-ever bailout package, worth US$57bn. But Argentina's situation in 2018 was less parlous than Venezuela's today, although its population is 50% larger. In February 2019, the head of the IMF, Christine Lagarde, said that the task of supporting Venezuela would be 'monumental'. The UK-based Economist Intelligence Unit projects that the costs could total US$46bn in 2020–23. This will come with stringent conditions, requiring a new macroeconomic framework and difficult structural reforms. These will include currency adjustments to eliminate exchange controls and distortions in the exchange-rate system (which will stoke further inflation in the short term) and deep fiscal cuts (Venezuela has not published complete fiscal data since 2011, but the deficit as a share of GDP is believed to be in double digits). This, along with tightened monetary policy, will almost certainly ensure that Venezuela's GDP will continue to contract in the short term. This will necessitate further humanitarian aid to alleviate the suffering of the population and prevent accelerated outflows of migrants until economic growth resumes.

The prospective restructuring of Venezuela's external debt is likely to be one of the most complicated endeavours of its kind ever attempted. The Institute of International Finance estimates that Venezuela's total external obligations stood at US$158bn in 2018 – more than double the level of 2008, and more than four times the size of its exports in 2018 (the median figure among Latin American countries for external debt as a share of exports is 99%). At the official exchange rate, debt is fairly manageable at roughly 48% of GDP. At the black-market exchange rate, however, it reached 138% of GDP in 2018 (the Latin American median is 41%). With its export revenue having plummeted, Venezuela has been in arrears since 2017 on most of its sovereign bonds and those issued by state-owned companies, notably PDVSA. Besides a restructuring with bondholders – with estimates of the haircut creditors will have to take ranging from 30 cents on the dollar to as high as 80 cents – Russia and China could be expected to renegotiate some debt as part of a broader economic-recovery package.

Those contemplating the challenges and opportunities of reconstruction might consider the oil sector, freed from sanctions, to be a ready source of increased government revenue and economic stimulus. However, lifting sanctions alone will not enable a recovery of oil output to the levels seen earlier this decade. Owing to years of mismanagement and underinvestment, PDVSA's output has been falling for years, but in December 2018 it plummeted more drastically to 1.2m barrels per day (b/d) – around half the level of three years earlier, according to OPEC data. Output fell further after the introduction of oil sanctions in January 2019, to 734,000 b/d in June, the lowest level since January 2003 when a nationwide strike brought PDVSA operations to a standstill.

PDVSA will need wholesale reform to open itself to the foreign finance and investment needed to revive its productive base. Guaidó's team proposes to create a new, independent regulator and to partly reverse the oil industry's nationalisation by allowing private firms a bigger role and shrinking the state oil company. They are considering new exploration and production contracts that would, for the first time in decades, permit private investors to operate oilfields themselves or in partnership with PDVSA. Until now they could only have minority stakes, without operational control. Private investors would also be allowed to operate refineries and retail petrol stations. New inflows of technical expertise may also be required; Guaidó has already proposed a programme to encourage Venezuelan professionals living abroad to return after a change in government, and PDVSA could be a beneficiary.

Restoring law and order will be another daunting imperative for a transitional government, and will be extremely challenging until economic conditions improve and it can gain a modicum of control over the security forces. Security conditions could potentially deteriorate further following a political transition, and security assistance from multilateral organisations or partner governments might be necessary.

Finally, the next government will have to work to rebuild democratic institutions and restore confidence in order to promote new domestic and foreign investment. In the short term it will be difficult for an interim government to implement the deep and wide-ranging policy and institutional changes needed to put Venezuela on a sustainable path to recovery. The first fruits of its work could well be spending cuts, higher taxes, rising prices and further economic contraction – usually a recipe for electoral defeat. The painful reforms demanded by bilateral and multilateral lenders could generate a popular backlash that constrains or derails pragmatic policymaking. In the best-case scenario, with the right policies and supportive external conditions, Venezuela's economy will initially experience a sharp additional contraction followed by sustained growth. Even then, however, it would take many years to restore the country to its former status. The risk is that the process of reconstruction and structural reform will be halting or could go into reverse, with the possibility that political dynamics will keep the country in a macroeconomic trap from which it cannot readily escape.

## Venezuela in Crisis

Venezuela's economic and humanitarian crisis has worsened to unprecedented levels in 2018–19. Inflation skyrocketed to one million per cent and food and power shortages encouraged still more Venezuelans to flee the country. In the wake of the escalating political crisis domestically and abroad, and with oil output falling further, Russia and China became more cautious about providing financial support to the government. US sanctions on the oil sector in January 2019, in effect closing the US market to Venezuelan crude, were particularly damaging. America is a major market and one of the very few countries with refineries configured to handle Venezuela's heavy, high-sulphur crude – and Venezuela is itself a customer for some of those refined petroleum products.

Puerto
Miran
Maracaibo
Bajo Grande

### HUMANITARIAN CRISIS

**4.3 million:**
Estimated number of Venezuelans
outside Venezuela
(UN, August 2019)

**7 million:**
Number of people in Venezuela in
need of humanitarian assistance
(UN, March 2019)

**5.3 million:**
Projected number of Venezuelans outside
Venezuela by December 2019
(UN, December 2018)

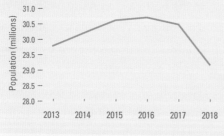

**Population**

**Unemployment (percentage of total labour force)**

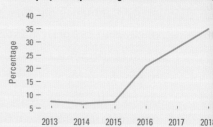

**Homicide rate, 2018**
Top three most violent cities, Venezuela

| City | Population | Homicide rate* | Global Rank |
|---|---|---|---|
| Caracas | 2,980,492 | 99.98 | 3 |
| Guayana | 823,722 | 78.3 | 7 |
| Ciudad Bolívar | 382,095 | 69.09 | 10 |

*per 100,000 inhabitants

**Top six host countries for Venezuelan migrants, June 2019**

| | |
|---|---|
| Colombia | 1.3m |
| Peru | 768,000 |
| Chile | 288,000 |
| Ecuador | 263,000 |
| Brazil | 168,000 |
| Argentina | 130,000 |

Sources: IMF World Economic Outlook Database; Economist Intelligence Unit; US Energy Information Administration; BP; Seguridad, Justicia y Paz; UNHCR; USAID

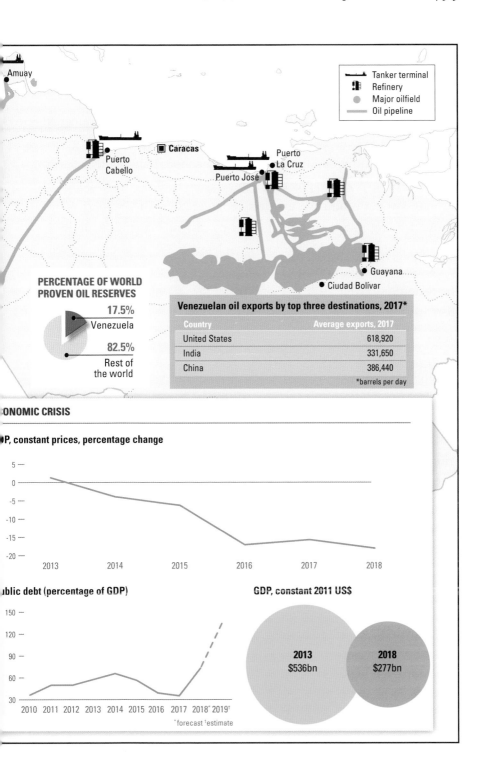

| Tanker terminal |
| Refinery |
| Major oilfield |
| Oil pipeline |

Amuay

Puerto Cabello

Caracas

Puerto La Cruz

Puerto José

Guayana

Ciudad Bolívar

**PERCENTAGE OF WORLD PROVEN OIL RESERVES**

17.5%
Venezuela

82.5%
Rest of the world

**Venezuelan oil exports by top three destinations, 2017\***

| Country | Average exports, 2017 |
|---|---|
| United States | 618,920 |
| India | 331,650 |
| China | 386,440 |

\*barrels per day

**ONOMIC CRISIS**

**P, constant prices, percentage change**

5
0
-5
-10
-15
-20

2013  2014  2015  2016  2017  2018

**blic debt (percentage of GDP)**

150
120
90
60
30

2010 2011 2012 2013 2014 2015 2016 2017 2018\* 2019†

\*forecast †estimate

**GDP, constant 2011 US$**

2013
$536bn

2018
$277bn

# The Challenges of Integration in Latin America

Latin America – Mexico and Central America and South America – boasts a plethora of regional and subregional institutions, yet its achievements in the field of integration are modest. This may seem surprising, given the supposed cultural and linguistic commonalities between the states, yet in fact history, geography and commerce, as well as current political realities, are not conducive to effective integration. The region has no natural leading state or group of states consistently committed to promoting integration, and economic complementarity within the region has always been, and remains, limited. Thus, while in the last 60 years the region has given birth to more than a dozen organisations, few of them have made a lasting impression.

## Integration past and present

The diplomatic history of the American hemisphere and of South America contains a number of attempts at organising greater union, beginning with Simón Bolívar's Amphyctionic Congress, convened in Panama in 1826, which was a patchily attended failure. The first US-sponsored gathering was held in Washington in 1889. It was not a universally popular initiative, the Argentines being particularly wary, but it did evolve into the Pan-American Union, which in 1948 gave way to the Organization of American States (OAS) – a body that, for all its limitations, remains the most serious forum for discussion of inter-American affairs.

The first modern attempt at economic integration was the five-member Central American Common Market, established in 1960. In the following 59 years, more than a dozen initiatives and organisations were established. Some have been disbanded, others are moribund. The large number of organisations, groups and accords is itself a source of confusion. Moreover, regional organisations have delivered few of the benefits associated with integration, such as increased levels of trade and investment. The growth of intra-regional trade has been disappointingly slight, and shows no clear continual upward trend; nor is it clear that the modest gains made can be attributed to conscious policies of integration. In some spheres it has gone into reverse: the once-important interchange between Colombia and Venezuela, for instance, has all but disappeared.

Most integration schemes have been hatched by politicians who are not always in tune with the economic realities of their own countries or those of their neighbours. Integration has frequently been a cause that can be embraced for short-term reasons with little political cost. In the last two decades, the prime exponent was president Hugo Chávez of Venezuela. His 'Bolivarian' regime, evolving into 'twentieth-century socialism', was essentially military populism dependent on the massive clientelism made possible by high oil prices. He adopted a pose of hostility towards the United States, not so much out of any profound, popular anti-American sentiment in Venezuela – a country that had little to complain of in that quarter, and whose culture was profoundly Americanised – but as a useful shibboleth for dividing adherents and opponents. With the country's high oil revenues, Chávez sought to buy support in the region through subsidised oil supplies in the Caribbean and Central America and with more direct cash incentives elsewhere. A Caribbean oil state, Venezuela has little in common with the rest of South America and consequently virtually no 'soft power' to back up its diplomatic ambitions.

A number of republics and politicians declared themselves 'Bolivarian': Ecuador under Rafael Correa, Bolivia under Evo Morales, Nicaragua under Daniel Ortega, plus a few Peruvian presidential hopefuls. Brazil under Luis Inácio Lula da Silva and his successor, Dilma Rousseff, from time to time made sympathetic noises; and with its characteristic opportunism, the Kirchner government in Argentina availed itself of Caracas's blandishments when offered. Venezuela was admitted to Mercosur, a customs union founded in 1991 made up of Argentina, Brazil, Paraguay and Uruguay, and pressed forward a series of wildly unrealistic projects such as the trans-Amazon pipeline that was to carry Venezuelan oil to be refined in Brazil. The Union of South American Nations (UNASUR) was created by Chávez in 2008, an organisation dedicated to the exclusion of the United States, with little other apparent purpose and with only shallow support from many who joined. Nor did the 'Bolivarian' republics follow similar economic policies. Economic management in Morales's Bolivia was sober and conventional, and Correa in Ecuador concentrated with some success on infrastructure development funded by Chinese loans.

This whole endeavour and structure fell apart with the collapse of the Venezuelan economy, which was already apparent before Chávez's death in 2013. As far as integration was concerned, general economic conditions in these times were not propitious. These were years of a commodity boom driven by Chinese demand, which reinforced the old export orientations of the Latin American economies.

Two relatively recent examples of moderate success have been sub-regional groupings with a political affinity and external economic focus. The Pacific Alliance, comprising Chile, Colombia, Mexico and Peru, unites a group of 'like-minded countries' which may yet have some success in making them more attractive to foreign investment through uniform policies on regulation, intellectual property and the like. However, the change of government in Mexico in 2018 has weakened the commitment of the member with the largest economy: Mexico's government has to attend first to the future of the North American Free Trade Agreement (NAFTA) and its own complicated relationship with the US.

Mercosur, from which Venezuela was suspended in 2016, has recently negotiated a trade agreement with the European Union. Argentina and Brazil, together with lesser partners Uruguay and Paraguay, are major commodity exporters in the world economy and have negotiated increased access to EU markets. The agreement is intended to boost international trade, not inter-regional trade, although were it to be successfully implemented, it would have a regionally integrating effect. However, the agreement has not yet been ratified by the parties, and Mercosur's two most important states may soon diverge politically, with Brazil under the right-wing presidency of Jair Bolsonaro and Argentina seemingly poised to turn to Peronism once again. That raises the prospect that Mercosur, like the Pacific Alliance, may struggle to build on its initial success with the EU.

While integration has been attempted more often at the subregional level, reflecting the difficulty in forging consensus among a sizeable number of states with distinct political traditions and non-complementary economies, the OAS has been the more durable and influential of the regional institutions. It has the advantage of being the oldest hemispheric forum, and enjoys some respect for its defence of human rights and democracy. It has been particularly active in its criticism of the regime of Nicolás Maduro in Venezuela. The relative success of the OAS may seem surprising to some outsiders in light of the fact that the US is a member, but in reality the region is much less uniform in its distrust of, and hostility towards, Washington than is often assumed.

## Inhibiting factors

The task of integration in Latin America is complicated by geography, history, politics and economics. The distances are vast. Natural communication channels – for example, the region's river systems – are relatively poor. Natural barriers are frequently formidable: aside from contact in the River Plate, the Amazon and Orinoco jungles have cut Brazil off from most of Spanish-speaking South America.

The old Spanish imperial divisions – the viceroyalties, captaincies general and presidencies – were not just 'lines in the sand', but were based on administrative imperatives derived from geographical realities. Despite leaving a legacy of minor border disputes at independence and thereafter, they have stood up well, and fostered proto-national feelings from an early stage.

In some ways the Spanish Empire can be seen as an integrating force. It was one of history's great catechising enterprises, imposing uniform laws and institutions, as well as spreading the Spanish language across much of its territory. It had an overall strategy of defence and communications, where needed supported by fiscal transfers from one part to another. However, the Spanish encountered a culturally diverse hemisphere, encompassing elements of the Aztec Empire in Mexico and the descendants of the Maya to the south; the complex of distinct societies in what is now Colombia; the Inca Empire; and the Araucanians of Chile. The extent of African slavery also varied: the institution was of great importance in Brazil, Venezuela, Cuba and parts of Peru and Colombia, while elsewhere it was marginal. These differences in many ways determined how these societies have viewed and still view themselves and each other.

There were other factors that limited the Spanish Empire's integration. Internal and external trade was strictly regulated, and remained scant between the empire's different parts. The most important exports – notably precious metals from the mines – were those that could bear the empire's high transport costs. All was held together by the Crown, and when Napoleon invaded Spain in 1808 and removed the Bourbons, disintegration inevitably followed. In its wake, 20 or so new republics emerged. These are now long-established states, older as nation-states than Germany, Italy or Belgium. It should therefore be no surprise that in 200 years of independent existence they have developed varied political traditions and cultures. For example, Venezuela, Colombia and Ecuador, although briefly joined together at the time of independence as Gran Colombia – a temporary facade to impress and gain the recognition of Europeans – rapidly diverged in their politics and today have little in common politically. While Venezuela and Colombia are neighbours, they have very different histories with regard to their own militaries: the constant political involvement of the Venezuelan army contrasts with the constitutionalist doctrine of Colombia's. For decades, the republics of Latin America took little interest in each other. Formal, permanent diplomatic relations between them often did not exist.

Distinct political identities and cultures are one factor inhibiting regional integration. Another is the economic structure of the countries and their lack of complementarity. At independence, these states entered into the world economy, unmediated by Spain or Portugal, with differing degrees of success. Some had commodities that the world demanded – for example, Argentine hides and salted meat – and did well. Others for long offered little. Yet all had in common an export orientation that determined the development of physical infrastructure: railways and roads connected their hinterlands with their ports; they rarely crossed national frontiers. Investing in connections with near or distant neighbours made no sense. The legacy of this rational orientation persists to this day. Republican governments were commonly dependent on income from customs tariffs, which reinforced their preference for foreign trade. Exports were almost entirely primary products, and imports were long dominated by British textiles. Inter-regional trade was insignificant.

Furthermore, because Latin America has for the past two centuries been a comparatively peaceful part of the world, at least in terms of inter-state conflict, one possible incentive for integration has been absent there. Unlike Europe, where the EU emerged after two world wars, Latin America has not been famous for its conflicts, which few outside or even inside the region can list.

Nevertheless, it has not been entirely peaceful. The nineteenth century saw one major war, that of Argentina, Brazil and Uruguay against Paraguay, and several lesser encounters, chief among them the War of the Pacific, in which Chile defeated Bolivia and Peru, gaining territory as a result and emerging as the leading military power in South America – an achievement viewed with reservations by Chile's neighbours. Despite the overall rationality of the old Spanish divisions, they left a number of border disputes, some of which were intensified by these conflicts. The dispute between Chile and Argentina over the Beagle Channel was acute in 1982, and there was speculation that the Argentine military junta might choose to attack Chile rather than invade the Falkland Islands.

All countries are sensitive in such matters, and Latin American nations are no exception. One characteristic they have in common is a strong tradition in public international law, marked by early texts such as Andrés Bello's *Principios de Derecho de Gentes* (1832) and the writings of the Argentine Carlos Calvo, perhaps the world's leading authority in the nineteenth century. This has produced a common legal culture, expressed strongly in a rejection of outside intervention, particularly by the US. Nonetheless, solidarity is not the same as integration.

## Weak engines of integration

Although integration efforts have generally been led by politicians, no state has consistently backed such enterprises. Latin America has no natural leading state. Brazil has rarely shown any interest in such a role, and the same can be said for Mexico and Argentina.

Starting its independent existence as a Portuguese-speaking monarchy, Brazil first looked down on the rest of South America, with which it had little contact. The very term 'Latin America', derived from the mid-century French fashion for the designation *l'Amérique latine*, was not thought to include Brazil, which was too vast and distant to feel threatened by the US. Many Brazilian thinkers were inclined to an alliance with the northern power rather than hostility or rivalry. They did not much favour bodies in which their country would have, like Nicaragua or Honduras, just one vote. The task of integrating Brazil itself, still incomplete, leaves little energy for integration beyond its frontiers.

Mexico, for obvious historical and contemporary reasons, is overwhelmingly concerned with its relations with the US, a conclusion confirmed by its founding participation in NAFTA in 1992. Mexico as a polity has little in common with the rest of Latin America. The Mexican Revolution of 1910 had no sequels elsewhere, and the political system that emerged from one-party rule by the Institutional Revolutionary Party (PRI) had no parallel. Apart from popular music and, for a time, cinema, Mexico has had little influence in South America. A persistent refusal to join in Washington's diplomatic isolation of revolutionary Cuba was little more than a gesture. Mexico has shown few if any signs of aspiring to leadership in Latin American integration, and the tentative steps that it took under its previous three presidents to play a more prominent role in Latin America and the world seem unlikely to persist under its new president, Andrés Manuel López Obrador.

Argentina too is no leader. For the first century and more of its independent existence, this republic was the most successful economically, a major exporter of wheat, meat and wool, and the recipient of vast foreign investment. It drew large numbers of immigrants from Italy and Spain, and created the splendid and populous city of Buenos Aires to rival the great cities of Europe and North America. This success generated a sense of superiority vis-à-vis the rest of South America. Despite experiencing decades of crisis, it is still inconceivable that Argentina should think of following the lead of any other country in the region except as a matter of temporary convenience. The legacy of Peronism has been long-term political instability, reflected in the erratic management of the economy.

The United States, particularly Congress, has been lukewarm in its interest in further free-trade initiatives in the hemisphere, and in Latin American integration in general. President Barack Obama sought to tie Canada, Chile, Mexico and Peru into the Trans-Pacific Partnership (TPP) to counterbalance China, but his successor's first decision was to withdraw from the TPP. President Donald Trump has evinced no interest in multilateral trade deals or integration of any sort.

In other regions of the world, business forms a powerful lobby for integration. This is less the case in Latin America. In certain commodities, Latin American enterprises are powerful actual and potential players, although there are not many Latin American multinationals. Mexico has the cement giant Cemex, the communications conglomerate of Carlos Slim and the baker Bimbo. In Brazil there was the now-bankrupt construction company Odebrecht, which maintained a whole unit – the 'Division of Structured Operations' – devoted exclusively to bribery and corruption. This came to light as part of investigations that began in Brazil and then fanned out across Latin America, leading to the ouster of presidents and ministers in several countries. The scandal has given this kind of ambitious enterprise a lasting bad name.

Latin American entrepreneurs do not find it easy to make money outside their own countries. The reason is essentially political. Import substitution, the origin of many companies that might seek the benefits of the wider markets that integration seems to promise, was a politically determined and dependent economic policy, and the legacy lingers. Much latent protectionism is contained not in tariffs, but in regulations and licences, to the advantage of well-connected nationals, not newcomers.

Nonetheless, the region's record on integration is arguably no worse than most other parts of the world, and the feeling that this is a problem is partly one of perception and exaggerated expectations. The interests of the disparate countries of a vast and geographically divided part of the world do not always coincide. Regional states' trade patterns and relations with the world economy have not favoured integration. Their politics are varied and sometimes antagonistic; there is no natural leading power; and, unlike the case of Europe, there has been no cataclysmic conflict to shock states and politicians across the subcontinent into a new frame of mind. There are grounds to be optimistic about the future of Latin America, but the likelihood of rapid further regional integration is not one of them.

# North America: Drivers of Strategic Change

- Special counsel Robert Mueller's long-awaited report on Russian interference in the 2016 election did not recommend legal action against US President Donald Trump or his family, reducing the risk of a legal threat that could terminate his presidency.

- Trump's Republican Party lost control of the House of Representatives in the November 2018 midterm elections, increasing the prospects of legislative deadlock. However, his solid support among Republican voters and improving approval rating among voting-age Americans suggests that he stands a fair chance of winning a second term.

- The US applied hefty tariffs on imports from China, and suffered retaliatory measures, as the president sought to fulfil promises to reset US trading relations with the rest of the world. The administration also marked its first achievement in the trade sphere when Canada and Mexico agreed to surrender some of the benefits of the North American Free Trade Agreement as the price of maintaining extensive access to the US market under a new US–Mexico–Canada Agreement (USMCA).

- The administration in February 2019 suspended compliance with the INF Treaty and gave six months' notice of its intention to withdraw from it. The decision is consistent with Trump's hostility towards constraining international agreements. The major remaining arms-control agreement, New START, is due to lapse in February 2021.

- The US stepped up its efforts to force Iran to negotiate over its nuclear aspirations and regional behaviour by increasing primary and secondary sanctions on Tehran, over the objections of EU allies. Although Trump is committed to 'maximum pressure', he has proved reluctant thus far to make good on threats of military action against Iran – despite some provocations.

## DEMOGRAPHY

POPULATION AND MEDIAN AGE
(IMF, April 2019; UN Department of Economic and Social Affairs, Population Division, 2019)

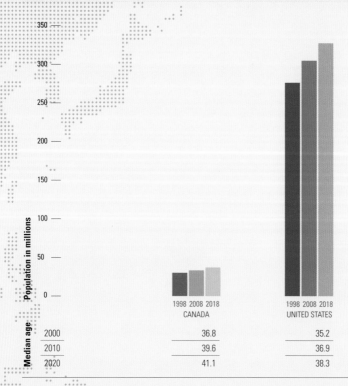

| | CANADA | UNITED STATES |
|---|---|---|
| 2000 | 36.8 | 35.2 |
| 2010 | 39.6 | 36.9 |
| 2020 | 41.1 | 38.3 |

AGE STRUCTURE
(CIA World Factbook, 2019)

| CANADA | |
|---|---|
| Under 25 years | 27.05% |
| 25–64 years | 53.86% |
| 64 years and older | 19.08% |

| USA | |
|---|---|
| Under 25 years | 31.74% |
| 25–64 years | 52.23% |
| 64 years and older | 16.03% |

# ECONOMICS AND DEVELOPMENT

## GDP AT PPP
Constant 2011 international dollars (IMF, April 2019)

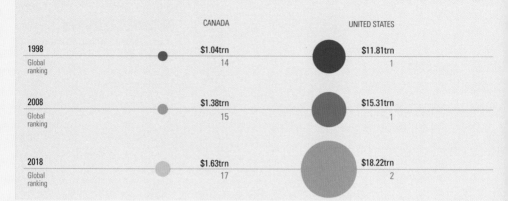

|  | CANADA |  | UNITED STATES |  |
|---|---|---|---|---|
| **1998** | $1.04trn |  | $11.81trn |  |
| Global ranking | 14 |  | 1 |  |
| **2008** | $1.38trn |  | $15.31trn |  |
| Global ranking | 15 |  | 1 |  |
| **2018** | $1.63trn |  | $18.22trn |  |
| Global ranking | 17 |  | 2 |  |

## GDP PER CAPITA AT PPP
Constant 2011 international dollars (IMF, April 2019)

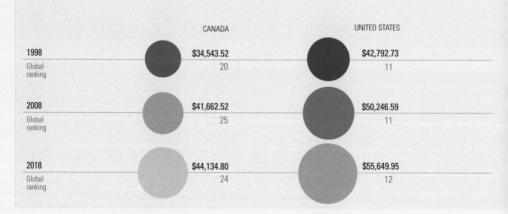

|  | CANADA |  | UNITED STATES |  |
|---|---|---|---|---|
| **1998** | $34,543.52 |  | $42,792.73 |  |
| Global ranking | 20 |  | 11 |  |
| **2008** | $41,662.52 |  | $50,246.59 |  |
| Global ranking | 25 |  | 11 |  |
| **2018** | $44,134.80 |  | $55,649.95 |  |
| Global ranking | 24 |  | 12 |  |

## HUMAN DEVELOPMENT INDEX (HDI)
(UN Development Programme, 2019)

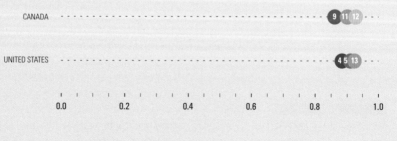

CANADA — 9 11 12

UNITED STATES — 4 5 13

0.0    0.2    0.4    0.6    0.8    1.0

 Global ranking 1998     Global ranking 2008    00 Global ranking 2018

Score between 0 and 1, where 0 denotes a low level of development and 1 a high level of development.

# INTERNATIONAL INTEGRATION

### TRADE
Exports of goods and commercial services, constant 2010 US dollars
(World Trade Organization, 2019)

Global ranking

| CANADA | | 10 13 |
| UNITED STATES | | 1 2 |

0    500   1000   1500   2000   2500

US$ billions

■ 2008
■ 2018

### INTERNATIONAL NETWORK
Total number of diplomatic missions, 2017
Lowy Institute Global Diplomacy Index
(2017)

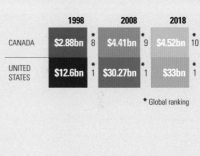

| | Missions abroad | | Global ranking |
|---|---|---|---|
| CANADA | 147 | | 17 |
| UNITED STATES | 273 | | 1 |

# DIPLOMACY AND DEFENCE

### DEFENCE BUDGET
Constant 2010 US dollars (Military Balance 1998,
and Military Balance+)

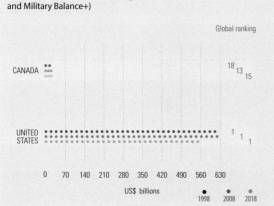

Global ranking

CANADA           18 13 15

UNITED STATES      1 1 1

0   70  140 210 280 350 420 490 560 630

US$ billions

● 1998   ● 2008   ● 2018

### OFFICIAL DEVELOPMENT AID
Constant 2015 US dollars (OECD, 2019)

| | 1998 | | 2008 | | 2018 | |
|---|---|---|---|---|---|---|
| CANADA | $2.88bn | *8 | $4.41bn | *9 | $4.52bn | *10 |
| UNITED STATES | $12.6bn | *1 | $30.27bn | *1 | $33bn | *1 |

\* Global ranking

### POLITICAL SYSTEM
(Economist Intelligence Unit, 2008, 2018)

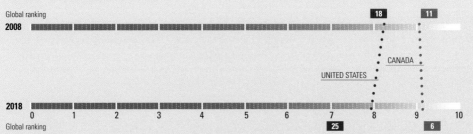

Global ranking

**2008**                                                          18        11

                                                          CANADA

                                    UNITED STATES

**2018**
0    1    2    3    4    5    6    7    8    9    10

Global ranking                                          25        6

Score between 0 and 10, where 10 denotes a fully democratic and 0 a fully authoritarian regime.

©IISS

Atlantic Ocean

Pacific Ocean

CANADA

UNITED STATES

NEWFOUNDLAND

QUEBEC

ONTARIO

NUNAVUT

NORTHWEST TERRITORIES

MANITOBA

SASKATCHEWAN

ALBERTA

BRITISH COLUMBIA

YUKON TERRITORY

Alaska (United States)

Ottawa

PRINCE EDWARD
NEW BRUNSWICK
NOVA SCOTIA
MAINE
NEW HAMPSHIRE
MASSACHUSETTS
RHODE ISLAND
CONNECTICUT
VERMONT
NEW YORK
NEW JERSEY
DELAWARE
MARYLAND
Washington DC
PENNSYLVANIA
WEST VIRGINIA
VIRGINIA
NORTH CAROLINA
SOUTH CAROLINA
GEORGIA
OHIO
MICHIGAN
INDIANA
KENTUCKY
TENNESSEE
ALABAMA
MISSISSIPPI
WISCONSIN
ILLINOIS
MISSOURI
ARKANSAS
LOUISIANA
IOWA
MINNESOTA
NORTH DAKOTA
SOUTH DAKOTA
NEBRASKA
KANSAS
OKLAHOMA
TEXAS
MONTANA
WYOMING
COLORADO
NEW MEXICO
IDAHO
UTAH
ARIZONA
WASHINGTON
OREGON
NEVADA
CALIFORNIA

# Chapter 10

# North America

## 2018–19 Review

The year to mid-2019 was notable for US President Donald Trump's apparent ability to shake off scandal and endure adversity. He experienced several serious setbacks, most notably the Republicans' loss of the House of Representatives in the November 2018 midterm elections. Yet the threat overshadowing much of his first two years in office – the investigation by special counsel Robert Mueller into Russian interference in the 2016 presidential election, the Trump campaign's alleged collusion with Moscow and Trump's possible obstruction of justice – seemed to lift with the submission of Mueller's report in March 2019. Meanwhile, Trump continued his attempts to fulfil campaign pledges, or at least to persuade his supporters that he had done so. The most obvious of these concerned immigration and his much-promised yet still unbuilt wall on the US–Mexico border.

In international affairs, Trump continued to combine aggressive rhetoric and willingness to abrogate international agreements with a marked preference for authoritarian leaders and an openness to negotiation with traditional adversaries. He met North Korean leader Kim Jong-un three times during the year, although these summits (or, in the final instance, an impromptu encounter at the Demilitarised Zone–DMZ) produced few tangible results. By the end of 2018, Trump had shed the last of those senior advisers many had hoped might constrain his more erratic foreign-policy impulses. Yet the first six months of 2019 revealed few signs of any significant discontinuity. In at least one instance, it was possible to observe a reverse dynamic, in which Trump himself seemed to be the voice of caution in the Situation Room. Trump's actions abroad, as well as at home, appeared to remain consistent with his two primary overarching goals: securing re-election and repudiating the legacy of his predecessor.

## US domestic policies

Trump's most obvious domestic setback was the Democratic Party's recapture of the House of Representatives, which had been in Republican hands for the previous eight years. In midterm elections in November 2018 the Democrats gained 40 House seats, as well as seven governors' mansions. Yet the Democrats lost two seats in the Senate, despite winning many millions more votes than the Republican Party, thanks in part to the latter's predominance in less populous rural states. Although the Republicans controlled Congress for the first two years of his presidency, Trump had struggled to push through key legislation. Most notably, the Republicans had failed to 'repeal and replace' the Affordable Care Act (ACA), one of former president Barack Obama's signature policies. With Congress now divided, legislative gridlock appeared even more likely, as did long-threatened Democratic investigations into the finances of Trump and his family. Trump announced in November that government would '[come] to a halt' if he were subjected to congressional investigation. In the immediate period after the Democrats' victory, however, the most probable stimulus for congressional action against the president seemed to be the special counsel's investigation.

For nearly two years, Mueller's investigation had provided solace for Trump's opponents, many of whom drew comfort from the notion that Trump's supposed crimes would be uncovered and punished. For much of 2018–19, periodic indictments and convictions sustained these hopes. In July 2018, Mueller charged 12 Russian military-intelligence officers with hacking the Democratic National Committee and Hillary Clinton's campaign during the 2016 presidential election. The following month, Trump admitted that, in summer 2016, one of his sons had met visiting Russians with Kremlin connections 'to get information on an opponent' but disclaimed any advance knowledge and argued that such practices were legal and commonplace. Over the following six months, several close associates of Trump were charged or convicted of financial crimes, lying to Congress or obstruction of justice, among other misdeeds. Meanwhile, Trump continued openly to lambast then-attorney general Jeff Sessions for his refusal to quash Mueller's investigation. Sessions resigned at Trump's request the day after the November 2018 midterm elections. His successor, William Barr, appeared more amenable to Trump's belief that the attorney general's responsibility was to defend the person of the president.

Mueller finally submitted his 448-page report to Barr on 22 March. Barr waited almost a month to release a redacted version. Within a few days, however, he had published a four-page précis highlighting Mueller's conclusion that, while Russia interfered in the 2016 election, he had found insufficient evidence for criminal charges relating to contacts between Trump's campaign and the Russian state. Mueller pointedly refrained from exonerating Trump of obstruction of justice and clarified that he had considered it impossible to indict a sitting president. Barr, however, determined that Trump's actions did not amount to obstruction.

Predictably, Trump declared himself exonerated by Mueller, whom he had previously accused of conducting a 'witch hunt' against his administration. During a subsequent television interview, Trump stated that he would be willing to receive a foreign source's harmful information about a political opponent in the 2020 election without reporting it to the FBI. Democratic Speaker of the House of Representatives Nancy Pelosi responded that Trump had given Moscow 'the green light' to repeat its electoral interference in 2020.

The Democrats were split over whether to impeach the president. Around 80 Democrats in the House voiced their support for impeachment, but Pelosi refused to proceed, calculating that Republican control of the Senate ensured that impeachment would be futile and could potentially be electorally counterproductive. Her opposing colleagues' counterarguments were on grounds of principle and pragmatism: that the prospect of a Democratic House investigating and impeaching Trump had mobilised many of their voters and that, to defend the rule of law, the president should be held to account for his perceived violations of the law and democratic norms, even if there were little prospect of convicting him. If the Democrats were lukewarm about impeachment, the Republicans were predictably opposed. Justin Amash of Michigan, the only Republican member who supported impeachment after reading Mueller's report, left the party amid signs that a pro-Trump colleague would challenge him in a Republican primary before the next elections. Nevertheless, as the year progressed, House Democrats sought ways to scrutinise the actions of Trump and his administration. In April, the chair of the House Committee on Ways and Means requested Trump's tax returns from the Internal Revenue Service, and the House Committee on the Judiciary voted to subpoena Mueller's full, unredacted report, for Mueller to testify before it, and to subpoena various Trump associates – including his son-in-law Jared Kushner and Sessions – relating to its investigation of potential obstruction of justice. Trump and his family also continued to face legal peril from various investigations mounted by entities in the state of New York, not least because convictions for state crimes are ineligible for presidential pardons.

Democratic deliberations over impeachment roughly reflected broader divisions in the party – both within Congress and in the crowded Democratic field for the 2020 presidential election – over which strategy was more likely to succeed: advocacy for radical change, in the hope this would tap the popular restlessness Trump had exploited in 2016; or a more moderate position representing the status quo ante Trump and a return to the normalcy many centrist voters craved. Advocates of the former position tended to be younger, while veteran Democratic figures such as Pelosi or former vice president Joe Biden often personified and championed the latter. While the younger, more radical wing of the party sought to erode Pelosi's dominance of the House, she demonstrated the value of her political experience in her initial dealings with Trump over immigration at the Mexican border.

From the outset of his presidential campaign, Trump had evoked imagery of a permeable border across which hordes of Hispanic 'parasites and criminals' flowed unchecked. The promise of a 'big, beautiful wall', the cost of which would be borne by Mexico, was perhaps his best-known policy, combining two of his more powerful convictions: that restoring American greatness required robust action to redress foreign exploitation of US goodwill; and that non-white immigration posed a threat to American identity and wellbeing. As with the ACA, Trump had failed to cajole any effective legislation for his wall while the Republicans controlled the House. With the midterm elections approaching, Trump and his political and media allies depicted a 'caravan' of several thousand Central American migrants approaching the southern border as a national-security threat, and 800 US troops were deployed to the frontier. Trump and his administration suggested that the caravan included 'unknown Middle Easterners' and possibly terrorists.

Trump's attention shifted almost as soon as the elections had passed, but he remained intent on using widespread concerns about uncontrolled immigration as an electoral wedge issue. With future Democratic control of the House making funding for his wall even less likely, Trump doubled down in the hope of forcing through a deal or, at the least, demonstrating to his followers that he had been thwarted only by Democratic intransigence. He announced he would be 'proud' to cause a shutdown of the federal government if doing so allowed him to secure America's borders. The incoming congressional Democratic leadership refused to accept Trump's demands for funding for a wall, and the shutdown began on 22 December.

Two weeks later, the Democrats assumed control of the House. They sought to reopen the government and allocated US$1.3 billion to border-security measures that did not include construction of a wall. Trump refused to authorise spending without specific support for such construction, and threatened to declare a national emergency that would allow him to bypass Congress. A week after that, the shutdown became the longest in US history. Pelosi demonstrated a shrewd assessment of Trump's priorities by postponing his invitation to deliver the State of the Union address to Congress on 29 January until after the shutdown had ended. She appeared to have outmanoeuvred the president. The shutdown was generally unpopular. Moreover, Trump had proclaimed beforehand both that it was unnecessary and that it was his responsibility. On 25 January, he agreed a measure to fund the government for the following three weeks without any provision for wall construction. The Congressional Budget Office estimated that the shutdown, which had lasted 35 days, represented a US$11bn loss for the US economy. It had also seen Trump's net approval rating fall by six points, while Pelosi's rose by three.

While Trump seemed to have suffered a humiliating defeat, he soon appeared to regain momentum. On 15 February, he declared a national emergency that would allow him to channel around US$6bn in military funds towards construction of the border wall. A month later he vetoed a Senate resolution against his declaration; later in March, the Democrats failed to obtain the House 'supermajority' required to overturn Trump's veto. While his measure was legally contested, and blocked at least in part by a federal judge's injunction in June, in July 2019 the Supreme Court overturned this injunction. Trump had succeeded in demonstrating to his supporters that he would stop at nothing to fulfil his promises to them. His apparent victory in forcing Mexico to adopt more stringent measures against northbound Central American migrants after threatening tariffs on Mexican imports to the US boosted this narrative. A furore had raged throughout the year over the separation of migrant children from their families and their maltreatment in detention. Seven children died between summer 2018 and summer 2019. Yet Trump seemed to have calculated that such actions made his re-election more, not less, probable. His 2020 election-campaign manager claimed in January that swing voters were likely to pick Trump because of border-security concerns.

By July 2019, although most Americans believed Trump's behaviour was unpresidential, his approval rating among Americans of voting age had risen to 44%, the highest of his term so far. While hardly stellar, this was only slightly below Ronald Reagan's approval rating at the same point in his presidency. Trump's net approval among Republicans was 72% – having risen by five points after he suggested that four non-white congresswomen 'go home'. Trump's appeal was not based solely on nativism: 51% of Americans approved of his stewardship of the economy. In April, the unemployment rate fell to 3.6%, its lowest in nearly 50 years, and GDP growth stood at a steady 3.1%. Trump appeared to be in a stronger position for re-election than many would have anticipated at the beginning of his administration.

## US foreign policy

For much of his first two years in office, Trump had supposedly been constrained by the so-called 'adults in the room' – officials such as the secretary of defense James Mattis, chief of staff John Kelly, secretary of state Rex Tillerson and national security advisor H.R. McMaster. It was reported that Mattis had resisted various bellicose impulses towards Syria's government and Iran. In September 2018, this notion was bolstered by an anonymous *New York Times* op-ed by a senior administration official who assured readers that he and others within government were working to thwart Trump's more destructive or illegal inclinations. By December, only Kelly and Mattis remained in post. Tillerson and McMaster had been replaced by Mike Pompeo and John Bolton respectively. The former displayed no inclination to contradict the president; the latter's history of bellicose policy advocacy offered few reassurances to anxious observers of Trump's behaviour on the world stage. On 20 December, following Trump's declaration that US forces would withdraw from Syria, Mattis announced his resignation, effective in February. Once he had been made aware of the criticism the resignation letter contained, Trump attacked Mattis's record and accelerated his departure. Kelly had also left government by the end of the year.

Yet as of mid-2019, there were few signs that US foreign policy had shifted or become more erratic as a result of Trump's unbridling. His attempted rapprochement with North Korean leader Kim Jong-un continued. While their initial Singapore summit in June 2018 produced few meaningful concessions, substantive diplomacy or a shared definition of what 'denuclearisation' entailed, a few months later Trump proclaimed that Kim had written him 'beautiful letters' and that they had '[fallen] in love'. At their second summit, in Hanoi in February, Trump defied expectations through his refusal (reportedly on Bolton's advice) to accept Kim's proposals for middling and reversible North Korean concessions in return for sanctions relief. While Pyongyang proceeded to emit various aggressive signals, including missile tests in April and May, Trump seemed to believe that, with continued flattery, his courtship of Kim could endure. On 30 June, they held an impromptu meeting at the DMZ. Bolton was absent, dispatched to another engagement in Mongolia. Within days, however, North Korea had warned that forthcoming US–South Korea military exercises could end bilateral dialogue and perhaps result in renewed nuclear testing.

Trump's Middle Eastern policy appeared consistent with his long-term critique of foreign entanglements, yet contradictory in that his reluctance to employ military force was combined with an incendiary approach towards regional rivals. Having fulfilled a campaign pledge in May 2018 by withdrawing from the Joint Comprehensive Plan of Action (JCPOA), Trump escalated his policy of 'maximum pressure' against Iran, reimposing previous sanctions and then surpassing them with additional measures. Following Washington's indication in April that it intended to eliminate Iranian oil exports entirely, Iran announced that it would incrementally violate the JCPOA's constraints on its enrichment activity. Tehran was also very likely responsible for several attacks on oil tankers in the Gulf. After Iran downed an American uninhabited aerial vehicle (UAV) in June, Trump claimed that US forces had been only minutes away from retaliatory airstrikes before he aborted the mission for fear of responding disproportionately; it was reported that his decision followed advice from a right-wing television commentator. Trump conveyed the impression that he had resisted the more aggressive instincts of his advisers. While his announcement may have been intended to signal a willingness to act decisively without suffering the negative repercussions of an airstrike, it mainly signalled indecision and a reluctance to employ force. Trump's repeated exhortations for dia-logue with Tehran also suggested he was attempting to re-enact his North Korean strategy: ratcheting up tension while advertising will-ingness to broker a 'better deal'. As of late June, however, there were few signs that his putative Iranian interlocutors were interested in reo-pening negotiations.

Trump's foreign policy remained consistent with long-held beliefs and campaign pledges. His trade war with China, which escalated throughout the year, demonstrated to his supporters that the days when foreigners exploited the US through free trade had passed, and was one of the few of his policies to enjoy broad bipartisan support in Washington. His hostility towards constraining international agree-ments manifested in the announcement in October 2018 of the US withdrawal from the Intermediate-Range Nuclear Forces (INF) Treaty (following long-standing Russian violations), a decision Trump con-firmed in February. In the spring, it was widely reported that Trump's decades-long complaints of foreign freeloading might result in a demand that foreign hosts of US forces pay for their full cost plus an additional 50% for the privilege, and perhaps a withdrawal from South Korea and/or Japan. It was even rumoured that Trump was intending to fulfil the threat he made at the July 2018 summit to withdraw the US from NATO. While none of these occurred, it was telling that few observers judged such moves impossible.

Trump's affinity for illiberalism was on display throughout the year. His declaration in October 2018 that he was a 'nationalist' was met by French President Emmanuel Macron's public response the following month that 'nationalism is a betrayal of patriotism'. Trump, in turn, attacked Macron's weak approval ratings and mocked France's wartime occupation. His confrontational tone with Western leaders contrasted with his submissive demeanour during his public meeting with Russian President Vladimir Putin in Helsinki in July 2018, during which he insisted that Russia had not interfered in the 2016 election. After this, he held a private meeting with Putin but without any other US officials. The following June, at the G20 summit, Trump joked with Putin about 'get[ting] rid of' journalists.

On one level, Trump's foreign policy could appear inconsistent and impulsive. His pledge to remove all forces from Syria, for example, was later watered down to maintaining a core of around 400 troops, probably due to Bolton's manoeuvring. On another level, there were several consistent coordinates around which his decisions tended to cluster. These included hostility towards traditional alliances; warmth towards authoritarian leaders; and a desire to win plaudits for being a tough yet conciliatory dealmaker who deserved re-election. In particular, Trump's urge to repudiate Obama's legacy wherever possible has driven both his foreign and domestic policy. This, as much as anything, explains his antagonism towards the JCPOA and determination to broker a 'better deal' with Tehran. While Trump may have had few tangible benefits to show for his policy, it seemed clear that for electoral purposes he would depict his actions as a decisive break from the past. Although much of the analytic community might decry his foreign policy as impulsive and wrong-headed, it remained unclear whether the electorate would agree.

## Canada

The supposed injustices of the North American Free Trade Agreement (NAFTA) featured prominently in Trump's election campaign. Trump's threats to revoke NAFTA posed a serious threat to Canada, whose exports to the US represent 20% of its GDP. In October 2018, Prime Minister Justin Trudeau agreed to join the 'US–Mexico–Canada Agreement' (USMCA), essentially an updated version of NAFTA that included additional restrictions, some of which were designed to increase US employment. The following May, Canada, the US and Mexico agreed to lift US aluminium and steel tariffs in force since the previous year. In June, Mexico became the first signatory to ratify the USMCA.

The year was also notable for Canada's troubled relations with China and Saudi Arabia. In summer 2018, in response to Canadian expressions of concern over imprisoned Saudi activists, Riyadh expelled the Canadian ambassador and planned to withdraw thousands of its students from Canada. Alarmingly for Ottawa, neither Washington nor its other traditional allies appeared eager to take Canada's side in the dispute. Following a US request in December, Canada detained Huawei's chief financial officer Meng Wanzhou (who is also its founder's daughter). In response, Beijing detained several Canadians, including a former diplomat, and suspended imports of Canadian canola.

At home, Trudeau faced allegations of impropriety that tarnished a prior reputation for uprightness. His former justice minister and attorney general, Jody Wilson-Raybould, accused him of having made 'veiled threats' to encourage her to allow a major Canadian firm to settle charges of corruption, in the fear that judicial action might result in job losses. She was eventually demoted to another post, before resigning. Jane Philpott, another cabinet member, also resigned, as did Gerald Butts, Trudeau's top adviser. By June, however, the consequent fall in support for Trudeau's Liberal Party appeared to be levelling out, and it remained unclear to what extent the scandal would affect federal elections scheduled for later in the year.

# A New US Consensus on China?

The new conventional wisdom states that the antagonism between China and the United States will be long-lasting and may escalate into a great-power struggle resembling that of the Cold War. Underpinning this theory is the assertion that there is now a hardline consensus in the US for a policy that not only seeks to rebalance the trade and commercial relationship between the two countries, but also views China as an implacable adversary and rival for global influence. There will be little opportunity for cooperation between the two powers in such a scenario: the US will need to actively challenge and contain China's efforts to increase its global influence. However, it is debatable to what extent this assertion reflects the current posture and practice of the US administration, or indeed whether such a consensus accurately characterises the nature of China's own stance.

## A Thucydides Trap?

In *Destined For War: Can America and China Escape Thucydides's Trap?*, Graham Allison revived the thesis of the ancient Greek historian Thucydides that when a rising power threatens to displace a dominant power, war is by far the most likely outcome. Since the book's publication in 2017, Chinese President Xi Jinping and US President Donald Trump have often seemed to be playing the roles assigned to them in the Thucydidean tragedy, while Henry Kissinger has endorsed the concept of the Thucydides Trap as the best lens through which to examine the US–China relationship.

China under Xi has become more assertive and ambitious: Xi has explicitly cast aside former Chinese leader Deng Xiaoping's doctrine that China should be cautious and restrained in its approach to the wider world, while China has stepped up the use of both coercive economic diplomacy and military pressure in Asia, especially in the South China Sea. Domestically, Xi's 'Made in China 2025' policy was an overt exercise to utilise protectionist industrial policies to seize global leadership from the US, Europe and Japan in several key high-tech economic sectors including robotics, biotechnology and artificial intelligence (AI).

On the US side, the Trump administration's approach to China was laid out in the December 2017 National Security Strategy (NSS). The NSS argued that the world had entered an era characterised by the re-emergence of great-power competition and declared the primacy of China as the main strategic threat facing the US, representing a fundamental shift away from the focus on Islamic extremism and terrorism that had animated US policy since the 9/11 attacks in 2001. Unlike previous periods of such competition, the economic dimension had become the central concern.

The Trump administration has laid out a long list of complaints about Chinese behaviour on the international scene not only in the NSS, but also in policy frameworks promulgated by other US executive departments. In a speech at the Hudson Institute in 2018 that outlined the motivations behind the administration's China policy, US Vice President Mike Pence accused Beijing of pursuing 'an arsenal of policies inconsistent with free and fair trade … directed its bureaucrats and businesses to obtain American intellectual property – the foundation of our economic leadership – by any means necessary'.

The administration's critique of China has also gained support among Democrats. Senate Minority Leader Chuck Schumer has stated that 'China takes total advantage of the United States' and suggested that 'what [Trump] did on China is right', while Senator Elizabeth Warren has said that Beijing has 'weaponized its economy' and is 'using its economic might to bludgeon its way onto the world stage'. In November 2018, a trio of Democratic senators (including Schumer) wrote a letter to Trump in which they praised the president's strong stance: 'we appreciate that you have initiated much more aggressive action than past administrations … We urge you to stand firm against China if meaningful concessions are not made.'

## The end of strategic convergence

Given this context, the widespread belief in a new US consensus concerning how to approach China is not surprising, and in a limited sense, it is true. The period of strategic convergence between China and the US – which began with then-president Richard Nixon's recognition of the People's Republic of China in 1978, accelerated after the collapse of the Soviet Union in 1991 and was transformed by more than 20 years of economic collaboration and engagement – has ended. The expectations that underpinned the long period of strategic convergence following the Cold War no longer hold.

During the period of strategic convergence, economic interdependence became the cornerstone of US–China relations. The US believed that growing economic and commercial ties between the US and China would lead China to become both more market-driven and politically open, and would result in Beijing becoming a more 'responsible stakeholder' on the global scene.

The Chinese theory of economic interdependence took shape in the aftermath of the demise of the Soviet Union and the rise of the US as the world's sole superpower, when Beijing worried about how it might forestall the US from blocking China's rise. Deng initiated his 'hide and bide' strategy – a form of strategic reassurance that China's rise would not disrupt the existing global order – combined with a policy of economic interdependence that would create US stakeholders in a successful China. China's commercial opening was principally driven by domestic economic motives, but these were supplemented by a geopolitical rationale: that a US with strong economic ties to China would be less interested in blocking China's rise.

In both the US and China, the expectation that economics would drive strategic convergence no longer dominates. Many in the US now believe that the theory of economic interdependence bringing about a more liberal China no longer provides a useful model for addressing the US–China relationship. There is also broad agreement concerning the increasing importance of geopolitical competition and of China's shift under Xi from restraint to a more assertive, ambitious posture. Indeed, there is general agreement on most of the individual elements of the 'indictment list' that has become the centrepiece of recent US policy statements on China. But the consensus does not extend to what the US response should be.

## Lack of coherence over policy implementation

Beyond taking a tougher approach to China, the Trump administration has had difficulty maintaining a coherent foreign-policy stance on China. On security issues, the US armed forces see the alliance system in Asia as crucial to countering China's ambitions in the region, but Trump is deeply ambivalent, having made comments veering between strong support and the view that the alliances are fundamentally 'unfair' to the US.

On trade, the president has focused on rebalancing the trade deficit and increasing US exports to China, while US chief negotiator Robert Lighthizer has given more attention to addressing structural issues of concern to US companies such as intellectual-property (IP) theft, the state subsidisation of domestic producers and forced technology transfer. While the US blamed the breakdown of negotiations in May on Xi's failure to support the deal his chief negotiator Liu He agreed to, China blamed Trump for allowing Lighthizer to push issues into the agreement that crossed Beijing's redlines.

On technology, there has been broad support for tightening up export controls and monitoring national-security risks in new inward investment into the US. In 2018, driven by concerns about China, Congress passed legislation that strengthened the arrangements to protect what the 2017 NSS called the 'national-security innovation base' – the broad ecosystem of tech expertise, talent and investment that has kept the US at the forefront of emerging advanced technologies. In May 2019, Trump approved a Commerce Department action to deny Huawei access to US software and high-end microprocessing chips. A month later, however, he suspended these restrictions to enable Xi to save face and agree to restart trade negotiations, again demonstrating the lack of a cohesive policy even on an issue where there has been broad bipartisan support.

## Trump's 'Team of Rivals' on China

To better make sense of current US policy on China, it is useful to think about the top levels of the administration being divided among three groupings, the strongest of which are the 'commercial rebalancers', led by Trump and including US Trade Representative Lighthizer. This group prioritises the economic dimension of the relationship over the security dimension, supports non-traditional policy tools to gain leverage, and does not seek a sweeping economic decoupling with China. US Special Representative for North Korea Stephen Biegun also belongs in this group.

More aggressive than the rebalancers are the national-security hawks, led by Pence, National Security Advisor John Bolton and Commerce Secretary Wilbur Ross, with support from elements of the military and intelligence services. They prioritise security concerns (including those related to economic issues) and support erecting permanent barriers around technology and security-related investments in both directions, which would lead to a partial economic disengagement between the US and China. They also advocate a robust military presence (especially naval) in the Western Pacific and have challenged the legality of China's activities within the so-called 'nine-dash line' in the South China Sea.

More cautious than the rebalancers are the 'macroeconomic pragmatists' led by Treasury Secretary Steven Mnuchin and White House Chief Economic Advisor Larry Kudlow, who are sometimes joined by Secretary of State Mike Pompeo. They argue for an approach that assures macroeconomic considerations and financial stability are taken into account in US actions, and are broadly seen as representing the interests of the US financial establishment and major US corporations in the policy process. For instance, following the breakdown of trade talks in early May 2019, Mnuchin put the Trump–Xi summit back on track during a meeting with People's Bank of China head Yi Gang two weeks before the G20 meeting in Osaka.

## Has US business turned against China?

Beyond the Trump administration, several key issues regarding China call into question the notion of a US consensus and the impending descent into a new cold war.

For many years, US firms in China were strong supporters of a 'soft-touch' approach to China, but this changed dramatically during the Obama administration, by the end of which US firms in China had become a strong voice for a tougher approach. US companies now perceive China as a more difficult place in which to invest and with which to do business. A set of US firms – those who have production operations in China – have become substantially more negative about their prospects, be they automakers, other manufacturers or high-tech hardware and software firms. These companies have been hurt most by IP theft, subsidisation of local competitors, forced tech transfer and an unequal legal playing field.

On the other hand, many US companies still regard China as an opportunity, given that in recent years it has become the leading contributor to global economic growth, while the Chinese economy has become much more consumption driven. Fifteen years ago, the main US commercial interest in China was the status of foreign direct investors, who used China for exporting (i.e., as a platform to penetrate other markets; today China is the market for many US firms). Today, the US export sector writ large has a stake in a growing China and an open Chinese economy. Farmers, energy producers and financial-services firms, among others, all view the Chinese market as an enormous opportunity. All these players view with scepticism the notion that a decoupling of the US and Chinese economies would be beneficial to the US.

## Understanding China's motivations

The US debate about relations with China is being shaped by the increasing focus on authoritarianism as a global alternative to Western liberalism. In a recent piece modelled on George Kennan's 1946 'long telegram' on the origins of Soviet external behaviour, Charles Edel and Hal Brands emphasise that China's increasingly assertive behaviour is less about US actions and 'more a product of shifting power dynamics and the ingrained nature of the regime'. On this basis, the authors argue that there is little the US can do to appease or reassure Chinese leaders.

However, many US observers of China believe that Beijing's policy goals and behaviour are not only driven by an authoritarian logic but are also informed by deeper historical considerations. China's pursuit of 'national rejuvenation' – with its emphasis on secure borders, national sovereignty and international respect – draws its inspiration from a range of sources, going back to the late Qing dynasty (1644–1912) and the Republic era (1912–49). Many US observers also believe that, despite Xi's efforts at recentralisation, the policy environment remains much more fluid than the blunt confrontational posture that the authoritarian model suggests. Prominent voices from Chinese academia continue to highlight the negative consequences of possible strategic overstretch in China's foreign policy, especially the incentives they provide for regional counterbalancing against China. These debates may reveal internal mechanisms that differ from China's increasingly authoritarian image. Xiaoyu Pu of the University of Nevada goes so far as to argue that the debates represent a form of 'strategic prudence' and the continuing relevance of a more accommodating foreign policy that predates Xi, while providing valuable insights for Chinese policymakers. US critics of an adversarial approach to China argue that ignoring such debates risks creating a self-fulfilling prophecy that empowers assertive nationalists in Beijing.

## Containment and decoupling: the right approach?

The analogy of the Cold War has often been evoked to describe the future of US–China relations. In Washington, discussions have centred on a new doctrine of containment, as well as the notion of at least a partial technological decoupling. However, the aptness of a Cold War-style containment approach is debatable, given the significant differences between the Soviet Union and today's China. The US and the Soviet Union had negligible economic ties with each other, while market connections between the US and China have created mutual interdependence and are of fundamental importance to both countries' future economic growth.

Even more significant is the difference between the Soviet Union's and China's roles in the world economy. The Cold War containment concept was directed at preventing the expansion of the Soviet Union's external influence by denying Moscow the ability to reap financial wherewithal from widespread global economic linkages. This policy was a stunning success, abetted substantially by the fact that the Soviet Union's centrally planned communist economy was not geared to such expansion in the first place. China, by contrast, is the world's leading trading nation. While some US officials have talked about forcing US economic partners to 'choose' between economic ties with the US or with China, the notion is fanciful. Washington can do this with Iran but not with China.

At the same time, it is easy to overstate the level of strategic influence that China's trade and investment networks buy Beijing. Many of China's most important economic partners in Asia are treaty allies of the US, and these alliance ties are not at risk. Even China's effort to gain influence through its Belt and Road Initiative has been vulnerable to considerable pushback from Southeast Asian states such as Malaysia and Indonesia.

In contrast to containment, the notion of a partial technological decoupling between China and the US has a much firmer empirical basis. The struggle around technology between the US and China appears set to continue into the foreseeable future. Former Australian prime minister Kevin Rudd has commented that 'we are already heading in the direction of two radically different digital worlds – one anchored in America, the other behind one form or other of the Chinese firewall'.

A similar process is now at work in telecommunications, justified in both countries on national-security grounds. While the US has backtracked on its restrictions applied to Huawei, it remains wary of the company's domination of 5G technology in much of Asia, Africa and Latin America. Washington is also seeking to prevent further encroachment by Huawei in Western markets, including among its closest military allies. Indeed, Huawei's rise to global prominence has been described as a second 'Sputnik moment' for the US.

There is, however, also a case to be made that the Sputnik moment may be in fact occurring in China. The ease with which the US was able to threaten the lifelines of ZTE and Huawei – two companies that have symbolised China's graduation from low-cost manufacturing – has alerted the Chinese leadership to the critical role that imported Western technology has played in China's meteoric progress. While China has officially dropped its 'Made in China 2025' campaign, there is little doubt that US moves against ZTE and Huawei will lead Beijing to put even more emphasis on the goal of technological autonomy from Washington.

## Looming technological decoupling rekindles the US policy debate

The danger in technological decoupling is: where does it stop? Can it be contained to elements of the digital space where there are clear national-security risks at play, or might it take on a life of its own, undermining much broader elements of the global economy and abetting the already rising forces of nationalism, populism and protectionism?

In the US, the increasing momentum of technological decoupling – with its ensuing risks – has generated a more overt pushback against a hardline China policy. In early July 2019, 100 former senior officials, business leaders and leading scholars signed an open letter that criticised the US approach to China. While recognising China's intention to weaken Western rules and norms, the letter argued that 'the best American response ... is to work with our allies and partners to create a more open and prosperous world ... A zero-sum approach ... would only encourage Beijing to disengage from the system or sponsor a divided global order that would be damaging to Western interests.' The letter concluded: 'there is no single Washington consensus endorsing an overall adversarial stance towards China, as some believe exists'.

In sum, while US attitudes to China have certainly hardened in recent years, important constituencies – sometimes including the president himself – dispute the hawkish view of China's intentions and the inevitability of a growing threat facing their country. Economic interdependence is today a fact of the relationship that was entirely absent from US–Soviet ties during the Cold War. That interdependence is a source of mutual concern, and certain constituencies in Washington (and Beijing) seek to unravel it. Some degree of technological disaggregation seems very likely if not inevitable; but it is premature to declare that the hawks have won the argument in the US, and therefore that a descent into unalloyed rivalry is inevitable. Even in a world where China is more assertive and the US accepts that 'convergence' is a flawed concept, there is scope for the US and China to cooperate where they can, as well as compete where they must.

# Home Front in the Trade Wars: US Trade Strategy in North America

Since his election, US President Donald Trump has pursued a campaign pledge to replace the North American Free Trade Agreement (NAFTA) with a 'better deal'. After 15 months, negotiators produced the United States–Mexico–Canada Agreement (USMCA), which was signed by Trump, Canadian Prime Minister Justin Trudeau and then Mexican president Enrique Peña Nieto (on his last day in office, 30 November 2018; his successor Andrés Manuel López Obrador took office on 1 December).

In North America, the USMCA is a tentative 'peace agreement' to end the trade war launched by the Trump administration; at the time of writing, it has received necessary legislative approval only in Mexico and may yet unravel. However, it is currently the best evidence available about what it may take to satisfy the US government's challenge to the post-war international trading system fashioned by Trump's predecessors.

## Trump's international economics

The Goldwater–Nichols Department of Defense Reorganization Act of 1986 (Goldwater–Nichols) included a requirement that the executive branch produce a report outlining the threats and risks to US national security on a quadrennial basis. The purpose is to inform Congress and the public with an unclassified explanation in support of spending requests submitted later. The Trump administration submitted its first National Security Strategy (NSS) in December 2017.

The 2017 NSS was noted at the time for signalling the Trump administration's assessment that a condition of great-power rivalry with China and Russia had displaced asymmetric threats from non-state actors as the principal threat to US security. Less noted was the analysis of the global economy in the 2017 NSS. It sets forth a revisionist aim for the international economic system:

> [The] international economic system rooted in [the] American ... eco-
> nomic system continues to serve our interests, but it must be reformed to
> help American workers prosper, protect our innovation, and reflect the
> principles upon which that system was founded. Trading partners and
> international institutions can do more to address trade imbalances and
> adhere to and enforce the rules of the order.

This preamble sets up five areas for action in the pursuit of national security: rejuvenation of the US economy; promotion of 'free, fair, and reciprocal' economic relationships; research and innovation; promotion and protection of US national-security innovation; and the embrace of US energy-sector dominance in world markets.

Replacing NAFTA with the USMCA was an effort to make US economic relationships with Canada and Mexico more 'free, fair, and reciprocal', but during the negotiation the other four elements were reflected as well, with the strong US economic performance during this period raising the stakes for Mexico City and Ottawa should talks fail.

While the 2017 NSS framed the strategic objectives that the US would pursue with its North American neighbours, the negotiation process was guided by the Bipartisan Congressional Trade Priorities and Accountability Act of 2015 (TPA 2015). This was the legislation passed to give Barack Obama's administration requisite authority to negotiate new trade agreements with Asian and European partners, namely the Trans-Pacific Partnership (concluded in 2016) and the Transatlantic Trade and Investment Partnership (talks towards which have stalled).

Congress was reluctant to grant trade-negotiating authority to the Obama administration in 2015. Democrats in Congress saw trade liberalisation as a corporate agenda and at odds with Obama's progressive rhetoric, and Republicans distrusted Obama deeply. TPA 2015 was therefore a compromise that established numerous conditions, restrictions and deadlines for any resulting agreement to receive congressional consideration without amendments. TPA 2015 covered any negotiations that produced an agreement submitted to Congress before 1 July 2018 but provided for a single extension of up to three years provided the administration could show significant progress on an agreement before that date.

The Trump administration inherited the TPA 2015 negotiation authority from Obama and did not request a new grant of congressional authority, even though Republicans controlled both the House of Representatives and the Senate in the 115th Congress elected with Trump in 2016. The negotiation of the USMCA was conducted under the constraints of TPA 2015, and in March 2018 the Trump administration requested and received an extension of that authority through July 2021.

## USMCA and NAFTA: a comparison

NAFTA was controversial in the US from the beginning, winning reluctant US congressional approval in November 1993 thanks to strong support from business and the political skills of then-president Bill Clinton. Trump was not the first presidential candidate to call for its renegotiation or cancellation; in every presidential election since 1992, at least one presidential candidate has campaigned against NAFTA (Ross Perot in 1992 and 1996, Ralph Nader in 2000 and 2004, Barack Obama in 2008 and 2012, Hillary Clinton and Trump in 2016).

The durable political opposition to NAFTA led the Washington policy community to advise against re-opening the agreement, fearing that it would result in NAFTA's cancellation. Many assumed that this was Trump's true objective.

The USMCA differs from NAFTA in several ways, but the most notable perhaps is in its name. The words 'free trade' do not appear in the name of the new agreement, which does little to liberalise trade or open markets. Instead, the USMCA is largely an agreement to redistribute the gains from continental economic integration in the United States' favour. The USMCA has higher rule-of-origin levels for qualifying for tariff-free market access (up to 75% for some automotive components), local purchase requirements for steel and aluminium, and reduced investor protection to drive disputes to domestic courts rather than international arbitration. NAFTA eliminated national-content requirements, and the USMCA allows them to return. And outside the USMCA talks, the Trump administration employed executive orders to set new standards for products to be counted as 'US-made' if they are at least 50% and in some cases 75% originating in the United States. This is the price the Trump administration has demanded for continued access to the United States' market, and however reluctantly, both Canada and Mexico have agreed to pay it.

This reflects the success of NAFTA in deepening the economic link-ages across the three national markets in the 25 years since it took effect in 1994. Then, North American integration was a strategic economic choice for all three countries. Today, specialisation within continental supply chains is the source of regional competitiveness in the global economy. NAFTA fuelled productivity gains that contributed to Mexico's dramatic rise to emerging-market status and to the ability of the US and Canada to maintain high wages and economic growth in the face of competition from China.

The USMCA retains key features of the NAFTA model. Like NAFTA, the USMCA conditions tariff-free market access on the basis of local (North American) content, calculated on the basis of a Rule of Origin (ROO) and requiring certificates of origin for each component in the supply chain. This adds to the compliance burden for firms, and the complexity of customs administration. It also exposes firms to the risk of retroactive duties and penalties resulting from a purchasing change that results in the product falling short of the required ROO threshold.

The automotive industry has been at the heart of North American integration since the 1960s, when the US responded to Canadian and Mexican attempts to use protectionist measures (including duty-remission schemes based on exports, subsidies and production quotas) in order to capture a larger share of regional employment, investment and production. The USMCA raises the ROO for automotive products from NAFTA's 62.5% to 75% regional value content. Indeed, USMCA goes further, setting higher content requirements for critical subassemblies such as engines and transmissions, and requiring that vehicles meet a separate 70% ROO for steel and aluminium content. Origin requirements on textiles require firms to source sewing thread, narrow elastic fabrics, pocketing and coated fabrics from within North America. Together, the USMCA changes will lead the automakers and parts suppliers headquartered in North America to source more inputs from the continent, and competitors from Germany, Japan and South Korea that produce and sell vehicles in the North American market to import fewer components or raise prices for consumers.

The USMCA innovates with the establishment of a Labor Value Content (LVC) measurement, which requires that no less than 40% of vehicle content be produced with labour compensated at no less than US$16 per hour. In practice, this measure will affect Mexican labour the most, and was a contentious US demand that achieved a break-through when Mexican president-elect López Obrador signalled his support for the requirement in the hope that Mexico would move away from a reliance on low-wage labour as a means to compete for regional automotive-production share.

In contrast with Europe's integration project, the NAFTA model relied on cooperation by the three sovereign national governments for the governance of cross-border flows of capital, goods and labour. To secure congressional approval, Clinton agreed to the establishment of weak trilateral institutions to facilitate environmental and labour coop-eration, as well as a North American Development Bank (which became a bilateral US–Mexico institution when Canada declined to make a capital contribution).

The USMCA places greater responsibility on domestic political institutions for regional governance than even NAFTA did. NAFTA's Chapter 11 established an investor-state dispute-settlement mechanism with trilateral arbitral panels that was mostly eliminated in the USMCA (it was retained for US and Canadian energy-sector firms in Mexico, as protection against expropriation) and as a result, investors will take dis-putes to domestic courts. Environmental and labour commitments in the USMCA are part of the core agreement, not left to the side without access to the enforcement mechanisms in NAFTA as was the case before. The Trump administration has written environmental and labour commit-ments into the draft implementing legislation for the USMCA, meaning that firms and non-governmental organisations have recourse to domestic courts to demand redress or enforcement from government.

NAFTA lacked the commitment to a single market that has been a core principle of European integration agreements since the Single European Act of 1986 amended the Treaty of Rome. Apart from tariffs and protectionist policies, regulatory differences have caused the fragmentation of the North American market. The problem of regulatory differences has been made worse by the federal nature of all three NAFTA countries where regulatory competencies are variously distributed or claimed by governments (federal, state and municipal) across the region.

NAFTA negotiators attempted to address this through the establishment of 12 trilateral working groups of officials charged with negotiating regulatory convergence over time. The NAFTA working-group system failed to make progress when officials, particularly US officials, interpreted NAFTA's unpopularity with the public and elected officials as a signal that support for further action was insufficient to justify heroic efforts to align or reform regulations with Canada and Mexico. Business groups in all three countries lobbied for successor efforts to promote regulatory cooperation, and convinced the George W. Bush administration to launch the Security and Prosperity Partnership of North America (an executive agreement outside the NAFTA model, in operation from 2005 to 2010) and the Obama administration to set up separate and parallel regulatory cooperation initiatives with Canada and Mexico in 2011. By separating regulatory dialogues with Canada and Mexico, the Obama administration made a shift towards making US regulatory standards and practices the most common, if non-explicit, outcome of regulatory cooperation with each smaller partner.

The USMCA follows the logic of government-to-government cooperation without shared institutions to embed agreement on regulatory approaches to certain sectors in the text of the agreement (eliminating the need for further debate on cooperation). The result is USMCA-driven Americanisation of rules on intellectual property, digital trade and financial services.

USMCA intellectual-property provisions commit Canada and Mexico to respect ten years of data protection and exclusivity of biologics and advanced pharmaceuticals, shifts copyright terms to the life of the author/creator plus 70 years, and enhances the protection of trade secrets in Canadian and Mexican law to match the protection afforded in US law.

In a necessary modernisation of NAFTA, the USMCA includes commitments on digital trade that prohibit duties, taxes or procedural discrimination for cross-border electronic media (from software and video games to e-books and movies) and establishes the right to cross-border downloads as well as a new charter of legally enforceable consumer-data privacy rights. Canada and Mexico agree that their governments and firms will cooperate in cyber security with US counterparts, and open public data for commercial use. The USMCA further limits platform liability for third-party content, a still-debated US approach to censorship of sites such as Facebook and Twitter.

The US also uses the USMCA to Americanise the regional approach to two critical sectors: agriculture and energy. In agriculture, the USMCA establishes enforceable requirements that sanitary and phytosanitary measures are 'science-based, developed and implemented in a transparent and non-discriminatory manner' and grants market access for bioengineered agricultural products of gene-editing and other innovative products.

Energy is the largest contributor by value to North American regional trade, but Mexico cited its constitutional prohibition of foreign ownership in the energy sector in refusing to negotiate on energy in NAFTA. Following the 2013 Mexican energy reforms, the USMCA expands tariff-free trade in energy flows to include Mexico, makes certification requirements for oil and gas moving between the three countries more flexible, and waives a US export-approval requirement for liquefied-natural-gas shipments to Canada and Mexico. The USMCA also addresses a problem arising when diluent is added to oil or gas to facilitate its transportation by pipeline by permitting origin certification as North American provided that non-North American diluent chemicals are no more than 40% of the volume of hydrocarbons transported.

In keeping with the broader economic-security strategy in NSS 2017, the Trump administration used the USMCA to send signals to other trading partners, in particular China. Unlike NAFTA, the USMCA includes provisions to monitor and permit trade retaliation for currency manipulation. Since NAFTA, the Canadian dollar and the Mexican peso have tended to follow the US dollar up and down relative to other world currencies, making North America a dollar bloc where currency manipulation has not been a concern. The USMCA provisions follow the US practice of debuting language at the first opportunity to try to establish a model for future agreements.

In its agriculture chapter, the USMCA includes a US signal to the European Union by expressly forbidding the recognition of geographic indicators as a barrier to US exports. This was prompted by Canadian concessions on 170 geographic indicators as part of the Canada–EU Comprehensive Economic and Trade Agreement, and Mexican recognition of more than 400 European geographic indicators in its updated trade agreement with the European Union concluded in 2018. Under the USMCA, US products labelled with a descriptor protected in the EU cannot be barred from or penalised in the Canadian or Mexican market. China was also put on notice in the USMCA through a provision that no USMCA member could enter into negotiations with a 'non-market economy for the purposes of trade remedy' without full transparency to other USMCA members. The peculiar phrasing of the ban is to link the determination of a non-market economy to a US Department of Commerce definition rather than to World Trade Organization (WTO) rules (which accept China as a market economy). Here, Canada was able to soften the US demand for a total ban on talks into a full-transparency commitment.

## The Art of the Deal

The content of the USMCA reflects the NSS 2017 goals for US economic security, apart from the 'promotion and protection of US national security innovation'. Yet US national security was a major topic during the negotiation of the USMCA.

This is because the Trump administration made use of a largely forgotten provision of the Trade Expansion Act of 1962 that empowered the president of the United States to impose tariffs on the grounds of 'national security'. Other US trade-remedy laws require investigations and evidence that delay the application of threatened tariffs; Section 232 of the 1962 legislation relies on the president to make the sole and generally unassailable determination of the national-security requirements of the US.

US negotiators carved out an exemption for national-security tariffs in the General Agreement on Tariffs and Trade that continued into WTO rules. Few governments wanted to see this exemption challenged, for fear that if it was upheld, national security would justify illiberal regimes to justify trade protectionism anew.

During the talks leading up to the USMCA, the Trump administration imposed national-security tariffs on Canadian and Mexican steel and aluminium and threatened similar tariffs on imported automobiles. When the USMCA was signed in November 2018, Canada and Mexico expected these tariffs to be lifted, but they were kept in place until June 2019. In the meantime, the US Commerce Department argued that national-security tariffs on imported automobiles could be justified if US 'technological leadership' in auto-related innovations was at risk, threatening another valuable export category for Canada and Mexico.

As the three countries moved towards legislative approval of the USMCA, the Trump administration announced that escalating tariffs would be imposed on all Mexican imports until the Mexican government took action to stop migrants from Central America from crossing Mexican territory to enter the United States. The López Obrador administration had advanced the USMCA through the Mexican Congress and was cooperating even then on the issue, but to avert the threat of new tariffs, López Obrador sent 6,000 troops to the southern border and 15,000 troops to the northern border to block migrant transit.

President Trump summed up his administration's view of trade policy succinctly in two statements. In NSS 2017 he is quoted directly: 'Economic security is national security.' And during the negotiation of the USMCA, he said of Canada and Mexico: 'They need a deal more than we do.'

Yet a deal is not a deal in the US until it is approved by Congress, and the 2018 midterm elections gave Democrats a majority in the House of Representatives. A tariff bill is a money bill under US congressional procedure, and so the implementing legislation for the USMCA must be introduced in the House, now led by Speaker Nancy Pelosi. For some observers in Canada and Mexico, this offered the hope that the USMCA might be altered or blocked. Trump's frequent threats to unilaterally withdraw the US from NAFTA were discounted since the US Constitution gives Congress authority over trade policy, and a clear right to challenge the president's notice of withdrawal from NAFTA in court.

However, prospects that Congress would check the Trump administration on trade policy have faded since the 2018 midterm elections. The 'America First' provisions of the USMCA, which hold out the hope of clawing back jobs and investment from Canada and Mexico to US states and workers, are popular with some labour-union members. Although they could be stronger, the environmental provisions of the USMCA are viewed positively by some environmental groups because they are more enforceable than anything in NAFTA. For Millennial-generation voters, NAFTA has been in effect for most of their lives and serves as a baseline. Like Canadians and Mexicans, Millennial Americans no longer see North American regional integration as a choice, but as a phenomenon that must be managed better. Combined, these reactions have split Democrats and provide little support for House Democrats to block the USMCA, even if Democrats are otherwise united in their dislike of Trump.

The future of the USMCA is now subject to the provisions of TPA 2015. The Trump administration has been scrupulous about meeting the requirements of TPA 2015, giving Congress no ground to refuse an up or down vote on implementing the legislation. Once it has been introduced in the House of Representatives, it cannot be amended and can be debated for 45 session days before the committee of primary jurisdiction (the House Ways and Means Committee and the Senate Finance Committee, respectively) before receiving just 15 session days of debate in the whole chamber. Those timelines, particularly if the Senate waits for the House to pass the legislation first, now have the potential to stretch into 2020, an election year.

Congress rarely wants to vote on trade in an election year, particularly to approve a trade agreement that is certain to be touted in Trump's re-election campaign. The USMCA is a loss for Canada and Mexico, but better than no deal at all. Trudeau, who faces an election on 21 October 2019, is unlikely to be harmed politically by the concessions he had to make to secure the USMCA. US business groups, having rallied against Trump's escalating tariffs on Mexico in June, now just want an end to trade uncertainty and will support USMCA ratification. All of which augurs for the USMCA to successfully replace NAFTA as the governing rules for North American economic integration before the end of 2019.

## The world is watching

The North American 'home front' in Trump's trade wars provides insights for other US trading partners, especially China. Firstly, Trump's trade policies are sustainable, as is his aggressive brinksmanship in negotiating. The Democratic opposition will not block an agreement that threatens friendly trading partners like Canada or a country like Mexico whose expatriates in the US are a valued Democratic Party voting bloc. Secondly, Trump has demonstrated the ability to link national security, aggressive threats and tariffs imposed suddenly to force concessions on his terms. It is possible to do a deal with the US, but it will be a deal on Trump's terms. Thirdly, if even the United States' popular, polite and friendly neighbour Canada can be treated roughly by US trade negotiators on the way to a deal, countries that the US views with concern (such as China) can expect little support from US business and political leaders when it is their turn to negotiate.

Nothing lasts forever, and Trump like any leader is vulnerable to mistakes of hubris or reckless misjudgement. Even if re-elected in 2020, Trump will still be out of office by January 2025. Taking the long view favoured by Chinese leaders, this is a minor period of discomfort, to be borne stoically, yet the report from the home front should caution anyone hoping to avoid the economic and political implications of Trump's rethinking of US trade strategy. Trump has achieved a reset in US trade policy that has bipartisan support and may outlast him. The old technocratic position on international trade has suffered a lot of damage – 2020 Democratic presidential contenders did not mention trade at their Miami debates in July 2019. China may yet decide that waiting out the Trump administration might not be prudent, for no one can say with confidence that this president is an aberration rather than the start of a new US attitude towards international trade.

# Index